MICMACS AND COLONISTS

MICMACS AND COLONISTS

INDIAN-WHITE RELATIONS IN THE MARITIMES, 1713–1867

L. F. S. UPTON

UNIVERSITY OF BRITISH COLUMBIA PRESS

VANCOUVER

MICMACS AND COLONISTS

Indian-White Relations in the Maritimes, 1713-1867

© The University of British Columbia 1979

This book has been published with the help of a grant from the Canadian Federation for the Humanities, using funds provided by the Social Sciences and Humanities Research Council of Canada.

Canadian Cataloguing in Publication Data

Upton, Leslie F. S., 1931–
  Micmacs and colonists

  Bibliography: p.
  Includes index.
  ISBN 0-7748-0114-X

  1. Micmac Indians—History. 2. Indians of North America—Maritime Provinces—History. 3. Indians of North America—Maritime Provinces—Government relations.
  I. Title.
  E99.M6U5   971.5'004'97   C79-091130-2

ISBN-0-7748-0114-X

Printed in Canada

For My Children

Contents

Photographic Credits

The Public Archives of Canada provided Plates 1(C–21112), 5(C–37056), 6(C–810), 7(C–36647), 14(C–11203), and 15(C–14143). Plate 13 is reproduced from microfilm number C.O.217/179, ff. 406–8, Public Archives of Canada; original is in the Public Records Office, London. Plates 10, 16, and 17 appear courtesy of the New Brunswick Museum. Plate 4 is reproduced by permission of the British Library. Plates 11 and 12 appear courtesy of the Nova Scotia Museum, Halifax, the former from an original in the British Library. Plate 8 is reproduced courtesy of the National Gallery, Ottawa. Photographs for Plates 2, 3, and 9 were provided by the Special Collections Division, the University of British Columbia Library, from, respectively, Baron Marc de Villiers du Terrage, *Les Raretés des Indes* (Paris: M. Chamonal, 1930), Abraham Gesner, *The Industrial Resources of Nova Scotia* (Halifax: A. & W. MacKinlay, 1849), and, by the same author, *New Brunswick, with Notes for Emigrants* (London: Simmonds & Ward, 1847).

Illustrations

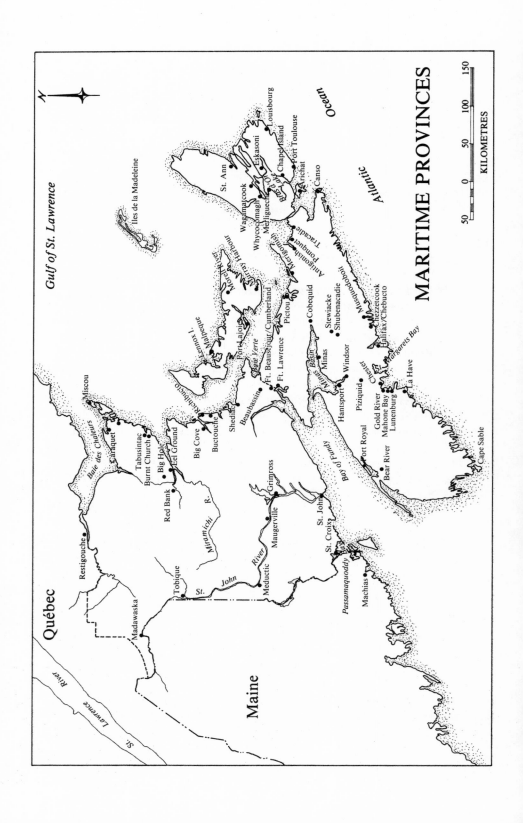

MARITIME PROVINCES

Introduction

The object of this book is to trace the interaction of the Micmac Indians and British colonists over a period of one hundred and fifty years.

Indian-White relationships in North America have passed through several well-defined stages. In the first contacts the Europeans were in a subordinate position, dependent on the sufferance of the Indians for advice, guidance, and survival. The newcomers had to accommodate to the natives' way of doing things and to accept their control of the relationship. However, the newcomers inadvertently introduced diseases that wreaked devastation on the receiving society and undermined its self-sufficiency. Paradoxically, those who survived this first onslaught were able to live better than before because they acquired European tools that allowed them to do what they had always done, only more efficiently: iron replaced stone, the cooking pot superseded the hollowed-out tree stump. Gradually, the traditional artifacts fell into disuse, along with the knowledge that produced them. The Indians became dependent on imported goods that they could not duplicate, and as their dependence grew, so the importance of the supplier increased. The tool that was servant became the master.

Nor is this all that changed. Even before the transformation was complete, European missionaries introduced new ideas and values to set alongside the new material possessions. However much a Christian missionary might profess his devotion to spiritual salvation, his teachings were inevitably received as a rationale for the new material environment created by the goods that were transforming traditional life. The missionary was seen as the interpreter of European civilization in all its aspects. The contact between old and new became personalized, for the missionary had a recognizable counterpart, the shaman or buoin, with whom he consciously competed for power. As European goods became dominant, so too did the missionary, and the traditional spiritual perceptions embodied in the person of the buoin declined steadily. Continuity was destroyed; the past ceased to exist.

The combined impact of these European innovations was to disorient the already weakened Indian societies and make the loss of their lands certain. The wars waged by settlers were fought against Indians who had already met the three horsemen of the European Apocalypse: disease, trade goods, and Christianity. The newcomers inevitably triumphed, and shattered tribes had to re-group and survive as best they could in the face of the omnipresent colonist. The process continued piecemeal across the continent and, since

Indians had no more concept of a common interest than did the Europeans, the tribes were picked off one by one, often with the help of other Indians who allied with the whites. When loss of land was added to loss of continuity, the Indians were forced to accept whatever the new masters determined for them. Sooner or later they were confined to reservations where government officials and missionaries attempted to assimilate them into white society.

The process was repetitious, predictable in its sameness throughout the three centuries that Europeans required to populate North America. The speed at which Indian societies were destroyed in any one area varied with the pressure of the immigrant population. In New England, scarcely a generation elapsed before the Indians were dispossessed; in New France, founded in the vacuum left by the disappearance of the St. Lawrence Iroquois, five generations passed without undue pressure; in Rupertsland, a territory long hostile to European settlement, ten generations passed before Canada made its first demands for land.

The apparently inexorable progress of these events gives the impression that Indians were, from an early date, passive individuals to whom things were done at the will of others. They are seen not so much as actors but as sufferers, sustaining a series of traumatic shocks that they cannot avert. This impression is misleading. The Indians retained a number of options in the face of events and were not entirely bereft of initiatives. They were, indeed, in the position of having to react to the advances of others, but they did have choices to make. They had to decide whether to resist the newcomers through warfare or to collaborate with them in a mutually profitable trade for as long as possible. Faced with dispossession, they might decide to remove from their original lands to retain tribal unity elsewhere or to accommodate to a new, lower status by accepting Christianity and other European values as individuals. Between removal and accommodation lay a third alternative, passive resistance, a determination to hold onto what shreds of the old life remained while steadfastly refusing to accept the new values. Only too frequently this response shaded off into a resignation so complete that white observers refer to it as a state of utter demoralization. Yet the perception of a distinctive past, however truncated, forms the nucleus from which a revived Indian culture may develop.

The Micmacs were the first North Americans to come into contact with Europeans, and they had two hundred years of experience behind them when the British arrived in their lands. The Micmacs were the first to be exposed to European disease, hardware, and Christianity. The survivors developed a resilience in the face of encroachment that set them apart from other Indians in Canada.

The Micmacs exercised a wide range of choices in their dealings with Europeans. By the beginning of the eighteenth century, the Micmacs had reached an agreeable *modus vivendi* with the French. They chose to collaborate with the French in trade and to accept their missionaries, for there were no martyrs in Acadia. They decided not to oppose the few French who came to settle in their territory. Nevertheless, these acceptable European contacts changed Micmac society, for disease brought in the sixteenth century ran its course and returned in intermittent epidemics; trade goods irrevocably affected their life-cycle; Christianity challenged their traditional values. Yet the new Catholicism did not replace their old beliefs, which stayed alive in a rich store of mythology. Trade goods became indispensable, but the price did not yet appear too high, and life remained a recognizable facsimile of what it had been. Such settlement as took place was confined to peripheral areas that could, if so desired, still be ignored.

However, the fortunes of the Micmacs declined as their territory rose in importance to the Great Powers. As long as it was left to itself, Acadia remained a home where they could continue their traditional life, albeit weighed down with some European impediments. But when the French built their fortress town at Louisbourg and the British countered with Halifax, control of the coastal region became of vital concern in a global contest. Unique among Canadian Indians, the Micmacs fought for their lands. They lost, but only when the defeat of France cut off their supplies.

The introduction of the British into the area presented the Micmacs with a new set of choices. Resentful at the interruption of their satisfactory relationship with the French, they chose to resist the British. The decision was not an unreasoned reaction against change, for the Micmacs were subtle enough to manoeuvre between the two European rivals, treating and trading with the British whenever it was necessary to prompt the French into fresh measures of support. Catholicism emerged as an important reinforcement to the distinctiveness of the tribe, setting it off from the British and furnishing a claim on French benevolence. In the course of their resistance, the Micmacs also began to adopt the idea that they had rights to their land, which could not be disposed of against their will. This was an argument that had had no place in the seventeenth century.

When the Micmacs did conclude peace with the British in 1761, it was in the expectation of re-establishing the equilibrium they had once enjoyed with the French. This was not to be. The British enjoyed total control of the Atlantic seaboard for only a few years, losing most of their colonies in the American Revolution. Halifax, unexpectedly, became their only base on the North Atlantic and so remained vital to imperial strategy. The British moved in Loyalist refugees to stabilize the area. Forced to contend with both settler and strategic interests, the Micmacs were rapidly dispossessed. They could petition for lands for themselves but claim none as of right; no government treated for the transfer of their rights as was done elsewhere in British North America. In the face of this catastrophe, they chose a form of passive resistance. They maintained the authority of their several bands and assembled each year to discuss matters of interest to all. The feast day of their patron saint, St. Ann, became the central point of their year. Its regular observance was an act of multiple defiance, for it commemorated their ties with the French rather than the British; with Catholicism rather than protestantism; with tribal rather than colonial government. The Micmacs retained a focal point that was clearly outside settler society and so kept the past alive. Even though many of them earned their living on the fringes of the white economy as makers of handicrafts and itinerant peddlers, they were still consciously Micmacs, deliberately putting a distance between themselves and the colonists. Their society remained alive, with its own focus, its own structure, its own religion, its own folklore, its own reason for existing.

In a sense, though they made peace, they refused to admit defeat. No government could make them sit down on reservations, and they continued to traverse their territory regardless of the political divisions created by the British. With their numbers fast diminishing to a low point of about 2,500 in 1860, they remained on the periphery of governmental concern and colonial society.

The Micmacs collaborated with the French and resisted the British. These were their choices to make, and they made them. When active resistance was no longer possible there were still choices. A few Micmacs, it might be argued, took the option of removal and went to Newfoundland to escape the intruding colonists. Some doubtless accommodated to white society and passed unnoticed into its ranks. But the majority opted for a passive resistance that drew strength from the past in the face of a desperate present.

The title of this book defines its bounds. A few Micmacs lived outside the three Maritime provinces. The Gaspé Peninsula was part of their traditional lands, and it came under the jurisdiction of Lower Canada. The British government at Quebec City had no place for such a remote people in its Indian policy and did its best to leave them to their own devices. The principal centre for the Micmacs of the Gaspé was Restigouche, just across the river from New Brunswick, where they pursued their livelihood and met the settlers. Another outlying group of Micmacs were the hunters who crossed from Cape Breton to southern Newfoundland. Given the nature of these people, it is impossible to identify any one group as "Newfoundland" Micmacs rather than mainlanders. There was little government and less settlement in the area, and there was no interaction between Micmacs and colonists.

East of the Micmacs lived Indian tribes whose fortunes often paralleled and sometimes intermingled with theirs. The Malecite Indians of the St. John River were their closest neighbours. They were not really challenged by the British until late in the eighteenth century, when their river valley became the core of settlement in New Brunswick. From then on, their experiences within the British colony were very similar to those of the Micmacs. The Abenakis, including the Penobscots and Passamaquoddies in what is now Maine, suffered white incursions at an early date, and their resistance was, for a time, loosely co-ordinated with the Micmacs' defiance of Britain. But the history of these people and their reaction to colonization is not the same as that of the Micmacs, and I have mentioned other tribes only when their activities shed light on the relations of Micmacs and colonists.

The colonists in this book are British. These were the people who wrested control of the land from the Micmacs and set up colonial governments. It was their society that confronted Micmac life at every level and substituted its norms for theirs. Consequently, the detailed portion of this study starts with the arrival of the British and the earlier period is treated as introductory to that event. The history of the French colonists of the seventeenth century and the later relationship of Micmacs and Acadians is matter for a different book. There was such a close connection between the early Acadians and the Micmacs that beleaguered British officials often complained that they could not tell the two apart. But the people concerned knew who they were and, despite the ties of blood and friendship, pursued their separate courses.

This book is divided into five sections. The first is concerned with the years before the arrival of the British. It provides a description of the Micmacs' life before white contact and their reaction to the French fishermen, missionaries, and traders who were the first bearers of European influences. The second section describes the resistance of the Micmacs to the British who established a tenuous presence in Nova Scotia after 1713. The British saw the Micmacs as simple people manipulated by unscrupulous Frenchmen. Indeed, the Micmacs frequently collaborated with the French, but they never lost sight of their own self-interest. The prolonged guerilla war fought in defence of their land apparently ended in 1761, but when the American Revolution broke out there were those who hoped to reopen the contest and use the Americans as they had once used the French.

After 1783 the British were securely in control of the Micmac lands and subdivided them into new colonial units. Each of the provinces was left to pursue its own policy towards its own Indians; there was no supervision from London as there was in the Canadas. The history of the Micmacs became fragmented as one people had to act and react to three separate settlers' governments. The third section analyses the particular situations that developed in each of the colonies of Nova Scotia, New Brunswick, and Prince Edward Island.

Separate governments created separate conditions, but not in all areas of life. The fourth section is concerned with matters that knew no provincial boundaries. I consider the interaction between Micmac and colonial society as a whole and emphasize two aspects of it. Catholic Christianity was one bond among the Micmacs that could not be severed by provincial jurisdictions. Frequently challenged by British colonists, Micmac Catholicism survived because it had become an integral part of the tribe's identity. Similarly, the traditional authority of the band chiefs survived, for although subject to the colonists' laws, the Micmacs were most often left to their traditional practices in governing their own conduct.

When the several Maritime Provinces passed into the Dominion of Canada, responsibility for the Indians passed to Ottawa. Ignorant of the Micmacs, the new policy makers built on their experience with the Indians of Upper Canada. Thus, Confederation marks a very real break. The final section surveys the Micmacs' position as a small people directed by a distant bureaucracy determined to ignore them for as long as possible. This study closes with an Epilogue. There is no Conclusion for there is no conclusion to the subject matter of this book.

I would like to thank Roger Nason, formerly of the Provincial Archives of New Brunswick, for his help in starting me off in this study; Brian Cuthbertson of the Public Archives of Nova Scotia and David Hume of the Public Archives of Canada for their timely assistance; Judith Fingard of Dalhousie University for her advice and encouragement; Philip Buckner for publishing my earlier essays in this field in his *Acadiensis* and for giving permission for incorporating them in this study; and Ralph Heintzman, editor of the *Journal of Canadian Studies*, for similar permission with regard to an article that first appeared in his journal.

PART I

The Micmacs: Introduction

1

The Micmacs

The historian Marc Lescarbot saw his first American Indians in 1606. They were a group of Micmacs coming out to meet his vessel in a shallop, under sail, easily outdistancing a similar boat manned by Basques.[1] That first sight held a deep significance: the untutored savages of the new world were sailing a European craft with more dexterity than Europeans. Lescarbot is among the first to write accounts of Micmac life, and he began his work a full century after the first contact with Europeans. In those hundred years the white man had brought with him diseases which not only killed off many of the native peoples, but also weakened the fabric of their society. He had brought trade goods that replaced the Indians' artifacts and challenged the rationale for much of their daily labour, and he had bought furs and created a demand which caused unprecedented destruction of the animal population. All these things had occurred before the first descriptions of Micmac society were penned; yet these late accounts must serve as the basis for reconstructing the nature of Micmac life before white contact.

The Micmacs occupied a territory of over fifty thousand square miles covering, in present-day terms, the whole of Nova Scotia and Prince Edward Island, most of New Brunswick outside the St. John River Valley, and the southern Gaspé Peninsula of the province of Quebec. The land imposed its own terms of life on its aboriginal populations. The growing season was too short for agriculture, and the people lived by fishing, gathering, and hunting. Their artifacts were proportionate to those needs, fashioned from what the forest provided: bark canoes, snowshoes, skin clothing and footwear, shelters covered with bark or skins, bark dishes and containers.

The number of people that such a woodland economy could support is still open to question, and there is no way to determine the pre-contact size of the Micmac population: how much forest land is required to support an individual? how large an animal population? how many miles of sea coast and river contributed how much marine life for human consumption? And even if these factors were known, there would be no proof that the Micmacs lived up to the full land support capacity of the area at any particular time. By 1600 the Micmacs were aware that their people had once been more numerous and had been dying off after the arrival of European traders and fishermen. Father Biard, the first white observer to hazard a guess at the size of the native population, stated in 1611 that their numbers did "not amount to two thousand"; five years later he gave the higher figure of between three thousand and thirty-five hundred. The wide variation between his estimates is nothing compared to the calculations of those who try to determine what the Micmac population might have been before the first coming of the Europeans: their population figures range from 6,000 to 100,000.[2]

The quest for food dominated Micmac life, but for most of the year nature provided a plentiful subsistence. The dangerous times came in February and March when the people were dependent on hunting for their support. Hunters on snowshoes stalked game, using their dogs to worry and exhaust the prey, but it was the condition of the snow that determined how much they caught. Ideally, the snow should be deep and crusted with a frozen surface which would break under the weight of a moose and hold him fast as the hunter approached for the kill; but a mild winter brought little snow, and a severe one meant that the snow froze hard to a considerable depth and provided firm footing. An abnormal winter brought on the starving time and acted as a natural control on the growth of population. The rest of the year could be guaranteed to produce more than enough to support life. There were many rituals to propitiate and attract large game animals and fur-bearers, none to honour the fish that nature infallibly offered for the taking.

The people moved with the seasons in a regular cycle. Small bands frequented the coast in January for smelt, tom cod, seals, and walrus. Slightly larger groups spent the critical months of February and March inland, hunting for game: beaver, moose, bear. By the end of March the people were moving back to the coasts to congregate in villages where they lived from April to October taking fish, shellfish, lobster, crabs, and eels in season and intercepting the spring and autumn migrations of wildfowl. From July to September their diet was supplemented by berries, nuts, and roots. As October approached, the villages began to break up as the people retired inland in smaller units to hunt, take fish from the rivers, and catch the occasional wildfowl. In January the Micmacs returned downstream to start the annual cycle again.

In the yearly diet as a whole, game provided only a small proportion of the

Micmacs' food resources, and it was one of the least satisfactory, for in the winter animals were at their leanest and their flesh was less nourishing than at any other time. Yet because it was the most difficult food to find, a man made his reputation on his prowess as a hunter. The hunt required a high degree of organized activity. Snowshoes, bows and arrows, and spears had to be made, and prefabricated tents and lean-tos were used for mobility. Men were responsible for the kill, and the women collected and prepared it. Success came from a man's knowledge of the countryside, of the salt licks where the animals gathered or the age of a broken twig that showed how long it had been since a moose passed by. Courage as well as skill was required to spear a demented animal at close range. There was challenge too in locating the winter beaver under snow and ice; skill in forcing him to come up for air at a predetermined spot, but not so much danger. Wildfowling was less honourable to the hunter, who drifted his canoe silently into sleeping flocks and pulled aboard birds dazzled by torchlight. Catching salmon in weirs, spearing eels, and gathering shells may have contributed most to the Micmacs' annual diet, but these activities were no challenge fit for a hunter.[3]

Given the nature of this life, the Micmacs had no permanent settlements, but there were traditional and well-defined sites that they occupied year after year. Summer was the time of easy living when the greatest number of people could subsist on the resources of the smallest area. Consequently, in the summer village the Micmacs came together in units of perhaps two or three hundred people. They lived in long houses accommodating twenty to thirty individuals. The only eyewitness account of such a village describes it as "a great enclosure upon a hill, compassed about with high and tall trees tied one against another, and within it many cabins great and small, one of which was as great as a market-hall wherein many households retired themselves."[4] This appears to have been a village prepared for defence, for the forty-six summer sites that have been identified show that the preferred location was usually at the mouth of a large river on a subsidiary stream near the main channel, convenient both for communicating inland by canoe and for harvesting seafood. Most sites were situated on level sandy soil with good drainage and access to spring water and sheltered from the ocean wind.

Settlements at other times of year were much smaller, were occupied for a much shorter time, and are therefore almost impossible to identify. It may be reasonable to assume that the same groups followed the same trails and returned to the same sites each year. Moose and beaver are relatively non-migratory animals, and familiarity with one particular area was distinctly advantageous to a hunter. The emphasis, however, was on mobility. In each new camp the Micmacs lived in wigwams that could house ten to twelve people around a single fire. Probably none of these camps was inhabited for more than six weeks at a time, and this state of perpetual motion contributed to the uncertainties of winter life. The Micmacs knew how to preserve food by smoking fish and meat, drying roots, and shelling acorns and wrapping them in bark containers. However, once this was done, the food was not transported; it was left suspended from trees out of the reach of animals. Thus, the presence of such preserves diminished the mobility of a hunting band. There were two choices: either stay put until the stores had all been eaten or move on and hope that the cache would be there when the band returned.[5] If preserved food was on hand when a real emergency arose, it was more by accident than design. Instead of averting hardship by stock-piling food, the Micmacs preferred to mitigate it by sharing whatever they did have. Their society placed little value on producing a surplus, either individually or collectively.

Provident or not, this life produced people with good health, a trait the Micmacs enjoyed in common with other native North Americans. The study of pre-Columbian skeletal remains indicates that the average life expectancy was thirty-seven, plus or minus three years, a degree of longevity not attained by Europeans until the nineteenth century; the chief medical trouble would seem to have been from digestive disorders in infants and the aged.[6] The appearance of the Micmacs testified to their health: they were "goodly men ... well-limbed, well-boned, and well-bodied, competently strong." They were, as an early missionary wistfully put it, "just as we would be if we continued in the same condition in which we were at the age of twenty-five. You do not encounter a big-bellied, hunchbacked, or deformed person among them."[7] It is difficult to believe that such perfection in human form was not the result of the hard physical life of the Micmacs. Those who could not keep up did not long survive.

Europeans had some difficulty determining the colour of the Micmacs. Some considered them to be of an olive complexion or tawny; others thought them naturally white but darkened by the omnipresent grease they put on their bodies to keep out the cold in winter and the mosquitoes in summer. All had black hair, which both men and women wore long, and black eyes. The men had little facial hair and customarily plucked out what there was. The dress of both sexes was similar, "a skin tied to a latch or girdle of leather which, passing between their buttocks, joineth the other end of the said latch behind." The women wore a girdle in addition to this. Extra protection was provided by a cloak made of skin "tied upward with a leather riband and they thrust commonly one arm out." Ornaments hung from their ears and about the neck, torso, arms, and legs. On their feet were thin moose-skin moccasins. There was separate finery for special occasions, brightly embroidered clothing deco-rated with broken chevrons and animal figures; the favourite colours were red, violet, and blue. Happiness or grief was demonstrated by body paint.[8]

The Micmacs were a healthy, colourful people sensibly dressed for the climate and protected from its extremes, yet according to medical evidence they were susceptible to digestive disorders. The practice of making baby's first mouthful a swallow of fish oil or melted fat may have contributed to infant mortality, but the danger for adults was undoubtedly the gluttonous mode of eating. The simplest way to preserve newly killed game was to eat it all at one time, a practice that was frequently followed by a fast of anything up to a week's duration. This alternation of feast and famine during the winter hunt would be hard on the constitution as age advanced. Food was eaten off skins placed on the ground, and from fifteen to twenty pounds of meat might be consumed by each person at a sitting. Meat and fish were roasted on sticks over a fire and eaten as the various portions became cooked; but the preferred method was to boil the flesh in water heated by hot stones in hollowed out tree butts. Further digestive troubles may have resulted from the fact that the food was undercooked; some parasites had a good chance of surviving and entering a human host.[9]

The group that ate together was the unit of social life. It consisted of an extended family around a chief and included some of his married sons and daughters and their families and sometimes other relations through either the male or female line, together with slave prisoners. Such was the unit that went on the winter hunt together, and it coalesced with other units in increasingly larger groupings as the food supply became more abundant in the spring. There were no clans, no regulations of exogamy, and no group totemism as found in the Iroquoian peoples. The restricted degrees of consanguinity were few, father/son, mother/daughter, sister/brother, so that marriages could take place within the bounds of the basic social unit.[10]

There was considerable ceremony at a man's first marriage, which was approved when the father of the bride said to his daughter, "Follow the youth, he is thy husband." But before that point had been reached, the suitor had had to serve a probationary period to demonstrate his ability to support his future wife and, if necessary, his prospective in-laws. The young man lived with her family, sleeping on the opposite side of the fire from his fiancée. Even after this probationary service, either partner could still refuse the marriage. No dowry was paid, and the obligation of providing the wedding feast rested on the groom. If no children were born to the couple within the first two or three years, the man could divorce his wife on his own volition. The marriage could be dissolved at any time on grounds of mutual antipathy, and either the man or woman could take that action. Divorce was, however, held in check since it involved an expensive exchange of presents. A man's second wife was acquired with much less formality, by making presents to her father, and the wedding feast did not have to be particularly elaborate. Polygamy was possible, and since it meant that a man was strong and skilled enough to support several families, it served to enhance his status.[11]

The role of women in this society was a subordinate one: they were servants, mothers, and food-gatherers. They did not have the responsibility of providing a staple crop as they had among agricultural Amerindians. They cooked the food, but they ate last, after the men had finished; at special feasts they remained to one side. They took no part in councils, and in this respect had the same status as young men before the first hunting kill. Woman's work was to prepare the wigwams and collect wood for the central fire. When the band moved, the women carried its equipment, on sleds in winter and canoes in summer. They sewed clothes, curried and suppled skins, stitched leather purses, made mats, created ornaments with porcupine quills, manufactured bark dishes, and decorated the wigwams with paintings. Each month a woman was guaranteed a few days' rest because of a complex of taboos surrounding menstruation. At that time she lived apart in her own wigwam and prepared and ate food out of her own dishes. She was unable to work for others; if she cooked food for the band, she rendered it unclean and offended the spirits. A young man who so much as brushed against her would consider himself deprived of the use of his limbs. She was taboo, and if she touched his bow and arrows, she would bewitch them, rendering them useless in the hunt. Widows were also subject to taboos: they were not to eat meat killed by a young man or to remarry until the death of their husbands, if violent, had been avenged.[12]

Childbirth was an uncomplicated process that took place in the open air, never inside a wigwam. After birth, the mother was subject to some of the taboos of menstruation; for a month or two she ate by herself from her own dishes. Her husband, who had not had intercourse with her since pregnancy was evident, customarily stayed away for this additional length of time. As soon as the baby was born, it was washed in cold water, which must have been a basic survival test, especially in the winter months. Mothers nursed their children for two or three years, and any pregnancy in that time was terminated by an abortifacient drug. The infant was carried everywhere by its mother on a swaddling board supported by a strap across the forehead, a device that left both her arms free for work while at the same time it protected the baby from twigs and overhead branches. Inside the wigwam, the board was propped up so that the child could still observe the life around him. The boards had their hazards, particularly for the male sex in freezing weather: "If it is a boy, they pass his penis through a hole, from which issues the urine; if a girl, they place a little gutter of bark between their legs, which carries the urine outside. Under their backsides they place dry rotten wood reduced to powder." The infants were unswathed once a day.[13]

The Micmacs loved their children and were permissive parents. There was no corporal punishment. No child had to cry for anything as his parents would even take the food out of their own mouths to placate him. The first tooth, the first walk, were causes for family celebration. Infants had small toys and beads attached to their swaddling boards, but once they were able to stand on their own, they began to enter the adult world. The boys' games prepared them for hunting, and they accompanied their fathers on the trail. A boy's first kill was an honoured event, and to drive home the need to share, the animals he took in early youth were given to others. Girls assisted their mothers in their work, at first in sewing and weaving baskets from rushes and, as they grew older, in the heavier tasks such as stripping bark off trees and setting up the wigwams. After puberty the young were allowed to engage in sexual play and were promiscuous without shame; but that licence ended with marriage.[14]

This upbringing produced a people who, although unaccustomed to personal restraint or denial, had a highly developed sense of the individual's responsibility to the group. The Micmacs were slow to anger with each other and made every effort to avoid giving offence by criticizing or advising or disagreeing. A person who had never been crossed from earliest infancy or made to do anything against his will was not trained to impose on others. The corollary of this attitude may well have been the cultivation of an emotional indifference to events and personalities lest such involvement provoke anger within the group. With no experience of external restraint, the Micmacs learned to exercise self-discipline. The band was too important to all its members, too dependent on the collaboration of all, to permit much indulgence. If anger was aroused, it was most often dissipated by mocking the antagonist behind his back. Extreme provocation could produce a fight, but it was a purposely ineffectual one, consisting mainly of hair-pulling. Major offences such as murder or adultery called for the personal vengeance of the aggrieved family and rarely occurred within a band. Discord was a luxury no one could afford.[15]

In these circumstances it is hardly surprising that lines of authority were vague. There was little need for a magistracy, little taste for giving directions. Decisions, of course, had to be made: the head of the family determined where to camp, his wife assigned seating places within the wigwam. But decisions above that level were made by persuasion, and the man with the most persuasive ways was the leader. Europeans found this arrangement baffling and, not yet having coined the word "consensus," had a difficult time describing it. A chief ruled "not with so much authority as our King over his subjects, but with sufficient power to harangue, advise, and lead them to war, to render justice to one who has a grievance, and like matters." The position certainly carried prestige: a chief would be accompanied by a retinue on ceremonial occasions; he had the seat of honour at feasts, the choicest pieces of meat, and he was served first. Young men who had not yet proven themselves remained silent in his presence. Yet these were the honorific rather than the substantive indices of position. The chief received tributes and could share in the produce of the hunt without himself taking part in it, but he did not accumulate an excess of goods over others, for his duty was "to provide dogs for the chase, canoes for transportation, provisions and reserves for bad weather and expeditions."[16] In other words, he was a trustee for the welfare of his band.

Despite the vagueness of authority, there can be little doubt that the

Micmacs had an order of precedence among themselves. There were three tiers of chieftainship for each unit; the winter band, the multiple bands of spring, and the bands that assembled for the summer months each had a recognized leader. The chief of the summer band was described as the sagamore "in these parts" using a geographical definition such as a bay or a river estuary. Micmac territory was divided into distinct areas: Gespegoitg in present-day southern Nova Scotia covering the counties of Queens, Shelburne, Yarmouth, Digby, and Annapolis; Segepenegatig, the counties of Colchester, Hants, Kings, and Lunenburg up to La Have; Esgigeoagig, Guysborough and Halifax counties; Onomagi, Cape Breton Island; Pigtogeog ag Epegoitg, Prince Edward Island and the neighbouring coastline around Pictou; Sigenigteoag, both sides of the Chignecto Isthmus and the counties of Westmoreland, Cumberland, Albert, and Kent, New Brunswick; Gespegeoag, "the last land," hence most recently acquired, ran from the Richibucto Valley along the north shore of New Brunswick to include the Gaspé Peninsula.[17] It is possible that the various branches of the tribe had totems to distinguish themselves from each other, but the evidence is slight. The missionary LeClerq mentions the cross of the Miramichi and the salmon of the Restigouche, and Lescarbot noted that the Indians who came out to meet his ship had a stag painted on their sail. If there were other distinguishing marks, they may have been lost to European observers in the mass of animal figures used in Micmac decorations.[18]

A tribe so dispersed had to organize a degree of collaboration when it came to dealing with other peoples. All or any combination of these regional groups could work together, and the most usual purpose was war on a common foe. There was some trade with other tribes south and west along the Atlantic coast for tobacco and wampum, but this did not require co-operation amongst the various Micmac groups, and it was conducted through the exchange of gifts. However, the conquest of the Gaspé, which took place in the sixteenth century, probably at the expense of the Laurentian Iroquois, would have been beyond the ability of any one section of the tribe. These wars remained in the collective memory through an exaggerated fear of "Mohawks" and tales of combat where the Micmacs won by outwitting their opponents rather than through superior strength. In the early seventeenth century, the southern portions of the tribe were at war with a people known to the French as the Armouchiquois, whose annihilation was probably completed by the great European-introduced plagues of the second decade. The Gaspesian Micmacs had as their traditional enemies the Inuit who frequented the opposite shore of the Gulf of St. Lawrence, and it is possible that there was conflict between the Cape Breton Micmacs and the Beothucks of Newfoundland, whose territory was being probed for additional hunting grounds.

The process of consultation that led to war was exhaustive. There would be a feast followed by a speech from the chief, who might or might not also be the war chief, explaining the reasons for taking action, indicating where the war would be fought, and setting the date. He addressed the assembled men and, after each proposition was put, awaited their reaction. Agreement was signified by all saying "Hau." If there was disagreement, it could not be expressed directly. Instead, an individual stood and made a speech extolling the virtues of what had been said up to that point and then gradually inserted his own views on the matter. There was no formal determination over who exactly was qualified to participate in this exchange, but the respect with which the older members of the band would be heard essentially meant that an informal council of elders usually carried the burden of decision-making. Thus a conference was a prolonged, but consciously equable, proceeding. One of the questions that would have to be determined was whether to call on other branches of the tribe for assistance, and the Micmacs were generally reluctant to ask for allies. If this was to be done, messengers were sent to arrange a conference, and summer was the only time when the people were sufficiently concentrated for this purpose. The visiting chief with his delegation would be given a feast of welcome before he proceeded to state his case and seek approval once again. Upon departure, it was the turn of the visitors to feast their hosts. Intertribal contacts were conducted with even greater formality and less goodwill. When Messamoet, chief of the Baie Verte region, treated for an alliance with Chief Olmechin of the Armouchiquois, he filled the latter's boat with gifts and was angered when Olmechin did not reciprocate immediately. On the following day Olmechin made presents in his turn, but it was too late: the delay was taken as an insult tantamount to a declaration of war.[19]

Wars were almost invariably grounded in matters of this kind: to take revenge for an insult or a blow at the self-esteem or to right a wrong were the usual justifications. Even when territorial gain ensued, as on the Gaspé or in Newfoundland, there is no evidence that the Micmacs were fighting for land or that they could be motivated to do so. There was an element of leisure-time activity in warmaking, for it gave a man an additional opportunity to prove himself to his fellows and to indulge in the satisfaction of a fight victoriously fought; and with increased esteem came status and a recognized voice in the councils of his group. The absence of violence within the tribe was offset by the frequency of violence towards other tribes. The festivities that surrounded a declaration of war and the return of the victors were outlets for emotions, pent-up within the group, that could be safely unleashed on outsiders. In defeat and the burial of the dead there was an even greater potential for emotional release. War had another major benefit. Since the Micmacs did not indulge in the rituals of torture practised by agricultural Indians, taking prisoners was functional rather than ceremonial. War could make up for losses in population by bringing enemy women and children in as prisoner slaves, while captive warriors could escape servile status if they were fortunate enough to be adopted into a family as a replacement for a man lost in battle.[20]

Wars were neither particularly bloody nor protracted. The killing or seizing of a few members of the offending tribe, men, women, or children, could be enough to justify a quick return home and a victory feast. Once war was decided upon, the warriors set out naked, armed with bows and arrows and clubs and a bark shield for defence. They attacked ferociously with "great clamour and fearful howlings." But wars were won, in the final resort, by a supernatural power, the *ginap*, of one leader being stronger than that of his opponent. In these terms, the individual warrior could do little to affect the outcome of a fight, although there was every reason to help the leader's *ginap*. Surprise and ambush were the required methods of assault, tactics that meant that no Indian could ever feel completely safe, for any noise in the undergrowth could signify a hostile war party. If the attackers failed to achieve a surprise, they were in a quandary, for they could not retire without losing face and they were not prepared for a campaign of siege and attrition. Thereupon, the war became more complex and more lethal than a simple ambush, for the chief of the band they had failed to take off guard could not ignore them. One solution was for the chief of the target village to invite his would-be attackers to a feast, treating them as honoured guests. At the end of the feast, each chief would perform his war dance and sing his war song, and then they would engage in personal combat. When one chief fell, the general battle began, with the advantage definitely on the side of those whose *ginap* had prevailed. The victorious cut off the heads of the defeated and carried them off as trophies. They danced with them at the first victory feast and then, lest the warrior became too proud, there was a period of near-penance. The band members "strip the conqueror and give him but some bad rag to cover himself withal." After a week, he was received with honour once again, and the festivities were renewed.[21]

The supernatural was as important in warfare as it was in every other aspect of Micmac life. Everything, animate or inanimate, had a spirit power, a *manitou*, which governed its existence and its relationship to human beings. Each person had his own *manitou*. A waterfall, a cove, or a particular stretch of river might have a *manitou* that required propitiation, for example, by the gift of an arrow from each traveller who passed by. Failure to observe this custom would offend the spirit of the place and set the careless at risk. The animals of the hunt had to be treated with a respect that showed a "cautious reverence for a conscious fellow-member of the same ecosystem." The hunter would address a sluggish bear in early spring to explain his need for food and clothing and to apologize for the kill. At other times, when the bear was more active, the ceremony could be performed posthumously. In either case, it was assumed that the bear assented to his own death so that man could be helped. The bear was treated with respect; when its carcass was brought into a wigwam, it came through a specially constructed opening to prove to the soul spirit of bears that the animal was still held in esteem. Beavers were dispatched with less ceremony, but they were eaten with care not to offend the species. Beaver soup could never be spilled on the fire; beaver bones were preserved and not given to the dogs or thrown into the fire for fear that the spirit of the bones would carry news of such maltreatment to the other beavers, who would thereupon refuse to give themselves to the hunters. The bones of marten and moose fawn were treated with similar respect and for similar reasons. The Micmacs accorded animals the same esteem they gave each other. They spoke of them as though the animals lived in the same way, each species a separate tribe living in its own villages under its own chiefs. The stories the Micmacs told each other were, more often than not, about the deeds of otter or beaver or moose. It was all one world indivisible.[22]

Access to the spirits lay through dreams, which were consequently highly valued. The hunting dream was almost a necessity of life, for there the dreamer would see the spirits of the animals and they would guide him to the best place for hunting. But dreams ranged much farther than the practical business of finding food. A true dream was regarded as just as real as the events of the waking life, for it was the experience of the dreamer's spirit. The reality of these dreams was such that the men would rise up in the middle of the night "and hail the omen with songs and dances." A true dream could be prophetic, an infallible guide to action. It provided the dreamer with authority, for, by using it as his justification, a man might demand action that he would not otherwise have dared to suggest. But there was always the possibility that a dream was not a true one and was therefore without validity. If the dream concerned the best place to hunt and no game was found there, then obviously it was proven false. Dreams that might lead, for example, to vengeance on another tribe, could not be so easily assessed. As a result, each band needed a specialist to interpret these contacts with the spirit world, the buoin.[23]

The prevalence of spirits was nowhere better demonstrated than in the practice of medicine. In common with other Amerindians, the Micmacs saw illness as a matter for both physical and spiritual attention. As in war, so in health, the final determination was made by a spirit power. There was much that could be done at the physical level. The Micmacs had an array of medicines fully up to the standards of those available to the European visitors. They kept themselves healthy by taking sauna baths in specially constructed pits or wigwams. They used herbs to produce expectorants and emetics and purgatives to cope with digestive problems; they had a remedy for epilepsy; set broken limbs in splints; practised resuscitation; healed wounds by licking and cleaning the cuts and then applying fir gum. They had nothing to offset toothache, for all had perfect teeth. There were set procedures for assisting at a difficult birth and a broth to ease the pain. Unless he was incapacitated by a broken leg, the patient was expected to keep up with the movements of the rest of the band, the only concession being that he was guaranteed a place close to the campfire.[24]

If the sick person did not recover after these treatments, it was obvious that his body had been invaded by a malignant spirit. There was no such thing as death from natural causes; every death was supernatural. Consequently, it was the duty of the buoin to pit his spirit against that possessing the victim, a process that required licking or blowing on the affected part and invoking spirit power through incantations. This treatment could be carried out coincidentally with the application of purely physical remedies. If the patient died, it was because the evil spirit had prevailed and still held his body, not because the physical remedies had failed. Diagnosis of the nature of the evil spirit was obviously very important. Sickness could be caused by the frustration of a desire that was agitating the body until it was gratified, a good reason for taking dreams seriously and indulging the dreamer in his wishes. But the desire could have entered the patient subconsciously, so that even he did not know he held it. Hence there was a need "to look into the inmost recesses of the mind." Sickness could also be the result of breaking a taboo, and it would then be necessary to determine which before proceeding to a successful cure. There was yet another possibility, that the victim had been possessed at the will of some malevolent person or persons unknown, who would have to be sought out and counterattacked before the patient would recover. With such a variety of possibilities, the buoin who occasionally lost a patient need not fear for his reputation; he could not always find the suppressed desire, triumph over the spirit of an offended bear or waterfall or contend with an unknown evil power.[25]

The practice of medicine was only one part of a buoin's duties, for his sphere of competence was vast. The source of his power lay in the leather medicine bag he carried around his neck containing the spirit objects of his profession. The contents of such bags were secret, but one handed over to an assertive missionary contained the following items: a stone the size of a nut, wrapped in a box, which was the buoin's personal *ouahich*; a piece of bark with the figure of a wolverine on it done in black and white wampum, which represented the master *ouahich*; a miniature bow and a cord interlaced with porcupine quills; a fragment of bark wrapped in a thin skin and decorated with pictures of little children, birds, bears, beavers, and moose; a tiny wooden model of a bird; and a rattle. The wolverine represented the buoin's animal helper in his contact with that spirit world; the personal *ouahich* was his entrée to the spirit world in general; the bow and pictures allowed him to use sympathetic magic and, with the one of the children, for example, to produce abortions. The ability to kill through symbols made the buoin a dangerous man, for he could substitute any figure that he chose.[26]

The secrets of shamanism were handed on from father to eldest son. The most important one apparently was how to make contact with the spirit world at will, while lesser mortals had to await revelations in dreams. The buoin would summon the supernatural by speaking in tongues, howling and contorting himself until the sweat stood out, and then relaxing into a trance. When the spirit entered him, he began to sing to it, and if the occasion was a public one, others would accompany him, dancing and chanting. Once the spirit had taken possession of him, he had power to exorcise, prophesy, speak with the spirits of the dead and animals past and present, heal the sick, and confound the enemies of his people. The wide range of this power put him in a position of authority, for no enterprise would be undertaken without first consulting him, and his advice would be needed in every time of stress. The chief who was also a buoin would be in a very strong position, but the two offices were not necessarily connected, and thus authority within the tribe was further diffused.[27]

The buoin possessed powers different in degree, not kind, from those of the ordinary mortal. Each person possessed three spirits: the life soul, the brain soul, and the free soul. When the life soul expired, death ensued; when the brain soul was destroyed, a man could live on but would be witless. The most important spirit was the free soul, for that existed both in life and in death. It was the shadow replica of a man and could leave him temporarily in dreams; if it was absent when a man was killed, it could bring life back to his body; and through this soul came the power of prophecy and contact with the spirit world. The free soul accompanied a man to the land of the dead, but it could also haunt the living, especially if it belonged to a warrior whose death had been unavenged. A sombre black image, it stalked the forests near the camps of its body's former relatives and was an object of terror and propitiation; food was regularly set aside for it at feasts. For fear of these ghosts, the Micmacs did not travel by night or wage war under the cover of darkness. The buoin could control his free soul and use it to work wonders, and any man could claim to be a buoin if he could prove by his dreams that he had similar power.[28]

If there were human spirits abroad in the land, so too were there animal spirits, for all shared the same qualities. In addition, there were totally supernatural beings possessed of a mystical power of unspecified potential. Different spirits held this power in different quantities; the principal one was the Great Spirit, possibly identified with the sun. A simple ceremony observed by missionaries was the greeting of the rising sun with a bow and a request that it guard the man's family, vanquish his foes, and bring him a good hunt. Next in rank after the Great Spirit came the *megumoowesoo*, giant beings of human form with enormous supernatural power. They lived much as did the Micmacs, in a far-away land where the spirit beasts were so abundant that there was never a starving time. The *megumoowesoo* could also live among mortals and even endow them with their powers and take them into their ranks. These spirits were generally benign, and their intervention in human affairs was minimal.[29]

Death and burial were governed by set rituals in order to prepare man for his transfer to the wholly spirit world. Correct form was necessary to prevent the evil spirit that had brought death from going with him to the next world. Ideally, the process of dying itself was ordered by custom. When the buoin pronounced a man mortally ill, he stopped eating, put on his best robes, and began to chant his death song. His relatives and friends would comfort him, saying that he was going to the place of the spirits and that he left strong children behind him to carry on his line. There was no overt mourning. Sometimes the dying person would use his surviving stock to put on his own death feast. If he lingered thereafter, cold water might be thrown over him to ensure his demise. At the time of death the body was bound in skins with the knees against the stomach in the foetal position. The corpse might be propped up thus while dancers circled around in full mourning. The nearest relative would deliver the funeral oration, reciting the dead man's genealogy and his heroic deeds and rejoicing that he was going to his friends in a better land. Then the corpse was lowered into a circular grave five feet deep and covered with a latticework of sticks. Into the grave went the things whose spirits he would need for life in the spirit world—his bow and arrow, hatchet, clothing, ornaments, pipe and tobacco, even his hunting dogs—and then the grave was covered with earth. The possessions that the dead did not take with him were burned. After further expressions of grief, the departed was never mentioned by name again, and if it was necessary to refer to him, a new name was invented. Relatives and friends observed a year of mourning.[30]

Obviously this elaborate sequence of rites could not be followed in all cases. Sometimes death came unexpectedly and without the presence of a buoin. In this case the survivors would beat the sides of the wigwam, crying out to make the spirit leave; then the death was announced to the other members of the band and and the appropriate ceremonies were followed. The Micmacs were accustomed to burying their dead in a common burial ground near to, but not part of, the summer camp site. If a death occurred elsewhere, during the winter hunt, for example, the body would be wrapped in bark and placed in a tree until it could be brought in for burial at the proper place. Infants were not necessarily brought to the common burial ground; instead they were interred at the side of trails, so, it was said, that their spirits "may slip into the bosoms of women passing by, and animate the yet undeveloped foetus." Death could not always be noble: incurables might be abandoned and the very old put to death as an act of mercy. The judgment of the buoins ensured that only the healthy people, so admired by European observers, survived.[31]

Death made apparent the gradations of rank and status in Micmac society. For one thing, death put on display the private goods that had been acquired in life and were taken by their owner to the spirit world. The ritual destruction of those goods ensured that the living would remain on a footing of equality with each other. Women and children were buried with much less ceremony than men, for the feasts were smaller and the mourning not so pronounced. They too took to the grave the possessions they would need in the land of the dead: for a woman, the collar she used to pull the toboggan, her hatchet, her needles and tools for embroidery, her ornaments; for a child, his toys. A famous warrior would be honoured above a lesser man and receive more than one funeral oration and feasts to match. The death of a chief or a chief's son demanded the full exercise of all the rites with a punctilio appropriate to the rank. The grave of a distinguished man was marked by a monument of interlacing poles as an especial token of esteem. If a matter of state was involved, as with a death that required vengeance on another tribe, the funeral services would be elaborated for political ends. The burial of Panonias, a trader murdered by the Armouchiquois, was one such event. A single funeral oration was not enough, for all had to speak; one day of grief did not suffice, for there had to be a whole week of mourning "by intermission every cabin his day, and every person his turn."[32] All men were not equal in death.

The Micmacs lived and died within the constraints of the world as they found it. They made no attempt to change the natural order to suit the convenience of human beings, for man was only one part of a totally interdependent system that saw all things, animate and inanimate, in their proper places. This view did not make life simple, far from it; every aspect of existence was highly complex. Fear was ever present: fear of offending spirits, fear of ghosts, fear of death at the whim of an unknown power. The basic offence was to upset the traditional order either by design or mistake, and the taboos served to maintain the balance within nature. The respect shown the spirits of animals ensured that the Micmacs killed only what they needed for food and clothing. Birth control guaranteed that the population did not grow beyond the means available to support it, and the buoin's power to judge the approach of death prevented the helpless from being an unproductive burden on resources. If men depended on nature, then they depended on each other as part of nature. The need to live harmoniously in small groups placed each individual under a severe code of self-restraint, but there were opportunities for emotional release in the frequent feasts and the excitement of songs and dances. These festivities in turn referred back to the holistic world that encompassed the people. Therein lay their strength: the acceptance of nature as a unity. Therein lay their weakness, for to change that society in any one particular was to undermine the whole.

2

Acadia: The First Contact

With the coming of the white man, the Micmacs entered into a process of acculturation that has continued to this day. This experience, common to all Amerindians, falls into two main phases: non-directed and directed acculturation. At first, two different cultural systems meet on a nearly equal footing and each chooses from the other those traits and materials that are of the most use to them; neither side is in a position to advance its culture by force. In the second stage, directed contact, one group develops the power to force change on the other and to decide what course that change will take.[1] Under the impact of white traders, missionaries, and settlers, many native people have passed from non-directed to directed acculturation within a generation. The Micmacs were able to resist that passage for almost two hundred years. From the first contact with white fishermen early in the sixteenth century until about 1700, they were able to absorb and to utilize European innovations which modified their behaviour in a manner they were able to control to a large extent. Outwardly they appeared to have maintained their traditional life within their accustomed territories, but contact with the French had in fact undermined their society.

Lack of power, not of desire, prevented the French from directing the acculturation of the Indians to European society. The first French to write of the Micmacs had no doubt that they were an inferior people who had wantonly wasted their opportunities and "through the progress and experience of centuries ought to have come to some perfection in the arts, sciences and philosophy ... ought to have produced abundant fruits in philosophy, government, customs and [the] conveniences of life."[2] No educated European could approach the Amerindians without preconceptions based on an already extensive sixteenth-century literature concerning the New World. At one moment the Micmacs were accorded the honour of living in the manner that "was in vogue in the golden age"; at another they were dismissed as beggars, poor hypocritical people.[3] Europeans, accustomed to a class system and a hierarchical ordering of authority, inevitably saw societies less structured than their own as primitive. Frenchmen needed a regular supply of food and shelter and clothing and the institutions that guaranteed such necessities; the Micmacs apparently needed none of these things, for they lived under four sticks in the ground, alternately feeding and starving.[4] The Indian fitted nowhere in the European scale of things: more intelligent than a peasant; measured and deliberate where the white was always in a hurry, equable where the French were quarrelsome.[5] It was quite obvious that such people should be moulded into something comprehensible.

Some Frenchmen had a perfectly clear idea of what they wanted to do with the Micmacs. Champlain hoped to pacify them and stop their intertribal wars in order that his country "might derive service from them, and convert them to the Christian faith."[6] He explained as much to a group of Indians in September, 1604, and promised to send them settlers to teach them how to cultivate the soil and free them from the miserable life they led.[7] When the Sieur de Monts settled at St. Croix, the Indians showed a proper deference by making him "judge of the debates, which is the beginning of voluntary subjection, from whence a hope may be conceived that these people will soon conform themselves to our manner of living."[8] On leaving his new establishment at Port Royal in 1607, de Monts promised the local Micmacs that he would return with "households and families ... wholly to inhabit their land, and teach them trades for to make them live as we do." The promise "did somewhat comfort them."[9] Not for a moment did French visitors show any desire to accept the Micmac way of life as it stood, and they blithely assumed that their hosts would be happy to see it thoroughly overhauled.

For their part, the Micmacs were generally unimpressed by the self-assurance of the Europeans they met. Frenchmen bragged of their riches yet haggled incessantly until they had struck a mean bargain for the simplest goods; men who were truly rich would bring splendid gifts to those they visited. Whites boasted of the wonders and comforts of home yet voyaged for weeks over dangerous seas to beg for furs that were too old to wear. Could France really be a terrestrial paradise if men were willing to abandon their families to visit the land of the Micmacs? The Indians were not so discontented with their lot that they wished to visit France.[10] Obviously, the actions of the whites belied their words, and the Micmacs could reply confidently to every criticism: "That is the Savage way of doing it. You can have your way and we will have ours."[11]

The first to bring European ways to the Micmacs were fishermen, many of whom, but by no means all, were from France. Trade with the coastal Indians was as old as the North Atlantic fishery, and its beginning cannot be placed more precisely than at some time in the first quarter of the sixteenth century. The trade must have started as part of the ritual of gift exchange that the Indians required on first meeting strangers. The fishermen found a ready market for the furs they acquired and were ready to exchange whatever goods they had at hand, including those parts of their ships' equipment that could be written off as lost on the voyage. Ships' masters and crews could make a profit at the expense of the owners, who, as soon as they realized what was happening, sent out trade goods on their own account. The resulting returns became an important auxiliary source of profit. Since the Micmac bands went to the same coastal sites each summer, they could be located easily and traded with on a regular basis. The value of this commerce was well enough established by the end of the century to become the financial justification for the first settlements and the first missionaries. But though both settlers and missionaries were occasional visitors for years to come, the fishermen returned year after year to barter with the Micmacs. Even at the end of the seventeenth century the fishing boats were still carrying off the bulk of the furs and hides collected by the Micmacs.[12]

The Indians incorporated the seasonal arrival of the fishermen into their annual life cycle. As the range and quantity of European goods increased, the bands were able to live through the summer with progressively less dependence on the gathering of local food. They awaited the arrival of one boat after another, consuming what they acquired from each. Brandy, introduced on these occasions, had a demoralizing effect and was of considerable assistance to the fishermen in their relations with Indian women.[13] The "French trade," as these seasonal visits came to be known, affected Micmac life at several levels. It changed the pattern of sustained food-gathering to one of summer hunts for moose hides, punctuated by long periods of relaxation; to greater dependence on a foreign rather than a country diet; to reliance on goods acquired and not made. Further, the traders promoted miscegenation and spread new diseases. Long before the first land-based merchant set up his post, the fishermen had introduced the Indians to the realities and abuses of the commercial world.

The French trade harmonized with Micmac life insofar as it required nothing new of a people who already hunted and traded through the medium of gift exchange. On the surface, European goods simply reinforced the old ways by permitting the Micmacs to do what they had always done more efficiently. A single discharge from a musket could kill five or six ducks where an arrow could only take one; a cooking pot saved endless hours of hollowing out tree stumps and heating water with red hot stones; an iron knife facilitated everything from skinning animals to making snowshoes. By using European tools in the traditional context, the band could now travel further and faster, feed and clothe itself better. The new implements could also be absorbed into the spirit world of the Micmacs, for it was the "spirit" of iron, not the metal itself, that made it superior to stone, the "spirit" of the kettle that determined its efficiency. As long as these innovations could be explained within the traditional pattern of thought, they were not necessarily a challenge to it. But such adaptations were doomed to failure in the long run, for the desire to acquire new goods made it impossible to use them simply in the traditional context. To buy European goods the Micmacs had to adapt to European demands and, imperceptibly, year by year, European standards. The result was a gradual disruption of every aspect of Micmac life, from the spiritual world to the daily routine.[14]

When animals became an item of commerce, the bond that had once united hunter and hunted was made nonsensical. The Micmacs lost their special relationship to the fauna as they adopted a more materialistic and European concept of the environment. What had been a resource for the use of the whole people became an opportunity to be exploited for the benefit of the most aggressive hunter. Once this notion was accepted, the way was open for an end to the idea that the land itself was for all to use. As the years of contact lengthened and trade was conducted with men outside the group, these outsiders became more important to the Micmacs' survival than their fellows. In the pursuit of the means to acquire European goods, certain lands were delimited as the preserve of one family rather than another. No longer was it imperative to co-operate with other band members, and the division of the land into hunting areas for individual families became all the more acceptable for that reason. Further, the European goods made the Indians more independent and more capable of moving and hunting and surviving in small groups. Hunting moose and beaver had never demanded the co-operation of large numbers of men: the moose was a solitary animal best stalked by the fewest hunters while the beaver was almost stationary and could be killed at leisure. European goods intensified the small-group nature of the Micmac hunt.[15]

Although the demands of the trade led to a greater individualization of economic enterprise, the Europeans preferred to do business with one acknowledged leader rather than with a conglomerate of individuals. Generous to a fault when it came to making gifts, the Micmacs were less than punctilious when it came to making payments for goods received. The Europeans found it necessary to hold one man accountable. If the existing chief was not amenable, then the whites would pick another person and conduct trade through him. Micmac society was pulled in two opposing directions: towards and away from a concentration of authority. Some of the chiefs with whom Europeans dealt tried to reach an accommodation between the two extremes; one, for example, abased himself before his fellow band members, conspicuously dressing in the most ragged clothes and consciously undervaluing his share of the total yield in order to avoid arousing jealousies. At the same time, the trading chief could demand some formal courtesies from the whites: a gun salute on approaching a trading post and feasts of welcome and farewell.[16] By virtue of this recognition he gained an authority within his own band that had no place in pre-contact society. If one man could become chief by choice of outsiders, so might another. The way was opened to a multiplicity of chiefs, who could now be defined as the leaders of the smallest groups with which Europeans cared to trade. Thus the determination of who was in authority passed out of the hands of the Indians and into the power of the French.

The emphasis on killing animals for commercial reasons distorted a way of life in which hunting had been only one of the seasonal activities in an annual cycle of food-gathering. Time spent hunting and trapping, even with efficient new tools, was time taken at the expense of the traditional routine. Moose were hunted in summer when they were the hardest to catch, and beaver were taken in the coldest weather when their fur was thickest and they were most difficult to approach. European goods had to make up the resulting deficiencies, but for all practical purposes the new products were inferior to the old ones. No European clothing could provide as much protection against the climate as fur, and European foods such as dried peas and prunes, even if they did not spoil on the Atlantic crossing, were less nutritious than country foods. Of course, the more animals killed for their skins, the more meat that was eaten; but overall the effect of trade was to leave the Micmacs less well-fed and clothed than before. The result was a general decline in health, more sickness, and less resistance to new ailments. Sickness diminished men's ability to hunt and, thus, to buy the new goods required to make up the new deficiencies, and this inefficiency promoted a further decline in physical well-being. And, since the physical and spiritual were never far apart in Micmac life, the traditional interrelation of man and spirit was also harmed by these new conditions.

The fur and skin trade introduced change to the Micmacs; their lives slowly altered over generations in a way frequently beyond their comprehension. The trader laid the groundwork for the missionary, who came to answer the unsolved riddles of white contact by propounding an alternative explanation for the whole of life. The missionary directly challenged the spiritual complex that had already been undermined by the economic impact of the French trader. The missionary's role was perfectly familiar to a people conscious of the spirit world and of the need to have an intermediary to maintain contact with it. Sickness, for both missionary and buoin, was a matter of spiritual concern, and the role of priest as healer was nothing new. Missionaries early appreciated the situation and were able to manipulate this coincidence of their functions and the buoin's to preach their own viewpoint. The Micmacs were able to verify the missionaries' claims about the superiority of their god without reference to Christian doctrine and only accepted what they had first screened through the filter of their own perceptions. Having selected only those ideas they found agreeable, the Micmacs were able to translate Christian beliefs into their own terms. As with the trader, so with the missionary, acculturation was a lengthy process.[17]

The first missionary, the Abbé Jessé Fléché, arrived with de Monts' settlers at Port Royal. Two Jesuits, Fathers Biard and Massé, went out with Poutrincourt's group and set up their own establishment at Mt. Desert Island. Both left in 1616, and among the more important of their scattered successors was another Jesuit, Barthélemy Vimont, who built a chapel at an inlet on Cape Breton that he named for St. Ann, mother of the Virgin Mary, who was to become the Micmacs' patron saint. But there was no continuous contact with the Indians. One of the longest established missions was founded by Father Maitre de Lyonne at Chedabucto in 1657; it was still in existence thirty years later. There were also missions on the mainland side of the Bay of Fundy, the most important being that of Father Chrétien Le Clerq, who began his work in Gaspesia in 1676 and stayed for almost a decade.[18]

The most striking attributes of the missionary were that he was white and French and therefore of the same kind as the fishermen who had frequented the coasts for many years before his arrival. Being to this extent a known quantity, the missionary had little difficulty in approaching the Micmacs. The formalities that governed the arrival of a guest allowed him the opportunity to state his business at length, and the gift of even a small amount of tobacco was enough to win an attentive audience.[19] The Micmacs regarded the first missionary, Fléché, as they did other newcomers, with a cautious curiosity and an eye to his usefulness. Since the French were apparently set on coming over in numbers, it was prudent to ally with them. When Fléché showed himself anxious to perform a ceremony that involved mysterious signs and sounds and water, 140 Micmacs were happy to oblige him; they saw baptism as a pledge of friendship and alliance with the newcomers.[20] Although later missionaries refused to baptize on this scale, the link between the French and the new religion remained basic to the Micmacs' acceptance of the missionary. He was useful, the only person who could communicate with the French, whether they were traders, settlers, or, later, soldiers. As the importance of the Europeans increased, so did the status of the one who performed the rituals recognized and respected by the whites.

The missionary had other uses beyond acting as an intermediary. One of the basic functions of the buoin was to predict where food might be found for the band. The missionary spent much time in prayer, communicating with his spirit. Could that spirit make useful predictions? Chief Membertou was impressed when, under Biard's direction, he prayed for food and found a good run of smelt on the following day. He checked on other occasions and found to his satisfaction that the Christian God had directed him at one time to moose and at another to herring.[21] Even after several generations of Christian contact, the new spirit was still expected to serve this old function. When

LeClerq refused to predict where the next game animals would be found, his guide triumphantly pointed out that since his spirit had given him clear directions he was obviously in touch with a superior power.[22] Over the years, however, the missionary was able to make a claim to spirit power of the same order as the buoin's. Nothing loath to pray for plenty, the priests were correct on enough occasions to prove the usefulness of Christianity.

Catholic practices also paralleled those of the buoin in medical matters, sometimes with an uncanny exactness. Just as the buoin carried bits of bone and other apparently everyday objects imbued with mystic power, so did the missionary. The frequent use of the crucifix as a healing agent was totally comprehensible to the Micmacs. When Membertou's son fell sick, "we put upon the sufferer a bone taken from the precious relic of the glorified Saint Lawrence, archbishop of Dublin in Ireland."[23] The man recovered, and the lesson learned was that the missionary's curative powers were at least as great as the buoin's. The mixture of medical and spiritual practice carried responsibilities too, and these might prove hazardous. The Indians of Mt. Desert Island told Biard that their chief was about to die, and since he had not yet been baptized, he would not go to heaven which was all the missionary's fault. Biard visited the man, who only had a cold, and he soon recovered: another triumph for Christian healing.[24] Naturally, the missionaries could not guarantee recovery every time, but their rate of success was enough to create a good impression.

The fact that the missionaries were able to pass such basic tests in the arts of prediction and medicine meant that the Indians were willing to gratify them by observing the formalities of the Christian religion. As early as 1611 some Micmacs were carrying "candles, bells, holy water and other things, marching in good order in the processions." Poutrincourt, it was claimed, had taught them the basic liturgical music for the mass.[25] They attended church services, but on their own terms, "to mutter there their ancient idolatries. They observed the appointed Saints' days, but it was while carrying on their sacrifices, dances and superstitions."[26] Father Perrault met some Micmacs in Cape Breton who were happy to make the sign of the cross and repeat "Jesus Christ" after him; all they asked in return was that he pray for their success in hunting and relief from disease.[27] As the years passed, Christian ideas gradually melded with traditional beliefs and the Micmacs began to talk of an afterlife that was miserable for the wicked and blissful for the good. A rough equivalence between Christian and native beliefs took shape: Jesus was the sun, guardian spirits were saints, tricksters were the devil.[28]

The success of the missionary took place at the expense of the buoin, who was hard pressed to maintain his traditional ascendancy. Honours were about even in the matters of prediction, and this fact itself meant a diminution of those powers that the buoin had once held as uniquely his own. The appearance of new diseases, some of which came with missionaries, totally confounded the buoin. A crucifix was no more able to cure smallpox than the entire contents of a medicine bag, but the missionary was demonstrably protected by his spirit power from an illness that could kill the buoin as easily as anyone else. Both sides continued to agree on the spiritual nature of the physical world, and the contest was fought along mutually recognized lines. When LeClerq reproved some Indians for licking the bodies of the sick and breathing over them, he was told that they were doing as he did at baptism: chasing out sin.[29]

The logical course for the buoin to adopt, if they wished to survive, was to incorporate some of the Christians' powers into their own rites by obtaining similar relics and performing similar rituals. LeClerq noted one instance where a picture traded from the French was being venerated as an image from heaven and another where Indians were hearing confession. One ancient woman used beads from an unthreaded rosary as the basis of her spirit power, while another had some beads, "a King of Hearts, the foot of a glass, and a kind of medal" as objects of worship.[30] The missionary's preoccupation with confession and holy water combined to modify shamanistic practices by the middle of the eighteenth century. The medicine bag lost its importance, and when called on for a prediction, the buoin consulted a bowl of water. If its surface was obscure or disturbed, he announced that he could go no further until those present revealed their inmost thoughts to him in private.[31] These attempts to adapt to the changing times did little to help the buoin and simply illustrated the Christianization of powers that were in an irreversible decline.

There was no need for the missionaries to dissemble or compromise their faith in paralleling Micmac experience. Both Indians and French saw culture and religion as a unit and neither expected them to operate independently of each other. Both believed in direction by a supernatural power which could be ritualistically consulted, and their common faith in the reality of mystical experience was an important bond. Missionaries could unabashedly pit the authority of their dreams against those of the buoin. Christian revelations were a viable form of persuasion. The ultimate experience in mystical contact, spirit possession, was prized by the Micmacs but feared by the missionaries as evil, a known evil with which they were prepared to cope.[32]

Despite the many parallels in belief, mission work among the Micmacs was far from simple. The first obstacle was language. The Micmacs were accustomed to not having to learn French. The lingua franca of the coast was a mixture of Basque and Micmac suitable for trading but little else.[33] Much of the scattering of French words that had preceded the missionaries came from the scatalogical vocabulary of the fishermen, and Micmac women were fond of trying out selections on embarrassed missionaries.[34] Learning the Micmac tongue meant paying Indians to act as teachers and, as Biard discovered, doing the menial work such as fetching wood for the fire.[35] The language was difficult; one student, Perrault, was convinced that the Indians added an extra syllable to each word deliberately to mislead him.[36] The missionaries were taught by the touch and identify method and quickly concluded that the language was replete with words applying to things but lacked those defining qualities. They had expressions, Biard noted, for good, strong, black, but not for goodness, strength, or blackness: "no words to describe things which they have never seen or even conceived." They had, admittedly, "a fair capacity for judging and valuing material and common things, deducing their reasons with great nicety, and always reasoning them with some pretty comparisons."[37] This limited view of the Micmacs' intellectual ability was the result of French ignorance, and it was not until the nineteenth century that white philologists finally discovered the extraordinary range and sophistication of the language.[38] The missionaries' belief that it was deficient in spiritual content confirmed what they had expected to find: a heathen people with few concepts beyond those of the material world.

The Micmacs indeed had developed no concept of an eternal life that would be either agony or bliss according to the individual's manner of life on earth. They were not aware of original sin nor, consequently, of the devil or of the need for salvation through Jesus Christ. The multitude of spirits with which they were familiar were neither good nor bad and could be mischievous or benevolent or threatening according to circumstance. Life hereafter was simply a continuation of life on earth in spirit form.[39] Since Christians had spent centuries refining the terms of their theology and its attendant vocabulary, it is hardly surprising that the missionaries had a difficult time relaying a highly technical subject in a language they little understood. They found the Micmacs to be slow learners, unable to retain anything by rote.[40] Given the importance of oral tradition in a pre-literate society, this inability could only be explained by the fact that the Indians were receiving little they considered worth remembering. LeClerq tried to overcome their chronic forgetfulness by inventing hieroglyphs to represent Micmac words that would keep Christian beliefs fresh in mind. The attempt was, to a degree, self-defeating, for the Micmacs were impressed by the spirit power that the missionaries had invested in words and paper and paid little attention to the meaning of the words themselves. This attempt to instil Christian precepts became yet one more demonstration of the shamanistic power of the missionary.[41]

As an element in white contact, the missionaries contributed to the decline of the traditional forms and beliefs of Micmac society, but not in the way they might have wished. Their success was as much the result of their being French as of being Christian. It was not Christian doctrine that persuaded the Micmacs, but the ability of the missionaries to perform on terms set down by those they wished to convert. A full century after the arrival of the first missionary the Micmacs described themselves as Christian, but their knowledge of the new belief remained rudimentary and suffused with their old concepts and attitudes. By then the missionary had replaced the buoin and his power had to be accepted, in a utilitarian sense, as the superior one. Persuasion operated through demonstration, not doctrine.

The activities of the missionary complemented those of the trader, and in many parts of North America both combined together to pave the way for the settler, the final agent in the destruction of the Indian. But as with trader and missionary, the impact of the settler on the Micmacs was so gradual over so many years that the changes might almost pass unnoticed. The French fell far short of De Monts' early promise to send families to inhabit the land. Acadia's chief importance to France was as an adjunct to the North Atlantic fishery and as a minor supplier of furs, and neither of these activities required extensive white settlement. This economic reality, coupled with political disputes in France and a general ignorance of the area, served to frustrate those whites who sought their fortune in Acadia. Moreover, the territory quickly took a place in the Anglo-French struggle for empire: King James I granted the land, under the name of Nova Scotia, to a Scottish entrepreneur who sent settlers to the old French site at Port Royal. Acadia passed under British control in 1629, but it was returned to France three years later. The Company of New France made its one attempt at colonization in 1632, sending three hundred people to La Have. After the contract labourers had gone home, there were only a dozen or so families left behind, and these concentrated at Port Royal. Distant from the authority of France, two rival grantees fought each other over their claims to the fur trade monopoly. War intervened to bring Acadia once again under nominal British control between 1654 and 1670. After that date, France tried to exercise some formal authority, at least to the extent of appointing colonial governors, but English ships sailed the coastal waters at will, trading or plundering as they saw fit.[42]

Although the violent and fluctuating nature of the European presence in Acadia did nothing to encourage its settlement, a resident population of French did establish itself and clung tenaciously to life. By 1650 there were some fifty European households at Port Royal and La Have; by 1686 the white population exceeded 900. Out-migration from Port Royal brought settlement to Minas and Beaubassin, and in 1707 the three contained 570, 271, and 585 Acadian French respectively. Less than 100 others lived dispersed along the north coast of the Bay of Fundy, where only isolated trading posts testified to their presence. When the British took control for the third and last time, capturing Port Royal in 1710, there were just over 1,500 native-born Acadians with roots going back from two to four generations.[43] The Micmac population stood at about the same number, having declined from the 3,000 or so at the beginning of the seventeenth century. In one hundred years the French had been able to establish a white population only one-half the size of the Micmacs' at their first arrival.

The legal forms under which the French took possession of Acadia were those of the seigneurial system: the king owned the land and could theoretically dispose of it at will. There was never any question of treating for the cession of Indian lands, no concept that the Indians had rights that had to be bargained for, no thought that they should be treated as a separate nation. Vast grants were made to individual Frenchmen for their profit: between 1632 and 1635 the Company of New France disposed of 3.7 million arpents. By the end of the century there were fifty-five grants of a seigneurial character still in existence.[44] As the French saw it, the Indians had no land they could legally call their own. When Récollet missionaries tried to establish farming communities to assist in the conversion of the Micmacs, they arranged to purchase the necessary lands from one of the French grantees.[45] But whatever the technicalities of form, the Acadian settlers themselves obtruded scarcely at all on Micmac territory. Farming on tidal flats that were dyked to permit cultivation, they were adding new land rather than destroying old hunting grounds. As far as the Acadians were concerned, there could be no question of dominating the Micmacs and bending them to their will. Mere survival dictated that they live in harmony with the natives. The king of France might claim ownership of all the land, but the realities of life made the claim meaningless.

At first glance, the Acadians appear to have been much less of a challenge to Micmac life than the traders and missionaries. The settlers tended to acculturate to the Micmacs, adopting their habits of dress and transportation. Many of the early French took Indian wives, and the community at La Have, for example, was a métis settlement. The relationship proved to be a source of security as well as population to the settlers, for blood ties ensured their protection and good treatment at the hands of the Micmacs. This mingling of the Micmacs with a settled population, however, tended to subtract from their numbers. Whether the children of mixed descent became hunters or farmers depended on which parent had the major responsibility for their upbringing. The white male settlers had an interest in retaining control of their children, if only as labourers on their farms. By contrast, the fishermen who preceded them had had no interest in the offspring of their casual liaisons, and those children were raised by their mothers totally within the Micmac culture. Hence the Acadian settlers presented a non-violent but very real threat to native survival; the half-breed child who stayed on the farm eventually assimilated to white society.

A few white traders planning permanent residence in Acadia also married Indian women. These unions, regular and sanctioned by the Christian church, made good sense to land-based traders because they provided them with connections among the native people on whom they depended for business success. Some of the leading families of Acadia, the Denys, d'Entremonts, and Saint Castins, for example, consolidated their position in this way. They lived in European-style trading posts behind wooden stockades, but they spent much of their lives travelling with their Indian relatives. Their children grew up to move freely in both worlds. The French called these men "capitaines des sauvages" and preferred to deal with them rather than with pure-blooded native chiefs. The captains were ideally suited to act as interpreters and intermediaries; and when French governors began the practice of giving the Indians annual presents, the captains took care of the distribution, which they made in their own names and in that of the king of France. This practice played further havoc with the traditional lines of authority already undermined by trader and missionary, for it introduced the notion of one whose power stood above that of all other chiefs. As the agents of that power, the métis gained great status, for it was they who demonstrably arranged for and distributed the gifts. The captains were hence much more useful to the Micmacs than were buoins and chiefs, and their source of power led inexorably away from the indigenous society towards a white king over the waters.[46]

PART II

The Struggle for Acadia

3

The Contest for Acadia 1714–1749

The Treaty of Utrecht in 1713 ensured that the northeastern Indians would remain in the centre of a global conflict. The British acquired Acadia within its never-to-be-defined ancient limits and exposed New France to attack from the southeast along the Kennebec and St. John rivers. Since Cape Breton was now the sole French possession on the Atlantic shore, the island took on high strategic significance. The new situation gave the native people a new importance in European eyes. Statesmen at Versailles saw them as auxiliary forces to be relocated at positions most suitable for the defence of New France. Britons saw them as subjects to be tied down by paper treaties to continue their trade and to share their lands with British colonists. The Indians themselves saw that they could use their position as a third force to wrest advantages from one side or the other by a mixture of threats and promises. Their desire was to be allowed to pursue their accustomed life in their familiar lands while enjoying a maximum of European goods. It is not too surprising that the strategic concerns of the underpopulated French empire should have impinged less on the natives than did the pushiness of the New Englanders. Land hunger meant that the Abenakis on their northern borders were the first to suffer aggression and the first to resist coherently. The Micmacs had more than thirty years' grace before their lands too came under attack; time to watch and learn what was in store for them, to practise and perfect their techniques of resistance.

The initial French reaction to the loss of Acadia was that the Indians should

†Quotations marked with a dagger are translated in the notes.

be relocated along the Gulf of St. Lawrence or on Ile St. Jean; but if, as seemed likely, they refused to leave the Atlantic coast, they should be moved to Cape Breton to strengthen the new establishment that was to be developed. The Acadian French should also move there. The minister of Marine wrote the missionary Antoine Gaulin that it was up to him to persuade the Indians; the task might prove difficult, but one who was inspired to serve the glory of God and the security of the new colony would doubtless overcome all obstacles. Three barrels of gunpowder and six hundred pounds of lead shot were despatched as presents.[1] The Indians would certainly want to move to the newly named Ile Royale: they were all Catholics and accustomed to the ways of the French nation. "The French and Indians of Acadia must look up to the Sun and the Stars from the same land; they must stand shoulder to shoulder on the battlefield; when the hatchet is buried, live together in peace and harmony; and when the time comes, sleep side by side beneath the sod of their common country."[2] Versailles proposed, the Micmacs disposed; they would not leave their ancestral lands at the whim of global strategists.

Since the Micmacs refused to be concentrated on Ile Royale, the French determined to use them where they lived. Hostility to the English was the corollary of their continued attachment to France, and it was to be encouraged "avec beaucoup de prudence et de secret pour ne point donner aux Anglois occasion de plaindre."[3]† Secrecy was necessary because Britain and France had formally concluded an alliance of friendship subsequent to the Treaty of Utrecht, and English officials frequently wrote their French counterparts reminding them of the "union" between the two crowns. Invariably, the French would reply that they had instructed their Indians that they should in no way disturb the harmony that existed between the two nations.[4] This deception was a useful formula for the French who never could, in truth, be sure that the Micmacs were acting under direction or from their own self-interest. But since the two coincided, it mattered little what the English were told.

The major weakness of the Micmac people was their lack of numbers. The first postwar estimate, in 1716, put the population in peninsular Nova Scotia and Ile Royale at only 260 families; in 1722 it was described as being 838 persons.[5] Their numbers increased steadily, and by 1730 French officials were reporting that they had increased by one-third in the previous decade. Despite outbreaks of smallpox in 1729 and 1733–34, there were some 600 warriors (men above the age of twelve) in 1739. Ten years later the estimates were down slightly, at 1,000 Micmacs for peninsular Nova Scotia alone.[6] None of these figures is very reliable, for they were based on the numbers at either the annual festivities at Catholic missions or at the distributions of French presents, neither of which would necessarily draw a complete attendance. At the same time there was always the possibility of an overlap, for the same Indians could be at more than one of these assemblies in a season. Again, in these figures there are no estimates of the number of Micmacs living on Ile St. Jean (the future Prince Edward Island) or the mainland side of the Bay of Fundy (the future New Brunswick), except insofar as they too would attend these annual gatherings. It is probable that the total population stood at just over 2,000 individuals by mid-century.

The French held an immense advantage in the contest for Acadia owing to the longstanding influence of Catholic priests amongst these people. French statesmen had no scruples about using religion for temporal purposes, and they commanded missionaries as they would military officers. Moreover, the missionaries did not hesitate to use their spiritual influence to secular ends, for the English were not only the enemies of France but of the true faith as well. Yet when the soldiers departed and the statesmen ceased to care, the faith of the Micmacs endured. Their attachment to the Catholic church was no transient affair, and it has survived to the present day. It was in the first half of the eighteenth century that the Catholic religion became an integral part of the Micmacs' identity, and they were to use it to put a distance between themselves and the conquering English in the years ahead.

The missionary's responsibilities to the Indians were succinctly described by Pierre Maillard: "Il faut que je les excite sans cesse à la pratique des actes de religion; que je les rende, autant que faire se peut, traitables, sociables, fidèles au Roy notre Prince, de qui ils ont constamment une haute et sublime idée, gens de probité, et surtout que je m'applique à les faire vivre en bon intelligence avec les François."[7]†

The missionaries never dignified their Indians with the adjectives "Christian" or "Catholic"; they were simply "hommes priants." The religion taught them was a very simplified version of Catholicism, but it was presented in the Micmacs' own language. Acquiring that linguistic skill was no easy task, and it defeated several who were sent to work amongst the tribe. But, once mastered, the knowledge almost insensibly altered the character of the missionary; he had crossed the dividing line between white and native, becoming himself "un presque-Sauvage, l'un de leurs en quelque sorte."[8]† The Abbé Gaulin, after twenty years' service, could apologize for berating his superiors by describing himself as "un pauvre mikmak."[9] He and his assistant Michel Courtin translated the catechism and other basic texts into Micmac to help those who would come after them.[10] Maillard, who arrived in 1735, went a step further and revived LeClerq's hieroglyphs, rendering them eventually into a system of some five thousand characters so that the Micmacs could learn selected prayers and chants, the catechisms, and the testaments as taken from the catechism of the Abbé Fleury. Significantly, Maillard chose not to use the Roman alphabet because, if the Micmacs learned to read and write it, "ils abuseroient infalliblement de cette science ... à sçavoir plutôt les chose mauvaises que les bonnes."† He taught the Micmacs to believe that a book was a sacred thing in itself and was scandalized when a Frenchman at Louisbourg read one of his Indians a story about Jupiter's amorous adventures. Such evil could not come from a book, Maillard insisted, the man was joking.[11] For all their identification with their charges, the missionaries did not trust them with knowledge.

The French felt that the best way to meet the religious needs of the Micmacs would be to induce them to settle and farm and receive instruction while sedentary. This idea had first been put in practice in New France in the 1630's. In 1716 Gaulin proposed the establishment of a mission at Antigonish within Nova Scotia, just across the border from Ile Royale. It would, he hoped, attract all the Micmacs and keep them safe from the evils of contact with the whites. The Indians who had come to the tiny settlement of Louisbourg had done nothing to strengthen it. They hung around all summer in idleness and so were forced to spend the winter there too. Governor Soubras complained of the great disorders "tant par l'yvrogneie que par la fréquentation continuelle des femmes dans les maisons des français."† If the Indians were placed at one spot at a distance from the French, then they would have to till the land for food and hunt for their clothing; they would come to Louisbourg only when called and leave their women and children at home. The Ministry of Marine approved these arguments and put up the money to build a church at Antigonish as a focal point for the settlement.[12] In 1722 Gaulin founded a second mission deep inside British territory along the Shubenacadie River, where he claimed 150 families congregated.[13] In 1724, at Gaulin's urging, the Antigonish mission was moved to Merligueche on Lake Bras d'Or, where he hoped the Indians could become self-sufficient by growing corn and fishing and selling their surplus at Louisbourg. Secure on French territory, the Micmacs would be ready whenever it was necessary "les envoyer inquieter les Anglois."[14]† In the early 1730's, Gaulin and his assistant, Michel Courtin, persuaded the Indians of Ile St. Jean to form a settlement at Malpeque, but within a few years it had sunk to "a very wretched and libertine condition."[15] The Micmacs did not agree with missionary plans to place them in sedentary communities. By the end of the decade the Cape Breton settlement was virtually abandoned. But, insisting that the failure was caused by poor land, a lack of fresh water, and bad hunting in the immediate vicinity, a new missionary was proposing a new move, to Vachebenacadie at the lower end of Lake Bras d'Or, where the soil was better and Indians had already planted gardens.[16]

By 1738 there were three functioning missions: Merligueche on Ile Royale, with a subordinate station at Antigonish, both the responsibility of Pierre Maillard; Malpeque on Ile St. Jean, with no resident missionary but visited once a year by Maillard; and Shubenacadie, described as being for "tous les Sauvages de l'Acadie," under the care of Louis-Joseph Le Loutre. The two men had an unenviable task, for the Indians were saints as long as the missionaries watched them, but "l'inconstance, la légèreté et la paresse de nos

Sauvages joint au commerce qu'ils ont avec les françois"† meant that they needed constant watching.[17] Although the missions had not become settlements, they were established as places of resort for the Indians scattered through Acadia, and since the men left their families in them while off on the winter hunt, the missionaries gave most of their religious instruction to the women and children.[18]

It was at these missions that the priest was best able to fulfil his second role, that of instilling loyalty to the king of France. This would be a subject more attractive to the warriors because it involved honour, courage, and often vengeance. Loyalty to the king was most easily exemplified in action against the English. The concentration of Indians for the protracted festivities surrounding St. Ann's Day was useful for French officials as well as for missionaries. In June, 1720, Gaulin sent word that the governor of Ile Royale should come to talk to the Indians assembled at Antigonish and listen to their grievances. But Joseph de St. Ovide refused to make a formal visit inside British territory and had the chiefs come to him at Port Toulouse on the Atlantic coast south of Louisbourg, where he told them of the nefarious things the English were doing and the steps he was taking to preserve the Micmacs' interests. In the following year, St. Ovide took the initiative and ordered Gaulin to assemble the chiefs at Antigonish. This time, however, the governor came to them.[19]

The first interest of the king, Maillard told the Micmacs, was to save souls; the second, "que l'on vous conservât votre pais, que l'on vous y laissat libres maîtres de vos volontez, tranquilles." The paternal care of His Christian Majesty was demonstrated by annual gifts. The need for that care was shown by the perpetual wiles of the English, who attempted to seduce the Micmacs by false promises or to deprive them of their lands by outright warfare. Resistance to the English, when preached by religious men, took on the fervour of a crusade with the sanction of divine vengeance behind it. "Ne voyez-vous pas que cette nation une fois éteinte, nous restons alors paisable possesseurs de tous ces pays-cy?" The English were animals, "mauvais animaux, dont il est absolument nécessaire que nous purgions la terre sur laquelle nous nous trouvons actuellement établis. C'est ainsi qu'un de nos rois fit autrefois exterminer tous les loups jusqu'au dernier, dans le pays d'ou nous sortons."[20]†

The third duty of the missionary, to maintain good relations between Indians and French, was partly accomplished by the inculcation of hostility towards the English. On the other hand, the missions had been established to prevent contact with the French at Louisbourg, whose actions were frequently unchristian, and it was dangerous to allow a Micmac to learn the French language. Separating the Acadians and Micmacs was more difficult. All priests, of course, served all Catholics, but there was a degree of specialization: Gaulin, Courtin, Maillard, and Le Loutre were missionaries to the Indians first and foremost, while at any given time there were usually another four priests in Acadia to serve the French inhabitants. The Indian missionaries roamed across international boundaries and were inevitably objects of English suspicion; the Acadian priests had fixed cures and were valued by English officials as the only intermediaries they had with the French settlers. There were different expectations at the diplomatic level too; while the Indian missionaries were instructed to incite their charges against the English, the Acadian priests were warned to behave with tact and prudence to keep their congregations out of trouble. The Indian missionaries had by far the harder life, and, as Gaulin pointed out, they received none of the tithes paid by the Acadians. In addition, they incurred expenses in living up to the Micmacs' high standards of hospitality and paying the charges for canoes and canoemen when they went on their travels.[21] Thus, maintaining a "bon intelligence" between Micmacs and French could at times be a difficult task.

However much they tried to identify with the Micmacs, the missionaries were never at ease with them. The Indians were by no means the unquestioning followers of clerical masters. Gaulin cautioned Governor St. Ovide that "Ces sauvages sont peu de choses estant nos alliés et pourraient devenir quelque chose de considerable estant nos ennemis."[22]† Maillard's fear of what might happen if the Indians became literate were close to hysteria: "Mais lorsque nous considérons encore que nous avons à vivre avec une nation qui, quoiqu'elle ait toûjours été jusqu'aujourdhuy très-attachée et très-soumise au gouvernment françois, pourroit peut-être à l'avenir nous manquer, nous trahir, enfin se détacher de nos intérêts, qui sçait s'ils ne se serviroient point à cette fin de cet art d'écrire que nous leur aurions communiqué?"[23]† If the missionaries could not be sure of their charges, it is not surprising that other French shared their misgivings. As fighting men the Micmacs were thought to be "bien moins guerriers que les Sauvages de Canada, ils serraient peu capable de conduire une entreprise considerable," but they were good enough to create small alarms and keep the English in fear of them. The nature of the Indian was such that the best defence was attack; a defensive war would soon exhaust his patience. "Si on nous attaque nous serons abandonnés et peut-être trahis par nos plus affidés Sauvages."[24]† Every statement condemning the unreliability of the Micmacs was in fact a testimony to their determination to make their own decisions despite the exhortations of French officials and missionaries. The contest in Acadia was being fought over their homeland, where French and English alike were intruders.

The French at least acknowledged that they were intruders by paying what amounted to a form of rent in the shape of annual presents of arms, ammunition, food, and cloth. Themselves generous in gift-giving, the Micmacs readily accepted gifts from the king of France. This policy was the second most powerful factor inducing the native people to support the French, for the English were never able to accept the idea of presents as anything more than *ad hoc* gratuities. In 1716, New France's governor,

Philippe de Rigaud de Vaudreuil requested thirty thousand livres a year for presents throughout French America, arguing that they were the only way to prevent the Indians from trading with the English and so bringing about an Anglo-Indian alliance against Canada. But Versailles was not in a spending mood, and the amount allotted Acadia was only two thousand livres. Such as it was, it was to be spent in the manner best suited for keeping English and Micmacs apart.[25] The distribution of presents became systematized in the 1720's. Each year the governor of Ile Royale journeyed to Port Toulouse and Port La Joie on Ile St. Jean. The Indians of Acadia, regardless of international boundaries, came to these assemblies. There they reported the latest moves by the English and by each other, complained that the presents were not enough, and swore undying loyalty to the king of France. In return they received supplies, speeches about the evil of the English and the kindness of the French, and occasional reproaches.

The English took it for granted that France had ceded title to Acadia at the Treaty of Utrecht and that the Indians were living on lands belonging to King George I. It was, however, prudent to make treaties of submission and friendship with those who lived in the areas of anticipated white settlement. The English placed great faith in these treaties, which had a once-and-for-all-time formality about them and did away with the need to be constantly nurturing the goodwill of the native people. These treaties stood in direct contrast to the French practice of persuading and befriending them year after year. Consequently, the treaty in itself was an innovation to those Indians who were dealing with the English for the first time. The English used commissioners, empowered to speak in the name of King George, with a set of demands: that the Indians should take the oath of allegiance to their new king; that they should trade only with his subjects; and that they should be prepared to share their lands peacefully with the settlers who would shortly be arriving. In all this, the English made one promise, that they would not interfere with the religious freedom of the Indians.

These demands forced the Indians to define their relationship to the newcomers much more precisely than they had had to with the French. The question of a formal oath of allegiance to an external authority provoked a chief of the Penobscot Abenaki to reply: "Jay mes roys naturels et mes gouverneurs, mes chefs et mes anciens." He had never been subject to a French king, so why should he submit to an English one? He would salute all the kings of the world, and the king of England in particular, if that pleased the commissioners. The Micmacs shared these feelings. The bald announcement that settlers would be coming to their lands also required that the Indians take a stand on an issue that had been of little consequence before. Again, to quote the Penobscot chief whose words are recorded in the only transcript of an exchange between English and Indians on the morrow of the Treaty of Utrecht: "Je ne veux pas neanmoins qu'aucun étranger fasse aucun fors ou etablissement sur ma terre. ils m'embarrasseront. Je suis assez pour occuper seul ma terre."[26]† According to a report reaching Vaudreuil, the Indians of the St. John Valley (Malecites) told the English quite clearly that they owned the land and that although they had been allies of the French king, they had never been his subjects.[27] The interpreter at these early contacts was usually a French missionary, which may be one reason why the English frequently came away with the impression that the Indians had cheerfully agreed to everything while the Indians remembered that they had not. As native resistance stiffened, the English saw the hand of the French in every hostile act. Governor Richard Philipps at Annapolis complained that they were inspiring the Indians "to assert their native right to this country in opposition to that of his Majesty."[28] The important point was not who was doing the teaching, but how well the student learned the lesson.

The insensitivity of the English in their dealings with the Micmacs tended to force the natives into a greater dependence on France than they would have wished. It required more imagination than London possessed to see that the wisest course to promote settlement would be to establish a system for the regular distribution of presents to those whose territory was to be used. Such a step would have gone part way towards appeasing the Indians, not only because it would have increased their material welfare, but also because as a token of Britain's awareness that they existed, it would have assuaged their pride. The newcomers would have been understood to be paying some form of tribute, or rent, for the resources they were using. British presents would have decreased the Indians' dependence on the French and increased the space in which the Micmacs could manoeuvre between the two. But while the French continued to see presents as a form of retainer for future services, the English did not. The English mind was so mercantile that the idea of giving something for apparently nothing was repugnant. A more congenial alternative was put forward in 1733 with the suggestion that truckhouses be established where goods could be traded at fixed prices under government supervision and where the drunkenness and fraud associated with private trading could be avoided. Truckhouses, however, tended to operate at a loss, as they did in Massachusetts, and a financial loss could not be balanced on the books by a gain in goodwill. The British government refused to authorize such a scheme until there was an elected assembly in Nova Scotia to bear the costs.[29] Without settlers there could be no assembly, and without the pacification of the Indians there were going to be no settlers.

The recalcitrance of the English forced the Micmacs to instruct them in the advantages of making presents. Several chiefs visited John Doucett, lieutenant-governor of the fort at Annapolis, in 1718 to explain that their continued friendship depended on receiving annual presents as they had done under the French king. Thereupon, Doucett explained to the Lords of Trade that presents alone could wean the Indians from their French priests and allow peaceful trade and settlement to take place. Reluctantly, their lordships agreed to send out "some Cloathing and Utensils of Small Value" for the Indians, "as an earnest of ye favour they may Expect on their dutiful behaviour towards His Majesty & Governm!"[30] Few of these presents were ever distributed, for the Indians' behaviour was not dutiful. Far from making distribution an annual event, the British government was still wondering what had happened to its solitary gift fifteen years later.[31]

The mere rumour that English presents were in the offing was enough to alarm the French and improve the Micmacs' bargaining position. In July, 1721, St. Ovide complained to those assembled at Antigonish that their young men had been receiving supplies from the English; not so, was the reply, all had been paid for. The only reason their young men had gone to the English, the chiefs continued, was that the French presents were so inadequate that they all might have to look elsewhere in the future. Chastened, St. Ovide could only reply that that was an evil thought, and he promised to do better.[32] When English colonials distributed a few presents in 1730 to induce the Indians to swear allegiance to the new king, George II, the French were outraged: "cette Nation que l'Interet domine se concile de façon avec les François et Les Anglois qu'ils reçoivent de toutes parts et sans un Menagement Infime tres capable de tous ce qu'il y a de Mauvais." Two years later, St. Ovide was still berating the Indians for having accepted those gifts.[33]† The Micmacs could, diplomatically speaking, make a few presents go a long way.

The strongest weapon in the Indians' armoury was their ability to keep Europeans off balance. The ambiguous nature of authority within each tribe and between tribes worked to their advantage. For example, a delegation of Abenakis visited Governor Vaudreuil in 1719 to ask for his help in ousting the English from the mouth of the Kennebec River. Vaudreuil temporized and offered powder and shot. Was that the way a father helped his children, the delegates asked, adding "avec un ris mocquer—Sachez... que quand nous voudrons tous, tant que nous sommes de nations sur ce vaste continent, nous nous réunirons pour en chasser tous les étrangers quel qu'ils soient."† Vaudreuil was understandably disturbed.[34] Had the Abenakis made an agreement with their neighbours to turn on Canada? Was the dread Anglo-Indian alliance about to take place? Similar ambiguities were presented Governor Philipps when he held a conference with the Indians of the St. John River shortly after his arrival in 1720. Chief Francis de Salle expressed his pleasure at being able to live in peace and quiet with the English, but he could only speak for his river people, and if some member of his nation insulted an Englishman he could not be held responsible.[35] Not knowing the limits of the chief's authority within his nation and being incapable of distinguishing a Malecite such as de Salle from a Micmac, Philipps was hard put to evaluate the worth of these assurances. And, within each tribe, there was the distinction between the elders and the young men, the former always blaming the latter for any action that displeased Europeans. Similarly, the French were to blame for what angered the English and vice versa. The Acadians too could play the game, to the discomfiture of the English; as early as 1717 they were refusing to take the oath of allegiance because, they said, they were afraid of what the Indians might do to them if they made a formal submission. Was this the truth, or were the Acadians simply biding their time before making common cause with the Micmacs in a powerful alliance to oust the newcomers?[36]

In the situation that had developed by 1720 the Micmacs had a fairly strong position. They were receiving support from the French to protect their land, something they would have done in any event. At the same time, the fact that the support was being provided *sub rosa* meant that they could always create some embarrassment for the French by revealing the true situation when they chose. The French feared that Anglo-Indian friendship would be a deadly threat to Canada and that it would come about if the two formed close commercial ties. The Micmacs let it be known that they preferred both the price and quality of English trade goods. If the French presents failed to satisfy, the Micmacs threatened to go to the English. And when official supplies were insufficient, the missionaries felt obliged to make up the difference. Gaulin estimated that between 1717 and 1719 he had spent 1,500 livres of his own money "pour l'entretien des Sauvages qui seroient sans moy aujourdhuy anglois."[37]† For all their overt hostility to the English, the Micmacs were still able to keep the French off guard. Instead of the Indians being dependent on French goods, the French were to be made strategically dependent on the Micmacs' acceptance of their presents.

In fact, there was no doubt that the English were the true enemies of the Micmacs. It was not that the native people were hostile to European settlement in itself; the French had lived among them for a century. The peremptory British approach to land, however, indicated that their settlement, when it came about, would leave little room for anyone else. The refusal of the Indians to accept English pretensions was shown by a series of hostile acts beginning in 1715. That year the Cape Sable Indians seized a number of fishing boats and held their crews for a ransom of £30 in goods. "The Indians," reported one of the sufferers, "say ye Lands are theirs and they can make Warr & peace when they please."[38] This type of raid was in the tradition of exacting tribute from those who would use tribal resources. Vengeance came into play when rumours spread that the English had poisoned a number of Micmacs that same winter: a ship was attacked, its cargo seized, and one of the crew shot dead in cold blood.[39]

The first major blow at the English came in 1720. The target was Canso, close by Ile Royale and some twenty-five miles from the mission at Antigonish. The area, with its offshore islands, had been in contention between English and French for several years. Under orders from Massachusetts in 1718, Captain Thomas Smart had seized several French vessels and some

200,000 livres in goods. In revenge for this deed, or so they later said, sixty Indians attacked Canso in the early hours of 21 August 1720, killing one man and driving the English out. On the following day French fishermen arrived and took what had been left behind: fish, cables, nets, sails, tobacco. The Indians generously insisted that they help themselves. On hearing of the attack, Governor St. Ovide expressed himself mortified and blameless, for "ses Nations suivoient lavis ny les conseils que de leur entiers et de leurs chefs."† The English insisted that Frenchmen had taken part in the attack and had stolen £9,000 worth of goods. St. Ovide sent an officer, Jacques de Pensens, to investigate, and while he was adamant that no French had been present in the assault, he could not deny that they had arrived the following day. Much of the stolen equipment was collected and returned by the French as proof of goodwill. Governor Philipps was not impressed, for he was convinced that the Indians had acted under orders from Louisbourg.[40]

The Micmac victory at Canso brought about a restatement of a position the English had no wish to hear and refused to believe when they did hear it. Returning from the raid, a small group of Indians plundered an English boat at Minas while the French inhabitants looked on. Called to account for this action, Antoine and Pierre Couaret, Micmacs, offered no excuses: "cete terre icy que Dieu nous a donné dont nous pouvons conté estre ausy tot que les arbres y sont né ne pouvez nous estre disputé par personne." They had no wish to see the English in their country and would oppose any who stayed without their consent, whether at Canso or at Minas. "Nous sommes Maistre independente de personne et voulons avoyr notre pays libre."† They were, they concluded, perfectly capable of making that decision for themselves and did not need to be instructed by the French on what course to take.[41] Before he had had time to digest the significance of this spirited reply, Philipps received friendly letters from both the St. John and Passamaquoddy Indians disassociating themselves from the attack on Canso and assuring him of their continuing desire to live at peace with the English.[42] The English governor might be pardoned if he felt that the alternate smiles and frowns he was receiving were part of a continuing campaign to drive him to distraction.

By 1721 Philipps' troubles were increased as a result of events on the disputed border between Acadia and New England. There, the pressure of white settlement on Abenaki lands brought matters to a crisis first. The Indians had resisted by shooting the newcomers' livestock as though it were wild game, and one particular foray where thirty cattle were slaughtered led to the imprisonment of several Indians.[43] The Abenakis of Norridgewock were divided over what to do next; the majority were for making peace with the English, and they sent four hostages as pledges of their good behaviour to Boston. A disastrous setback for France was now foreseen. If the English were to settle along the Narantsouack River, they would be within three days' journey of the St. Lawrence in the next war. This calamity was averted thanks to the efforts of the resident missionary to the Abenakis, Sebastian Rasle, who received orders direct from King Louis to excite the Indians to resistance. By bringing Canadian Indians in to strengthen the locals, Rasle put on a bold front at a meeting with the English at Arowsick Island. The Indians offered two hundred beaver pelts as compensation for the slaughtered cattle, demanded the return of the four hostages, and told the English to get out of the country.[44] Letters of protest passed between Boston and Quebec. The French insisted that the Abenakis were their allies and lived on land that was outside Acadia; the English that they were British subjects on British land.

The worst English suspicions were fully documented when a raiding party captured Rasle's private papers. Vaudreuil, far from honouring the alliance between the crowns of England and France, had been encouraging the Indians to fight and using a missionary as his agent. Unabashed, Vaudreuil denounced the English colonists' continuing encroachment on the Abenakis.[45] He suggested to the Abenakis that they take some English hostages as security for their own men in Boston, and in May, 1722, the war began with a connected series of raids and reprisals.[46] In August, Massachusetts declared war on the Abenakis; in the following month 160 Indians were sent from Canada, with orders to fight along the line of the Narantsouack River. This war was going to be much harder than the last one, Vaudreuil wrote the governor of Massachusetts; the Indians would defend their lands to the last and see to it that all their brethren took up the hatchet as well. From Versailles came the decision: "Les Français ne doivent pas paraître entrer dans cette guerre; mais ils doivent sous mains inspirer aux autre nations d'aider les Abenakis."† The fund for presents was tripled, to be used "sous le nom des jésuites" who would distribute the supplies.[47] France would fight—to the last Indian.

Although this war lay on the margins of Nova Scotia, it was inevitable that the colony would be involved. Vaudreuil rejoiced in the prospect of the Abenakis and Micmacs uniting to drive the British from Annapolis and Canso, thus restoring to France everything she had lost by the Treaty of Utrecht.[48] Indeed, the handful of soldiers at those two posts was the only British presence in the land, and Governor Philipps was getting no help from London to strengthen his position. The supplies he had requested arrived three years late in bad condition and in only half the quantity ordered. He had to apologize frequently to visiting Indians for his failure to give them presents and spent £150 of his own money to reinforce his fair words. At times he doubted that even £100,000 would win the Indians over from their missionaries.[49] Lieutenant-Governor John Doucett was equally pessimistic. His suspicions, especially of Father Gaulin, increased when he heard that stolen English goods were ornamenting a new Indian chapel. Gaulin wrote Doucett to announce the founding of the mission for the Indians at Shubenacadie "ou nous pourrons plus facilement detourner leurs Mauvaises enterprises."† Doucett nearly burst with indignation: who let loose the "Mauvaises enterprises?"

The Indians would do anything for the Father Gaulin who talked so disingenuously about their being their own masters. Despondently, he wrote the Lords of Trade: "This is the Pass we are att Every day, our Traders rob'd and Plunder'd"; and at the centre of this violence was that half-breed, the bigoted and indefatigable Gaulin.[50]

In June, 1722, Philipps was at long last able to distribute some of the king's presents at a feast for the Micmacs. In July the bands struck at English shipping, capturing eighteen vessels on the Atlantic coast. They then took off in their prizes, so it was reported, to cruise the fishing banks and attack Canso. The fishermen at the port, crowded at mid-season, panicked and prepared to flee, but they were rallied by Philipps. Two sloops were fitted out and took to sea with their crews and some soldiers from the garrison; within three weeks they had recaptured the ships. Fighting was fierce at times, and the Indians lost heavily. Among their dead were four of the chiefs who had come in weeks before to receive the English presents. Why had they attacked? All "agreed on one Storey that they were sett on by the ffrench Governors." Doucett forestalled an assault on Annapolis by seizing twenty Indians he found in the neighbourhood and holding them hostage. The war chief, Captain Laimable, captured two boats in the Bay of Fundy and appeared before Annapolis, but he did not press an attack. By September, Philipps considered the crisis over: "wee are now as easy and quiett as if there was not an Indian in the Country."[51]

The quiet lasted through 1723, punctuated by the occasional raids that had become the pattern of life in Nova Scotia. Late in June 1724, some thirty Malecites and twenty-six Micmacs attacked Annapolis. They killed two of the garrison, wounded several others, and took some civilian prisoners before retiring. By way of reprisal the English shot one of the hostages they had held in the fort for two years. Early in 1725 sixty Abenakis and Micmacs struck at Canso, destroying two houses and killing half a dozen civilians. By June, armed Indians were once again reported sailing the Atlantic coast and seizing fishing boats. The newly arrived lieutenant-governor of Nova Scotia, Lawrence Armstrong, expected a full-scale attack by Micmacs and Acadians in the ensuing winter; he proposed to take a tour of the province in the spring and force both groups either to take the oath of allegiance or leave. Thirty-six Wampanoag from Martha's Vineyard, with three whale boats, were hired to terrorize the Micmacs in the area of the fisheries.[52]

The war, however, had run its course. In October, 1725, a delegation of Abenakis went to gain Vaudreuil's consent to their making peace with the English. Sick and close to death, the governor put up little resistance: "cette guerre ne regardait point les François";† it was in the Indians' own interests to defend themselves.[53] On 15 December, articles of peace were concluded at Boston between the English and the Abenakis, Malecites, and Micmacs. The treaty was ratified at Annapolis in June, 1726, by John Doucett and sixteen chiefs. The Indians, he felt, had been so exhausted by the war that they would never fight again in Nova Scotia. By the treaty, the English promised not to molest the Indians or interfere with them in their hunting, fishing, and planting grounds, nor in the exercise of their religion through approved missionaries. Any injury done to an Indian by a white would be prosecuted according to English law "whereof the Indian shall have the Benefitts Equal with His Majesty's other Subjects." In return, the Indians acknowledged that the Treaty of Utrecht had made King George "the Rightful Possessor of the province" and submitted to him in "as ample a manner" as they had formerly done to the king of France. Further, the Indians promised not to molest any settler, present or future; to bring in deserters from the army; to release English prisoners; and to forego private revenge to redress injuries.[54] The treaty could obviously mean different things to different men; since the Indians did not consider they had ever "submitted" to the king of France, their promise to observe a similar allegiance to the king of England was somewhat less than the English might have desired. Nevertheless, this treaty became the cornerstone of British Indian policy in Nova Scotia, and it was carefully renewed after every subsequent rupture as the definitive statement of the relationship between Indians and whites.

The Indians' decision to end the war was, in the words of a Memoire du Roy, "un inconvenient auquel on ne devait pas attendre," which left the southeastern flank of Canada dangerously exposed. The news that the English colonials had feasted the Indians and given them presents at the treaty ceremonies prompted the president of the Navy Board to comment that they would do anything to win over the Indians. The news of peace "n'est que trop véritable,"† but the lull would not last long. St. Ovide was ordered to do everything he could to frustrate English designs.[55] On his circuit in 1726, he did his best to dissuade the Indians from making peace, and when he found that they had done so, he summoned fifteen chiefs to Louisbourg for a scolding. Why, he asked, had they concluded peace? It was the work, they said, of greedy, empty-headed youths anxious—a not so subtle hint—for presents. For themselves, the chiefs would gladly give their lives for their father in France. At Port Toulouse in 1728 St. Ovide repeated his question. This time the Indians told him they never had made peace and in any event had burned the copies of the treaty given them by the English. The story was repeated at Ile St. Jean: Why had the Indians not let St. Ovide know what they were doing and accepted his advice? No man could have two fathers. Which did they choose?[56]

The French seized eagerly on every indication that the war might be renewed. Indians took an English boat, but the crew recaptured it, killed some of the attackers, and carried the others back to Boston. "Je ne fais nul doute que cette affaire rallume plus fort que jamais, la haine, et la mefiance quy est entre les deux Nations,"† wrote St. Ovide. His superiors responded that this was indeed an opportunity "pour fomenter ces querelles," and the Bostonians obligingly hanged the Indians as pirates. In reprisal, thirty Indians seized an English boat at Port aux Basques, Newfoundland, and sailed it back to Merligueche. Anxious to remove any English suspicions of his complicity, St. Ovide bought the cargo from the Indians and told the boat's owner where he might pick it up. His caution was understandable, for the attack had been carried out under French colours.[57] Following the annual distribution of the presents at Ile St. Jean in 1728, some fifteen Indians on their way home tried to board an English fishing boat. They were repulsed, but the scare thrown into the English was enough to send eighty boats scurrying for shelter.[58]

For all the news of Anglo-Micmac hostility that French officials sent home, the fact remained that the Indians had followed their own counsel in making peace and that, despite frequent exhortations, they had refused to embroil themselves in another major war. The English presence in Nova Scotia, limited to the fort at Annapolis and the fishing base at Canso, was no real threat. English civilians could be counted in the dozens, and their numbers were declining; the military garrisons, when they were at full strength, stood at 350 men. The defences of Annapolis were in a perpetual state of disrepair, and much of the earthworks washed away in the rains each spring. There was not even a blockhouse or a magazine to support the troops at Canso. By contrast, both the French and native populations were increasing dramatically, the Acadian by 50 per cent and the Micmac by a third in one decade. If English power were ever to match English claims, it would have to be through massive settlement; but settlers required a minimum of security which the two small garrisons could not provide. No oath had yet been devised that the Acadians could not render ambiguous or the Indians ignore. Administering oaths was cheap enough, but it was no substitute for loyal subjects.

In 1732 the council of Nova Scotia made a major attempt to encourage immigration from Massachusetts by planning to divide the area of the lower St. John into townships with grants available on the payment of quit rent. No one was interested. Armstrong tried to establish a visible English presence at Minas, the principal growing area in the province and the centre, such as it was, of Acadian settlement. He decided to build a blockhouse there, but not daring to call it that, he let a contract for a granary. This deception did not succeed for long, for the Indians told St. Ovide all about it on his visit to Ile St. Jean that year. Naturally, he encouraged their preparations to oppose this extension of British power.[59] The Indians came to Minas in July, and the leader of the delegation announced that he was the king of the area; King George might have captured Annapolis, but he had never taken Minas. Shortly thereafter, other Indians attacked the tiny colliery being developed by Bostonians nearby, destroying a house and store. They claimed they were owed a rent for the use of the land and camped on the site throughout the winter to prevent any further intrusions.[60] Armstrong was powerless. He tried persuasion, sending Micmac-speaking Acadians with small presents for the women and children of various bands, promising full support if the Micmacs would not oppose his establishment at Minas. It was all in vain, and an attempt to revive the plan in 1738 proved equally futile.[61] Meanwhile, the English fishery declined rapidly since the Indians would not "suffer an Englishman to settle or cure fish in any of the ports on the south side [of] Nova Scotia." At each post was an Indian, styled captain, with a commission from the French "to command a particular district." The English could not expand their sphere of influence in face of the overt hostility of the Indians.[62]

As the European powers once more drifted into war in the early 1740's, rumours spread throughout Acadia. Major Paul Mascarene, president of the council at Annapolis, issued a proclamation in October, 1743, against ill-designing persons who, playing on the "Chimerical Notions" of the Indians, led them into pillage and plunder on the pretext that war had broken out between Britain and France. He added point to his warning by writing to Alexander Bourg, an Acadian notary at Minas, who acted as an intermediary, that the Indians should be made to understand that their depredations, far from being of service to the Acadians, would only hurt them. If war broke out, Mascarene hoped that both Acadians and Indians would be able to live in peace with the English.[63] In the following May a group of St. John Indians led by the son of Chief Joseph met the council at Annapolis to learn whether there was peace or war. Mascarene replied that war was probable but had not yet broken out; the Indians professed their desire to remain neutral. Mascarene gave them a few presents and sent them home on a ship going to load limestone at Musquash Cove. Tactlessly enough, he said that he expected the Indians to help with the loading, for which they would undoubtedly receive some small compensation.[64] No greater insult could have been offered warriors!

The war was closer than Mascarene knew. Less than three weeks after the St. John Indians were sent to load limestone, Canso fell to a surprise attack from Louisbourg. The Indians were soon back at Annapolis, accompanied by the missionary Maillard. Three hundred gathered for an assault on 1 July 1744, but with the arrival of seventy soldiers from Boston on 5 July, they withdrew to Minas. In dire straits, Mascarene requested the services of Indians and rangers from New England. Indians were the best people to fight other Indians, and the next best were the white wood rangers, "People who are used to hunt the Indians" in a way regular troops could not. Warfare took a new and uglier turn. A force consisting largely of Mohawks arrived from Boston under Captain John Gorham and immediately went to work attacking the Micmacs indiscriminately.[65] Their first victims were five women, two of them pregnant, and three children. Pierre Maillard recorded numerous atrocities ranging from the desecration of burial grounds to the distribution of infected clothing.[66] However, Gorham did not break the Indians' spirit; a combined force of six hundred Canadiens and Indians lay siege to Annapolis in May, 1745.[67] After three weeks they left, at Maillard's urging, to go to the aid of Louisbourg, too late to prevent its fall to British colonials from New England. Maillard went to Louisbourg to treat with its conquerors under a flag of truce and was unceremoniously shipped off to England. Le Loutre was captured on the high seas, and, as the British closed in, he threw Maillard's books and possessions overboard.[68] But the fighting was not over. In February, 1747, a New England expedition was cut to pieces at Minas by a force of Canadiens and Indians.[69]

The war wound down in Europe and hostilities dwindled in America. Before the complex process of peacemaking with the various tribes could begin, the terms of reference for Nova Scotia changed dramatically. Louisbourg was returned to France, but it would no longer go unchallenged on the north Atlantic coast: Halifax was founded. This decision sealed the fate of the Micmacs. Together with the French they had held the English for thirty-five years to a tiny garrison at Annapolis and a seasonal port at Canso. The foundation of a military base at Chebucto Bay, however, meant that the British were making a major investment in Nova Scotia. They had finally fit the province into their global strategy, as the French had years before. To protect Britain's investment, its back country would have to be as secure as its seaward approaches. The homeland of the Micmacs would come under sustained British aggression for the first time. They would now experience what the Abenakis had suffered over the previous three decades, but with more intensity, for the stakes were now military and international, not just frontier land. The Micmacs would resist as the Abenakis had resisted. They would use the French, and the French would use them; both had had years in which to perfect that collaboration.

4

The Loss of Acadia 1749–1761

The Treaty of Aix-la-Chapelle, which ended the War of the Austrian Succession, was proclaimed in Annapolis in May, 1749. In July, an English expedition under the command of Colonel Edward Cornwallis arrived at Chebucto Bay with twenty-four hundred settlers. The British government, which had long balked at the slightest expenditure on Indian presents, proved ready to back this venture with over £400,000 in the first six years.[1] Britons were coming to British territory to do with it as they pleased. They chose to use settlers in much the same way as the French had, more economically, used the Indians, that is, to support their strategic requirements. Cornwallis was ordered to establish two townships at Chebucto, each with twelve hundred settlers, and townships at Minas, Whitehead (south of Canso), Baie Verte, and La Have, each with five hundred settlers.[2] From their site at Chebucto the English spread to the opposite shore to found Dartmouth and then along the coast ten miles to Chezzetcook; they went southeast to Mahone Bay and sent German immigrants to Lunenburg. In all these areas the newcomers found cleared land, for the sites had long been used by the Indians. Surveyors were sent up the Shubenacadie River, which was the junction for the most important canoe routes in the province. A fort was established at Minas controlling access to the Bay of Fundy, and with Minas secured, the English moved on to the Chignecto Isthmus where they had never before attempted settlement. The British government got its money's worth in those first few years, and anyone who stood in the way was a rebel.

†Quotations marked with a dagger are translated in the notes.

Since the new town of Halifax lay indisputably within the limits of Acadia ceded to Britain in 1714, France could not protest its foundation. Her counter was to assert her claims to the Chignecto Isthmus and the mainland side of the Bay of Fundy. On the diplomatic level this meant reviving the Anglo-French Commission that had last met in 1719 in a futile effort to agree on the limits of Acadia; the result this time was a two-volume report, published tardily in 1755, that determined nothing.[3] On the military level, the French garrisoned a post at the mouth of the St. John River to show the flag and serve as a rallying point for the local Indians. With support from Canada, the Abenakis briefly took up the hatchet against the New·Englanders once more, but their enthusiasm was not what it once had been. The major French effort went into holding the line of the Missiguash River on the Chignecto Isthmus where they built Fort Beauséjour and a satellite post on Baie Verte in 1750. The first line of defence for the whole French position, however, lay not in fixed positions but in the support of the Micmacs.

Versailles adopted the same attitude to the founding of Halifax as it had to the English colonial incursions into Abenaki lands thirty years earlier.[4] The governor of Ile Royale was ordered to employ the Indians "sans vous compromettre, a interromper les etablissements des anglais."[5]† When the Abenakis were concluding peace in 1751, he sent Micmac messengers telling them to break off the negotiations.[6] Governor General La Jonquière at Quebec assured Spencer Phips, the president of the Massachusetts Council, that the Indians were free men and nothing could stop them from doing whatever they wished: "bien loin d'animer les Sauvages contre les Anglois, je fais mon possible pour les contenir en paix avec vous."[7]† He was not telling the truth. Again, as in the Abenaki Wars, missionaries were expected to act as the agents of French policy. This position was fully accepted by the influential and non-resident vicar-general of Quebec, the Abbé de l'Isle Dieu. The missionaries, he wrote, "ne devraient rien entrepriser que de concert avec le ministère et les personnes qui sur les lieux sont revêtues de l'autorité du Roi."[8] From the other side, Cornwallis wrote Bishop Pontbriand. Was it to the Micmacs' advantage, he asked, that missionaries should incite them to war and prevent them from joining with a civilized and Christian people?[9]

There were only two missionaries to the Indians in Acadia, Maillard and Le Loutre, both of whom had returned by 1749 after their misadventures in the hands of the English.[10] They were joined by a third, Jean Manach, in 1751.[11] Maillard acted as spokesman for the Micmacs in arranging the renewal of the annual presents and in articulating their resistance to Britain. He was no longer as active as he had been, and he was somewhat disappointed at the difficulty he met in gaining a pension similar to that awarded his junior, Le Loutre, for services in the previous war.[12] However, his enthusiasm for the cause still ran high, and he now saw the interests of Acadians and Micmacs as one: "Je ne donne pas plus de cinquante ans à ceux-cy [Micmacs] et aux

Marichites [Malecites] pour qu'on les voye tellement confondus avec les François colons, qu'il ne sera plus possible de les distinguer."[13]† From his post at Louisbourg, Maillard watched Le Loutre's activities with admiration, finding it incredible that the man did not succumb to fatigue: "luy seul donne courage à tous."[14]†

Le Loutre brought the first news of the Chebucto settlement to Louisbourg. He realized immediately that the British intended to spread out to Minas and from there to Baie Verte and Beaubassin. The war that had begun in 1744 would go on without a break. He decided to return to Acadia "pour exciter les Sauvages à continuer la guerre aux Anglois et leur faire dire qu'ils ne souffriront point de nouveau établissement dans l'Acadie."† Governor Desherbiers gave him presents to distribute.[15]

From the first, Cornwallis acknowledged him as a most dangerous opponent and eventually put a price on his head.[16] Le Loutre's missionary fervour gave an added edge to his conduct in the war, and the tension between his ideals and his enthusiasm led him at one time to ransom English prisoners and at another to pay for English scalps.[17] There is little doubt that he connived at, if he did not actually arrange, the assassination of an English negotiator, Edward How, under a flag of truce in 1750. Maillard spent many pages explaining that murder to a French correspondent and justifying it because, twelve years earlier, How had insulted a statue of the Virgin Mary.[18] The confounding of Catholic zeal and military misconduct was such that even French officials were afraid the missionaries went too far.[19] Sometimes Le Loutre himself was alarmed at what he was doing and feared repudiation by his secular superiors.[20] During this time, Le Loutre abandoned his mission at Shubenacadie and retired to Beaubassin. After Fort Beauséjour was built, he stayed there until it was captured by the English in 1755. As the years of campaigning went by, he became less of a French missionary and more of a war chief with the powers of a buoin.

The war placed the Micmacs once again in the position of a third force pushed relentlessly to the French side by English aggression. They tried their best to maintain some room to manoeuvre between the two, and whenever it was rumoured that they might come to an agreement with the English, the old plea that "c'est une nation que l'on ne menne que les présens et les vivres à la main"† was still forwarded to Versailles.[21] But the logic of the situation left the Micmacs no choice; their concern was, as never before, for their land. Although the British continued to insist that the Indians were simply the dupes of the French in asserting such an interest and refused to take it seriously, this second generation of Micmacs to face the British had learned something about the value of land from their elders. The very importance that the British placed on land ownership was a lesson in itself. The precision with which they fixed on sites long used by the Micmacs—at Chezzetcook, Minas, Lunenburg, and Shubenacadie—would have been enough to produce conflict without the need for any general theories. And whether or not the Micmacs had any idea of land ownership before the whites came, they certainly had acquired it by 1750.

Cornwallis was new to America. His disposition was unbending, and unlike any previous governor of Nova Scotia, he had the forces to indulge his will. As he saw it, his task was to make peace with the various tribes who had broken their allegiance in the recent war and to do it by renewing the treaty ratified at Annapolis in 1726. Any tribe that did not renew automatically continued in a state of war with Britain, for the general peace made at Aix-la-Chapelle could not include rebellious subjects within its scope.[22] Accordingly, when he was visited by some Indians within days of his arrival, he gave out a few small presents, offered his friendship and protection, and promised more presents when they were ready to enter a formal treaty.[23] The only Indians to come in were a delegation from the St. John River, empowered to speak for the Passamaquoddy and Chignecto bands, and they ratified the renewal of the 1726 treaty in August.[24] But the Micmacs conspicuously stayed away. On 19 August 1749, they seized twenty Englishmen at Canso and took them captive to Louisbourg, where they were ransomed by the French. Early in September the English began their push out from Halifax when Cornwallis ordered Mascarene to set up a blockhouse at Minas and garrison it with one hundred men. Micmacs attacked two English ships at Chignecto, and on 30 September they raided a sawmill close by Halifax itself. If the Micmacs wanted war, Cornwallis wrote the Lords of Trade, the British should never again make peace with them, but "root them out entirely."[25]

When the French resumed the annual distribution of presents, the Micmacs assembled once again at Port Toulouse. There, on 24 September, they formally declared war on the English. The document was written by Pierre Maillard in Micmac (in the Roman alphabet) and French, and a copy was sent to Halifax. The chiefs restated a familiar position: the land belonged to the Micmacs and they would not abandon it without a fight. Unless the English abandoned Halifax there would be war.

> L'endroit où tu es, où tu fais des habitations, où tu bâtis un fort, où tu veux maintenant comme t'inthroniser, cette terre dont tu veux présentement te rendre maître absolu, cette terre m'appartient, j'en suis certes sorti comme l'herbe, c'est le propre lieu de ma naissance et de ma résidence, c'est ma terre à moy sauvage; oui, je le jure, c'est Dieu qui me l'a donnée pour être mon pais à perpetuité... montre-moy où moy sauvage me logerai? tu me chasses toy; où veux tu donc que je me réfugie? tu t'es emparé de presque toute cette terre dans toute son étendue. il ne me restoit plus que Kchibouktouk [Chebucto]. Tu m'envies encore ce morceau.... Ta résidence au Port Royal [Annapolis] ne me fait pas grand ombrage, car tu vois que depuis long tems je t'y

laisse tranquille. mais présentement tu me forces d'ouvrir la bouche par le vol considérable que tu me fais.[26]†

The French, Cornwallis noted, had "begun their usual game." The council of Nova Scotia debated whether or not to declare war on the Micmacs and decided that to do so would be to "own them a free & independent People; whereas they ought to be treated as so many Banditti Ruffians, or Rebels to His Majesty's Government." Drastic measures were proposed: fifty rangers should be recruited locally and a further one hundred in Boston to go over the whole province killing Indians. However, the St. John's tribe which had come in and renewed the treaty should be sent an extra one thousand bushels of corn to keep them well disposed. Cornwallis issued a proclamation on 2 October commanding all "to Annoy, distress, take or destroy the Savages commonly called Mic-macks, wherever they are found." As was the custom in America, ten guineas would be paid anyone producing a savage or his scalp. Any person found helping the Indians would be treated as though he were one.[27] Cornwallis was as worried as governors before him about the Acadians, who being "not unlike" Indians could easily aid them in disguise.[28]

Within a few days fifty local volunteers were raised, and together with Gorham's Rangers, they began scouring the woods for Indians.[29] Cornwallis ordered Silvanus Cobb to go to Boston, collect a hundred men, and then sail straight to attack Beaubassin. If he called in at any bay or harbour on the way, he was to seize or destroy all Indians he found. When he arrived at Beaubassin, he was to continue destroying Indians, search the Acadians' homes for warlike stores, and find and destroy Le Loutre's house. For every Indian scalp or prisoner brought it, "Man Woman or Child," Cobb would receive £10. If Le Loutre were taken, the ship's crew would receive £50, and a further £50 would be granted on his delivery alive to an English post.[30] These draconian orders never went into effect. When Cobb arrived at Boston, he put recruiting advertisements in the newspapers, causing great excitement and publicizing the whole venture. Cornwallis ordered it abandoned.[31]

The Lords of Trade in London proved to be less than enthusiastic about the steps Cornwallis was taking against the Indians. Experience in other parts of America, they wrote him, indicated that "gentler Methods and Offers of Peace have more frequently prevailed with Indians than the Sword, if at the same Time, that the Sword is held over their Heads."[32] Never had he thought of exercising cruelty on the Indians, Cornwallis protested in relaying the gist of his orders to Cobb. When there is a good fort on the Chignecto Isthmus, then it will be possible to "harass & hunt them by Sea & Land" until they either sue for peace or leave the colony.[33] This unrepentant letter crossed another one coming out from London to emphasize that the wisest course any governor in America could follow was to secure peace with the Indians.[34]

The sword would not merely be held over the heads of the Indians; it was to be thust hard at them. The overland route from Halifax to the Bay of Fundy lay along a cattle trail that ended at Minas, which became the first object of tactical concern. The force ordered there in September, 1749, held a key position. In December, a call, probably issued by Le Loutre, went out from "Nous les Sauvages Micmacs, Mariches, Cinabres, Hurons, Abenaquis, Esquimaux" ordering the inhabitants of Minas to defend the area: it was in their interest, and in God's, they were told, to chase the English away.[35] The Malecites came out of their brief neutrality and joined with the Micmacs to attack the fort. They captured a patrol of one officer and twenty men, who were ransomed by Le Loutre and sent to Quebec; they fired sporadically at the blockhouse for a week before retiring to Beaubassin. Cornwallis ordered Gorham to Piziquid to arrest various Acadians suspected of joining with the Indians in the attack. In March, 1750, Gorham was sent back to build a blockhouse and mount a garrison at Piziquid. There was a skirmish and a company of regulars was rushed from Halifax in reinforcement. With Minas and Piziquid secured, Major Charles Lawrence was despatched to Beaubassin at the head of four hundred men. The Micmacs resisted and, on Le Loutre's orders, burned the town as the English approached. Lawrence retired to Minas and spent July strengthening the fort at Piziquid, the future Fort Edward. In August he was back at Beaubassin, breaking through a line of Acadians and Indians ensconced behind the dykes. This time he stayed and built Fort Lawrence facing Fort Beauséjour across the Missiguash River.

The English campaign to destroy Micmac power could go no further in this direction without serious international consequences. The French claimed the territory south and west of the Missiguash River, and conventional forces were on hand to defend that claim. Neither side wished to take the next step, and for almost five years there was an uneasy truce along the line of the tiny river. Throughout this period the French succeeded in maintaining their fort at the mouth of the St. John River, resisting several demands to leave. The English seized French vessels carrying supplies to the garrisons of both posts, but not until June, 1755, did they finally attack Fort Beauséjour. When it surrendered, the satellite fort at Baie Verte also capitulated, and the fort on the St. John was evacuated. The eastern defences of Canada were severely eroded, and by the time war was formally declared between the great powers, only Louisbourg was left to France. But this conflict was only one of the two wars being fought in Acadia.

The Micmac war of resistance was a response to the extension of English settlement, not an expression of high strategic concerns. That resistance was helped by the French at Beauséjour and Louisbourg, who supplied the weapons, but it existed in its own right as elsewhere on the North American frontier. The Micmacs wanted the English to leave them alone, and they made their position clear. Their response to the building of Fort Lawrence was to demand that the English abandon the Chignecto Isthmus and give up half the country, "with such like Stuff," as Cornwallis reported: demands "so preposterous and Ridiculous that they can't be in Earnest."[36] But the resistance itself was far from ridiculous. Sixty Indians attacked Dartmouth in June, 1750, killing eight and capturing fourteen. Halifax was kept in a state of fear, and its population dwindled. When twenty families went to settle at Chezzetcook, they were escorted by two hundred soldiers. A prefabricated blockhouse was sent ahead to Mahone Bay before settlers were allowed there. Because the fort planned at the mouth of the Shubenacadie River to make that area safe for settlement was not built, the settlers never came.[37] Newly arrived Germans were attacked outside Halifax in 1751, and when they moved to Lunenburg, the war followed them. They "mutinied" in December, 1753, hoping both for an end to Indian hostility and "to affect the same kind of Independency that the French Inhabitants have done" so that the Indians would not treat them as Englishmen.[38] Micmac resistance slowed British expansion dramatically and made it so costly that Cornwallis was never able to carry out those instructions that called for him to locate settlers at Minas, Whitehead, and Baie Verte. Nor, incidentally, was he able to root out the Micmacs.

The first apparent break in Micmac resistance came shortly after Peregrine Hopson succeeded Cornwallis as governor. On 14 September 1752 Major Jean-Baptiste Cope of the Shubenacadie band appeared before the council and proposed that "the Indians should be paid for the land the English had settled upon in this Country." He spoke, he said, for the forty men he had under him and offered to contact other bands to bring about a full-scale conference at Halifax. Two days later the council replied, studiously ignoring any question of paying for the land. They pointed out instead that they were all the children of King George and that the Indians had acknowledged him as their great chief and father. The English promised not to interfere with the Indians' hunting and fishing and said they would not "meddle with the lands where you are." If Cope wished to settle at Shubenacadie, he was free to do so. The governor would open a truckhouse where his band could trade at fair prices. Cope should spread this good news around and would receive handsome presents on his return; indeed, there would be annual presents for all the Indians as long as they behaved themselves.[39]

Governor Hopson expected little to come of this conference,[40] but Cope returned in November to conclude a formal agreement. The treaty of 1726 was confirmed and all recent warlike events "buried in Oblivion with the Hatchet." The English gave their friendship and protection, and presents of blankets, tobacco, powder and shot were promised for each October first "so long as they Continue in Friendship." The band was to enjoy "free Liberty of Hunting & Fishing as usual," and the Indians were invited to come to Halifax at any time for trade. The *Treaty or Articles of Peace and Friendship* was quickly embodied in a printed proclamation to ensure the widest distribution.[41]

Hopson gave the band, now ninety persons strong, provisions for six months, a costly business, he admitted to his superiors, "but as the French have done it we cannot be behind hand with them, when indeed we ought to outbid." The Lords of Trade expressed great satisfaction and entirely agreed that presents were necessary. The money would have to come from economies elsewhere in the province, such as taking the soldiers off rations during the summer months.[42]

News of the treaty naturally provoked French indignation. Maillard wrote of the "faux frères," and Prevost at Louisbourg denounced the "mauvais Micmac" named Cope and the "mauvais sujets" who had ratified the treaty.[43] But these worries proved premature; the treaty was soon wiped out by a deed of revenge. On 15 April 1754 two sailors arrived at Halifax carrying six Indian scalps. The men said that they were the survivors of a ship's crew that had been seized by Indians and that they had escaped when they caught their captors off guard. The truth was totally different, for the two men had been on a schooner that had robbed the Indians of forty barrels of government provisions at Jeddore. A short while later the crew was shipwrecked, and the two survivors were taken in and cared for by friendly Indians whom they murdered for the scalp money.[44] Such treachery required vengeance. On 16 May Cope's son requested the use of a government ship to move provisions given the Indians from Jeddore. A sloop was accordingly sent, and the crew was civilly received ashore by Cope. Then, without warning, the whole party was seized and killed with the exception of the Acadian pilot. He was taken to Cobequid where Cope threw his copy of last year's treaty into the fire "telling him that was the way they made Peace with the English."[45] The first exercise in Anglo-Micmac peacemaking had come to a dramatic end.

In November, 1754, Charles Lawrence succeeded Hopson as governor. His attitude was soon put to the test, for two Cape Sable Indians came to Halifax to say that their band, sixty in number, was in great distress since their friendship with the English meant they got no supplies from the French. Despite the Cope débacle, the council decided to send them food, blankets, powder, and shot.[46] The fact that the English were still ready to treat with the Indians and at last had presents to back up their words continued to worry the French. Governor Duquesne at Quebec decided that he must see to it that negotiations were broken off, that the Indians were pushed "à frapper sans qu'il paraisse que cela vienne de moy."[47]† But the time for French leadership was fast running out.

Le Loutre was still at Beauséjour, but his influence was increasingly restricted to an area where the needs of imperial strategy were beginning to clash with those of home defence. He was constantly pressed by Indians who wanted to fight the English close by at Fort Lawrence, an enthusiasm which did not, in 1754, accord with French plans. If the Indians could not fight, they felt they might as well make peace and buy the goods they needed from the

English.[48] To head off these arguments and prove his own good faith, Le Loutre wrote Governor Lawrence in August to propose that the greater part of eastern Nova Scotia be ceded in perpetuity to the Micmacs and left free of fortifications. The governor and council dismissed the approach as "insolent and absurd" and ordered the commander of Fort Lawrence, Captain Hussey, to communicate their answer. At the same time, they added, the English still wished for peace on reasonable terms and the Indians should go to Halifax to treat for them.[49] Le Loutre had the answer he had expected, but in January, 1755, Chief Algimou decided to take the English up on the offer. He applied for a safe-conduct, hoping "that the government will grant us a domain for hunting and fishing, that neither fort nor fortress shall be built upon it, that we shall be free to come and go wherever we please."[50] When it became apparent that this approach also included a demand for a vast reservation, the English dropped the matter.[51] There were no further negotiations. The land question was settled by force.

With the fall of Fort Beauséjour, both the French forces and Le Loutre were permanently removed from the scene. Fortified by this victory, the colonial government issued an ultimatum to the Acadians: swear allegiance or be deported. The Acadians refused the oath and the expulsions began in 1755. Those who were caught were shipped out of the province with nothing but what they could carry. Those who had warning scattered through the forests and made for the safety of French territory. In these circumstances, many who had given passive support to the Micmacs now joined in their struggle, which increased in intensity. Raiding parties continued to strike at the outskirts of Halifax, and in 1756 Lawrence issued a proclamation ordering "hostilitys to be committed on the Indians" with cash for prisoners or scalps. Three groups of volunteer rangers responded. Travellers were ambushed and scalped on the roads, and Lawrence called for more troops from England to track down the enemy.[52] The French continued their annual distribution of presents at Port Toulouse and organized the Indians into four detachments, two to defend Ile Royale, two to attack Halifax. The raiders brought back intelligence and scalps, for which they were well paid.[53] But the British blockade was beginning to have its effect. In July, 1757, a force of 100 Canadiens and Acadians, together with 280 Indians, assembled at Port Toulouse, but there was little to offer them beyond harangues and promises. A desperate appeal went to Versailles for presents to distribute to the Indians in the autumn, emphasizing "l'extrême besoin que nous avons de l'un et de l'autre."† The Navy Board despatched twelve large and six small medals. As many as 700 Indians were optimistically shown on the French records as requiring subsistence to aid in the defence of Ile Royale.[54] The last raiding party left Louisbourg for Halifax in December, 1757. The Indians returned the following month with two English scalps and the news that the harbour was practically deserted.[55] The missing ships were on their way to Louisbourg.

The official returns still listed five hundred Indians among the defenders of France's Atlantic citadel, but the figure was a wild exaggeration. Moreover, the Micmacs had lost their zeal for a foreign cause, and Pierre Maillard himself joined in their despair. He had been visiting Louisbourg when the English arrived and left on the evening of the first attack. With him went sixty Indians who, once outside the walls, unearthed supplies that had been cached to support guerilla warfare. In all, Maillard estimated, two hundred Micmacs stood by as Louisbourg succumbed for the second and final time to English assault.[56] It was now only a matter of time before the Micmacs too would have to surrender, for Louisbourg had been their source of supply. They were still ready to fight in their own cause; as late as December, 1758, they raided Lunenburg and forced a panicky evacuation of the country lots.[57] That was the last blow. Maillard moved to the mainland and took refuge with a large group of Indians on the banks of the Miramichi River. He wrote to Quebec for guns and ammunition so he could organize his men into guerilla bands to strike the English. They, in turn, heard rumours that Maillard and his Micmacs had been ordered to Quebec to help in its defence.[58] Yet any hope of maintaining communications with the remaining French forces was illusory. The Micmacs held on through 1759, but the winter broke them. Without powder and shot they could neither hunt game nor fight the English. Micmac resistance ended as it ran out of ammunition.

In February, 1760, the Malecites and Passamaquoddy Indians who had been on the fringes of the war came to make peace at Halifax. The resulting articles recited the treaty of 1726, renewed in 1749, and fixed the Indians with the blame for having violated it. Mitchell Neptune of the Passamaquoddies and Ballomy Glode of the Malecites swore their allegiance and submission to King George in renewing peace and friendship with the English. Each promised that three men of his tribe would go to the newly refurbished Fort Frederick at the mouth of the St. John River as hostages.[59] The treaty provided for a truckhouse that would sell trade goods at fixed prices, and the colonial government appointed a commissary to supervise its operation. The chiefs met twice with the council to set the rates, in beaver skins, for a large variety of articles.[60] The Indians began to trade for desperately needed supplies and the English distributed presents to the value of £3,000 within a year.[61] Individuals came to Halifax to make their personal submissions: Claude René, chief of the Shubenacadie and Musquedoboit band; Francis Keehosgeith of Cape Sable; Jean Ball, identified only as a Micmac.[62]

Pierre Maillard accepted the inevitable. He moved with some of his followers to Merigomish, and there, realizing that they had been completely abandoned, treated for peace with an English officer in November, 1759. When news of his decision reached Montreal, Governor Vaudreuil accused him of treason. He penned a furious reply but refused to recant. "Pour moy, m'étant fais victime pour tous, et ayant dû le fuir dans des circonstances où il n'étoit pas possible d'agir autrem^t je tiens inviolablem^t la parole que j'ay donnée. telle est ma façon de penser."[63]† Jean Manach also made his peace. In March, 1760, he brought two chiefs to old Fort Beauséjour, now Fort Cumberland, to make their submission: Paul Lawrence, whose tribe had lived at La Have before the war, and Augustine Michael of the Richibucto band. Manach gave the surprised commandant a list of fourteen other bands that would be coming in as soon as the winter hunt was over: from Miramichi, Shediac, Ile St. Jean, Pictou, and Minas.[64] Maillard wrote Governor Lawrence on behalf of the Acadians and Indians, expressing the hope that religious zealotry would not stand in the path of reconciliation. Lawrence reciprocated by agreeing that Manach and Maillard should stay among the Indians "for the Public good." Manach proved intransigent and was arrested and deported in April, 1761.[65] Maillard, however, moved to Halifax and played a central role as mediator between Micmacs and English.

On 25 June 1761 elaborate ceremonials were held at the governor's farm at Halifax on the formal conclusion of peace "with the several Districts of the general Mickmack Nation of Indians." Once again, the treaty of 1726 was confirmed. Lawrence had died the previous October, and the honour of peace-making fell to Lieutenant-Governor Jonathan Belcher. The council was there, as were the principal military officers and citizens of Halifax. Father Maillard acted as interpreter. Belcher addressed the chiefs: "Brothers . . . I assure myself that you Submit . . . with hearts of Duty and Gratitude, as to your merciful Conqueror." He then led them to a pillar erected in the field, where he received their public vows of obedience. "In this Field you will reap support for yourselves and your Children." Afterwards he distributed presents to each chief. "Your Religion," he continued, "will not be rooted out of this Field—Your Patriarch will still feed & nourish you. . . . The Laws will be like a great Hedge about your Rights and properties," but, he said, it was necessary for them to build a wall to protect the rights of the English. From the pillar they moved to another part of the field for the ceremonial burying of the hatchet, and along with that, as Belcher put it, was buried the memory of faith broken by the Indians. Ominously, he added, "Lenity despised may not be found any more by your Submissions and the Razors set in Oil will cut with the keenest Edge." The party then returned to the pillar for the signing of the treaties, one for each band: each was to the same effect, renewing the treaty of 1726. Finally, Belcher announced triumphantly, the Indians were "in full possession of English protection and Liberty."

The chief of the Cape Breton Indians replied to "My Lord and Father!" They had intended to yield unconditionally, for they had been impressed by the help given them and the poor French inhabitants in the past winter. British generosity had made them decide to come out of their hiding places in the woods. The British were the masters now, according to the will of God. It was a great misfortune that "we have so long neglected to know you" and did not listen to the missionaries when they said the British were also Christians whose blood should not be shed. "As long as the Sun and Moon shall endure" and regardless of whether "things in these Countries be restored to their former State or not," the Indians would hold this treaty inviolable. That said, the ceremony concluded with dancing and singing and toasts to His Majesty's health. An honour guard fired three volleys to mark the joyful occasion.[66]

There was a sequel. The Micmacs, through their spokesman as interpreted by Maillard, had only *intended* to surrender unconditionally. Presumably then, they had not. Was it possible that there were unstated conditions to the treaties? At the last recorded treaty-making, in November, 1761, the La Have chief, Francis Muise, balked at burying the hatchet, for his people would be left defenceless. Maillard assured him that if any wrong were done he might take it up again.[67] This is one condition that may have been communicated to the Micmacs without finding its way into the official reports.

There remained the question of land ownership. The British issued additional instructions to all colonial governors to prevent Indian land being taken in violation of treaties; there was no particular reference to Nova Scotia, for the orders were meant to correct specific abuses arising over Mohawk lands in New York.[68] Nevertheless, in May, 1762, Belcher issued a proclamation that His Majesty was determined to maintain the just rights of the Indians to all lands "reserved or claimed" by them. This naturally raised the question of what were the Indian lands within the bounds of Nova Scotia. He enquired "into the Nature of the Pretensions of the Indians for any part of the Lands within this Province. A return was accordingly made . . . for a Common right to the Sea Coast from Cape Fronsac onwards for Fishing without disturbance." In the proclamation itself this was presented as a claim for

> Fronsac Passage and from thence to Nartagonneich, and from Nartagonneich to Piktouk, and from thence to Cape Geane from thence to Emchih, from thence to Ragi Poutouch, from thence to Zedueck, from thence to Cape Prommentia, from thence to Mirimichy, and from thence to Bay des Chaleurs, and the environs of Canso, from thence to Mushkoodabroet, and so along the Coast, as the Claims and Possessions of the said Indians, for the more especial purpose of hunting, fowling and fishing.

There was a marked similarity between this claim and the "insolent and absurd" demand made by Le Loutre on the Indians' behalf in 1754. Without doubt, Belcher consulted Maillard before drafting the proclamation, and the missionary had performed this last service for his people. Belcher must have had some qualms, for he pointed out to the Lords of Trade that this claim in no way vitiated English title "since the French derived their Title from the Indians, and the French ceded their Title to the English under the Treaty of Utrecht." But he did not publish his proclamation "at large" for fear that if it were known it might incite the Indians to "extravagant and unwarrantable demands."[69]

5

An Uneasy Peace 1762–1783

The memory of fifty years of enmity could not be buried at one ceremony at the governor's farm. Micmacs and English continued to regard each other with suspicion and distrust over the next twenty years. Later, all that changed was that the English gradually ceased to regard the Micmacs at all. But in 1762 the Indians still appeared dangerous, and a revival of French fortunes might have easily set them on the warpath once again. The contaminating French influence continued after the peace of 1763 since the Indians tenaciously demanded the services of Catholic priests and travelled hundreds of miles in search of spiritual consolation—and presents. For their part, the Micmacs resented the English dominance and the refusal to allow them their religion as promised by the treaties of 1761. Opposition remained mostly latent, however, because the slow development of the province minimized the threat to Indian lands, and the English were able to provide uncharacteristically generous support for a few years. When the American Revolution broke out, the Micmacs preferred to stay neutral, yet they had to take precautions to remain in the favour of whichever side emerged victorious. Their affections were not engaged in a war between Englishmen, although the crisis did emphasize their continuing position as a separate power within Nova Scotia. One war gave them status, another took it away; the flight of the Loyalists from the triumphant republic to the only remaining Atlantic colony overwhelmed the Micmacs for all time.

A set-piece opportunity to demonstrate the continuing fears of the English and the abiding resentment of the Indians came very shortly after the Halifax treaties. In June, 1762, a French force attacked Bay Bulls and captured St.

John's, Newfoundland. The news spread quickly throughout Nova Scotia. Lieutenant-Governor Belcher ordered the militia to concentrate at Halifax. From Lunenburg came a plea not to strip the settlers of their defence, since the Indians "by their Motion and Insults for the last twenty-four Hours" appeared to be on the verge of attacking. Once again, farmers were quitting the outlying districts and moving to the safety of the town. Belcher excused the Lunenburg militia from marching to Halifax, and sent a warship to reinforce them. The Indians then came in to explain that their threatening behaviour had just been a drunken spree.[1] When it convened in September, the four-year-old assembly denounced the remaining Acadians for inculcating "those ignorant Wretches" the Indians with hatred of the English. The insolent behaviour of both groups showed that they were ready to chase out the settlers at the first opportunity.[2] After the crisis had passed, Belcher permitted himself some mild self-congratulation in reporting to the Lords of Trade the measures he had taken to check and disperse the Indians.[3] But one of the casualties of the scare was undoubtedly his proclamation regarding their claims. The assembly's London agent blamed the impudence of the Indians on that "silly & too precipitate Proclamation" which had led them to threaten settlers on the coast. Everyone knew, he continued, that the proper place for the savages was the interior, where they could hunt for skins, "which is their Lazy occupation"; they should be allowed to come to the coast only if they did not disturb the white settlers and fishermen.[4] That was the last that was heard of Belcher's proclamation.

Peace, but not mutual trust, came in 1763. In that year King George III issued the proclamation that has been recognized as acknowledging the usufructuary rights of the Indians to the lands of British America. Their special status was to be safeguarded by regulations against the private purchase of their lands. Montagu Wilmot, newly installed as governor of Nova Scotia, acknowledged receipt of the royal proclamation "relative to the newly conquer'd Countries in America" and promised to give it the widest circulation.[5] That was all he said, for he obviously did not consider that it related to his province, which had been conquered fifty years earlier. Both he and his successors ignored the proclamation, and when they came into existence, so did the governments of the other Maritime provinces. It was as though it had never been made.

The Royal Proclamation was one part of a new imperial policy aimed at bringing the management of Indian affairs under central direction. The continent was divided into two departments, north and south, and the Micmacs became the nominal responsibility of Sir William Johnson, a resident of northern New York. The appointment of the famous ranger, John Gorham, as his deputy in Nova Scotia was hardly the most tactful decision. In 1768 the British government dismantled the superintendency under pressure from all the colonies, restoring the regulation of the Indians to each individual province. Lieutenant-Governor Michael Francklin was profoundly thankful, since the Micmacs differed greatly from the interior Indians and could not be treated the same way, being for the most part "dispersed Among the General Settlement of His Majesty's other Subjects."[6] Within a year, the British government reversed itself, and the Indians of Nova Scotia were once again placed under the control of the remote and heedless Johnson.[7] These changes in the higher bureaucracy had little meaning within the province, which continued to meet its problems in its own way.

From the colonists' point of view, the Micmacs could be made useful and peaceable by incorporating them into the empire of commerce. The programme developed in 1760 as part of the peace settlement called for a restricted trade through government sponsored truckhouses. The idea was doubly doomed, for it was easily subject to abuse by a monopolist and ran counter to the imperial government's predilection for competitive and licensed trade. Truckhouses were set up in the full knowledge that losses might be incurred, but such losses were less costly than the expense of fighting the Indians or of giving them the goods for nothing. The existence of an assembly with full taxing powers fulfilled one of the basic conditions that London had laid down thirty years earlier. However, the assembly did not want to underwrite the venture, preferring simply to ban private trade and legislate against fraudulent dealings with the Indians.[8] A schedule of prices was set up based on 5 shillings as the price for one pound weight of spring beaver skin. Other pelts were related to this value. Thus, six mink skins equalled one pound of beaver, one black fox skin equalled two pounds and so on. Trade goods were expressed in the same way: thirty pounds of flour, two gallons of rum, or fourteen pounds of pork equalled one pound of beaver (or six mink pelts or one half a black fox skin). The whole complex scheme was struck down in London, but not before it had collapsed of its own accord in Nova Scotia. Benjamin Gerrish, the commissary, provided the truckhouses with goods from his own store at high prices plus a commission three times what he had contracted for; his accounts were "confusing and irregular." By January, 1763, the best interpretation that could be put on those accounts showed an enormous deficit of £6,296.14.2¾.[9] The provincial budget of Nova Scotia was a little over £1,000 a year.

The losses on the Indian trade, Belcher primly informed his superiors, would "remain for the consideration of Parliament."[10] New regulations came from London ordering that trade be conducted under licence only at fixed locations: Halifax, Fort Cumberland, and the lower Saint John River. Governor Wilmot protested that this plan was too restrictive and successfully urged that additional posts be set up at Lunenburg and Canso.[11] The new system was ineffective as a pacifier, for the Indians still expected presents. The problem was how to persuade the English, who apparently gave presents only when they negotiated treaties? Jenot Piquid Oulat and Bernard, two Micmac chiefs, went aboard a warship and informed the captain that they were there to renew the treaty. Then they asked for goods: cloth, gunpowder, shot, kettles, muskets, hatchets, shirts, twelve cod lines, a salmon net, a compass for a shallop, canvas, and twine. Somewhat taken aback, the captain agreed to bring them what they had requested. He informed the Lords of the Admiralty, and they wrote the Lords of Trade, who replied that it would be highly improper for a ship of the Royal Navy to deliver Indian presents. The Admiralty then informed Governor Wilmot of the situation and stated that if the Indians concerned were of "sufficient rank and consideration," he might meet their demands.[12] By that time Oulat and Bernard were long forgotten.

If the Indians could not get presents from the English, they could still receive them from the French. In 1763, Britain returned the tiny offshore islands of St. Pierre and Miquelon to France. The Micmacs knew these islands, for they had long crossed to Newfoundland, which they regarded as an extension of their hunting grounds. From 1720 on they had a more or less permanent settlement at St. George's Bay on the east coast. For the Micmac traveller it was a fairly simple proposition to go along to the Bay of Despair opposite the French islands. The first report of Micmacs at St. Pierre came within months of the French re-occupation. The chief of the Cape Breton Indians stayed there with his whole band, and the reasons for French hospitality could not be entirely altruistic.[13] It was vital that the English continue to make presents, argued Wilmot, for the custom had been too long established to be broken with safety. The presents were not luxuries, but the necessities of Indian life, and to cut them off would provoke the enmity of a people with six hundred warriors in a thinly populated colony garrisoned by a scattered five hundred soldiers. The deficit on the Indian account stood at £12,000 by June, 1764.[14] The Lords of Trade replied that the Indians must be weaned from presents and taught to live on the sale of furs; but if in fact they were going to St. Pierre and Miquelon, Wilmot should give them necessities up to the value of £250 from contingency funds. It was vital to cut the Micmacs off from their contacts with the French. When the expenses for the year went over £750, the imperial government, while insisting that the charges should be met out of provincial funds, grudgingly agreed to pay.[15]

Nova Scotians could be just as hospitable as the French, especially if there were a chance that the imperial government might pick up the bill. Indeed, in a Halifax gripped by postwar depression, Indians were big business and important patrons. Between 11 September and 6 December 1763, no less than 777 Indians came to Halifax and all apparently lodged with William Fury; from November 1764 to May 1766 he accommodated a further 2,263 visitors. Chiefs were boarded and lodged at two shillings and sixpence a day, ordinary Indians at two shillings. Any damage they caused was paid for by the government, ten shillings for a broken door, ninepence for a square of glass. Dr. Alexander Abercrombie attended sick Indians and boarded some of them. He received £95 for his services up to September, 1763, and a further £72.10.0 by

May, 1766.[16] With the assembly steadfastly refusing to pay for this outpouring of public money, it simply went on to the provincial debt in the hope that the British taxpayer would eventually shoulder the load.

The Indian threat helped to spread the wealth around and thus performed a useful service. Nova Scotians did not allow the British to forget that the French hold over the Indians remained unabated.[17] It was, after all, true. The Indians continued to assemble each year at Port Toulouse on Cape Breton, where the French had once distributed presents. Passing through English settlements on the way, various Indians announced that they were off to meet the French fleet and would destroy the colonists on their return. The settlers stood to arms and lost much precious time. At their assembly in 1765, the Micmacs resolved not to allow any settlement around Pictou.[18] In the circumstances, the commander at Louisbourg was only too happy to see them leave the mainland and gave out passports to Newfoundland. Hugh Palliser, governor of the island, was furious and said so.[19] His composure was little helped by the receipt of a letter from Francklin telling him to set up a coastal patrol to prevent Micmacs from crossing to St. Pierre.[20] Palliser ordered the whole tribe out of his island, but to no avail. By 1767 there were some 175 on the coast in the Bay of Despair area trading with French merchants.[21]

The link with St. Pierre was all the more important to the Micmacs because they could find Catholic priests there to marry, baptize, confirm, and confess them. Although they had been promised free exercise of their religion in the Halifax treaties, there was no Catholic priest in the province after Pierre Maillard died in August, 1762. Frequent approaches to the colonial authorities to find a replacement were turned aside. The British government had determined that the Indians should be protestantized, both for their spiritual benefit and for the security of Nova Scotia. It was axiomatic that Catholicism meant loyalty to France. The agent of conversion would be the Anglican missionary Society for the Propagation of the Gospel, whose first man in Nova Scotia, the Reverend William Tutty, had identified the Indians as "bigotted Papists" under the control of French priests back in 1749.[22] He attempted no conversion, but the need for it was kept alive by the publication, in 1758, of a long letter describing the customs of the Micmacs and Malecites. The study was an English translation of a manuscript by Pierre Maillard, but there was no account of how it had been acquired. The preface gave the message: Catholic priests must be countered by offering the Indians "a much more pure and rational" religion which would free them from bondage to the French.[23] After the defeat of the Micmacs, when Maillard begged that bigotry be put aside and helped in arranging the peace treaties, the colonial government thought that they might have found the man to ease the transition to protestantism. In his final days, Maillard was accompanied by the Reverend Thomas Wood of the SPG, who attended him at his death. Maillard's status with the English was attested to by the presence of the president of the council, the speaker of the assembly, and four other gentlemen as pallbearers. Wood read the Anglican burial service in French before a large gathering at the graveside. He hoped that this visible proof of continuity would establish him as Maillard's successor and lead his people to abandon the superstitions of popery.[24]

Indians approached Governor Wilmot in July, 1763, asking for the services of a Catholic priest, and he promised to find one. He reasoned that if they were denied, the Indians might be able to get priests secretly from France and suggested that two or three loyal French-speaking Catholic priests might be sent from the King's German possessions.[25] The Lords of Trade did not agree and approached the Society for the Propagation of the Gospel with a request to send three protestant missionaries who understood French. The Society ordered its missionaries on the spot to give all the attention they could, consistent with their other duties, to the Indians and promised to appoint special ministers as soon as possible. When the Indians come again, Wilmot was instructed, say nothing more than that the king would attend to the situation; on no account was he to let it be publicly known that protestant missionaries were on their way.[26]

Besides Thomas Wood, the only SPG missionary in Nova Scotia was J.-B. Moreau, a French protestant stationed at Lunenburg after 1753. He claimed considerable success in making Indian converts, baptizing twenty-seven children, marrying two couples, and having sixty-two communicants at his Easter service in 1764. The Micmacs "behave with great Decency in religious Ceremonies," but like the Catholic missionaries before him, he found he had to go to great expense to entertain them whenever they came to visit. There were five hundred Indians in the vicinity of Lunenburg, and a wedding or baptism unfailingly drew fifty guests to his house.[27] The colonial government was willing to pay his expenses for wine and other refreshments dispensed, as his claim put it, to persuade the Indians to bring their children to be baptized and married in the Church of England.[28] Moreau did not work unopposed. The local Indians received copies of a letter written by Jesus Christ to the Bishop of Luca threatening eternal damnation to those who failed in any point of the Catholic faith and promising eternal bliss to those who shunned protestantism. The letter was signed by two men long associated with Maillard at the Ile Royale mission, Louis Benjamin Petitpas and J.-B. Roma, who were distributing it. The devout wore copies of the letter, as in a buoin's bag, next to the heart.[29]

Thomas Wood "providentially" came into possession of the papers of Pierre Maillard, which included a Micmac grammar and numerous translations of a devotional nature.[30] Earnest in assuming Maillard's mantle, Wood set out to study Micmac with the object not only of being able to preach in the language, but also of translating the Book of Common Prayer and of eventually publishing a grammar, a dictionary, and the whole Bible in

Micmac. He quickly ran into difficulties with Maillard's hieroglyphics, suspecting them to be of Assyrian origin.[31] He was able to hire Roma, the man who had been circulating Christ's letters, to help him in the work.[32] By 1766, Wood had transcribed some seventy-five pages of Maillard's grammar and sent them off to the society as "An Essay towards Bringing the Savage Indian Mickmack Language to be Learnt Gramatically [sic]," dedicated to King George III. For years, he wrote, the Catholics had taught the Micmacs to kill heretics, and "until these poor deluded Indians [are] Convinced by plain Arguments of the falsity and Absurdity of many of the Tenets of that bigotted Religion," they would remain lost. He also addressed the Archbishop of Canterbury, urging him to instruct the Micmacs in the way to salvation.[33] But there the matter rested. The society did not print the grammar, and the translations were never made. Wood became busy with his new work as rector of St. Paul's Church, Halifax. And no protestant missionaries left England to devote their lives to the Indians.

In one of his letters to the society, Wood expressed the hope that the Catholic faith of the Indians would "wear off" if they never again saw a French priest.[34] Just how long this process would take was a moot point, and those responsible for the day-to-day administration of the province were not willing to wait to find out. They were not impressed with Anglican missionaries. Governor Wilmot found the Indians "very impatient and Dissatisfied without the Exercise of their Religion" and thought that attempts to convert them were doomed to result in nothing but exasperation.[35] Lieutenant-Governor Francklin was even more direct; the refusal to provide priests amounted to a breach of English faith. The Indians had been promised freedom of religion, he recalled, as part of the terms arranged by Maillard in 1759 and 1760. The council had promised to find a priest in July, 1763. Not too surprisingly, the Indians were saying that they had been deceived. Even without their priests, they still assembled of their own accord each year for the St. Ann's Day festivities. Although there is no direct evidence, it would be reasonable to assume that the basic rituals were kept alive by band captains acting as catechists and using Maillard's ideographs. The Indians received books and "superstitious baubles" from St. Pierre to authenticate their services and thus strengthened their connection with France. All this danger could be averted by allowing them a loyal priest or two: surely the governor of Quebec could send someone?[36]

These arguments, together with the failure of the Society for the Propagation of the Gospel to provide any new missionaries of its own, persuaded the British government to allow in one Catholic priest as an experiment. Charles-François Bailly came from Quebec in 1768 and went to Halifax, where he stayed with the Reverend Breynton, rector of the Anglican St. Paul's Church. Breynton was optimistic that the Indians would "be soon brought to listen to Instruction, & live peaceably under the Government," and doubtless he communicated these sentiments to the young priest. Bailly then met the new governor, Lord William Campbell, who gave him a glowing commendation that he forwarded to the bishop of Quebec, Jean Briand. After this welcoming start, Bailly went to visit the Malecites on the St. John in June, and from this vantage point he surveyed a vast and empty mission field. He advised Bishop Briand that missionaries should be stationed at Restigouche to serve St. John's Island, Cape Breton, and the Magdalen Islands; at the Miramichi to serve the Indians there and at Richibucto; and, permanently, on the St. John River to serve that area. The best locations for bringing the Micmacs together were at Miramichi and Caraquet. As yet, he reported, he had no stipend, but Campbell had promised him $200 from the funds administered by Sir William Johnson. Until them, he had to live off the charity of the Indians.[37] The firm of Simonds and White, trading along the St. John, noticed that the Indians had many fewer furs to sell in 1768. Bailly had been paid for his services in fur and had disrupted the hunt by making the Indians break it off a month earlier than usual.[38]

In July, Bailly was back in Halifax; in October, Briand appointed him vicar-general of Nova Scotia and parts adjacent. By 1769 he was receiving a salary of £100 from the king. He toured the province and came to the conclusion that he would rather live at Halifax, for his health had been impaired by two winters' sojourn on the St. John. Despite his own earlier warning against locating Indians near Halifax for fear of drunkenness, he now proposed to bring them together in a settlement on the outskirts of town. Lord William Campbell thoroughly agreed, for the English would then be able to keep the Micmacs under close watch. Bailly, he wrote, was "unbigotted, candid, and of a Liberal turn of Mind," willing and able to eradicate old prejudices and teach the Indians obedience to government.[39] In short, Bailly was the perfect Catholic priest. Unfortunately, not everyone agreed, for a few zealous souls raised the cry that if the king could install a papist in Halifax, why not also in Boston?[40] Between August and November, 1771, Bailly toured Cape Breton; he then wintered in Halifax and departed in May of the following year to become bishop coadjutor of Quebec. That left J.-B. de la Brosse as the nearest missionary, and he was located on the Quebec side of the Baie des Chaleurs. He was replaced in September, 1774, by Joseph Mathurin Bourg, the first native Acadian missionary. But he stayed far from Halifax.

In the decade following the Halifax treaties the Micmacs were more interested in priests and presents than in land. The priests were important because they had become an integral part of life, an element in the Micmac identity that had to be preserved in the face of the conquerors. Presents were vital because they furnished both the necessities of life and a measure of self-esteem, a token that the English were not riding roughshod over the tribe. Land came third in importance because the English had not yet acquired enough of it to damage the customary pattern of existence. The portents were there, but not, as yet, the reality; surveyors went out, but few settlers followed. Samuel Holland surveyed Cape Breton and encountered bands of roving Micmacs congregating to meet their aged chief Janot, who was expected to return shortly from Newfoundland. Holland assumed they wished to seek his advice on how best to secure a French priest. When they saw what his party was doing, the Indians "seemed dissatisfied at the Lake [Bras d'Or] being surveyed, saying we had discovered now all their private Haunts, which the French never attempted to do." He talked to them, and they told him of the traders who made them drunk and took their goods at half-price. He said they would be glad to have a tract of land "granted them by His Majesty for the Conveniency of Hunting in which they might not be molested by any European Settlers." Holland estimated that 808,000 acres of Cape Breton could be set aside as the "Savage or Hunting Country."[41]

There was still room for all in Nova Scotia. Francklin assured the secretary of state, with a certain pride, that whatever injustices might be wreaked on the Indians in other colonies, Nova Scotia was entirely free of such wrongdoing. In fact, "we are at perfect Peace with the Indians," he wrote, forgetting for once the existence of St. Pierre and the baneful French.[42] However, the peace was not so perfect that the withdrawal of troops to pacify unruly Boston in 1768 did not cause him some concern. Prudence dictated that he avoid annoying the Indians and cajole them into self-sufficiency. Happily, one family had already bought a few cows and many others had applied for lands to cultivate; some had taken to catching and curing cod for sale. These activities would "have a tendency to Civilize them and to make them more resident among our People."[43] The absence of troops brought a marked increase in the number of Indians arriving in Halifax to ask for provisions. They received some presents and much advice: take up farming and "pursue the same Plan of Life, which they observe their Brethren the English follow."[44] Assimilation was the wave of the future.

As long as the Micmacs had plenty of living space, descriptions of the virtues of farming had little effect, and they were not concerned to secure their land. But the Malecites were more wary, for they faced the first postwar roving bands of colonials. In May, 1762, twenty men of Newburyport, Massachusetts, led by James Simonds, sailed up the St. John to St. Ann's, where they found cleared land and the remains of a settlement. They pitched their tents and began a survey of what was really an Indian burial ground and the site of a mission church. A party of Malecites appeared in full war dress and informed the English that they were intruders on Indian land. If they did not stop the survey immediately, the Indians said, they would be forced to do so. The English protested that they had authority from the governor to carry out the survey, and the Indians replied that the treaty forbade any English settlement above Grimross. Accordingly, the intruders withdrew twelve miles down the river and surveyed a township, Maugerville, without challenge.[45]

The importance of St. Ann's was reaffirmed when a delegation of Malecites from the area, led by Pierre Thomas and Ambroise St. Aubin, conferred with Francklin in July, 1768. They came to Halifax shortly after Bailly's stay among them, and it was probably he who suggested the agenda. The first question was whether the new priest could stay with them? No, was the answer; he would serve all the Indians. Could anything be done to staunch the flow of rum and spirits? Everything possible would be done. The chiefs expressed their wish to forgive and forget past hostilities and to remain neutral in any future war between Europeans. They indicated that they disliked Major Gorham's power to "Command and Direct" them, and they received approval for the expulsion of two Acadian families living in their village and causing trouble. But the central concern was their desire for "land for Cultivation." The council agreed. Accordingly, a grant was issued on 20 August to "give grant and confirm unto Pierre Thomas & Ambroise St. Aubin in trust for and in behalf of the Tribes of Indians inhabiting St. John's River" 500 acres of woodland, the 200 acres of Indian Island in the river across from St. Ann's, and the 4 acres covering the site of the burial ground. These 704 acres were granted "forever," with an annual quit rent of ¼d an acre due after the first ten years. No part of the land was to be alienated without the prior consent of the governor. This first grant of land to Indians was made in a form similar to that issued whites, except for the restriction on resale. The use of the specific word "forever" was in marked contrast to later practice where Indians were given their lands "to occupy during pleasure." No one raised the question of how lands that had never been acquired from the Indians according to the terms of the Royal Proclamation of 1763 could legally be granted back to them or why such a process should be necessary. Officials did notice, and rejoiced at, the willingness of Indians to take up agriculture. Tools were provided to help with the cultivation that, the chiefs explained, would "support our old People and pay our debts." The Malecites were ready to consider farming as a supplement to the hunting life.[46]

The need to develop additional resources to pay off debts was the result of a considerable trade along the St. John River Valley. Between 1764 and 1774 the firm of Simonds and White took out furs valued at £11,295. They found that the Indians constantly required fresh credit to pay off old debts.[47] Nevertheless, the profits were good enough to attract others. Charles Jadis set up a store at Grimross, right on the boundary claimed by the Indians who confronted the Newburyport settlers in 1762. He had bought the land for just over £100, sight unseen, before leaving England. Pierre Thomas and others warned him not to settle there and told him several times that he would be burned out. On 6 February 1771 a fire that was started at his door destroyed his house and, so he claimed, £2,000 in goods. Settlers as well as traders who stepped over the line were punished. In one such exploit, Pierre Thomas forced a white to drag him, atop a sleigh full of provisions, seven miles up the

St. John River ice and then back again. The Malecites did not accept intruders meekly, and the dismantling of Fort Frederick at the mouth of the St. John meant that there were no armed forces to restrain them.[48]

Prudence dictated that the colony continue to take some responsibility for the welfare of the Indians. John Cunningham had been the Indian agent in the early 1760's and had presided over the first expenditures of public money. He was replaced in November, 1767, by Major Gorham, and there is no record that anything was spent under his agency. But in less than eighteen months Cunningham was back at his post and the payments resumed, albeit on a reduced scale. There was less for medical services and supplies, while visitors to Halifax were lodged at a flat rate of only a shilling a day. The phrase "indigent Indians" made its first appearance in his records as a description of those for whom he bought miscellaneous goods.[49] This term involved an important new concept, for it fitted the native peoples into a recognized segment of white society: the very poor whose maintenance was traditionally a charge on the community. With Nova Scotia now a settled colony, the Micmacs would have to learn to accept their new status.

The time for that had not yet quite arrived in 1775, where Cunningham's accounts end. Great events were taking place elsewhere in America, in fact, almost everywhere else than in Nova Scotia. The onset of colonial resistance to British rule left the colony acutely isolated on its stretch of the Atlantic coast. Governor Francis Legge was understandably distraught; three months after the skirmish at Lexington had signalled a general revolt, he had thirty-six effective fighting men to protect Nova Scotia, far fewer than Governor Philipps had had in the dismal days when there was only a frontier post on the Bay of Fundy and a seasonal fishing station at Canso to defend.[50] Legge was responsible for a colony of eighteen thousand settlers who he feared were republican New Englanders to a man, and his fears were reasonably well founded. He had a fractious assembly, someone had lost the financial records of the province, and the government itself was in a state of almost unbelievable chaos. Perhaps he might be excused for forgetting the Indians under the press of these events.

The men of Massachusetts did not overlook the Indians. On 15 May 1775 the Provincial Congress addressed an open letter to the "Eastern Indians" explaining that the British ministry was planning to take away the liberty of colonial and Indian alike; they would not even allow the Indians to shoot game. The letter asked the "good Brothers" what they needed—guns, powder, cloth, stores—and promised that they would be supplied. In September, the Malecite leaders Pierre Thomas and Ambroise St. Aubin, alerted by their Penobscot brethren, decided to investigate these offers. They dictated a letter allying themselves with the Penobscots and agreeing to "oppose the People of Old England that are endeavouring to take your and our Lands & Libertys from us." They offered to trade furs for arms and provisions and asked the spiritual descendants of the *Mayflower* to find them a priest.[51] The only sign of interest on the British side was when Governor Legge sent an emissary to the St. John's Indians in November. He travelled as far as Annapolis and then, faced with bad weather in the Bay of Fundy, returned to Halifax bearing further gloomy accounts of the rebellious nature of the whites he had met on his abortive mission.[52]

The loyal colonials of Nova Scotia found little comfort anywhere. Their isolation was almost complete. The defences of Canada fell before the revolutionaries' onslaught and only Quebec itself remained, with the British forces there penned inside as securely as was the royal army besieged at Boston. Had the governor's emissary been able to proceed to the farthest reaches of Nova Scotia he would have found rebellion there no mere sentiment but a reality, for the majority of whites in Cumberland County and along the St. John River were in favour of throwing in their lot with Massachusetts. Distance made them immune to whatever feeble authority Halifax could exert. Fort Cumberland, decaying and undermanned, stood alone as an apologetic reminder of the days of imperial power. Both Micmacs and Malecites, seeing the collapse of the English throughout the continent, wisely decided to make their peace with the new force that was changing the face of America. The republican government of Massachusetts was more than willing to meet them halfway. They followed up their first overtures by establishing a truckhouse at Machias, on the northern coast of the commonwealth, to attract the trade of the St. John's Indians and bind them to the revolution.

Late in January, 1776, Malecites joined Caughnawaga and Penobscot Indians at General Washington's camp outside Boston. The Caughnawaga, living near Montreal, had seen the success of revolutionary arms with their own eyes and were insistent on making an alliance; the others were more reticent. Washington hoped they would all stay neutral, because he feared the expense of supporting them, but he did conclude a treaty with the Caughnawaga. He sent a letter to the eastern Indians calling on them to remain at peace and offering to defend them against the English if the need arose.[53] Micmac leaders professed to adore Washington as a saint for the nobility of these sentiments. In June, a deputation visited John Allan, a leading rebel of Cumberland, to discuss the situation. They had, they said, just been to see Major Gorham, commander at Fort Cumberland, who had offered them ample provisions if they would take up arms against the rebels; now they must decide what to do. "How comes it," they asked Allan, "that Old England & new should Quarrel & come to blows? The Father & Son to fight is terrible— Old France & Canada did not do so, we cannot think of fighting ourselves till we know who is right & who is wrong." Allan obliged them by explaining why the revolutionaries were justified in their resistance.[54] He had to be all the more persuasive as the Americans had by then been driven out of Canada and battle honours were even. The Micmacs were once again in a position to manoeuvre between contending parties, but they wondered whether it was wise to do so. They wanted to keep their options open; they had no desire to take arms in a war of son against father, but they had no wish to offend a future victor.

The Micmacs could afford to bide their time. A widely dispersed people, they had dealt with the whites for over one hundred and fifty years, and they were accustomed to seeing them scattered in small groups across their land. By comparison the Malecites were much more concentrated in their tribal lands. As soon as they received Washington's letter, they went on a witch hunt for Loyalists, without making too much distinction between white faces.[55] The handful of settlers and traders who had established themselves along the St. John River in the 1760's had provoked strong resentment. Rebel claims that the British were taking away the Indians' land found a ready response among the Malecites, who were also looking for a commercial alternative to Simonds and White, to whom they were perennially indebted. There was no imperial presence on Malecite land, not even a Fort Cumberland, and communications with peninsular Nova Scotia were cut for months at a time by privateers operating out of the rebel base at Machias. Geography and the fortunes of war combined to bring the Malecites within the orbit of Massachusetts. The result was a split within the tribe: one party, under Ambroise St. Aubin, was consistently ready to support the rebels, while the other, led by Pierre Thomas, was cautiously pro-English.

The war continued to go badly for the revolutionaries. The British had disengaged themselves from Boston and were attacking with great success at New York. George Washington decided it was time to use the Indians and urged the Continental Congress to engage men from the Penobscot, Malecite, and Micmac tribes in its service. On 11 July he wrote the Massachusetts legislature that he had been authorized to enlist the Indians, if necessary at full continental pay, for two or three years. They should be engaged immediately and marched to New York.[56] Even as Washington was writing this plea for help, a delegation of ten Micmac and Malecite chiefs arrived in Watertown, the seat of Massachusetts' government-in-exile. Their main interest was to see that the truckmaster at Machias offered better prices and longer credit than Simonds and White, but the politicians of Massachusetts had other concerns. They agreed to increase the grant to the truckmaster and then grasped at the opportunity to fill their chronically undermanned quotas for the continental army by resolving to employ Indians from the two tribes. They authorized the raising of a regiment of 500 Indians and 250 whites. The field officers were to be white, and other commissioned officers half white, half Indian. This was the basis for a treaty concluded on 19 July in which the Indians acknowledged the independence of the United States, agreed to assist the republic and to urge other tribes to do so, and promised to send men to join the army. Ambroise St. Aubin was the first to make his mark; there were two other Malecites and six Micmacs, including John Battis and Sabbatis Netobcobroit.[57]

The Micmacs at large gave this treaty no support. John Allan conferred with the chiefs of the Miramichi, Richibucto, Shediac, Chignecto, and Cape Sable bands in September. They told him that they had not authorized the treaty and that it was the work of a few of their young men. John Battis said that he had been misled in translation and did not realize that the Micmacs were binding themselves to fight alongside the revolutionaries. All wished to stay at peace, as Washington had said they should in his letter to them. Further, they intended to show the treaty to the British at Fort Cumberland and then return it to the Bostonians. Dismayed, Allan amassed his whole stock of arguments to prove the rectitude of the American cause from the time the first settlers landed. Politely, the chiefs agreed with him, but they insisted that their people were too few in number to perform the military services stipulated in the treaty. Their present support came from Old England, and if they offended her, she would send "big Vessels in our Rivers & prevent us from fowling & Fishing... we know we must submit to the strongest Power." They asked Allan to transcribe the conversation so they could show the British written proof of their good intentions. Allan refused and persuaded the chiefs to write the Massachusetts government instead, explaining their refusal to take up the hatchet.[58]

The Micmacs' decision to remain neutral was taken despite the lack of any overtures from the British side to offset rebel initiatives. Perhaps the British discounted the Indians' strength, but that seems unlikely given the recent past. Perhaps they refused to get involved in the bargaining game, relying on their big ships as the ultimate persuaders. Most probably, however, they simply forgot about the Indians. Certainly, Michael Francklin thought that the Indians had been most shamefully neglected and the opportunity to use their services left to waste. Relieved of his position as lieutenant-governor, he was anxious to be appointed Indian agent and use his influence among them.[59] Such accounts as there were of British initiatives—a full-scale conference at Halifax late in 1775, offers by Gorham at Fort Cumberland—came from Allan's reports of what the Indians told him and do not appear in the official British records. Admiral Marriott Arbuthnot, the new lieutenant-governor acting in Governor Legge's absence, was not inclined to worry about Indians. At the very time they were negotiating with Massachusetts and being sought as recruits for the rebel army, Arbuthnot wrote the secretary of state: "The Indians have not hitherto gone further than to discover a spirit of insolence, by interrupting the Trade on the St. Johns river and taking away a few Cattle."[60]

This complacency received a severe jolt in November, 1776. For months there had been rumours that the rebels would attack Fort Cumberland, and

Jonathan Eddy, a local settler, finally succeeding in raising a force. He led almost two hundred men to the attack. They had some initial success, wading through the tidal mud in a fog to capture a sloop, but they failed to take the fort. They withdrew at the end of November. Only a few Indians took part in the assault, fifteen Malecites and four Micmacs, but the British did not know just how few they had been. The mere fact that "the Indians" were once again on the warpath was sufficient to arouse all the old fears. Many believed it would never have happened "had the smallest attention been paid to their Chiefs...which by some strange mistake has been entirely omitted."[61] The revolutionaries continued to pay attention to them; Pierre Thomas went to Boston and there received a fulsome letter from George Washington congratulating him on keeping the chain of friendship unbroken.[62] The British finally decided to pay some attention too, and in the spring of 1777 they sent a big ship, HMS *Vulture*, up the St. John River.[63]

The expedition came with olive branch and sword, to offer amnesty to all those who had strayed from the path of loyalty and to build a fort at the mouth of the St. John River as a security against future trespass. Councillor Arthur Goold spoke to a delegation of Indians, led by Pierre Thomas, who visited the *Vulture*. He had them take the oath of loyalty on the Bible, offered to let bygones be bygones, and told them that he had invited the missionary Bourg to come amongst them on the same footing as M. Bailly had once been.[64] Within a month, John Allan, newly appointed as Massachusetts' superintendent of the eastern Indians, made his countermove. He travelled to Aukpaque, the cluster of river islands and riverbank that had been granted the Malecites in 1767, where he held a number of conferences with the tribe. He faced an uphill task. The government of Massachusetts was making preparations, on paper at least, for an invasion of Nova Scotia, but it was losing interest in the Indians. They, in their turn, were complaining that the state was not observing the treaty and was overcharging at its truckhouses.[65] Allan only had fair words and his own enhanced status to bargain with, little enough to set against a thirty-four gun sloop. However, St. Aubin's pro-revolutionary group was in the ascendant. Allan was ceremoniously inducted into the tribe, and after three weeks of waiting and persuading, he drew up articles of trade and commerce with them. By then it was the end of June, and the *Vulture* was slowly making its way upstream. Pierre Thomas and four others went to meet the British, but the rest refused to go, and the young men were eager to attack any force that put ashore. The result was a draw. Thomas failed to carry his people over to the British side, but he did prevent bloodshed. Rebels and Malecites began a long retreat, via Meductic, to the coast at Machias. The British consolidated their position. In the middle of August they attacked Machias, and by November, 1777, they had completed Fort Howe at the mouth of the St. John.[66]

Once again, outside events began to play their part. The British defeat at

Saratoga in October threw their ultimate victory in doubt, and when reports arrived that France was entering the war, these doubts were doubled. Micmacs and Malecites still had fond memories of the French, and Britain would now have to bargain hard to win their support. John Allan had a correspondingly stronger bargaining position than before. In August, 1778, he informed the Indians assembled at Machias that the United States and France were allies. "I Demanded of them to thro' aside that Indolence & Lethargic Spirit"; all responded they were ready. "War seems to be the Cry from all Quarters," he happily recorded. He drew up a declaration of war, and the Malecites sent it to the commander at Fort Howe. They were, they said, unanimous that Old England was wrong and New England was right, for "our Father the King of France takes their part." The English must leave the Malecites' lands forthwith: "The River on which you are with your soldiers belongs from the most ancient times to our Ancestors, consequently is ours now, and which we are bound to keep for our posterity."[67]

The Indians' behaviour was so changeable, Allan once observed, that "it brings on an unsteadyness in my own conduct with them."[68] Such a fit of unsteadiness must have seized him just over a month after his declaration of war, when he received a letter dictated to the same Indians by his opponent Michael Francklin. It repeated that all differences with Britain had been resolved and demanded that Allan stay at Machias and bother them no more. The volte-face was a triumph for Pierre Thomas, who was able to summon shamanistic powers to his aid. Approached by James White, one of Francklin's deputies, Thomas "said that he must consult the Divine Being and throwing himself upon his face in the sand lay motionless for nearly the space of an hour." At the end of that time he announced he would keep the peace with King George.[69] Further spiritual assistance for the British arrived in the person of Father Bourg, authorized by the bishop of Quebec to excommunicate all those who acted against the constituted authorities of Nova Scotia. The Indians came to meet their long-awaited missionary at Fort Howe on 24 September. Pierre Thomas and Francis Xavier of the Malecites were there as well as delegates from the Miramichi, Chignecto, and Minas branches of the Micmac tribe. Bourg told them that loyalty was a condition of their receiving the sacraments of the church. They took the oath of allegiance on bended knee, handed over presents once given them by George Washington and also the 1776 treaty with Massachusetts, and promised to stay neutral and shun the rebels at Machias. To emphasize the seriousness of their pledges, members of each tribe delivered a string of wampum, a rare event in Anglo-Indian negotiations on this part of the continent. Francklin gave them supplies and presents, including religious objects, as well as speeches. Such was the Treaty of Fort Howe; the Indians long retained a memory of it as the time when they and the English became "all one brother."[70]

In reality, the treaty settled nothing, for both sides continued to bid for

Indian support. Admiral d'Estaing, commanding a French squadron cruising the western Atlantic, issued a proclamation calling for a general uprising against the English throughout the old realms of France. The French consul at Boston sent individual copies to various Indian leaders, among them Ambroise St. Aubin and Joseph Claude. He apologized for not having a priest for them but, meanwhile "love Jesus Christ with all your soul and go in peace."[71] Allan despatched a secret agent to Cumberland to distribute the summons. In July, 1779, he sent out a war belt which resulted in twenty canoes from the St. John and a small delegation of Micmacs arriving at Machias to learn what was afoot.[72] But the odds against Allan were lengthening, and he lacked the resources to compete with the British. Francklin maintained a steady flow of supplies to the Indians: food, medicine, ammunition. The Treaty of Fort Howe had cost over £500 and in the year following he spent a further £1,000. He rewarded the Cape Breton Micmacs for beating off a privateer and averted a threatened Indian attack on Pictou by distributing presents. The Council of Nova Scotia reissued the grant of Aukpaque to the Malecites, dropping St. Aubin's name from the list of trustees.[73] Francklin's efforts won approval in London, and he was ordered to recruit Indians into the royal service. He drew back at this suggestion, for it involved the expense of caring for the families of the warriors while they were away. In any event, their loyalty was still suspect, and if a French warship hove into sight their old affections would be immediately set aflame.[74] But the French ships did not appear. The British steadily extended their control over the Bay of Fundy throughout 1779, capturing Penobscot and isolating northern Massachusetts from the rest of the United States. Britain was unquestionably the stronger power in the homeland of the Micmacs.

Just how strong was shown by the swift and decisive reaction to Micmac raids on the stores of John Cort, a merchant on the Miramichi River. The Indians may have been encouraged in the attack by emissaries from d'Estaing or Allan, but they were most probably venting an accumulation of grievances against the traders. No matter; HMS *Viper* was sent to the spot flying the French flag and put out a long boat under American colours. After a brief scuffle, the landing party seized sixteen Indians. The vessel then sailed for Quebec, where it deposited the captives. This punitive act provoked widespread concern but no resistance from other Micmacs. Ten "Consequential Indians" visited Francklin to find out what was to happen to the prisoners and to arrange for supplies for their families. Francklin took the opportunity to conclude a treaty making the Indians assume the blame for not stopping those who had plundered the stores and promise both to protect British subjects in future and to have nothing to do with John Allan. All Francklin gave in return were some presents, an assurance that the Indians would not be molested, and a promise that traders would supply their needs in exchange for furs. John and Francis Julien signed as first and second chiefs of the

Miramichi Indians, Augustine Michael and Francis Joseph Arimph for the Richibucto.[75] Nothing was said about the return of the prisoners. As far as the colonial government was concerned, they could stay in Quebec. Governor Haldimand did not agree, and he sent them all to Halifax. Detaining the two ringleaders, the council decided to send the others home.[76]

With the British in control of the waters of Nova Scotia and northern Massachusetts, the final years of the Revolutionary War passed uneventfully. Allan still held an occasional conference where Indians came in search of supplies and trade, but their support no longer made any military difference, and they were allowed to follow their own inclination to remain neutral. Allan lamented the lack of help from his government, while Francklin found himself engaged in an unseemly three-way struggle between the secretary of state, the colonial assembly, and the controller of army funds over who should pay the costs of his diplomacy.[77] By the time the fighting stopped in 1782, the Indians were no longer of account as allies, enemies, or people. Nova Scotia was inundated with Loyalist refugees from New York. Its population tripled to forty-two thousand within one year. And in all the flood of correspondence concerning the details of that great migration, there is not one word about the Indians who would be dispossessed by the new settlers.

PART III

The Micmacs and Colonial Governments

6

The Micmacs and Government: Nova Scotia

The arrival of the Loyalists completed Britain's conquest of Acadia. For the first time she was able to establish permanent settlements on lands long claimed but never grasped. The Micmac Indians, already broken as a military power, were now overwhelmed as a people. They were no longer a threat to Britain, nor was their support worth courting. Henceforth, the imperial authorities would take as little interest as possible in their fate, concerned only when there was a threat of foreign war. As Anthony Blackwood of the Colonial Office would one day explain, the Micmacs possessed "an undeniable Claim to the Protection of the Government as British Subjects," but that obligation did not call for the direct interference of the Crown. They had no "military title" to assistance as did the Canadian Indians who had fought at Britain's side against both French and Americans. Micmac claims for fair treatment were not based on any debt of gratitude but simply "resolve themselves into an equitable right to be compensated for the loss of lands." This being so, there was no reason for the imperial government to involve itself in their affairs.[1]

The spread of British settlement quickly led to the division of Acadia into separate political units. Nova Scotia was partitioned in 1784, with the mainland side of the Bay of Fundy becoming the colony of New Brunswick and Cape Breton being given (until 1821) a measure of autonomy from Halifax. Ile St. Jean, then known as St. John's Island and shortly to be Prince Edward Island, had enjoyed its own government since 1769. Acadia was split into three major jurisdictions. Decisions that would affect the life of the Micmac people in their own land were now going to be made by three different colonial governments. Since the imperial government had no Indian policy to guide these colonies, each treated the Micmacs in its own way. Consequently the relations of whites and Micmacs became as fragmented as Acadia itself and varied according to the political boundaries that now divided the area.

The dispossession of the Micmacs took place very rapidly after the arrival of Loyalist refugee settlers in Nova Scotia. The Micmacs were still largely dependent on the produce of salt and fresh water, and both they and the whites prized the same areas, namely coastline and river frontage. Whites quickly disrupted the pattern of life since they preferred to settle the easily accessible places first: the coast for the fisheries and the river valleys, not only for the best soil and fisheries, but also for the potential of water-powered saw mills. The indented coastline and numerous rivers of the province ensured that this white settlement intruded almost simultaneously into every part of the land, and as a result the Indian, in moving from forest to river to coast, inevitably encountered the newcomers. Since Nova Scotia was small, there was nowhere the Indians could maintain even a semblance of the old life in ignorance of whites. These changes had become apparent to all by 1783.

As a survival from the days of Micmac power, the province retained the office of superintendent of Indian affairs in 1783. Established and paid for by the imperial government, it was continued as a temporary expedient to tide the colony over a period of rapid transition. George Henry Monk, the newly appointed incumbent, had the task of easing settlement by "quieting" the Indians.[2] One of his first missions took him to Antigonish where a group of veterans claimed to be in dread of the Indians. Monk found that the natives feared they would lose their seasonal settlement in the neighbourhood and that they were content to have a small area including their church and burial ground reserved to them.[3] But it was not always possible to get the whites to concede even that much. From Cumberland he heard that settlers were threatening to call in the Micmacs' legendary foes, the Mohawks, to run them off the land granted them by the government. Not so, retorted one of the settlers, Edward Barron. Indians, he said, complained about trifles, pretending that their game was frightened off by people cutting down trees and building houses; and anyway the Indians never had a grant. Barron promised to treat them in a kindly fashion, but that did not mean giving them a reserve on his own land as Monk had suggested. "I do not mean to have an Indian Town at my Elbow." There was nothing Monk could do. Faced with the stereotype settler, he had no power to "quiet" the whites.[4]

The spread of settlement showed that the Indians were accorded no rights to the land but that they were expected to follow the white man's practice of petitioning for grants. However, such grants as were made the Indians were in the form of licences of occupation "during pleasure."[5] A tract of 550 acres was set aside for the use of the La Have Indians at St. Margaret's Bay in June,

1782, and 11,500 acres vaguely described as being near Belcher's estate was accorded another group in September, 1783.[6] Then, in December, came what the colonial government no doubt saw as its definitive answer to the Indian problem. Licences were issued to eight groups for lands along the Stewiacke, Remsheg, Antigonish, Philip, Merigomish, Macan and Shubenacadie rivers, and at St. David's Bay.[7] With this much done, there was no longer any need for a superintendent of Indian affairs, and the abolition of the office was recommended by Nova Scotia's London agent early in 1784.[8] The office lapsed, the few grants that had been made went unsurveyed, and no new petitions were forthcoming. There was no cause for alarm; the Micmacs might be "displeased" with the loss of their land, but, as one contemporary author pointed out, "their weakness, added to their prudence, will certainly prevent them from making any disturbances."[9]

And so it stood until the outbreak of the third Anglo-French war in as many decades brought the great Nova Scotian invasion scare of 1793 and revived old fears of the Micmacs as allies of France. Monk patriotically recalled his past responsibilities, offering his services once more as super-intendent of Indian affairs (unpaid) given the "present causes for Alarm."[10] Lieutenant-Governor Sir John Wentworth ordered him to investigate reports that large numbers of Indians were encamped near Windsor, stealing sheep and frightening the settlers. If necessary, Monk was to seize hostages, men, women, and children, and confine them in Fort Edward. On second thought, Wentworth considered that it would be better to try to win the Indians over by gifts of food and clothing, so "that the peace of our scattered Inhabitants may not be disturbed by them, and also that they will join us in case of an invasion."[11] Monk sent a deputy, and after he had consulted with the local major of militia, it was agreed that no immediate hostilities were in view, although the wretched condition of the Indians might provoke them. Wentworth authorized immediate supplies and an issue of bread and beef for the Indians of the Halifax area as well. In his report, Monk took the opportunity to urge regular supplies for all Indians to guard against disturbances.[12]

Monk spent much of December and January talking to various Indians and distributing supplies of cloth for the women and shot for the hunters. He became convinced that rations of food would have to be issued on a permanent basis to avoid further trouble. Charles Alexander of Cape Sable told him how generous the British had been until they had taken all the land they needed. Alexander's son took up the theme: "What Country was left for the Indians now the English give no more provisions and clothes.... What must the Indian do?" James Paul was among those who wanted to know if he could expect any supplies from the government and, if so, of what kind. When told that no food was immediately available, John Paul went so far as to murmur: "if King George was so poor that he could give no more to Indians—

the Indian better take nothing." This flicker of independence so outraged Monk that he subsequently denied relief to John Paul's family three times before allowing the starving man to make a formal apology for his "misbehaviour" before a magistrate.[13]

The slight on King George was proof of the dangerous state of mind exhibited by the Micmacs. Monk found them "more restless and dissatisfied with their condition than I have ever known them to be" and emphasized the fears expressed to him by the isolated white settlers. There were reports of strange comings and goings between bands which suggested that a master organizer might somewhere be at work in the interest of France. But Monk also recognized that the Indians' grievances were real, and he embodied them in a petition to Wentworth. When the Indians first made peace with the English, he wrote, there had been room for all, and until the end of the American Revolution the Micmacs had received provisions and clothing from the government. They had been told to live with the whites like brothers and promised help whenever they were in need. The English, however, had come and penetrated every part of the province. The hunting grounds were destroyed and there was no back country for the Indians to retreat to; when government supplies stopped, many died from starvation and all would soon perish without "general relief." Monk strongly urged that rations be issued all Indians for a few years so that it might be possible "to rehabilitate the rising Generation to labour in some of the various works of farming till they know how to earn a livelihood for themselves."[14]

Wentworth took these recommendations seriously. He saw subversion replacing invasion as the main threat to the colony's security. Citizen Genet might well have agents at work in the province, and he instructed Monk to look for any signs of "Democratic french practices among these Savages." Monk commissioned a peddler, Job Ross, to stay alert for news of any French emissaries that he might pick up in his travels. Apparently he had little to report, for he was only paid ten dollars for his counter-insurgency activities.[15]

The major recommendation, that the Indians receive a general scale of rations, was much more expensive, but Wentworth was sympathetic since he found a way to place that financial burden on the shoulders of the British taxpayer. As early as May, 1793, he had described the Micmacs' sufferings to the Home secretary, Henry Dundas, adding that he had explained the war to them and that they were willing to raise from sixty to one hundred men for the defence of the colony. In the circumstances, an imperial grant of £200 would be desirable. The expenditure was authorized, and Wentworth drove his point home by relaying the story of the Windsor alarms "during the expectation of a [French] Descent."[16] He forwarded Monk's petition and explained that the royal bounty had been spent on potatoes, meal, fish, bread, and clothing and that several Indian families had been given seed and tools to get themselves started as farmers. Within a few years they would be in the habit of supporting themselves, he continued, but it would not happen next year, for which a further £200 was needed. Again the British government agreed, convinced it would be "unpardonable" to ignore the plight of the Micmacs. The best use for the money, wrote Dundas, would be in equipping the Indians to become self-supporting farmers, and the grant was to be understood only as a temporary and diminishing one.[17]

The emergency, of course, did not go away. Each winter posed a new crisis which only imperial money could alleviate. Wentworth drew in advance for Indian relief and overspent by £656. The charges were protested in London, and the Indian subsidy finally disappeared in the general chaos that overwhelmed Wentworth's finances.[18]

Responsibility for the Indians now fell squarely on the province. In 1800, Monk chaired a committee to consider the condition of the Indians and rehearsed the already familiar themes: the destruction of game, fur, and fishing resources, the absence of any area as a refuge for the natives' way of life, and, a new point, the responsibility of the very people represented in the legislature for these calamities. What was to be done? Charity in the form of relief was not the answer, for it intensified the worst traits of the Indian character, indolence and drunkenness. The only solution was to make them over into farmers, "useful members of society." This could be accomplished by offering aid to those who would settle and withholding it from those who would not.[19]

The assembly was in an optimistic mood, voting money with a lavish hand, and it authorized £350 for the relief of the Indians. A committee was struck to supervise the expenditure of this sum, and commissioners were appointed to report on the condition of the Indians in each county and to distribute supplies to them. No mention was made of an Indian superintendent.[20] The next step was a joint committee of assembly and council which drew up a questionnaire to determine the number of Indians and the leadership of the various bands, the lands suitable for settlement in their "usual places of resort," the state of the fisheries, the expected cost of building huts, providing potatoes, clearing an acre, the opportunities for training Indian women in spinning and knitting, and the possibility of inducing them to place their children with neighbouring whites "to learn our domestic arts." The number of replies received, five out of a possible ten, was disappointing, but those who took the trouble were convinced that there was some chance of leading the Indians to settle and become self-supporting. Such a plan, the committee recognized, would face many obstacles and require much perseverance, but it would lead ultimately to the "rescue of our wretched fellow creatures." It recommended the survey of suitable lands and the settlement of some of the "best disposed" Indians as an example to the rest.[21]

Plans were one thing, execution quite another. Lands were not set aside and surveys were not made. Funds on a reduced scale were voted in 1801 and 1803 and then lapsed.[22] The committee administering relief grew a little testy. In forwarding £20 to James Archibald at Truro they expressed their exasperation at the sight of able-bodied Indians passing the summer in idleness and then demanding support through the winter. "How many white men are now struggling about this Capital to support families of five, six seven & Eight Children, upon three & four shillings a Day—and in bad weather not even that much."[23] Once again the Indian had to shift for himself as the money dried up.

By 1807 a new war threat developed as the Anglo-American crisis intensified. Nova Scotia had to look to its defences, and, as before, one result was that the Micmacs were rescued from oblivion.[24] Monk again emerged from his lapsed office of Indian superintendent and wrote the various commissioners for their "Aid in the hour of alarm." Each was to report the number of male Indians in his area and his reaction to the embodiment of the local militia, their general disposition, and all their movements. The object was to "keep the Indians friendly and render them serviceable." Wentworth even promised to furnish aid in clothing, arms, and subsistence if absolutely necessary.[25] The replies to Monk's anxious queries on what would happen "should there be an American war" showed that there was little to worry about. Most of the Indians were too close to starvation to concern themselves with rumours of war, and those commissioners who hazarded a guess as to their allegiance assumed they would follow the winning side. Despite this response, Monk's report was quite emphatic that the Indians expected the colony to be invaded and planned to remain neutral. Then he reversed himself and cautioned that though few in numbers "they might harass and distress the scattered Inhabitants of new settlements." As before, he urged the establishment of a regular system of relief for all Indians. A copy of the report was forwarded to London.[26] But the Colonial Office was not to be stampeded into providing money for Indian relief, and only with the actual outbreak of war did it authorize the issue of occasional presents. Their object was not so much to enlist the Micmacs' support as to keep them neutral, for a dread of savage warfare lingered long in the corridors of Downing Street.[27]

One aspect of the renewed interest in the Indians was a resumption of petitioning for land. In 1807, Samuel, Francis, and Gorham Paul asked for two hundred acres for each of eleven families so they could farm and learn to live independently. Wentworth approved one hundred acres each "for the present time" at Shubenacadie.[28] In 1810 the surveyor-general ordered an investigation into an application by an Indian named Panhall for lands near Chester.[29] There were other applications in the following years, enough that Surveyor-General Morris made a report to the provincial secretary on the whole situation in 1815. He urged against making grants to individual Indians, for too many sold their holdings for cash or liquor; the only acceptable procedure, he thought, was to reserve lands for their use in "such situations as they have been in the habit of frequenting." There were lands reserved for them in numerous localities, but none had been surveyed. Further protection could be given by passing a law to preserve moose and other game for their exclusive use, and government could guarantee them a moderate price for their handicrafts.[30] The report was filed.

Lieutenant-Governor Lord Dalhousie made the first full-scale attempt to face the government's responsibilities to the native peoples. Despairing of any initiative from the assembly, he took the matter up in council and proposed the establishment of a reserve in each county, not to exceed one thousand acres, to be held in trust for those Indians who were disposed to settle. On 8 May 1820, the surveyor-general reported to council with descriptions of reserves in each county.[31] The lands were a mixture of old and new allocations, and no money was provided for the costs of a proper survey. The descriptions were of little value either as a legal defence against encroachment or as a guide to what was in fact set aside for the Indians, many of whom used and continued to receive the use of lands outside the reserves.

Much remained to be done, as Dalhousie's successor, Sir James Kempt, told the assembly in 1827. The sufferings of the Indians were much greater than was commonly recognized, and many of them were now disposed to settle. But until each reservation was surveyed and each Indian family had its own "Potatoe Plantation" allocated to itself within the reserve, settlement would remain unattractive. He asked the assembly for funds to carry out correct surveys and subdivisions and to provide some seed, an axe, and a hoe to each family willing to farm and a small supply of provisions and coarse clothing for the weak and sickly.[33] The assembly granted £250 for relief.[34] "Let not the lip be contemptuously curled at the idea that an Indian may become an industrious farmer," wrote "Micmac" to the *Nova Scotian,* "if under the auspices of our legislature such a procedure were extensively persisted in, may not the happiest result be anticipated?"[35] But the legislature had answered no; it refused to be drawn into any but the most immediate and temporary measures of relief.

One major obstacle to any attempt at settlement was the fact that whites never allowed an Indian land claim to stand in their way. They were accustomed to squatting where they pleased on crown lands and making their peace with the authorities sooner or, preferably, later. They saw no reason to treat Indian lands any differently and assumed the government would take an equally indulgent view of their presence on them. Generally speaking, the squatters were right. It was very easy for a white official to see the virtuous hard work of a squatter with a large family to support, less easy to remember that those who had been dispossessed had some claims on colonial justice.[36] The inhabitants of Wagamatcook on Cape Breton were eloquent in listing the disadvantages of having a large tract at the river mouth "Permitted to a Parcell of Indians." Their presence effectively cut off land communications around Bras d'Or, "Which occasioned the Death of Individuals and Endangers the Life of Eny who are cast upon the Inhuman Feelings of these Indians."[37] There were ways of expelling unwanted Indians. In a contest over river frontage, for example, a basic white tactic was to net all the fish at the mouth of the river so that the fishermen upstream got none.[38] The Indian response to these harassments was almost inevitably to move to a less desirable location, without offering any resistance beyond a petition to the government drawn by a local sympathizer.[39] When the government did try to evict squatters, it found that it could only bluster, for it had neither the money for the necessary court actions nor the force to remove undesirables.[40]

In the face of these adversities, the Indians began to develop a leadership that could learn the new ways and bring its own influence to bear on the government. The first example of this trend was the appearance before the bar of the assembly of Andrew Meuse, who successfully opposed a bill that would have ended the porpoise hunt in the Gut of Annapolis. J. B. Uniacke witnessed the scene as a boy, and years later recalled the deep impression it had made on him. Meuse spoke of the legislators: "I see among them but one face that I know, and that man is trying to take away from the Indian the source of his livelihood."[41] Meuse later became the chief of the Bear River settlement, from which position he lobbied both the colonial government and London philanthropists for support.[42] Meuse organized a petition that Chief Charles Glower presented to the assembly on the very basic issue of liquor, calling for the prohibition of its sale to Indians. The chief was heard with great respect as he explained that "himself and friends were led to trouble the House from having daily witnessed the disgrace and misery which spiritous liquors spread among the Indians."[43] The result of his appeal was the passage of a law—the first one, despite common belief to the contrary—to "prevent" the sale of alcohol to Indians. It was far short of what Glower had wanted, for all it did was to authorize magistrates to make regulations in their own districts to prevent such sales. If there were no regulations, then presumably sales would continue, as they in fact did. While they were dealing with Indian matters, the council took the opportunity of tacking on a clause providing for the instruction of Indians free of charge at any publicly supported school.[44]

With the enactment of this law the legislative interest sparked by Chief Glower died away. However, from 1827 on, the assembly regularly voted between £100 and £150 a year for Indian relief to be spent at the discretion of the lieutenant-governor. The goods purchased with these funds were distributed by local commissioners throughout the province. Individual petitions for sums up to £50 to build a chapel or a school or a barn were approved sporadically. The Cape Breton reserves, which had been outside the jurisdiction of Nova Scotia in 1820, were roughly surveyed in the early 1830's.[45] But it had been apparent for sometime that the reserves everywhere existed in name only and that the policy of settling Indians had collapsed.

In 1829, the lieutenant-governor tried without success to have the council devise "some means to protect from encroachment and trespass the various tracts of land reserved for the Indians."[46] However, no ripple disturbed the surface of inertia. In 1834 the British House of Commons began extensive inquiries into the condition of aboriginal peoples throughout the empire. The government of Nova Scotia ignored a request to provide information. Only after the enquiries were over did Lieutenant-Governor Sir Colin Campbell respond to a direct order from the colonial secretary and circularize a number of leading local citizens to learn the condition of the Indians. The abstract of Martin Wilkin's report from Pictou is typical of the despondent tone of the replies:

> With the destruction of their hunting grounds came vagrant and intemperate habits, and decrease of their numbers, chiefly from drunkenness, partly from emigration. All Roman Catholics—low morals— [when] settling driven away—no lands for them—attributes their degeneration to maltreatment of whites.

Campbell neglected to forward the reports to London.[47]

But for another Indian initiative, there is little doubt that matters would have rested there. The wall of colonial indifference was finally broken through by a petition from Chief Paussamigh Pemmeenauweet direct to Queen Victoria. Beautifully written, it was couched in language that even the least romantic Whitehall bureaucrat could recognize as the authentic voice of the noble savage. It was an address to an equal. Chief Pemmeenauweet said:

> I cannot cross the great Lake to talk to you for my Canoe is too small, and I am old and weak. I cannot look upon you for my eyes not see so far. You cannot hear my voice across the Great Waters. I therefore send this Wampum and Paper talk to tell the Queen I am in trouble. My people are in trouble.... No Hunting Grounds—No Beaver—no Otter... poor for ever.... All these Woods once ours. Our Fathers possessed them all.... White Man has taken all that was ours.... Let us not perish.[48]

The petition was received at the Colonial Office on 25 January 1841. Five days later a despatch was on its way to Nova Scotia's new lieutenant-governor, Lord Falkland. Her Majesty was deeply interested in the appeal, but the colonial secretary did not have the necessary information to advise her on the subject. Falkland was ordered to resume the enquiries immediately.[49]

Lord Falkland gave the matter his best attention. He issued his own circular letter calling for yet another survey of the condition of the Indians.[50] He found the neglected replies to Campbell's circular and forwarded them to London together with his own digest of information and critique of past policy. "Most Colonies have done something for the relief of this class of their people," he wrote, "but the records of Nova Scotia hardly shew any intention of that kind." He recommended that settlements be established as rallying points rather than year round domiciles and cautioned against hoping for too rapid a change in the Indians' way of life. In the past decade, he continued, relief had amounted to the donation of a few blankets each year to Indian bands, a practice that should be discouraged; "a few presents now and then" would suffice. Public money should be devoted to founding correct surveys, alloting land, and providing tools and seed and minimum relief for the infirm. There was one further suggestion: the appointment of an Indian commissioner to supervise the whole programme.[51]

With this office in mind, Lord Falkland requested Joseph Howe to give his thoughts on a policy for the Indians. Howe, who had already made his mark as a reform politician, took up the task. In so doing, he discovered an interest that was to stay with him the rest of his life, and he eventually became dominion superintendent of Indian affairs. His first thoughts were that the government should appoint an official who would work through the chiefs as much as possible to bring about that predictable solution, settlement. Squatting must be stopped. Each chief should be given plans of the reserves within his jurisdiction, and he should advise on the subdivision of them among individual families who would have the right to sell or bequeath their holdings to other Indians. Assistance should be given to those who set up as farmers, and each village should be provided with a chief's house, a school, and a church. The status of the chief was to be publicly acknowledged by making each one a captain of militia and issuing medals every three years. Selected Indians should go to white schools to learn to become teachers of their people. Apart from his emphasis on the chiefs, few of Howe's ideas were new, as he himself admitted. But, he argued, the recent rapid spread of temperance made them much more practicable than they had been even three or four years earlier.[52]

By January, 1842, Falkland's administration had prepared a bill based on Howe's recommendations. The law, passed in March, provided for the appointment of an Indian commissioner to supervise the reserves, act against squatters, consult with the chiefs to encourage settlement, and arrange for the admission of Indians to local schools.[53] No mention was made of relief, but the assembly did vote £300 each year for the Indians from this time forward. Falkland proudly informed the colonial secretary that the law would "afford protection to this helpless race, and elevate them in the scale of humanity." The attorney-general observed that nothing had been done before to improve the conditions of the Indians and that they had to adopt a "less desultory mode of living" if they were to survive. The objects of the act were to prevent intrusion by whites, to use public and private benevolent funds to induce the

Indians to "submit" to civilized life, and to encourage their education.[54] The new law brought about one change that was not mentioned in the official correspondence. Previously the assembly had voted money for the Indians to be spent at the discretion of the executive, but henceforth they would be accountable to the assembly, whose committee on Indian affairs became the ultimate authority on policy towards the native people. If Lord Stanley, the colonial secretary, caught this drift of authority, he ignored it. He was quick to approve the law. As Anthony Blackwood of the Colonial Office noted, everything depended on the assiduity of the man to be chosen as Indian commissioner. If he were supine, the whole edifice would collapse.[55]

Falkland's choice for the office, not surprisingly, was Joseph Howe, who had no intention of being supine. The instructions he received were a paraphrase of his own recommendations.[56] He set out to learn about the Indians at first hand. In May he visited Shubenacadie, where he found only Gorham Paul in residence, living in a wigwam since his house had been turned into a barn. Much of the flat, cultivable land had been flooded by a dam.[57] In October Howe set off on a five-week "western tour," visiting eleven reserves and encampments. He was most impressed with Bear River, "sufficiently removed from the corrupting influence of whites" to be a potential "centre of Civilization and information around which the Indians of the North Western portion of the Province might gradually be collected." He spoke to all he met about the intentions of the new law, the need to settle on farms, the virtues of education. He made arrangements with local teachers to take in Indian children and adults and ordered surveys and subdivisions made.[58] He corresponded with local commissioners in areas he had been unable to visit.[59] As a result, his was the most extensive contact with the Indians since the days of George Monk.

Howe's first report as commissioner struck a sombre note. There had been 1,425 Micmacs in the province in 1838, but their numbers had declined so rapidly in the previous four years that they would disappear completely within forty. "Our grandchildren ... would find it as difficult to imagine the features or dwelling of a Micmac, as we do to realize those of an ancient Briton." There were 22,050 acres of Indian reserves, but the lands and sites were generally poor. Five counties had no reserves at all, and there were none near Halifax, although the capital attracted Indians from all over the province who were "consequently compelled to build their camps on private property, and are tempted to destroy the wood, and commit [vexatious] depredations." Howe then listed the sums he had spent in his official capacity, ensuring his financial accountability to the assembly.[60]

The role of the Indian commissioner was very much a full-time job, and there was no pay. Howe found what later commissioners were also to discover to their dismay—that his home became a resort for Indians with all sorts of pleas and complaints. Moreover, since there was no separate warehouse for relief supplies, the basement and spare rooms served as storage for blankets, greatcoats, and other paraphernalia. Howe's enthusiasm ebbed. His second report was his last. He had promised, but never made, a visit to the Cape Breton reserves, and most of what he wrote came out of his tour notes for 1842. He reported some progress in settlement, some in education. He was, at best, wanly optimistic and shortly thereafter resigned.[61]

One of Howe's principal aims had been to persuade at least some of the Indians to go to school and master the English language.[62] He was able to note some initial successes, but the project quickly collapsed. It ran into opposition from all quarters: local school boards unwilling to see shabby and hungry Indians mixed in with white pupils,[63] men like Bishop Fraser who considered it humbug to educate Indians before settling them,[64] and the assembly itself, which refused to pay the bills for placing Indians in school.[65] There was also resistance from the Indians to the discipline of the schoolhouse and curriculum.[66] A number of Indian women expressed disapproval "of any of their children being educated in the White Man's school—because, when so educated it would break off the natural ties of affection and association between them and their Tribe, and mutual dislike and contempt would be the result."[67]

The touchstone of Indian policy, however, remained settlement. Howe had been diligent in ordering the laying off of one-hundred-acre lots for future Indian farmers, seed and tools had been distributed as encouragement, and every glimmer of success carefully noted. And then farming throughout the province was destroyed by widespread potato blight for three seasons from 1846 to 1848. The disease made a mockery of all the much touted comfort and stability of the farming life. It affected whites and Indians alike, but the accompanying diseases ravaged the natives most severely. Dr. Robert Leslie reported a "Bilious Remittant fever attended with great Prostration of the Vital Powers" amongst those at Bear River. The sickness affected only Indians, he asserted, because of the great scarcity and unwholesomeness of their food over a long period and their "damp lodging on the ground."[68] Edward Jenning commented on the passivity of the Indians he visited, "careless about their own pain and the pain of others," whose children shed no tears when enquiring after ailing parents.[69] From Sydney, Commissioner H. W. Crawley wrote of imminent starvation among the Indians of Cape Breton and received £105 in emergency funds.[70] Years later his successor reported a marked increase in tuberculosis among the Indians of the area "since the commencement of the failure of the crops in their different settlements."[71] Chief Gabriel Anthony appeared before the bar of the assembly pleading for recognition of his labours and help for his people.[72] As the cost of aiding sick and starving Indians rose dramatically, local overseers of the poor began to petition the assembly to meet their bills.[73] And bills started to come from physicians who listed their services, seeking to charge them off against the annual Indian grant.[74]

The Indian Act had failed in one of its primary objectives, education, and now hope of settling the Indians had been dealt a serious blow by the crop failures. The customary system of relief, which education and settlement were to have made unnecessary, became more important than ever. At this critical stage a new Indian commissioner, Abraham Gesner, was appointed to fill the post that had been vacant for three years. A conscientious man, he was fully aware of the condition of the dispossessed and broken-spirited Indians who had "a real but almost unknown existence within the colony." Their vagrancy and poverty were taken for granted, and it was assumed they would wander until the day the last one died. No attempt, Gesner asserted in his first report, had ever been made to change the Micmacs from "wild pursuits to sober industry," and he urged that they be formed into settlements, with farms supported by workshops and Micmac-language schools.[75] He considered the assembly's grant quite inadequate for the task, for the immediate demands of relief had to be met. Yet settlement, not relief, was the only solution: if not, then "instead of the 'Last of the Mohicans' the historian will record the last of the Micmacs."[76]

Gesner was able to settle fourteen families at Shubenacadie in 1848, and in the first season their crops were destroyed by blight. Undeterred, he held a meeting of chiefs in Halifax to convince them of the need to cultivate the land. The result was yet another petition presented at the bar of the assembly:

> Some of your people say we are lazy, still we work. If you say we must go and hunt, we tell you again that to hunt is one thing and to find meat is another. They say to catch fish, and we try. They say make baskets, but we cannot sell them. They say make farms, this is very good; but will you help us till we cut away the trees and raise the crop. We cannot work without food. The potatoes and wheat we raised last year were killed by the poison wind. Help us and we will try it again.[77]

Ten chiefs bore the petition from their conference at Dalhousie College to Government House and back to the legislative building. They were men, enthused the *Acadian Recorder*, of "admirable proportions and symmetry ... dressed in their gay and ancient costume." It was sad to think that their race was fading away "like a withering leaf in a summer's sun." *The Church Times* primly expressed the hope that something might yet be done to "preserve the rising generation from the degradation of their parents." The *Times and Chronicle* ran a long editorial on the evils the Indians had suffered and the need for prompt legislative action to save them from extinction.[78] These journalistic outpourings signalled a revival of interest in the

Micmacs that was reinforced by their prominence in the centennial celebrations of Halifax.[79]

Concern for the Micmacs was fully justified. Their numbers continued to decline in the early 1850's, and Commissioner Gesner continued to insist that settlement was their only salvation, carefully noting every report of a successful start at farming. But he grew weary and was replaced in 1853 by William Chearnley, whose knowledge of the Indians came from the contacts he had made while big-game hunting.[80] Chearnley contradicted all the previous suppositions. The Indians, he stated in his first report, would always be unwilling to work and settle; their reserves were mostly barren and those parts that were not had already been taken by whites. Since the Micmacs were "fast passing away," he proposed to ease their last days by supplying them with blankets and greatcoats and, if any money was left over from the annual grant, a few seed potatoes. Any additional funds should come from the sale of such of their lands as squatters possessed.[81] These economical proposals met the approval of the assembly, and although there was some ridicule of Chearnley's obsession with blankets, there was no outcry at his refusal to promote settlement. The administration of Indian affairs was so disgraceful, wrote one editor, that it might be as well to give up the annual vote of funds and teach the Indians some much-needed self-reliance.[82]

Ironically, the disgraceful state of affairs was not the fault of the Indians themselves; it was the result of the increasing claims that overseers of the poor were making against the Indian grant. These charges included expenses for food, clothing, and even board and lodging for indigent Indians; but the largest sum, year after year, was for medical fees. Howe had cheerfully turned back one such claim in his time on the grounds that "in general the Indians are better Doctors than the Whites,"[83] but this attitude had gone by the board in the famine years. The assembly was early aware of the possibility of abuse in medical claims and insisted that services had to be authorized by the overseers of the poor and attested to before a justice of the peace.[84] Even with these safeguards, the bills kept coming. Ministering to the Indians was bitterly resented by some doctors who had to run the obstacle course of attestation and petition and sometimes wait for years before being paid. "Blast the Indians!" exploded Dr. Shaw of Horton, who had spent many nights climbing fences on repeated visits to the camp of Peter and Sally Paul, "I sincerely hope I shall never again have one to attend."[85] Indian doctors also sought compensation; Peter Babey, for example, explained that he used simple plant extracts while whites "use Minerals, and noxious Medicines calculated to destroy life."[86] A patent-medicine man claimed he had been giving tonics away for over twenty years to various Indians and requested support in the future.[87] In 1857 the assembly committee decided to put an end to such importunities and recommended that no medical bills be paid henceforth "except in cases of surgical operation or accouchements." The assembly took the opportunity to

Plate 1. Copper plate engraving, coloured by hand, of "Homme Acadien," by J. Laroque and J. G. St. Sauveur. Controversy exists over whether body markings are tattoos or body painting.

Plate 2. Woodcut of Micmac man, by a Mrs. Elliot, from Abraham Gesner's *The Industrial Resources of Nova Scotia.*

passinassionek se decris cette pesche aillour qui est une des
choses tres meruailleuses touchand la f. 19. etc.

kouabâgan

alinamek

Batchkoupan

grand eskan

A DRAUGHT of the ISTHMUS which joyns Nova Scotia to the Continent, with the Situation of the ENGLISH and FRENCH Forts & the Adjacent BAYS and RIVERS by W: Tonge Chignecto Fort Lawrence 1755.

Scale of Miles

ate 4. Legend and illustration from map of the Chignecto Isthmus, 1755.

te 3. "La pesche des Sauvages," from "Codex Canadiensis," an album manuscript from late seventeenth century containing 180 sketches of natives, flora, and fauna of New nce, reputedly drawn by Charles Bécard de Granville (1675-1703).

Plate 5. "Micmac Indians," watercolour by Millicent Mary Chaplin, 1839. Original is in the Royal Ontario Museum.

Plate 6. Watercolour of Micmac women on Prince Edward Island, by Harcourt Taylor, c. 1850.

ate 7. Micmac Indians, watercolour by I. G. Toler, 1808.

ate 8. Portion of painting of Micmac Indians by an unknown artist, c. 1820–30, now in the
tional Gallery, Ottawa.

NEW BRUNSWICK;

WITH

𝕹𝖔𝖙𝖊𝖘 𝖋𝖔𝖗 𝕰𝖒𝖎𝖌𝖗𝖆𝖓𝖙𝖘.

COMPREHENDING THE EARLY HISTORY, AN ACCOUNT OF THE INDIANS, SETTLE-
MENT, TOPOGRAPHY, STATISTICS, COMMERCE, TIMBER, MANUFACTURES,
AGRICULTURE, FISHERIES, GEOLOGY, NATURAL HISTORY, SOCIAL
AND POLITICAL STATE, IMMIGRANTS, AND CONTEM-
PLATED RAILWAYS OF THAT PROVINCE.

BY ABRAHAM GESNER, ESQ.

SURGEON;

FELLOW OF THE GEOLOGICAL SOCIETY OF LONDON; CORRESPONDING MEMBER OF THE
ROYAL GEOLOGICAL SOCIETY OF CORNWALL; MEMBER OF THE LITERARY AND
HISTORICAL SOCIETY OF QUEBEC; CORRESPONDING MEMBER OF THE
ACADEMY OF NATURAL SCIENCES OF PHILADELPHIA; AUTHOR
OF "REMARKS ON THE GEOLOGY AND MINERALOGY
OF NOVA SCOTIA," ETC.

LONDON: SIMMONDS & WARD,

6, BARGE YARD, BUCKLERSBURY.

1847.

Plate 9. "Micmac Family Travelling in Winter," title page from Abraham Gesner's *New Brunswick, with Notes for Emigrants*. This comprehensive book reflected contemporary interest in the area for colonization and resource development.

Plate 10. Pastel by an unknown artist of a "Micmac Woman," probably Christina Morris (c. 1804-86), who was renowned for her great skill in native crafts.

Plate 11. Photograph taken by members of the *Challenger* expedition near Halifax in 1873.

HIS EXCELLENCY

LEUTENANT-GENERAL
Sir John Coape Sherbrooke,

Knight of the Most Honorable Order of the BATH.

Leutenant-Governor and Commander in Chief in and
over His Majesty's Province of Nova-Scotia,
Vice-Admiral of the same,
&c. &c. &c.

J. C. Sherbrooke.

To *Louis Benjamin Pominout* Greeting.

Whereas an address has been presented unto me by the Reverend John
Mandetus Segogne in behalf of the Indians of the Micmac Tribe stating among
other things that the said Tribe have made choice of you the said Louis Benjamin
Pominout to be their chief. Wherefore relying upon the loyalty zeal sobriety and good
Character of you the said Louis Benjamin Pominout I do ratify and confirm the choice
which the said Tribe has made and do hereby appoint you Chief of the Micmac Tribe
of Indians this Province. You are therefore to use your utmost endeavours to keep all
persons belonging to the said Tribe Loyal, Industrious and Sober, and to render them
good Subjects and Christians, and the said Tribe are hereby required to obey you as
their Chief.

Given under my Hand and Seal at Arms at Halifax
this Twenty eighth day of April 1814 in the Fifty fourth
Year of this Majestys Reign.

By His Excelleneys Command

Henry H. Cogswell

N. Secy

Plate 12. Commission given by the Lieutenant-Governor of Nova Scotia to "Louis Benjamin Pominout," appointing him "Chief of the Micmac Tribe of Indians this Province" in 1814.

134, N. Scotia

To the Queen

Madam,

I am Paussa-
migh Pemmenauweet, and am called
by the White Man Louis Benjamin
Pominout.

I am the Chief of my
People the Micmac Tribe of Indians
in your Province of Nova Scotia
and I was recognized and declared
to be the Chief by our good Friend
Sir John Cope Sherbrooke in the
White Man's fashion Twenty Five
Years ago; I have yet the Paper
which he gave me.

Sorry to hear that the King is
dead. Am glad to hear that we have
a good Queen whose Father I saw
in this Country. He loved the
Indians.

I cannot cross the great
Lake to talk to you for my
Canoe is too small, and I am
old and weak. I cannot look
upon you for my eyes not see
so far. You cannot hear my
voice across the Great Waters. I
therefore send this Wampum and
Paper talk to tell the Queen I am
in trouble. My people are in
trouble. I have seen upwards of a

Thousand Moons. When I was young
I had plenty: now I am old, poor
and sickly too. My people are poor.
No Hunting Grounds—No Beaver—
no Otter—no nothing. Indians
poor—poor for ever. No Store—
no Chest—no Clothes. All these
Woods once ours. Our Fathers
possessed them all. Now we cannot
cut a Tree to warm our Wigwam
in Winter unless the White Man
please. The Micmacs now receive
no presents, but one small Blanket
for a whole family. The Governor
is a good man but he cannot
help us now. We look to you the

Queen. The White Wampum tell
that we hope in you. Pity your
poor Indians in Nova Scotia.

White Man has taken all
that was ours. He has plenty of
everything here. But we are told
that the White Man has sent to
you for more. No wonder that
I should speak for myself and my
people.

The man that takes this
talk over the great Water will
tell you what we want to be done
for us. Let us not perish. Your
Indian Children love you, and
will fight for you against all
your

Plate 13. Part of a letter sent by the same Chief Pominout, using his real name,
"Paussamigh Pemmeenauweet," to Queen Victoria twenty-six years later, complaining of
negligent treatment of Micmacs by colonists. (Full text of letter follows p. 188.)

Plate 14. View of Halifax from the Micmac encampment at Dartmouth, from *Sketches in Nova Scotia and New Brunswick*, by Lieutenant R.

Plate 16. Place mat decorated with porcupine quills (black, red, purple, green, and yellow), dyed purple split spruce root binding on the edge, Micmac, c. 1880.

Plate 17. Chair seat and back of birch bark decorated with porcupine quills (mainly green and white with brown lines) and split spruce root binding, Micmac, c. 1870.

cut down the activities of the overseers of the poor in other areas as well. Aid in any form would first have to be fully paid out of the poor rates and only then would the assembly refund one-half of the sum. Indian funds were now safeguarded for the all-important annual distribution of blankets and great-coats.[88]

With the principal Indian commissioner and the assembly committee both restricting their activities to the most basic relief, concern for the Indian reserves passed almost by default to the office of the commissioner of crown lands. The encroachments of squatters were regularly reported, especially from Cape Breton Island, where friction centred on Wagamatcook (Middle River) and Whycocomagh. These were both desirable locations; Wagamat-cook was at the mouth of a river valley containing some of the best land on the island, and Whycocomagh, the furthest inland point on the interior waters of Cape Breton, was a road and steamboat junction.[89] The area had been settled by Scots in the 1820's and 1830's, many of them with tickets of location to lands that overlapped Indian reserves. Some claimed to have rented fields from local chiefs; others had simply moved on to apparently empty lands.[90] Pleas came in regularly from the Indians. Peter Gougou of Whycocomagh reported in 1850 that it was no longer safe for Indians to walk down the road and that whites were threatening to shoot their children for supposedly stealing potatoes.[91] Closer to Halifax, the Indians at Ingraham's River were being driven away by the construction of a dam upstream, the floating down of logs to break their weirs, and flooding.[92] But as before, the executive had neither the finances nor the muscle to prosecute squatters.[93] In most cases there was still no legally defensible survey of a reserve, and attempts to plot one at Gold River and, later, Middle Stewiacke showed how confused title and division lines had become.[94] In these circumstances the crown lands commissioner, J. B. Uniacke, was vested with title to all Indian lands and ordered to prepare a report on the reserves. He recommended that the government regain control of lands lost to squatters and pass a special law against intruders.[95] But nothing punitive was done, for such action would be much more disagreeable than adopting Chearnley's idea of having the squatters pay for their lands.[96]

Samuel Fairbanks, who succeeded Uniacke as crown lands commissioner, was the first to grasp the nettle: squatters must either go or pay to remain.[97] The result was "An Act concerning Indian Reserves," passed 30 March 1859, that allowed squatters to buy their holdings. A clause to permit the sale of unoccupied reserve land (as in New Brunswick) was in the original draft of the bill, so the idea of a general dismemberment of the reserves had been considered, only to be put aside.[98] The moneys raised from the sales were to be paid into an Indian Fund and the interest, at 6 per cent, applied to relief as a first charge and then to the promotion of settlement. In the future, intruders were to be liable to summary ejection. A new officer, commissioner of Indian reserves, was created to supervise these proceedings. Thus, if law alone could do it, the problem was solved. Squatters would become legal freeholders, no further Indian land would be lost, and a fund would build up to the point where the assembly no longer had to subsidize the Indians out of the general revenues.

The responsibility for Indian affairs was now clearly split between the Indian commissioner, who provided blankets and greatcoats, and the Indian reserves commissioner, who tried to conserve Indian lands against the day of settlement. Chearnley's proudest achievement was to bring the cost of army surplus greatcoats down from three shillings to two and sixpence. Appointed to the new post, Fairbanks ordered more surveys and the setting off of individual lots for Indians on long leases.[99] With Chearnley's resignation in 1862 the way was clear to unite the two functions in one person, Samuel Fairbanks, who also remained crown lands commissioner.[100] Although restricted by law to using the assembly grant for "blankets or necessary clothing" only, he continued to do his best to urge settlement on the Indians. The crown lands office stood ready to grant leases to one-hundred-acre lots on reserves and to permit their alienation to other Indians. The assembly committee now supported these efforts and informed an Indian delegation from Cape Breton that it would devote the money raised from the squatters to encourage settlement and recommend the establishment of schools, a subject that had been almost forgotten over the previous twenty years.[101] Fairbanks' surveyors went to work, and in 1864 he reported that the bounds of the Indian reserves "are now placed beyond dispute."[102]

The new wave of optimism rested on the acquiescence of the Indians to being settled and the willingness of the squatters to pay for their land and so create a fund to assist settlement. Neither group played its role as desired. The Indians made "many unreasonable objections" to having their reserves subdivided, wishing rather "to have everything in common, even their wigwams—they wish to be as children of the same family."[103] By the end of 1866, Fairbanks could only report having settled ten Indian families.[104] The squatters were no more co-operative. There were disputes over the price they should pay for their lands, which was always assessed at more than the crown land charge of forty-four cents an acre. Few of the squatters paid anything, and none paid in full. By the end of 1866 only $1,531 had been collected. Fairbanks sent out printed reminders of moneys due and refused to issue grants until the final payment was made.[105] But the squatters preferred to stay put until this latest enthusiasm of the government had run its course.

The imminent transfer of responsibility for the Indians to the government of Canada led Fairbanks to review his achievements in his final report, dated 31 December 1866. He estimated the total native population at between 1,400 and 1,800 persons, but made no comment on the marked increase in their numbers. There were 20,730 acres reserved throughout the province for 637

Indian families, but very few had taken up farming on the terms offered to them. Squatters on Indian reserves had bought their holdings at a "fair evaluation," and no further sales were contemplated. The remaining Indian lands were now as well protected from intruders "as either the Crown property or the unsettled land of grantees." The assembly's Indian committee had the last word in April, 1867, with some advice to the new government: grant the same amount as the provincial legislature had done and appoint a commissioner for Nova Scotia to continue the distribution of greatcoats and blankets. The province had done all it could to encourage the Indians to settle, "and if they do not avail themselves of the advantages thus offered, it is owing to their own nature and habits." Or as Fairbanks more lyrically put it: "Their means of livelihood in other occupations are fast diminishing; and as it has been justly observed, *that one of the greatest blessings conferred by Providence upon man, is the necessity for labor*, it is to be hoped that the same motive may operate to assist the efforts which are made to elevate their condition."[106]

7

The Micmacs and Government: New Brunswick

The British had regarded the portion of Acadia that lay on the mainland side of the Bay of Fundy as part of Nova Scotia since 1714. The area had, however, remained beyond their control during the wars with the Micmacs, and it was not until the 1760's that the first British entrepreneurs began penetrating it along the lines of the principal rivers. This territory was organized as the colony of New Brunswick in 1784 to be the home of Loyalist refugees. The few whites, mostly Acadians, who had previously established permanent settlements within its boundaries were pushed aside for the benefit of the newcomers. The land was heavily forested, well-watered by navigable rivers, and much larger in extent than the now truncated Nova Scotia. Nevertheless, the white invasion had an immediate effect on the native people, for here as elsewhere both they and the whites valued the same locations. The core of Loyalist settlement was in the fertile valley of the Saint John River, the home of the Malecites, who were the first to suffer. As whites sought out fishing sites and accessible commercial timber, the disruptions spread to the traditional homeland of the Micmac people along the Richibucto and Miramichi rivers. The presence of regular soldiers, stationed at the new capital of Fredericton on the Saint John, was a powerful deterrent to resistance. But further north, beyond the range of the troops, "the insolence of the Savages" and their "many acts of violence" nearly led to the abandonment of the first settlements in the Madawaska area. Lieutenant-Governor Thomas Carleton had to borrow the 6th Regiment from Quebec in order to protect the whites.[1]

It is surprising that there was not more resistance. There was no attempt at any orderly transfer of Indian lands to the whites; everything belonged outright to the Crown. No government agents came to the Indians bearing gifts and annuities and parchment treaties as they had in that other Loyalist colony being founded along the shore of Lake Ontario at the same time. There, everything was done according to the terms of the Royal Proclamation of 1763, which meant that Indian land could only be alienated by the agreement of the Indians concerned and then only to government officials. Moreover, each treaty delineated a tract of land that was to be reserved for the use of the Indians. In New Brunswick there were no treaties. Just as in Nova Scotia, it was the responsibility of the Indians to petition for any lands they might want to keep for their own use.

The only Micmac reservation within the boundaries of the new province was the 20,000 acres along the Miramichi granted to John Julien under a licence of occupation by the Nova Scotia government in 1783.[2] New Brunswick did not recognize grants made by its predecessor, and Julien had to request the confirmation of his lands in 1785.[3] Four years later his band was given licence to 3,030 acres, known as the Eel Ground Reserve, on the Northwest Miramichi.[4] Following numerous complaints about white encroachments, licences of occupation were issued in 1804 and 1805 for 8,700 acres at the Big Hole tract and 750 acres at Indian Point.[5] A further five-mile stretch along the Northwest Miramichi and Sevogle rivers was licensed in 1807,[6] but in the following year Deputy Surveyor-General William F. Odell assembled the Indians at the Miramichi court house, pointed out to them the boundaries of the various tracts of land allocated them, "and informed them that they must not expect or claim anything more." The original 20,000-acre grant had been reduced by half.[7]

By the turn of the century, other Micmac tribes were complaining of pressure from whites and requesting licences for land. The first protests from the Richibucto band dated back to 1788 when Carleton issued a proclamation against those who had settled "within the district of the said Village" whose limits would be ascertained in "due time."[8] Weary of waiting for the due time to arrive, the Indians began to ask for their own land grant on the advice of their missionary; they received licence for 51,200 acres in 1802.[9] The Tabusintac Indians petitioned Carleton in 1801, explaining that they had "allowed the English to settle on the lower end of Tabusintack, on Lands which your Memorialists forefathers possessed," but as the newcomers were moving upstream, "a permanent Licence of Occupation" was necessary to preserve the Indians' rights to the eeling grounds. The request "appears to be reasonable and can interfere with no settlement," noted the surveyor-general. A licence was accordingly issued in 1802 for 9,035 acres on the Tabusintac River, 240 acres at Burnt Church Point, and 1,400 acres on the north side of Burnt Church River.[10] That same year saw the Indians of the Buctouche River granted a reserve eight miles long and four miles wide on each side of the river.[11] The Indian reservation had become an accepted feature of New Brunswick life. The haphazard pattern of the first licences continued; Indian initiative or the needs of white settlers dictated whether new grants were made or old ones whittled down. The first listing of reserved lands was published in 1838. It identified fifteen reserves ranging in size from 10 to 16,000 acres, for a total of 61,293 acres in the whole province.[12]

The exact size of New Brunswick was a matter of dispute for almost sixty years. Up to one-third of its territory was claimed by the United States, as a result of the imprecision of the line drawn in the Anglo-American peace treaty of 1783. At an early stage in the protracted negotiations, both sides tried to use Indian testimony to substantiate their claims. "When was this place first called St. Andrews?" Captain Nicolas Awawar was asked in October 1796. "Since the time St. Andrew put up the crop."[13] That same month, the Americans called Indians from the Machias and Passamaquoddy bands on oath to testify for their side.[14] When, by 1808, the dispute threatened to be submerged in a general Anglo-American war, the New Brunswick government was already sensitive to Indian contacts across the border. Lieutenant-Governor Martin Hunter looked to his defences and had to consider the danger that might arise from Indian discontent. He felt that the New Brunswick Indians were "less enterprising" than others and would be of little use as allies but that they could become formidable enemies if war with the United States gave them the opportunity. Although some lands had been allocated to them, they still retained their nomadic way of life, and the colonial government's refusal to do anything further for them had led to the complaint of "an injurious distinction between them and the Indians of Canada, on one side, and those within the limits of the neighbouring American States on the other." Prudence, Hunter concluded, called for some attempt at redress, and he asked the British government for £500 a year for occasional relief to the Indians.[15] His assessment failed to impress Lord Castlereagh at the War Office, who was not to be panicked into increasing Britain's financial burdens. The proper thing to do, he replied, was to refer the matter to the provincial legislature, which should make it its "particular business" to convert the Indians into "an useful People of the Community." Simply giving them presents was not enough, for the Canadian experience showed that while the practice did keep the Indians friendly, it did nothing to improve their way of life.[16]

There matters rested until the outbreak of war brought reports that the Indians of the Saint John and of the Penobscot in the United States were about to meet. Somewhat alarmed, the council agreed "to make a donation of Provisions to these [Saint John] Indians on this particular occasion," the cost to be charged to contingency expenses. The result was most gratifying, for on 10 July 1812, the council received an agreement guaranteeing the neutrality of the Indians of Charlotte County.[17] The Micmacs of the Miramichi, Richibucto, and Tabusintac rivers pledged themselves to remain faithful and promised they would "not molest or injure or disturb any of His Majesty's

Subjects or their Property or Effects during the present War." They would remain "peaceably and quietly occupied in their ordinary pursuits." In return, the British would not require them to take up arms against the Americans.[18] A year later, £50 more was taken out of the contingency fund for Indian relief.[19] In 1814 the Indians near Fredericton were able to get £300 to add to their holdings at Kingsclear, a decision justified "more especially at this particular crisis."[20] Once the crisis had passed, the contingency funds closed down.

New Brunswick had no governmental agency responsible for maintaining contact with the Indians. All correspondence concerning them passed through the provincial secretary's office. Local unpaid Indian commissioners had been designated *ad hoc* from the earliest days, but it was not until 1825 that there was the first indication of a change. Upon taking office, the new lieutenant-governor, Sir Howard Douglas, was greeted by two hundred Malecites at Kingsclear. Impressed by their demonstration of both loyalty and poverty, he issued provisions to them. Discovering that no provincial moneys were appropriated for their relief, he wrote the colonial secretary for authority to make annual presents as was done in other British North American provinces. He received approval to spend up to £60 a year out of the colony's casual revenues, but he was cautioned not to encourage the Indians to look for such bounty on a regular basis.[21] Nothing daunted, Sir Howard was able to persuade the assembly to vote £200 for the Indians on three separate occasions during his tenure of office. He decided to use the casual revenue money to provide farm tools and seed to encourage agriculture, while the assembly's grants went strictly for the relief of the aged and infirm. He appointed a group of commissioners in 1826 to supervise the distribution of these funds to the Indians of Richibucto, Buctouche, Kingsclear, and the Miramichi. The commissioners' instructions were to persuade the Indians to abandon their "desultory pursuits" and lead them to civilized life through education and agriculture. In reporting back, the commissioners were most optimistic and not a little unctuous, urging an "unremitting cultivation of a Hope which at length seems to dawn upon the hitherto benighted prospects of these original Masters of this Soil." Those original masters had expressed their eagerness for education and their willingness to take up farming, and when they had received seed and tools for the following year's crops all would be well.[22] But there are no further commissioners' reports for over a decade, no records of funds to buy farm tools—only a grudging payment of relief when it became unavoidable.

Inertia remained the rule in Indian affairs; inertia so strong that it was even able to withstand an imperial initiative. When Colonial Secretary Sir George Murray overhauled the administration of Indian affairs in the Canadas in 1830, he wrote Douglas to inform him of the changes and told him to be guided by the new instructions "in any measures which you may adopt for improving the condition and promoting the interests of the Native Indian Tribes."[23] Apparently no measures were contemplated in New Brunswick, for there was no reply. The omission passed unnoticed, and so did the colony throughout the extensive British parliamentary enquiries of 1835 and 1836 into the condition of the aboriginal peoples of the Empire.

If there was little concern for the Indians themselves, their lands were still highly valued. White squatters settled on, or stripped the timber off, what they insisted was unclaimed land. They were without the shadow of a title to their holdings and could get no credit from local merchants; they lived in a state of constant uncertainty which discouraged any but the most slovenly type of farming. When the existence of the squatters could no longer be ignored, the executive government made the proper denunciations, but the elected assembly was most sympathetic to their position. The first official notice was taken in 1841, with two proclamations requiring those who had illegally occupied lands reserved by the Crown for the benefit of the Indians to leave immediately and desist from cutting the timber.[24] A list drawn up that same year showed 118 squatters on Indian lands, with the largest single group, 87, in Northumberland County.[25] In fact, the government did not have the ability to remove these trespassers. There was no doubt that they had the legal right to do so, but the necessary procedure, by an action for information for intrusion before the Supreme Court, was too expensive.[26] The assembly would not have supported any such move, for, as a select committee reported in 1843, the "actual Settlers" on the reserves had contributed greatly to the progress of New Brunswick by improving waste lands that otherwise lay as barriers to the extension of thriving settlements. The "industrious poor Squatter" should not be harried off the land which necessity had forced him to seek out for a livelihood.[27]

Everything would have been much simpler if the Indians could have been persuaded to sell their reserves. In 1832 the Miramichi bands agreed, in a legally witnessed document, to relinquish their land. They asked that each family be given a small lot for its own use and that the money raised from the sale of the surplus be put "in a fund for support of the Sick, aged and infirm Indians belonging to their Tribes." Even though they were presented as taking the initiative, it is highly doubtful whether the Indians really wanted to dispose of their reserve. In any event, nothing further was done in the matter.[28] But in 1838, the whole question was raised in the assembly with a motion for information on all the reserves.[29] The next month there was a motion to authorize the sale of reserve lands in Kent County and the use of the money so realized to provide relief for the Indians under the supervision of commissioners. A lively debate ensued. William End moved to strike all references to land sales and proposed a policy of ameliorating the Indians' condition with public money distributed by commissioners for "agricultural implements, clothing, bounties on whatever potatoes, grain or other produce they may be induced to raise, and generally in such manner as may allure them to the arts of civilized life." John Street was agreeable to the commissioners distributing public money, but at the same time he wanted them to recommend what portion of the reserves in general could be sold to establish a fund for the benefit of the Indians—and relieve the assembly of an annual charge. These alternatives failed to win approval, and the original motion was passed, fifteen to twelve.[30] End tried again a few days later and received approval for a motion to defend the equitable rights of the Indian tribes in Gloucester County by having commissioners appointed to determine the best way the reserve lands could be made of benefit to them.[31]

Six months after these demonstrations of legislative concern, embodied in addresses to the lieutenant-governor, Sir John Harvey received word that the Colonial Office was once again interesting itself in the fate of the native people of his province. Right at the end of his term of office, Lord Glenelg sent out a letter with specific instructions. Harvey was to report to him "on the State of any of the Aboriginal Inhabitants who may still exist in the Province"—their numbers, whether they were increasing or declining, their condition, and their morals. More awkwardly, Lord Glenelg wanted to know what efforts had already been made to civilize them: how many were actually settled farmers? how many still hunters? how much land did they hold? what were the local statutes concerning them? And what did Harvey suggest should be done to improve the Indians' lot?[32]

Glenelg's letter was transmitted to the commissioners for the Miramichi, Richibucto, and Gloucester county Indians. Their reports, although brief, did attempt to answer the questions put by the colonial secretary.[33] On the Miramichi there were some 400 to 450 Indians living from hand to mouth, for the hunting had been ruined by the great fire of 1825, which destroyed six thousand square miles of prime forest. To make matters worse, whites had superseded Indians as casual labour in the timber industry. The local Indians, so the commissioners asserted, were loyal, harmless people, living in bark huts in the forests during the winter and spending the summer on the riverbanks. Their "natural indolence" prevented them from farming, and there was no prospect of change in this respect. Their numbers had increased in the previous five years, and their morals had improved too, but not one Indian could be called "civilized." The report strongly urged the sale of portions of the reserves to provide a fund for the aged and infirm, but had nothing to suggest for the able-bodied Indians. The commissioners for the Richibucto Indians also felt that some scaling down of the size of the reserve would be useful. If the Indians had less land, they would appreciate what remained all the more. There were only 120 of them, half what there had been in 1825, and only fourteen farmers, all unsuccessful, because their practice was to sow seed and then leave the crops unguarded in unfenced fields. Too many of the local Indians were addicted to liquor and spent their time hanging around stores and shipping in the harbour, trying to sell baskets. The commissioners in Gloucester County were not very sympathetic either. Their Indians had declined in number by one-third in the previous decade, and only 183 were left. Since the Indians did not wish to farm, the reserves were of little use to them. The best thing that could be done was to furnish relief through provisions and clothing.[34]

These reports covered only a minority of the native population, but Harvey sent them off to the Colonial Office with a brief and unhelpful covering letter. Giving relief to such improvident people as the Indians, he wrote, only confirmed them in their indolent ways; yet he had nothing better to suggest than that provisions and clothing requested by the commissioners should be supplied.[35] The tone of the letter caught the prevailing mood at the Colonial Office, where there was a note of weariness after almost a decade of zeal for aboriginal peoples. The new secretary, Lord Normanby, replied that rapid progress in civilizing the Indians could not really be expected, although he did not despair of their becoming farmers one day. He would not venture to give any instructions on how to improve their condition, since he felt sure that Harvey and the provincial legislature would know best. Selling part of the Indians' reserves to provide a fund for their benefit was a good idea and had been helpful in other colonies. He told Harvey to consult his executive council and any other persons knowledgeable of the Indian character and if anything came to mind, to get in touch with the Colonial Office.[36] Harvey had received the answer he had been hoping for: approval to do nothing.

With a new administration came a fresh perspective. Owing to the efforts of Lieutenant-Governor Sir William Colebrooke, something approaching an Indian policy emerged in the 1840's. Colebrook's interest was aroused and maintained by Moses H. Perley, his adviser on Indian affairs throughout, who assumed the role of public spokesman for the Indians' interests. Perley was the grandson of a Newburyport pioneer who had led a group of settlers to the Saint John River in 1763. He himself had spent much of his youth travelling, hunting, and trading with the Indians. Called to the bar in 1830, he kept his contacts through several unsuccessful business ventures in sawmills, coal mines, and land speculation and was appointed a commissioner in 1837.[37]

Colebrooke and Perley reached some general agreement on the subject of the native peoples by June, 1841. Both opposed giving presents, as was done in Canada, and both wanted to secure the Indians in permanent possession of the reserves. Colebrooke was especially concerned to educate both boys and girls in integrated schools near white settlements, "as it is not desirable to bring up [Indian] children as an exclusive class or caste, but rather to blend them with others." He thought it might be possible to found schools on the pattern of those recently established in the West Indies. He also recommended that the government establish loan funds to encourage agriculture and, meanwhile, that the annual distribution of seed corn and potatoes should continue. Indian farmers should be allotted lands for their individual occupation, and their general interest in the reserves should be protected by taking steps to prevent their granting timber-cutting or occupancy rights to outsiders. Colebrooke followed up on his consultations with Perley by appointing him to consult with, and report on, all the Indians in the province.[38]

Perley visited the Malecite Indians of the Saint John Valley in July and the Micmacs of the Miramichi to the north in August and September, 1841. To all he carried the same message. The government wished to make the reserve lands benefit the Indians, to improve their condition by forming them into settlements with secure title, and to educate the young not only in academic subjects but also in farming and useful trades. The response was pleasing. For the Micmacs assembled at Oxford Brook, near Newcastle, "The announcement that the Executive was about to take some interest in their affairs, created great satisfaction, and caused much rejoicing."[39] Those assembled at Burnt Church were quite willing to let the government take sole charge of their lands and expressed their desire for schooling. Perley felt that the greatest ambition of each Indian there was to have his own frame house, and if assistance to build could be tied in with the encouragement of agriculture, the Indian would indeed turn farmer. The Micmacs elected Perley "Wunjeet Sagamow" (Head Chief), a title he was to use with pride over the years.[40]

Whether his recommendations entirely justified the honour bestowed on him is questionable. Most of the suggestions he made following his visits to the Indians were those he had agreed on with Colebrooke before he set out. They had decided that the scattered Indians of the province should be concentrated in a few settlements: the Malecites at Kingsclear and the Micmacs in the Miramichi Valley, in villages that contained land held both individually and communally. However, Perley cautioned against a too-rapid break with the hunting way of life. Once settled, the Indians' children could be sent to school, and any parental objections, he wistfully explained, would be overcome by issuing school uniforms. It would be best to place the new villages near rural white settlements (not towns), so that the children of both races could go to school together. In order to combat the appalling mortality rate, medical attention could be guaranteed by paying a retainer to a local doctor. The cost of these relocations and services would be met by establishing a fund from the proceeds of leasing to whites all the reserve lands no longer needed under the new arrangement. One or more Indian superintendents, under a board of commissioners, would be responsible for carrying out government policy, improving the social and religious state of the Indians, gathering and settling bands, encouraging agriculture and education. Thus the Indian would be paying the cost of his own "civilization."[41]

Perley's recommendations were, not too surprisingly, in line with the policy that had been worked out for the Indians of the Canadas in the previous decade: assimilation by way of "civilization" through agriculture—and at no extra cost to the taxpayer.[42] He had read the voluminous parliamentary papers containing correspondence and testimony about the aboriginal peoples of the Empire, and so he knew the sentiments approved in England. In fact, he included unacknowledged excerpts from those papers in his report.[43] He subscribed to the idea of the Indian as "an infant requiring a guardian," who had to be under the paternal care of the Crown.[44] Perley was a white man of his time, more sympathetic than most, but still encumbered with those presuppositions he had taken with him from his earliest visits to the Indians. For example, he fully realized that the Indian hunt was an integral and eternal part of life, yet he often referred to it as though it were a self-indulgent sporting activity that should be dispensed with in favour of work.[45] But, of course, Perley was writing for other white men, not for Indians.

Colebrooke was happy with the report. He sent a copy to Lord Falkland in Nova Scotia, expressing his conviction that "settled habits" and "industrial pursuits" would be the salvation of the Indians and offering to co-operate with Falkland's own plans to help them.[46] But the important reaction would be that of the Colonial Office. When Stanley finally acknowledged Perley's report, he expressed his approval of the "proper and judicious representations therein," but in a vague and brief letter that gave no direction for the next step.[47] However, imperial approval was demonstrated in a more tangible way when Governor General Sir Charles Bagot offered Perley the office of superintendent of Indian affairs in Canada in 1843. The offer was later withdrawn, but not before Perley had accepted with enthusiasm.[48] This near-achievement was to heighten his exasperation with his own colony's politicians in the years ahead.

The publication of the report had set in motion a sequence of events within the colony. The attorney-general and solicitor-general gave their opinion that the executive council could lease Indian lands on its own authority, but that it would require instructions from London before they could be sold.[49] Since numerous petitions were coming in from those identified in the report as squatters, the executive council decided to take action. Perley had urged that the occupants of Indian lands be given the chance to legalize their position, and it was decided to place an advertisement in the *Royal Gazette* setting out the conditions for leasing such holdings. Those who wished to settle on Indian lands, or, by implication, who were already settled, were advised to petition the lieutenant-governor through the surveyor-general's office describing the location sought. After a survey made at the applicant's expense, leases would be granted. The whole operation, the advertisement maintained, was to reclaim and improve the reserves for the benefit of the Indians.[50] It soon became apparent that leasing was not the way to do it. No squatter would put out the cost of a survey merely to get a leasehold.

Something had to be done. In 1843 the assembly began to show some excitement at the prospect of ridding itself of the annual grant for Indian relief, then running at £300. A motion to compensate Reverend Michael Egan, a Roman Catholic missionary singled out for praise by Perley, was defeated because the reserve lands should pay "for the temporal and spiritual wants of the Indians."[51] A select committee appointed in February, 1843, to consider the subject of the illegal occupation of crown lands and Indian reserves concentrated exclusively on the latter. After noting that squatters performed valuable services to progress, the committee recommended that such land as was not required for Indian villages be sold in fifty- and one-hundred-acre farm lots and that leasehold arrangements should be restricted to meadow lands for grazing. Lots would be offered for sale at an upset price, and payment could be made over five years. After the first instalment, the purchaser would be given a ticket of location, although the actual grant was made only with the final payment. The money accruing from sales and leases would go into an Indian fund account bearing interest at 6 per cent, with the interest appropriated annually for the benefit of the Indians, proportioned according to the amount raised in each county. Indian villages were to be laid out in town, pasture, and wood lots, and those wishing their own land within the village could be given non-transferable location tickets. If an Indian consistently improved his land, he might one day expect to own it freehold.[52] This was a solid statement of the policy of despoliation cum assimilation.

Legislation was now in the offing. Moses Perley was asked by the council to draft a bill "for the Management of the Indian Lands, and the Settlement of the Indians."[53] It was nothing more than a courteous gesture, for the resulting bill, much to his disgust, was obviously the work of the assembly's committee. The act (7 Vict. c. 47) passed with a suspending clause in April, 1844, and was proclaimed in September. The preamble noted that the reserves greatly retarded the settlement of the province and yet were of no use to the Indians. To turn these reserves into an asset, it would be necessary to survey them definitively and distinguish between the qualities of land they contained and then, under commissioners appointed by the act, to sell or lease at auction whatever tracts were thought fit to be offered. The resulting funds would be used for the exclusive benefit of the Indians, for the relief of the aged and infirm, and for the provision of seed and agricultural implements. The local commissioners were empowered to create Indian village tracts on the reserves, but no mention was made of the costs involved in relocation.[54] The hopes raised by Perley's report had been shorn away. There was no longer so much as a token gesture towards ameliorating the Indians' condition. They were no longer even supposed to pay the costs of "civilizing" themselves. The sales and leases would simply generate enough money to provide their relief payments from one year to the next.

Perley was quick to lodge objections, but the council brushed them aside.

No one, they said, intended to sell so much land that the Indians would be injured thereby; and as for education or religious instruction, mention of these had been omitted from the act because they were mere details. As things stood, it was asserted, it would be possible to raise money from valuable tracts never before used, and the interests of the Indians were stringently safeguarded.[55] When his turn came, the colonial secretary was a bit more cautious, warning against alienating too much of the reserve land. But he approved the law and professed to see it as a measure for the benefit of the Indians. He did not wish to pursue Perley's objections any further, trusting to the discretion of the provincial executive.[56] Thus the imperial government washed its hands of the matter.

The government of New Brunswick, now for the first time armed with legislative authority, issued its instructions to the several commissioners. The first task was to determine how much of the Indian reserves should be given to the Indians, at the rate of fifty acres per head of family. When this was done, the Indians were not to "interfere" with the balance of the land in their reserves, which would be offered for sale by advertisement in the *Royal Gazette*. No mention was made of Indian villages with a mix of private and communal land. Each individual was to receive a location ticket immediately, and after ten years' continuous occupancy he would be eligible for a free grant of his fifty-acre lot. When he had received a free grant, an Indian would be able to alienate his land, but not before. To those Indians who complained of the arrangements it would be necessary to explain "that the Act must be carried out for their general benefit." As for the squatters, they had to take immediate steps to legalize their position by applying for a survey. To encourage this process, the commissioners were instructed to cancel any arrangements whites had made with local Indians to cut hay or timber or occupy any part of the reserve lands.[57]

These instructions were even more callous and impractical than the act itself, and so thought Moses Perley. Despite his earlier criticisms, he accepted appointment as a commissioner "to act in conjunction" with local commissioners, apparently hoping that he would be given some overall supervisory control.[58] Thwarted in this expectation, he penned a devastating critique of the policy early in 1846. Nothing had yet been done under the terms of the act, and nothing ever would be, he said. Since no squatter could be ejected, there was no reason for him to legalize his position. The trifling sum raised to date did not nearly cover the costs so far; and the multitude of commissioners prevented any uniform programme from being followed.[59] "The Squatters are dissatisfied, reckless and troublesome, the Indians are not much better, and matters will thus continue until a settlement of existing difficulties takes place." He recommended that the whole process laid out in the act and instructions be abandoned, that the 1844 law be repealed, and that a modification of the Canadian policy take its place. He argued that the provincial government should make treaties for the surrender of all the Indian reserve lands to the Crown, while safeguarding, in specific words, the Indians' rights to the land they actually occupied. In return for this surrender the Indians should receive annuities, worth about £1,000 across the entire province. The Crown would thus have a large amount of land to sell without complications, enough to fund the annuities; the annuities could be used for the Indian's "moral, social and physical" betterment and for the encouragement of his settlement on land clearly acknowledged as belonging to him; and the assembly would be free of the need to spend £250 to £300 a year for relief.[60]

These suggestions aroused no interest. Perley found time out from his new post as government emigration officer at Saint John to return to the struggle in December, 1847. Once again he urged the conclusion of treaties and the payment of annuities; again he cited the Canadian example. As he informed Surveyor-General Thomas Baillie, he had himself laid the groundwork for such a policy in conferences with the Indians of Northumberland and Pokemouche, where all had agreed on what land could be surrendered for an annuity. Similar agreements could be made with the Indians of Richibucto and Buctouche to cover all the Micmac people. There should be no trouble in negotiating with the Malecites over the Tobique reserve, and "At Madawaska, all the Indians, save one, died last Season, and Consequently there would be no difficulty as to that reserve." The executive council decided to let the message stand over.[61]

Meanwhile, portions of Indian reserve lands were being offered at public auction. The first to be put up were tracts already occupied by squatters, and the presumption was that the squatters themselves would buy in at the upset price established by the local commissioner. Anyone else who bought would have to pay the assessed value of the improvements extra. The seven acres held by William Wishart at Wishart's Point, Tabusintac reserve, for example, were listed at £10 the lot; 425 acres held by Donald M'Kay on the Eel Ground were offered at 3s. an acre.[62] But if the squatter did not bid the upset price, and no one else showed any interest, what happened then? No one was satisfied with the progress made, and no one but Perley had any alternative to offer. An assembly committee reporting in April, 1847, urged sale "as soon as possible," and another committee a year later simply repeated the hope.[63]

"On behalf of the Indians of New-Brunswick," Perley made his last bid to influence policy in March, 1848. Reporting directly to Lieutenant-Governor Colebrooke, he argued that as long as the emphasis remained on selling Indian lands to accelerate settlement, no worthwhile amounts of money would be raised. If the government continued to sell the land cheaply on credit, there would soon be no land and no funds for the support of the Indians. The government should either lease the lands on a long-term basis, or legislate an annuity for the Indians as compensation for the low prices being realized. There should be no further sales until the amount of land required by the Indians had been precisely determined.[64] Colebrooke was sympathetic, but he recognized that there was no way he could persuade the assembly. He agreed that it was impossible to raise an adequate fund from land sales and urged that some method be found to get higher prices and prompter payment. He hoped the assembly would reconsider those provisions in the act and would guarantee the Indian Fund before allowing any further sales.[65] As one of his final gestures in office, Colebrooke wrote a gloomy report to the colonial secretary concerning the fate of the Indians. He followed Perley's critique exactly; the act had not worked, and since the assembly refused to grant an annuity, the only hope was to raise some money for the Indians by putting part of their lands out on long leases. Lord Grey referred the letter to the imperial commissioners of colonial lands and emigration.[66]

Colebrooke's dejection was replaced by the vigour of Sir Edmund Head. Instructed to give his views on the situation of the Indians, he quickly forwarded Grey a lengthy report. There were, he explained, only two ways to deal with aboriginal peoples throughout the world: give them full legal rights or treat them as children, thereby limiting their "discretion and capacity . . . for dealing with their own affairs." Only the latter course was possible in New Brunswick, where the Indians could be too easily cheated out of their land by whites. Head illustrated his views with excerpts from Perley's report that were extensive enough to take up the bulk of his dispatch. But although he may have relied on Perley for information, he did not draw the same conclusions. In fact, he agreed with the assembly that the act of 1844 had never been given a fair trial. Head proposed to give it a chance with a new set of instructions. He hoped to raise enough revenue to provide relief for the Indians, applying any surplus to the industrial education of the young. He did not really expect any improvement, however. The Indians were a harmless people and their numbers continued to decline. It is not hard to imagine the future Sir Edmund Head saw in store for them.[67]

Certainly that future held no place for Moses Perley. Sir Edmund informed Grey that he would not employ Perley in any capacity among the Indians. His zeal had antagonized both council and assembly and led him to think of himself as the "diplomat of an independent power," treating between the Indians and government. Apparently Perley had let slip the fact that when he announced the 1844 act to the Indians at Burnt Church, he had read along with it his own criticisms of the law. Head did not approve of such conduct in an officer of the government, although he emphasized that he was faulting Perley for an excess of zeal rather than incompetence. As a farewell tribute, the lieutenant-governor enclosed Perley's memorandum on the history of the Indians of the province with his despatch.[68] That sad review showed how accurately Perley saw what was happening and how such perception had made him a sore embarrassment. As he summed up the history:

The first step was a joint occupation of the country by the Indians and British settlers: the second was assigning to the Indians certain districts of counties, within which they were not to be disturbed, the next, confining each Tribe to a certain tract or portion of land called a reserve and finally, reducing those reserves by degrees until in 1842 only one half remained . . . and to conclude by selling all that remains . . . without any provision for their [the Indians] future welfare.[69]

The colonial secretary approved Head's suggestions,[70] which were embodied in new regulations drawn with the avowed object of making the Indian Act work more efficiently. Head's continuing interest is shown in his own handwritten contributions to the draft of the document. Sixteen commissioners were appointed or re-appointed, two for each district, by name. Striking at one abuse that had already appeared, the new regulations forbade the sale of any land actually under cultivation by the Indians. To slow down the process of alienation, only those who were actually squatting on Indian land before the passage of the act were to be allowed to apply to buy their lots. All such requests were to be in by 1 March 1850, and those applying after that date would forfeit any claim to the value of the improvements made. Payment was to be over three years, not five, with a 15 per cent discount for a lump sum. The cost of surveys, to be paid by the applicant, was fixed at twopence an acre. The regulations emphasized that commissioners reporting lands for sale must also recommend portions of the reserves suitable for Indian village sites.[71]

But regulations are made to be broken, and it seems unlikely that the new restrictions were always observed. The demand for land was not as great as the advocates of rapid settlement hoped. Sometimes there was collusive bidding when auctions were held, sometimes no response at all. In 1862 Commissioner John Dibblee reported only one person appeared at the last auction he had arranged, and the solitary bidder, "thinking there was so little interest manifested, got discouraged and gave it up."[72] Instalment purchasing did not work as well as the government expected. Visiting the Tobique reserve in 1865, Commissioner Wilson found that no payments beyond the first had been made on the four lots sold there in the previous three years: six hundred of the eight hundred dollar purchase money was in arrears. Matters had been further complicated by the fact that two of the lots sold and not paid for had been re-sold. Three squatters who had paid the survey charge had paid no instalments at all, yet they were still in possession of the land. The general hope was to sell the improvements after investing as little money as possible in land title. One enterprising individual had paid the first instalment on one lot and was squatting on two others. Further along the Saint John River the situation was the same, only of longer duration. There, sales had been made before the appointment of the incumbent commissioner, who had been unable to find out from the crown lands office who owed what. When asked why he was behind on his payments, the standard squatter response was that since others had not paid, why should he?[73]

The land sales policy that had begun in 1844 had run its course by 1867 when the new government of Canada assumed control of Indian affairs. 10,679.5 acres of reserve land had been sold to 109 whites; £2,853.10.0 had been raised for the Indian fund. Thirty-one of the purchasers, with 3,235.5 acres of land, were in arrears to the extent of £565.6.6.[74] By its own estimation, the crown lands office had sold 16 per cent of the 66,096 acres of reserve land. None had been leased, and possibly as much as 10,000 acres were still held by squatters.

The Indian fund never met the demands upon it for relief, let alone social and moral improvement. The assembly continued to pass annual grants, with what ill grace may be imagined. Between 1855 and 1857 they had to find £1,083, an increase over the average of the previous decade.[75] The administration of Indian affairs remained chaotic. Matters beyond the scope of individual commissioners continued to go directly or via the provincial secretary's office to the surveyor-general, the crown lands commissioner, the executive council, or, if extra money was needed for emergencies, the assembly itself. Severe outbreaks of sickness entailed special pleading for relief funds.[76] The building and repair of fences had to be discussed in council.[77] Three orphans from the Meductic reserve were given executive permission to attend parish school.[78] Commissioner Dibblee was authorized to pay the estate of Peter Fraser up to £200 for land to be given the Indians in exchange for a lot on the Meductic.[79] Another dispute at Burnt Church over the election of chiefs came before the council.[80] Lola Selmore and twenty-four Indian descendants of those who at one time lived at St. Andrews petitioned for lands they had been deprived of by the Loyalists.[81] Angry Indians had to be told that the moneys arising from their particular lands were not being embezzled by the commissioner, but had to be paid to the Indian fund and only released on executive order.[82] As at the beginning, so at the end, everything referring to the Indians was treated on an *ad hoc* basis.

Everything considered, it is remarkable that the native peoples of New Brunswick survived at all. Completely on their own, they had been totally neglected for years, and when a policy was finally instituted, its aim was to dispossess them of their reserve lands in the name of progress and to free the white taxpayer from the costs of relief. This policy, challenged by Colebrooke and confirmed by Head, could have led to the total disappearance of the reserves in a very few years and the expulsion of the surviving Indians into white society without a shred of support. That this did not happen was no fault of the colonial or imperial governments. New Brunswick was not very attractive as an agricultural society, and the Indians' lands, marginal at best, were not required by whites for their family farms. But the New Brunswick pattern, had it been applied in Canada, would have proved to be one for the "final solution" of the Indian problem.

8

The Micmacs and Government: Prince Edward Island

Ile St. Jean, Prince Edward Island, lay outside Acadia, at least as eighteenth-century diplomats understood the term. The British laid no claim to it under the Treaty of Utrecht but conquered it in the wake of the capture of Louisbourg in 1758. At that time the island's tiny population of resident Micmacs and French fishermen was swollen by Acadians seeking refuge from the expulsions. The British moved most of these people on and left the island almost empty.[1] For a few years after the conquest the Micmacs' life continued in its usual course. By the end of the American Revolution, however, the pressures of British settlement were beginning to have their usual effects: the Indian's freedom of movement was restricted by farmers, his game was disappearing as the forests were cleared, and his access to the river and coastal fisheries was challenged by the newcomers. If the Indians of a large land mass such as New Brunswick were deprived of their livelihood, what would be their fate in an area as small as Prince Edward Island? The peculiar development of the colony, unique in the annals of British imperialism, further served to guarantee that the Micmacs were of even less concern to its government than they were in the other Maritime provinces.

In 1767 the whole surface of the colony, 1.4 million acres, was divided into sixty-six lots and granted to a group of absentee British proprietors. The only portions of the island not allocated were three sites for county towns with attached "royalties" or food-growing areas and Lot 66, 5,800 acres of land-locked left-over ground about one-quarter the size of the average holding.[2] Until Confederation, the principal concern of the residents was to get rid of the proprietors; and of the proprietors, supported by successive British administrations, to hold on to their lands. The colony was thus unique, and its government was uniquely handicapped, for the land had been transferred to private ownership at one stroke. In all other colonies the bulk of the land remained in the possession of the Crown, enabling colonial governments to exercise some control over settlement, raise revenue from its growth, and, if necessary, find some few acres for an Indian reservation.

Lieutenant-Governor Edmund Fanning received numerous appeals from Indians for lands of their own with access to water. But where could the land be found? The government had none. From the official point of view the ideal place for a reservation would be a small offshore island. Its isolation would prevent the Indians from annoying white farmers, protect them from the evils of liquor, and enable them to live in something approximating their accustomed way. The most remote, and hence the most attractive, spot was Lennox Island off the northwest coast, 1,400 acres in extent. This island had been overlooked in the original partition, and only in 1772 was it attached to Lot 12 and granted to Sir James Montgomery. Fanning wrote Montgomery, who gave his permission for the Indians to reside on the island and offered to sell it for £300.[3] The government did not purchase it, but by 1800 several Micmac families were established on Lennox Island. They received regular visits from a missionary, the Abbé de Calonne, who began the lengthy task of persuading them to clear land and plant crops. He had them build a chapel to St. Ann, and Lennox Island became the meeting place for the whole tribe every 26 July on the saint's day. In 1806 the abbé petitioned the British government to buy the island for the Indians, "as being the aboriginal owners they had a right at least to have some portion" of their ancestral homeland. Manual labour was now their only hope, Calonne argued, and it would take at least a generation to convert them to farming. The process was hard enough without the knowledge that the improvements they were making were on someone else's private property.[4] Nothing came of this initiative. A few Indians maintained permanent residence on Lennox Island, and by 1841 there were twenty-five acres cleared, mostly for potatoes. It was not the most attractive place for potential farmers. The trees were mainly fir and spruce, and the light, sandy soil was of inferior quality. Between five and six hundred acres were barrens and swamp; the most attractive feature was the adjoining marsh, which yielded hay for those who had livestock.[5] The Indians had none. The hay and timber proved to be an irresistible attraction to nearby whites who took what they wanted for fodder and fuel despite the protests of the Indians. One of the neighbours, James Yeo, tried to legitimize his position by offering to buy the island from Montgomery in 1827 for £400, but the resistance of the Indians caused the plan to collapse. Yeo neither forgave nor forgot. He continued to make his presence felt on the island, and as he progressed through the assembly to the council of the colony, he did the Indians considerable harm by posing as a spokesman for their true interest against the quirks of fanatical reformers.[6]

Apart from its chapel, Lennox Island was of little importance to the majority of Indians, who continued their accustomed way of life as best they could. Only two or three families, principally the Francis family, lived there, while the rest continued to move around, hunting and fishing with diminishing success. Because of Prince Edward Island's small size and the need to range ever wider in the hunt, it is impossible to say how many resident Micmacs there were. Families made frequent crossings of Northumberland Strait, keeping in close touch with the Indians of northern New Brunswick and Cape Breton. A petition of 1838 stated that the tribe had been reduced "to a skeleton of five hundred individuals" within the colony, but Lieutenant-Governor Sir C. A. Fitzroy thought that their numbers did not exceed two hundred, all in as depraved a condition as it was possible for humans to be. Those who were visible spent the summer months, as did Micmacs in the other colonies, visiting white households to sell baskets, birchbark toys, and similar handicrafts. They were also conspicuous as beggars on the streets of Charlottetown.[7] But the situation did not disturb whites unduly. As one visitor explained, the Micmacs "inherit less of the energy, but not less of the independent spirit, of their ancestors, than the Indians of the tribes better known in Canada. All that need be here added concerning them is, that they form no obstacle to the progress of the settlers, before the effects of whose industry, they are perceptibly dwindling away."[8]

The first approach to the assembly on behalf of the Indians came in April, 1831, in a petition from an Irish immigrant, Thomas Irwin. He deplored the gradual decline of the tribe toward extinction and urged that the benefits of education be extended to them and that a grant of land be made "as a means of fostering a taste for agricultural pursuits amongst them." A committee was struck to consider the best way of ameliorating the Indians' condition.[9] There the matter rested until the next session when Louis Francis Algimou and four other chiefs presented a petition: "Fathers,—Before the white men crossed the great waters—our Woods offered us food and clothes in plenty—the waters gave us fish—and the woods game—our fathers were hardy, brave and free— we knew no want—we were the only owners of the Land." It was not the most tactful of appeals, for it contrasted the benevolence of the French with the callous disregard shown by the British and reminded the legislators that the Micmacs once "took up the tomahawk against your fathers" only to put it down on being offered protection. "They promised to leave us some of our land—but they did not—they drove us from place to place like wild beasts— that was not just." We need "part of that land once our fathers'—whereon we may raise our wigwams without disturbance—and plough and sow." The other branches of the Micmac people had as much, whether they were in Nova Scotia, Canada, New Brunswick or Cape Breton.[10]

The day before the presentation of this petition, the committee of the previous year began to make enquiries about the possibility of buying a small island somewhere. They considered the Boughton Bay area, the Murray Islands, Governor's Island in Hillsborough Bay, and St. Peter's Island. None was available. They wrote the agent of Sir James Montgomery only to learn that Lennox Island had just been sold for £400 to David Stewart of London. The report was premature, for the sale was not completed until 1839. Stewart had visited the colony in 1831 and later claimed to have bought Lennox Island out of compassion for "the poor harmless Indians [who] were much harassed and annoyed" by trespassers.[11] The island was only one of the tracts of land he acquired as the future home of settlers he would send out from Wexford and Kilkenny counties. Despite his professions of benevolence, Stewart was hesitant about the Indians at first, hoping to pay for Lennox Island "only in proportion to what could be recovered" from them. But he did change his mind, declaring he would defend them and allow them as much land as they wanted on the easiest terms. He suggested marketing some of their handicrafts in London, and assured Chief Peter Francis of support against white trespassers, Yeo in particular. When Bishop McEachen enquired if the island was for sale in 1834, Stewart boldly answered that he had made the purchase for the express purpose "of protecting the Indians and to prevent their being annoyed and driven about."[12]

The imperial government became involved in the future of Lennox Island when a petition from Chief Oliver Thomas Le Bone found its way directly to the Colonial Office in August, 1838. Le Bone was careful to avoid making invidious comparisons between French and British attitudes in the past and diplomatically stressed that with the loss of their hunting grounds his people were ready to turn to farming. They needed land "on which we may reside and cultivate without fear of removal or molestation." Forwarding the petition, the colonial secretary called on Lieutenant-Governor Fitzroy for his recommendations, and he suggested buying Lennox Island. The Colonial Office wrote David Stewart in December, 1838, and he eventually replied that if the government thought they could "better provide for the security and comfort of the Indians," he would not stand in their way. His business agents would name the price: they demanded £1,500. The colonial secretary thought the amount too high, but since the Treasury had no intention of putting up the money the assembly would have to decide.[13] Fitzroy, fully aware that Stewart had just bought the island for £400, thought that £600 would be quite enough. The assembly ordered a survey, decided that the land was not worth more than £200, and resolved not to vote any money for it.[14]

Before the Lennox Island negotiations the assembly had shown no interest in the Indians. Thereafter there was a minimal concern. A gesture was made towards obtaining some land for them when £50 was voted in 1843 for the purchase of one of the Murray Islands, without result. The same year saw a distribution of presents to the Indians, just over £25 worth, but this did not become an annual practice.[15] Some public money was voted for the education of a handful of Indian children: £4.10.0 in 1843 for three students for six months; £2.10.0 to the Ladies' Benevolent Society in 1846 towards educating "two aborigines"; £2 for the education of Millicent Mitchell at St. Peter's in 1848. The grants reflected no set policy, only the whims of individual members of the assembly.[16]

A gradual change in the climate of opinion was demonstrated by the passage of a law in 1856 that accorded the Indians legislative recognition for the first time. Reluctantly following the lead of Nova Scotia and New Brunswick, the provincial government received authorization to appoint commissioners to supervise and manage "any lands belonging to [the Indians] or which may hereafter be granted or given to them." The commissioners were to report on any sales of these lands and prosecute trespassers; they were to encourage the resident Indians to settle, assist them in the purchase of farm seed and implements, and parcel out holdings on the reserves to each family. Since there were no reserves in the colony, it is difficult to say what precisely was expected of the commissioners; their job would be very much what they made of it. But, as one of them observed, the law was at least "a step in the right direction, by giving the Indians a *status* in the land of their birth, and so far placing them on a footing with their brethren in the neighbouring provinces."[17]

The law made no mention of providing relief for the Indians, although this item now became a more or less regular charge on the public revenues until Confederation. After 1856 the assembly voted sums ranging from £10 to £100 a year either for Indian relief in general, for the aged and sick in particular, or simply for the Indians without any qualification. A few individual petitions by or on behalf of Indians were received and answered through these annual grants.[18] The Indian commissioners, Theophilus Stewart and Henry Palmer, quickly found themselves at odds with each other over relief. Palmer insisted that "the more you attempt to support the Indians by furnishing either provisions or clothing, the worse they are."[19] Stewart, on the other hand, overspent his allocation every year, mostly on direct relief. The published accounts show that he distributed the money in numerous small sums to individually named Indians for such things as flour, bread, sugar, tea, coffee, molasses, pork, beef, mutton, potatoes, leather, flannel, socks, blankets, and mitts, and for medicines and medical services. The Indians, he explained, still wandered across the colony trying to sell their baskets and other handicrafts on a market glutted by goods imported cheaply as a result of free trade. When the Indians were unable to make a sale, whole families faced immediate starvation.[20]

The only alternative to basket-making was settlement on the lands so freely mentioned in the Indian Act. Yet where were those lands? The commissioners regarded Lennox Island as being in the possession of the Micmacs, although title to it was still held by a proprietor. In addition to the three or four families who lived there year round, several more spent the spring and summer on the island; and the whole tribe still congregated there for about three weeks at the time of the St. Ann's Day festivities. As had been true twenty years earlier, the island remained the obvious location for any concerted attempt at introducing the Indians to agriculture. The nucleus of a settlement was there: a chapel, a cemetery, several houses and barns, and a few cleared patches of ground. However, the right to cut hay in the nearby marshes was rented out to local whites, and as long as that practice continued there would be no fodder for Indian livestock. When Stewart applied to the assembly for funds to buy two yoke of oxen and a plough for the Indians, he was turned down.[21]

The alternative to concentrating the Indians on Lennox Island was to provide them with scattered areas throughout the province located near their accustomed campsites. Henry Palmer made a start in this direction when he arranged with the Board of Ordinance for the loan of ten acres which had long been visited by Indians on the east side of Charlottetown harbour. The surveyor-general laid off small lots and eleven branches of the Louis and Mitchell families went to work. The neighbouring white farmer refused them permission to cross his land, so they first had to build their own access road, then clear and fence the area. The first crop of potatoes, in 1857, yielded almost six hundred bushels; Palmer had never seen a finer crop. Cultivation continued for a few years, and then the government built a fever hospital on the site.[22]

Another piece of land that the Indians might have been able to use lay in the proprietary of Charles Worrell, who had divided 204 of his acres amongst half a dozen Indian families. After they had made some improvements, the Indians were bribed and bullied out of their holdings by Irish immigrants. The widow of Augustine Nicholas applied to Stewart for reinstatement in the twenty acres she had occupied. Stewart made two trips to nearby St. Peter's and had the trespasser bound over to keep the peace. Mitchell Nicholas applied to be restored to the eighteen acres he claimed had been filched from him, but by that time the Irish settlers had launched a petition against the commissioners' activities. Stewart and Palmer countered with a petition of their own, requesting that the assembly restore the Indians to the lands Worrell had given them or else provide an equivalent alternative. An exchange was effected, with 204 acres along the Morell River in Lot 39 being transferred to the commissioners in 1859. The new land was surveyed and pronounced ready for sowing in the following spring, although half of the grant proved to be unfit for any practical purpose. Meanwhile the Irish squatters received title to the land they claimed on payment of the regular price to the crown lands office.[23]

The tiny Morell River settlement was the only successful transfer of lands to the Indians. A few rather poor acres were set aside in the Boughton River area of Lot 55, while some better quality land on Lot 15 near Cape Egmont was quickly taken over by whites. In 1861 Mr. Perry of Prince County petitioned on behalf of Peter Francis to allow the Indians to re-occupy Indian Island in Murray Harbour at the other end of the province. This was the island the assembly had made a gesture towards purchasing in 1843 after refusing to bid on Lennox Island. When they found that the owners wanted £400, the legislators dropped the matter again. To end this story of failure, Stewart himself recommended that the sites in Lots 15 and 55, which the Indians had never used, be sold and the proceeds put to the acquisition of more suitable lands elsewhere. The sale was agreed to, but no more land was bought.[24]

As the normal procedures of recommendation and report failed to stir the assembly to any useful action, Theophilus Stewart began to reach beyond them by publicizing the plight of the Micmacs. He arranged for a group of Indians to meet the Prince of Wales on his visit to Charlottetown in 1860. Standing on the front lawn of Government House shortly after breakfast, Stewart harangued the prince on the "depressed and unhappy condition of the resident Indians." They had no land of their own except for their refuge on Lennox Island, which they had held against every effort to dispossess them. All they needed was assistance from the government to become farmers and so shake off their poverty. After the speech, Mrs. Augustine Nicholas presented His Royal Highness with a miniature canoe and some baskets she had made. The prince retired and Stewart chatted with members of the retinue. The royal artist, Dr. Ackland, sketched two or three of the Indians. The party then broke up, the Indians making their own way back to their camps. "Well, what did the Prince give you?" Mrs. Nicholas was asked on her return home. "Why, *noting*." "Did no one give you anything?" "No.....me no beg. Squaw poor now—Squaw always be poor—me no care."[25] The prince, however, had been sufficiently moved to donate £50 for the benefit of the Indians; the money was used to buy fifty obsolete muskets from army surplus.[26]

The *Examiner* praised the "persevering energy of Mr. Stewart [in] what we hope may be the first of a series of efforts to enlist general sympathy" for the Micmacs. A second opportunity offered itself a few weeks later with the public hearing of the land commission appointed in an attempt to resolve the proprietorial claims on Prince Edward Island. Stewart presented the Indians' case. It was a familiar story: they had received nothing when the colony had been divided up amongst the proprietors; they could no longer hunt or fish and depended on the sale of their artifacts for subsistence; the only place where they could become self-supporting was Lennox Island. They had never recognized the claims of any proprietor there and had been known to eject agents sent to collect rents from them. "There is a want of sympathy for these poor people even on the part of the Government itself; and ... for the neglect of them a stigma rests both upon our Legislature and our Government of the day; without assistance they must perish." The land commissioners were sympathetic, especially Joseph Howe, who had been brought in from Nova

Scotia as one of the members. Even before the findings were published, he let it be known that the rights of the Indians to Lennox Island and the adjacent hay marshes would be confirmed or, in the words of the report itself, that "this very small portion of the wide territory their forefathers formerly owned, should be left in the undisturbed possession of this last remnant of the race."[27]

Robert Bruce Stewart, David's heir and the then proprietor of Lennox Island, did not wait for the formal report. He sent off a protest to the colonial secretary on the basis of the newspaper stories of Howe's opinion. The island, he stated, was clearly his property and the land commissioners' misguided views on Indian claims went quite beyond the scope of their powers; the local Indians were also being misled, particularly by Theophilus Stewart, who had persuaded them to threaten to kill anyone who went to the island on behalf of the proprietor. Even so, R. B. Stewart expressed his willingness to sell the island for £400, the same price as his father had once paid for it. Lieutenant-Governor Dundas received the ensuing enquiry from the Colonial Office before he saw the land commissioners' report. Of one thing there was no doubt: R. B. Stewart's legal title was unassailable.[28] The only solution to the impasse was to find £400.

There was no chance that the assembly would come forward with such a sum since it was becoming increasingly niggardly in providing for the Indians. Only £30 was voted in 1862, nothing in 1863, and a mere £10 "for indigent squaws" in 1864. These trifling sums were to be spent by named individuals, and none of them was Theophilus Stewart.[29] The assembly turned aside a petition by both commissioners urging the punishment of whites who gave or sold liquor to Indians or advanced them credit, and a similar appeal from a Micmac, John Mitchell, requesting some restrictions on the sale of alcohol was also refused. Vain attempts were made to have the Indians exempted from ferry charges, which amounted to a considerable sum in the course of their annual migrations. A list of aged and destitute Indians, compiled by Stewart, was referred to the committee on paupers and lunatics where it lay untouched.[30] After the rejection of his plea for the purchase of oxen and a plough for the Lennox Island Indians, Stewart turned to raising money by private subscription. Collecting some £10, he took £17 from the previous year's grant and bought the equipment anyway.[31] In return, the assembly made sure he did not touch public money until 1865, when members rediscovered a modicum of faith and generosity. Beginning in 1867, the annual grant of aid was increased to £100. In addition, money was voted for a nondenominational school at Lennox Island. The curriculum covered the basic skills of reading, writing, arithmetic, grammar, geography, and dictation. Even though there were only four families in year-round residence in 1868, Stewart pronounced the school an immediate success. Six years later, after more families had settled, he reported that forty Indian children—40 per cent of the total—were in attendance.[32]

The assembly's change of heart was related to the fact that at long last someone was going to resolve the problem of Lennox Island for them. Following his first venture into private philanthropy, Theophilus Stewart determined to see what more could be achieved from this source. In June, 1862, he founded the Micmac Society with the object of assisting "the native Indians in rendering the cultivation of the soil an auxiliary to their ordinary manufacturing pursuits, and in forwarding the education of their rising generation." The society had a president, two vice-presidents, a treasurer, a secretary, and a committee of ten. Stewart was the secretary, and it was his duty to make collections to help the cause.[33] He wrote the Aborigines' Protection Society, a London organization founded in 1838 to hold a watching brief for the native peoples of the world. The society had never shown much interest in the Maritime provinces, its published notices over twenty-five years being limited to an abridged version of Perley's report on the New Brunswick Indians and an open letter to Lieutenant-Governor Gordon on his going out to that same colony.[34] Nevertheless, Stewart's description of the distress of the Prince Edward Island Indians found a sympathetic response. He estimated the cost of providing the thirty-three families in the colony with the supplies necessary for spring planting at £47.7.6 a year, and a further £50 was needed to build permanent homes for them. The Society agreed to send a small sum to help Stewart meet these charges and, more importantly, opened a subscription in 1865 for the purchase of Lennox Island. The president of the society, R. N. Fowler, headed the list with £100.[35]

Negotiations for the sale of Lennox Island were completed in 1870. All the money was raised in Britain, and the society decided to hold the island through a board of trustees which included Lord Alfred Spencer Churchill, several members of Parliament, and the secretary, F. W. Chesson. Stewart's Micmac Society was kept fully informed; the draft of the conveyance was submitted for their approval, and they were asked to nominate a local committee to supervise the settlement. They recommended three *ex officio* members, the lieutenant-governor, the chief justice, and the Indian commissioner, and named an additional five persons. Stewart stressed that only Indians native to the province should enjoy the use of Lennox Island, as ample provision had been made for Indians in the other British colonies. All was agreed. The Aborigines' Protection Society passed a resolution commending Stewart for his services; and the Micmac Society returned the compliment.[36]

The local committee took over the direction of Lennox Island in 1871. Stewart paid eight visits that year. In his role as Indian commissioner he dispensed public money to settle the Francis, Bernard, Mitchell, Snake, Dominick, Toney, and Labob families. As a member of the local committee, he consulted frequently with the surveyors who were laying out settlers' locations and blazing a road through the island. Indians were employed in the survey as chainmen and labourers, and Peter Francis and Joseph Francis were appointed overseers or wood rangers to prevent whites from taking firewood off the island. The survey showed that the property contained 1,320 acres, of which 1,100 were optimistically described as excellent for agriculture. In addition, it was estimated that the adjacent marshes under proper management would yield eighty tons of hay a year. By 1874 there were almost 90 acres under cultivation, producing four hundred bushels of potatoes, forty of wheat, thirty of oats, and small quantities of turnips, corn, peas, carrots, and cucumbers. Martin Francis owned a horse, two cows, a bull and a hog; Peter Francis had two cows and two calves; two yoke of oxen and two cows were held in trust for the use of all. The importance of fishing in the island's economy was shown by the fact that between them the families owned twelve small boats.[37]

Once Lennox Island was under the care of a London society, the interests of the Indians received attention at the highest level. A provincial law was passed in 1871 to regulate the inland fisheries, allowing, *inter alia*, for the sale of exclusive rights to oyster farming in Lennox Channel. A petition in the name of the Indians protested that the law would deprive them "of one of those means or sources graciously provided by a kind and beneficient Providence" and cause them "great discouragement and dismay." Thereupon, the provincial government postponed the sale for three months. Alerted by Stewart, the Aborigines' Protection Society took up the cause. Chesson wrote the colonial secretary that the law was very injurious both to the Indians and to the society. He pointedly reminded Lord Kimberley of the names of the trustees and advised that the law be disallowed by the imperial government. Kimberley promptly wrote the lieutenant-governor, who agreed to further postpone any sale until the law had been reviewed in London. The usual reason for the disallowance of a colonial law was that it contained provisions repugnant to the laws of Great Britain. There was nothing of the sort in this law, whose main purpose was to establish closed seasons for oysters and trout. Nevertheless, the assembly repealed that part of it referring to exclusive oyster farming in Lennox Passage to meet the objections. One letter from a London lobby had stirred more action than a hundred years of patient suffering.[38]

When Prince Edward Island entered Confederation in 1873, responsibility for the Indians passed to Ottawa. The Department of Indian Affairs had its standard list of questions: on what tenure did the Indians hold the land, where were the lands, what did they contain, which bands held what? How far had the Indians progressed in agriculture and where did the support come from for schools "and other useful objects?" Stewart provided what information he could, and, in return, he was appointed visiting superintendent at $200 a year with $100 for travelling expenses. By way of guidance, he was told only to prevent intemperance, to make parents send their children to school, and to send in quarterly reports.[39] His first report arrived somewhat tardily in January, 1875. The province had handed over to the Dominion 302 Micmacs, of whom 99 were children; 1,524 acres of land at Lennox Island and on the Morell River as Indian reserves; ten frame buildings, one dilapidated log house, and about fifty-six "old fashioned camps" scattered across the countryside. Stewart welcomed the dominion government to the challenge of improving the condition of those who had always had to live from hand to mouth: "Now that their position has been altered, and that they are to share or participate in the glory of Canadian policy . . . the most ardent aspirations, if not anticipations, may be indulged with reference to the future progress of these people."[40]

PART IV

The Micmacs and Colonial Society

9

Micmacs and Colonists

Colonial governments affected the Micmacs differently in matters of policy, but the people themselves retained their identity regardless of political boundaries. They continued to regard their homeland as a unit, and the whims of individual governments affected only a portion of their existence. They refused to give up the seasonal rhythm of their lives; they refused to stay put on reserves, and they continued to travel across the land as before. Consequently, the full range of their relationship with white society cannot be measured province by province. They encountered common problems, common challenges, common responses throughout the area. One people, albeit under three jurisdictions, remained one people. Their numbers were in decline, and sickness was endemic among them. With their traditional patterns of work disrupted, they supported themselves as best they could in the settler economy. They spoke with the whites, when they had to, in a staccato broken English that deprived them of the subtleties of expression in their own language. They solaced themselves with stories about the past when they had been powerful in their own land, but were forced to express their views to officials through the unsatisfactory medium of English-language petitions. The whites viewed them with contempt or compassion, but always as a dying breed whose usefulness had passed. Yet through it all, the Micmacs retained their coherence, their distinctiveness and their sense of the past.

The scattering of the Micmacs across several provinces makes it difficult to arrive at an accurate idea of their numbers, and the first systematic counts were not taken until the 1840's. Moses Perley listed the Micmac population of New Brunswick at 935 in 1841, and Abraham Gesner reported 1,166 in

Nova Scotia in 1847. No one tried to count the Micmacs in Prince Edward Island, but the total was usually put at about two hundred.[1] All reports described them as a sickly people. Moses Perley, visiting all the bands in New Brunswick, spoke to many elderly, childless couples who claimed to have had from eight to twelve children, all of whom had died in infancy. Measles, whooping cough, scarlet fever, and croup were all endemic, and typhus and smallpox still appeared.[2] Sickness was ever-present and conditioned the terms of existence. Obligations to sickly members decreased the mobility of whole bands and narrowed their possibilities for earning a living. Fishing and hunting could still provide a better income than that enjoyed by most white labourers, but if the Indian was unable to move his family to the resources, he was reduced to poverty.[3] The widespread failure of the potato crop in the mid-1840's broke the tenuous hold that many Indians had on life.[4] Even without this additional adversity, the general level of health remained low and winter was a killing time. Sixteen of the Micmacs of the Miramichi area died within four months early in 1856, the adults from rapid consumption, the children from whooping cough and similar ailments to which they had no resistance.[5] When smallpox broke out amongst a band at Musquodoboit late in 1860 there were twelve deaths; five of the victims were children and five were adults over forty. Fifteen persons, all but one less than twenty years old, caught the disease and survived; three adults who had been vaccinated escaped the outbreak altogether. The increasing professionalism of white medical services was shown by the fact that the attending physician, William Pearson, had the survivors thoroughly washed, fumigated, and disinfected with chlorine gas before allowing them to leave the area. They were given new clothes, and their old ones, along with their camp, were burned.[6]

Endemic sickness is a tragic drain on a people's energy, and whites, who characterized the Indians as lazy, never saw any connection between the two conditions. Yet the fact is that most Micmacs continued to work, trying to adapt their customary way of life to the new conditions. They came to Halifax regularly in the early years to sell the produce of the hunt, moosemeat and birds, fish and eels. They were shrewd bargainers who knew "the value of money quite thoroughly and cheated at least as often as others cheated them."[7] But after 1783 and the arrival of the Loyalists there was a rapid decline in game, and the Indians lost one of their staple sale items. According to Titus Smith, writing in 1802, the Micmacs had previously divided their hunting grounds among their families and were scrupulous to take no more game than was absolutely necessary. Any Indian forced to kill game for food in another's area would acknowledge the proprietor's right by offering him the skin; and any Indian trapping on another's territory might forfeit his entire stock of undried pelts. These arrangements could not withstand white intrusions. Clearing fires set by the newcomers destroyed the slow-growing moss which was the chief food of the caribou.[8] The moose of Cape Breton were hunted by organized gangs of whites for the skins: the kill in 1789 alone was estimated at nine thousand.[9] There was even some suggestion that the Indians themselves slaughtered game rather than share the resource with the colonists, killing ten times more than they needed for their own immediate use.[10]

The most obvious result of this destruction was that the Micmacs lost a basic supply of food; an ancillary result was that it drove them to rely on the sale of artifacts, not provisions, for much of their support. A pattern of relations emerged in the 1790's that was to endure for generations. In summer, Micmac families would camp near a white village to sell the goods the women made, such as baskets, quill boxes, and brooms. The men worked in wood, manufacturing axe handles, butter tubs, and barrels. These, like the baskets, were sold from door to door, and the men were further ready to do odd jobs and repairs about the house. Sales were made by haggling, and Indians complained that they were all too often fobbed off with old clothes and spoiled food.[11] However, a benevolent lady of Windsor was pleased to note that the women made a point of asking for food or old clothes rather than money which their men would squander on liquor.[12] Micmacs travelled far and wide to sell their wares; one unfortunate peddler froze to death on the winter ice outside Quebec city.[13] By the middle of the nineteenth century they had branched out into the tourist trade, with stalls set up at strategic points such as the steamboat landing at Rivière du Loup in Lower Canada.[14] The Micmacs were proud of their handiwork, particularly the quill boxes. One woman sent some to Queen Victoria "as a mark of her special love," and after much bureaucratic rumination the Colonial Office forwarded them to Windsor, even though the "acceptance of this present is contrary to the rule which is usually observed."[15]

The quill box and the woven basket had become the mainstay of Micmac commerce, but some few were still able to make a living in the fur trade. The wildlife had re-established itself sufficiently by 1820, so Nicola Tenesles later recalled, that he was able to support his young family by a two-month hunt in winter and one of three months in the spring. With one companion, he would range over a trapline of a hundred miles with an outfit of snowshoes, toboggan, blanket, gun, hatchet, and six steel traps. Between them, the two could take some one hundred beaver pelts on each expedition.[16] But, as the years passed, the hunting skills of the Micmacs were diverted and they became guides for white sportsmen. Moses Perley began the vogue for hunting in the Maritimes with a letter in the *London Sporting Review* in 1839. He described the big game available in this little known area and "the lynx eyed, active, half amphibious Indian boys" who were excellent bearers and guides.[17] The sportsmen came, first from England and, later, from the United States. In 1870, Micmac guides received royal approval when they were entrusted with Prince Arthur on his venture into the woods.[18]

Wages paid by the touring sportsman became an important source of income for the Micmacs, and their reputation as guides was second to none. The work had psychological as well as financial rewards. In the forest, the Indian still had the upper hand. An outcast in the eyes of most whites, he was here the master. Those he guided depended on him not only to find the game, but also to provide the very food and shelter necessary for survival. As a result, the two peoples found they could relate to each other in a way impossible on the outside; the Indian talked and the white listened. "Last night Nicholas and Nowell were singing French songs in duet," recorded one visiting sportsman, "or complaining of the usage of the Indians in this province, or telling me of the wars in olden times, or of the Mohawks."[19] Around the campfire, Lieutenant-Governor Arthur Gordon heard and wrote down stories of Gluscap and other mythic heroes.[20] Only in the forests could white and Indian meet on such a basis, and only there could the whites begin to appreciate the culture of the natives.

Since whites only hunted for diversion, they could never accept that hunting or anything connected with it was "work." The prototype of the industrious, energetic person was the farmer, and "work" was measured against his labours. This sedentary, repetitive, and slow-moving life held few attractions for the Micmacs. It was not only a strange form of work, but the very assumptions behind it were instinctively recognized as a threat to their existence. The Micmacs, as Titus Smith observed, "have as strong a prejudice against our way of living as we can have against theirs." He noted that the few Indians who had taken up full-time farming gave "great uneasiness to their relatives and countrymen," who tried everything to discourage the habit. In one case, the farmer's wife took off to the woods when she could no longer stand the strain, and the husband had to give up farming while he went searching for her.[21]

Conditions, at least in New Brunswick, were such that farming, supposedly the norm for the white colonist, was in reality less remunerative than work in the logging camps. Here, Indians were ready to do white man's work. Along the Restigouche they were known as "excellent axemen ... they receive the highest rate of wages, and spend a large portion of the year in the forest." In the Richibucto area they were both loggers and dock workers. One employer, John Jardine, who hired them at his deal wharves and shipyard "found them as useful and profitable men as any he could get ... very strong, as well as active, and would do far more work in a day than the ordinary run of labourers."[22] The Micmacs at Eel Ground had made their accommodation to the white economy by "getting lath-wood, bark for tanning, treenails, and timber."[23] There was less opportunity for such employment in the other two provinces where the forest industry was not important. And even in New Brunswick, it would appear that competition from poor whites for jobs at the lowest end of the economic scale, always fierce, eventually ensured that few Indians could find such work.

The working Indian received little notice, but the drinking Indian became a conspicuous feature of colonial life. Public drunkenness among poor people was endemic to the age, and the Indian stood out mainly because he was easily identifiable. Some of the drinking took place in a festive context. Along the Miramichi the Micmacs observed each New Year's day by visiting white householders "dressed in the tip-top of Indian fashion," firing salutes, waving flags, and going from door to door yelling "habby new year."[24] But most of the time there was no carnival air. Brawls between drunken Indians were relished as a spectator sport, and they frequently attracted crowds of onlookers with "pleasure depicted on every face."[25] Each summer, "small groups of wretched Indian men and women, in various stages of intoxication, bearing unfortunate squalid infants, and followed by half-starved dogs, were continually to be met with in our streets," lamented the *Acadian Recorder* of Halifax. Only the onset of winter drove them back to the forests and put an end to the "miserable spectacle."[26] A few Indians did not leave town, and the confirmed alcoholics could be found among them. An Ann Gloud died in a deserted house in Halifax, and her body lay there several weeks before anyone discovered it. At the coroner's inquest, Joseph Cope of the Dartmouth band testified that she was not of good character and drank hard; she rarely lived amongst her people and had resisted his every effort "to make her good."[27]

Alcohol had been present among the Micmacs for over two hundred years. It may have been accepted at the outset as an occasional release from demoralizing change, but it had had plenty of time to become a deadening opiate. The pressure of the whites had increased dramatically after 1783, but the Micmacs were far from accepting their fate. They were eloquent in denouncing what had happened to them; but their eloquence was screened through a filter, the English language. Broken English was the means of communication between whites and Indians, replacing broken French in the generation following 1760.[28] Few whites knew the Micmac tongue. They often reported Indian speech in a pidgin English that could have served equally well in Africa or Asia or the southern United States: for example, "No, neber see me one man, all same like dat man."[29] The language barrier meant that only by chance could whites plumb the depths of Indian fears. Charles Ward reported with astonishment that an assembly of Micmacs on Cape Breton Island had refused to give any information about themselves for fear they would have to serve in the militia, where they would be placed in front of the regulars and driven, at bayonet point, to face the foe.[30] The Indians had only broken English with which to convey their point of view to the authorities. Chief Gabriel Anthony had to address the Nova Scotia assembly in English in support of a petition: "Sir, I don't understand English—don't speak him very well. If I could speak my language to you, I could tell you better. I could tell you in one word ... in two words, in three words; and you would know what I have to say." When asked by several members to speak to them in his own language, he was "most impressive, pleasing and dignified, and his dark eye eloquently appealed to his auditors although they could not understand a word he said."[31]

Amongst themselves, the Micmacs kept memories of the recent past alive. One of the basic stories in the Micmac repertoire concerned their treaty with the British in 1761. The kings of England and France were competing for the Micmacs' support, and the English had been successful.

> The King said to Ginnish, "This is the last time I shall come ashore with my proposal. As long as the sun shines, and the grass grows, I will support you. I shall give you your living: food and clothes. If you die, it will not be because of any fault of mine; if I die, it will not be because of any fault of yours." The Indian said, "All right." They dug a grave four feet deep. The Indian said, "Put your bayonet in first, the French bayonet on it, and the Indian will put his battle-axe on them. You see me put them in. I shall never take one out. If I do take mine out, I promise you that I will finish you. But I will never take it out, unless it is through your fault.[32]

The tone of the story was that of a strong people bargaining from an advantageous position and capable of taking revenge if necessary. There were similar folk memories of the origins of many of the reservations, frequently blended with the knowledge that whites had stolen large portions of the lands. According to these traditions, the Eel Ground Reserve in New Brunswick was delimited as the result of a treaty made between King John Julien and King George, who had been in a ship that anchored at the mouth of the Miramichi. The English king had given the band six miles on both sides of the Southwest and Little Southwest Miramichi, considerably more land than they subsequently possessed.[33]

Other tales did not concern agreements between equals but rather cast the whites in the role of guilty men making reparations for the injuries they had inflicted on the Micmacs. "Bill Dumfry's Story" tells how a group of English traders killed some Indians and stole their furs. Bill Dumfry reported them to the authorities and they were hanged, but ever after the whites gave the Indians money for necessities and for the support of their old and infirm. "This is their way of paying back for the furs which the English took from those Indians. That is why King George made the treaty with them." Guilty whites were punished even more dramatically by the great fire on the Miramichi in 1825, for they had plotted to kill all the Indians in the area on the very day it broke out. Only two whites, one a mill owner and one a ship's captain, refused to join in the conspiracy. As the fire spread, it destroyed all the whites' buildings and ships, except those belonging to the two men. The flames stopped short at each wigwam, and not one Indian was harmed.[34]

Through such stories handed down within the bands, the Micmacs showed their wounded pride and suppressed resentment with far greater clarity than they would deign to reveal to a white man.

Some Indian views of the whites may be determined by a cautious use of written records. There were numerous petitions made by whites on behalf of Indians seeking grants of land. Many of these documents included statements on what had happened to particular bands since the arrival of the settlers. Another class of petititons consisted of those, usually subscribed with the totems of chiefs and captains, that presented more general observations about the condition of Indian life. None of these sources is particularly reliable, for the Indian of necessity appeared through the whites' medium, and he was completely in the hands of those who actually wrote the petitions in English for him. Sir August d'Este was faced with three Indians from the Restigouche who had unexpectedly arrived in London to speak to the queen. He went over the reasons for their visit with them and wrote a statement on the basis of what he had elicited. He, for one, appeared to capture the quality of bewilderment and resentment that characterized the Indians' reaction to the way their lands had been filched away: "we cannot understand the dealings of many of the white men—there seems to be a right and wrong with the white man which Indians cannot comprehend."[35] Few of those who helped the Indians with their petitions cut that close to the bone.

The first petition made in the name of the Micmacs in general was written by George Monk, Indian commissioner of Nova Scotia, in 1794. It was the result of his contact with those who came to his home-cum-storehouse at Windsor seeking aid. The conversations he then noted must stand for many thousands of similar exchanges over the years that went unrecorded, but which effectively instilled certain precepts into the Micmacs. The winter of 1794 was an anxious time in the colony, with the government convinced of the imminence of a French invasion and afraid of trouble with the Indians. As a result, it had been decided to issue modest rations to those in dire need. Monk imposed a severe means test on applicants, being most generous to the most wretched, a family with five children "stupefied almost to Idiotism by being long exposed to cold and hunger." He had no provisions for "stout young men" or those who did not show a becoming humility. He did give his unreserved approval to one well-clothed hunter who had only his aged mother to support and nothing to ask for himself. This man, Francis Emable, did, however, want to know "what was to be done about the Indians . . . what are they to do to live. What has the Governor ordered for them?" That theme returned several times: if only the governor knew what was happening, he would provide all the supplies necessary. Charles Alexander of Cape Sable pointed out that the English had given the Indians all they wanted until their lands were taken; then, nothing. His oldest son made it clear that he regretted having given up so much without a fight. John Paul described the scarcity of game and professed it would be better to die than live in such poverty. Were the Indians to be allowed provisions on a regular basis or not? Monk could not be informing the governor of their distress. Stung by their accusations, Monk did his best to present the Indians' case, using the Indians' own arguments, in a petition to the governor. When the Micmacs had made peace with the English, he wrote, there had been room for all, and until 1780 they had received provisions and clothing on a regular basis. Then the supplies stopped; many had died of starvation and all would soon perish. Yet Governor Parr had promised them they would never be in need. Implicit in the argument was that the British would surely stand by their treaties. It was Monk's task, first, to disabuse the Micmacs of that notion, and, second, to teach them how to beg.[36]

The failure of the colonial governments to provide relief as a matter of right left the Micmacs in no doubt over what was happening to them. "White man settle this side, that side, every where. Indian no see moose, caraboo; Indian no like 'em starve,—force 'em go farm."[37] Should some Indians by chance miss the point, there were sympathetic whites ready to articulate their griefs. In 1831 Reverend William Morris transmitted Chief Pemmeenauweet's petition to Sir Peregrine Maitland describing how the sound of the axe had scared away the game, how the sale of baskets and buckets was a precarious substitute for hunting, and how Indians would need time to learn farming just as those "accustomed to civilized life" would need time to adapt to the Indians' ways.[38] This petition was thoroughly English both in concept and presentation. The chief's second petition, in 1840, was of a very different kind, for here the style and order of expression were consistent with Indian use of the English language. The appeal was sent to the queen herself, who was addressed with courtesy but without obsequiousness:

> My people are in trouble. I have seen upwards of a Thousand Moons. When I was young I had plenty: now I am old, poor and sickly too. My people are poor. No Hunting Grounds—no Beaver—no Otter—no nothing. Indians poor—poor for ever. No Store—no Chest—no Clothes. All these Woods once ours. Our Fathers possessed them all. Now we cannot cut a Tree to warm our Wigwaum in Winter unless the White Man please. The Micmacs now receive no presents, but one small blanket for a whole family.[39]

Numerous petitions bearing Micmac totems singled out the destruction of game as the main source of their troubles. One went so far as to request that a law be passed to protect this resource for the native people. Indians, the petitioners asserted, killed only what they needed, while the whites hunted with dogs for the sport of it, destroying whole herds simply for the hides.[40] But such plaints were futile, and some Micmacs professed themselves willing to try settlement. Again it is impossible to extricate what was actually said from what the colonist who wrote the document thought should be said, but such petitions presumably gave some idea of what the Micmacs thought the colonial government expected of them. A group seeking land near Guysborough explained that they were loyal British subjects, fully aware of the advantages of being settled and civilized now that the game had disappeared; in fact they had raised potatoes for a number of years on land that whites had let them use.[41] Another petitioner, Gorham Paul, explained that his group, all of whom had taken the pledge of total abstinence, needed sixteen hundred acres where they could remove themselves from the temptations of drink and be fortified with the teaching of religion.[42]

Abraham Gesner tried a different tack by organizing a petition with an eye to its publicity value. Following a meeting at Dalhousie College, he accompanied ten chiefs in procession to Government House and the assembly building. The event was duly reported in the press, where the Indians appeared as fine figures of men, dressed in traditional costumes complete with medals. Their petition was a litany of familiar woes and was given favourable editorial comment. In days gone by sickness had been unknown, old men were wise, young men strong. Whites had come and destroyed the forests and fish and game. Things had never been as bad as they were at present, with too little food and clothing, no sale for handicrafts, and crops blighted by disease. But, given help, "We will get our people to make farms, raise grain, feed cattle and get knowledge."[43] The analysis of the problem was Indian, the solution was white.

The most ambitious petition of them all was presented to the queen in 1853 with a certificate from the Baptist missionary, Silas Rand, that it had been dictated by Louis Paul (a veteran of Gesner's petition) and approved by Chief Francis Paul in council. The Colonial Office received a copy in Micmac, written in the Roman alphabet, together with an English translation. The petition explained that it was difficult for the Indians to forget that the whole colony had once belonged to them and that when peace had been made with the British, they had been promised continued possession of the major part of it. What had happened? Settlers had destroyed the game, and whatever land the Indians still held had been obtained by humiliating entreaties to the government. The whites who had dispossessed them and destroyed their resources refused to share the resulting bounty with them. "In words of bitter reproach and contempt we are often repulsed. . . . Because of our poverty we are despised." Yet who was it who made the Indians poor? And what gave the colonist the right to despise and deceive them "simply on the ground that the color of our skin is somewhat different from his own"? Indians could not speak English very well, and no one in authority spoke their language, hence the need for translation. Rand had decided that the Indians should subscribe as loyal subjects. Chief Francis Paul objected: "We treated as an independent nation. . . . We are not the 'subjects' of Queen Victoria." As a compromise the petitioners styled themselves "Your Majesty's dependent and dutiful children."[44]

The last opportunity to reach a royal ear was at the state visit of the Prince of Wales in 1860. Louis Paul was there, but the spokesman and author of the accompanying petition was an Englishman, John Thomas Lane, who had been elected medicine man of the Shubenacadie band. He had evidently been telling the Indians to accept their fate, for the petition acknowledged that the tide of civilization was going to sweep over all wild peoples as it had already swept over the Micmacs, leaving them only with the memory of once having been a people. The petitioners offered their services in any future war, especially their skills in forest craft and the construction of camps. If only there had been an Indian Camp Corps in the Crimean War![45] The royal visit was recalled a few years later by Peter Charles, who offered thirteen good marksmen to help out at the height of the Fenian crisis. Lane's petition had been altogether too English in tone; Charles's was excessively Indian. "Good Brothers of the Great House of Assembly, who give to almost every one who asks of you, give some help." But Charles too struck a note of resignation, for he described the Micmacs as subdued by fate and superior weapons and as submitting to their lot more cheerfully than anyone had a right to expect.[46] After one hundred years, the Micmacs were learning to accept what had happened to them.

The Micmacs had become curiosities in their own land. When the city of Halifax celebrated the marriage of Queen Victoria, a group of Micmacs were paraded "with badges, ribbons, flowers and Indian ornaments—Indian boys with bows and arrows and badges,—Squaws (female Indians) with their picturesque costume, of high peaked caps, and various ornaments." A venerable chief appeared, drawn in a carriage by a beribboned horse. Tables were set on the Parade Ground and the Indians ate, watched by a large gathering. The band of the Royal Welch Fusiliers played "Even as the Sun goes down." "A shade of melancholy mixed with the pleasure of the occasion," commented the *Nova Scotian*. "The chief and his poor followers, a remnant of his tribe, reminded one of the captives which the Romans led in their triumphs, and which told the conquests of the masters of the soil."[47]

Few whites doubted that the sun was setting on the Micmac race. Within each colony, parades excepted, the ideal Indian was the invisible one. The young white was spared the trouble of learning anything about the natives. Dawson's *Handbook ... for the use of Schools and Families* carefully named the first settler in each county of Nova Scotia and lovingly described the flora and fauna, but of the Indians it made no mention.[48] Yet outside the colony readers would always find some mention of the Indians in the popular travelogues of the day. Some visitors were disappointed in their hopes of finding noble savages: Capt. W. Moorsom was distressed at his "first sight of abject beings who loiter about the wharfs, or infest the barbers' shops of

Halifax—meagre, squalid, dirty in person and habit."[49] From a European perspective, however, the Saxon Johann Seume found the Halifax Indians "not much worse dressed than...Letts, Esthonians and Finns."[50] Those visitors who came with gun and rod, as well as pen, in hand were eloquent in praise of the Indian. They wrote stories of the campfire, the canoe, the wigwam and of superhuman feats of tracking and endurance. Their Indians retained dignity even in the unfamiliar surroundings of the town: "Outcasts, as it were, in their own country, and sensible of their position, they bear themselves with becoming haughtiness towards the mob of staring Europeans in the crowded street; and, hastily purchasing their few necessities, they retreat, as they came, to their hunting grounds in the interior."[51]

Every mention of the Indians in books of travel was an embarrassment to colonial boosters who feared that the stories of wigwams and forest life would frighten potential immigrants into thinking that their lives would be in danger as soon as they stepped off the boat. It was necessary to assure newcomers that, far from plunging themselves into the midst of "Indian squalor," they would be settling in an area where there were less than 2,000 natives to half a million whites. When the reader in chemistry and mineralogy at the University of Durham calculated that New Brunswick alone had land enough to support a population of 5.6 million, the thought that the publicity the Indians were receiving might be interfering with this glorious destiny was hard to bear.[52] Abraham Gesner's *Notes for Emigrants* gave an honest account of the natives, with emphasis on the fact that they were inoffensive and diminishing yearly.[53] But it was easier by far to ignore them altogether, as did the prize-winning essay, *New Brunswick as a Home for Emigrants*.[54] Other frankly promotional literature, such as Atkinson's *Advice to Emigrants*, had a difficult time when it noticed the Indians. They were degenerate but friendly, harmless, and trustworthy, content in their shiftlessness, "ignorant, selfish and degraded" and dishonest.[55] The reader could choose what to admire, what to deplore, just so long as he was not deterred.

The persistence of the Indian was offset to some extent by prophecies of his imminent extinction. Colonials deplored the event but with few exceptions, they could face the prospect calmly. Many believed it the nature of native peoples the world over to die out in the presence of whites. "Now we seldom see a Moose or an Indian"; their continued existence was incompatible with civilization.[56] A correspondent in the *Nova Scotian* pleaded with the legislature to help the Indians lest the very name Micmac "be blotted out from the enrolment of the living."[57] "What will posterity think of this species of man," asked T. C. Haliburton, "who will exist no more but in the accounts of travellers?"[58] Moses Perley, who championed the cause of the New Brunswick Indians and was presented to Queen Victoria in the full regalia of a chief, could tell his audience at the Mechanics' Institute that "civilization, as it rolls its restless course over this favoured land, bids fair in a few years to sweep off the last trace of the Red man."[59] The visiting sportsman, Lieutenant Campbell Hardy, saw clearly that there was no way to save the Indian "except by [the] evacuation of the broad lands which have been wrested from him for the starving thousands of Europe."[60]

The starving thousands who had come to the Maritime provinces showed what they thought of the Indians by deed rather than word. They ignored the natives as much as they could and never allowed an Indian land claim to be taken seriously. The Indians' failure to use the land as intensively as the whites was a conclusive argument for dispossession. The tough Scots who squatted in the Whycocomagh area repeatedly justified themselves by stating that two thousand acres was much too large an area to be reserved for six or seven native families who only visited it occasionally.[61] What many settlers felt but rarely expressed in writing may be deduced from an address to the first public meeting of the Nova Scotia Auxiliary Society, formed to improve the moral and religious character of Scottish immigrants. The speaker emphasized that he was not interested in the Indians who had once owned the land and murdered whites so wantonly. The Indians had not changed:

> The spirit of revenge is still smothering in their bosoms and although they make their canoes, and their snowshoes, and their baskets ... and are indebted to the inhabitants in whose neighbourhood they live for the sale of them it is only the lack of opportunity, or the settled conviction that their hostility is unavailing, which prevents that spirit from breaking forth in all the fury of its wonted cruelty.[62]

For some whites the Indians were an ill-used people whose condition deserved careful analysis. Thomas Irwin of Charlottetown was one of the most perceptive commentators. The Indian "considers us *usurpers, (as in truth we are)*, therefore he despises us." Often deceived, he was suspicious of those who offered to help him and accepted such relief as came his way as a right. Whites regarded the very existence of the Indian as a reproach, and seemed to desire his extinction; their prejudices were rooted in a past where the cruelty of one side was remembered and that of the other forgotten. He had an answer to why the Indians did not better themselves as the whites did. They refused to copy the manners of those who had dispossessed them, repaid contempt with scorn, and still respected the way of life of their forefathers.[63] "Publicola" argued that the Indians could no longer survive by the hunt and had adopted only the vices of civilization; they were a helpless people, "infants as regards defect of knowledge in their new situation."[64] There were still some traces of nobility, thought Haliburton, a philosophic contempt for the "artificial wants and migratory habits of the Europeans," weaknesses from which they themselves were exempt.[65] James Sprott contributed the phrase "nature's gentlemen" in an article that included most of the standard analyses of the time. With their better days gone by, the Indians had descended from powerful lords to beggarly chiefs; still independent, they were cursed with lack of foresight and aversion to work, living in seclusion, inoffensive, "without arts, science, and laws—without the temples of religion."[66]

There was in every generation a handful of whites who undertook to champion the Indian cause as they saw it, men such as Walter Bromley, Moses Perley, Abraham Gesner, and Samuel Fairbanks. Theirs was a lonely task, for their enthusiasms were faintly suspect. As a cautious sympathizer explained, too much "cant and humbug" tended to get mixed up with attempts to help the Indians.[67] When Gesner became Indian commissioner of Nova Scotia in 1847, he saw his task as being that of "a mediator between a civilized and semi-barbarous people." The destruction of the Micmacs was proceeding rapidly, he wrote, and unless something was done they would go the way of the Beothuks. Before the whites came, the Micmacs had had their priests, their chiefs, their councillors, orators, and warriors. They worshipped the Great Spirit. They cared for their aged and ministered to their sick. "Their attachment to their tribe, their patriotism for its honor and welfare, were not exceeded by the Greeks and Romans." Naturally they resisted the whites as long as possible and only abandoned the struggle in return for promises of royal favour and protection made by treaty in 1761. "More than once I have seen the tears trickle down the furrowed cheeks of aged Indians as they recounted the losses of their Tribe by what they always call an impolitic Treaty." Since nothing had been done to fulfill the treaty promises, their condition had steadily worsened until it was now far more miserable than when Cabot first set foot in the New World. Ravaged by European disease, dispossessed by settlers, they were now vagrants wandering from door to door seeking charity. Clad in filthy rags, they ate filthy foods: "The offal of the slaughter-house is their portion." Denied the right to cut firewood, they suffered extremely from the cold of winter. The result of these living conditions was a high rate of infant mortality and consumption among the survivors. And yet all this misery was unnecessary, for Indians were "quite equal to the whites in natural understanding and ability." To say they could never be civilized was simply to evade a Christian duty.[68]

Whites could see only one way to improve the temporal conditions of the Indians and that was to assimilate them to a social organization based on the family farm. Consequently, the first desideratum was to convince them that they must restrict their movements. Colonists, who had wandered all the way across the Atlantic Ocean, were instinctively hostile to Indians who wandered across the countryside. The fact that the Indians did not gladly embrace the whites' superior way of life was bad enough; that they persevered in their own was even worse. As early as 1783 John Young suggested that regulations be devised so that "every Indian shall be obliged to Stay att his Respective place or River and Not be Running from one place too an Other."[69] Jonathan Odell put the matter succinctly: "If they are ready to learn, we are willing to teach them ... all the methods of agriculture by which an unfailing Subsistence is secured to all civilised and industrious Planters."[70] Governor Wentworth of Nova Scotia managed to get cash grants from the British government for a few years to establish Indians as farmers, and the New England Company was prevailed upon to put its funds into a scheme that would promote husbandry amongst the Indians of New Brunswick.[71] But as outside sources of support dried up, regulations were suggested once again. Lands should be laid out for the Indians, supplies granted for two years, and clergymen given wide discretionary powers to withhold provisions from those who would not work. Any Indian going off his allotted settlement would be required to carry a pass, and any found without one would be treated as a vagrant. Whites were compelled to work if they had no means of support. Why not Indians?[72]

It is obvious that many colonists had very little real expectation that they could alter the Indians' way of life. But it was a visitor to Nova Scotia, Anthony Lockwood, who brought the issue out into the open. His account of the province, published in 1818, opened with an unsparing denunciation of the Micmacs. All attempts to settle them had failed, and they had learned to beg rather than to work; the money spent could have better gone to the support of poor whites. "An Indian never can be cured of the wandering habit," and the best thing that this "useless, idle, filthy race" could do for the province was to leave it.[73] This polemic was quickly challenged by Walter Bromley, who retorted that such charges were commonplace among those who sought to justify their usurpation of native lands. Bromley did not support the continuation of the nomadic life, but he did argue that Indians were capable of adapting to the routine of agricultural work.[74] He set out to prove this point with a settlement at Shubenacadie, but neither that venture nor a later private foundation at Bear River did much to show that Indians could become successful farmers in the image of the colonists.

The Micmacs remained a standing denial of all the ambitions the colonists held dear. Nova Scotia's future was put on display for the whole world to see at the Great Exhibition in London in 1851: a province "capable of supplying the whole British Empire with steel and charcoal iron, equal to the best foreign articles, and at greatly reduced prices." But the most numerous items in the colony's display were "specimens of native manufacture of the usual simple description": a canoe, paddles, a dress, cradle, chairs, mats, cigar cases, fans, purses, hoods, moccasins, baskets. New Brunswick, which regrettably sent no information with its exhibits, had as its centrepiece a canoe with three full-size figures in state costume.[75] "At that ever memorable exhibition," fumed Alexander Monro, "how did New Brunswick figure? *By a lump of asphaltum, the figure of an Indian, and a bark canoe!*"[76] Faced with the need to represent themselves to the outside world, the colonists could find little that was original in their own society, whose dearest striving was to imitate that of the mother country. To display something distinctive, emblematic in its way, they had to turn to the crafts of the native people. Yet inside each colony those same natives were the lowest of the low, ignored as much as was humanly possible.

Peter Paul looked back over his long life at the age of eighty-five. The old days had been good, everything had been plentiful. But, by 1865, "vessels sail about, steamboat make water dirty, and scar'em fish; Railroad and steam engine make noise; everything noise, bustle, all change—this not Micmac country... poor Indian—he have no country now—call'em stranger here."[77]

10

Micmacs and the Law

A society expresses itself through its laws, and colonial society was no exception. The legal status of the Micmac Indians was presumably based on the 1726 treaty which had placed them on the same footing as other British subjects. This has to be a presumption because, characteristically enough, the relation of the Indians to the law was never definitively determined in the Maritime provinces. The records indicate that the Indians remained largely apart from the criminal law, an area covered by tribal codes for which they held themselves responsible. In the totally artificial world of the civil law, however, the Micmacs' concept of property naturally came into conflict with the laws of the newcomers, and the results were usually to the detriment of the native people. When the several provinces did eventually pass legislation concerning the Indians, its intent was to settle them as individuals, regularize the position of squatters, and make the reserve lands pay the costs of Indian relief. By contrast, the Canadian practice of the same period was based on the safeguards in the Royal Proclamation of 1763, which forbade the alienation of Indian land except to the government. Further interpretation of this provision had denied Indians the ownership of freehold land and, by extension, the right to contract debts. The Micmacs could own land freehold, alienate property to individuals, and go into debt. They exercised all these civil law rights, more by accident than design. They had to make their own adjustments to the colonists' laws without the guidance of the protective bureaucracy that existed in Canada.

Judge T. C. Haliburton of Nova Scotia summed up the situation: the Indians are British subjects, he wrote in 1823, "yet they never litigate or are in any way impleaded. They have a code of traditionary and customary laws among themselves."[1] The extent to which the Micmacs remained apart may be measured by the extent to which they retained their tribal authority. The British, in theory, preferred to work through native power structures in all corners of their world empire. They would endow tribal chiefs with authority and have them do the Empire's bidding. To an extent, this was what happened in the Maritime provinces, but the puny bureaucracies there were unable to impose any uniformity or routine in the matter. They were able to go so far, occasionally, as to back up a new chief with a paper commission and a silver medal as the visible symbol of his authority. Unfortunately for them, the British were unable to make much use of Micmac chiefs because there was no agreement among the Indians as to the exact power of a chief or whether he should be appointed by hereditary right or election.

The ideal procedure, from the official point of view, can be seen in the appointment of Louis Benjamin Pominout of Shubenacadie. He was elected chief of the Micmac tribe in Nova Scotia in 1814 and received a commission signed and sealed by the lieutenant-governor: "You are therefore to use your utmost endeavours to keep all persons belonging to the said Tribe, Loyal, Industrious and Sober and to render them good Subjects and Christians, and the said Tribe are hereby required to obey you as their chief."[2] Barnaby Julien was elected chief of the Miramichi bands in 1836 and went to Fredericton to have his appointment confirmed. He carried with him a "Writ of Election by all the Chiefs & Captains of the different Tribes in his favour." Barnaby succeeded his brother Andrew, who had "resigned through incapability," and the appointment was announced by a gubernatorial proclamation. The commission was for life, which created trouble when the Indians replaced Barnaby by Nicolas Julien in 1841 and he refused to surrender his authority.[3]

The power to grant commissions assumed the power to take them away as well. Following the rebellion in Lower Canada, Chief Thomas Barnaby of Restigouche was approached to take the oath of allegiance. He refused, saying that his Indians would not take up arms to help the government fight the Canadians. When he was told this was his duty as a British subject, he replied, "No, No, I know better." The government cancelled his commission and took away his medal, though both were restored within six months as a result of the intervention of the bishop of Quebec.[4] Sometimes the initiative for deposing a chief came from within the tribe. A petition of 1815 denounced Andrew Julien of the Northwest Miramichi as a "palpable drunkard" whose bad example was leading his people headlong to destruction: either Denis or Peter Julien would make a better chief. The memorial bore the marks of numerous Indians, but an accompanying certificate from the local missionary indicated its authorship.[5]

Most of the surviving documents mention the election of chiefs, but there was throughout this period some sentiment in favour of hereditary succession.

The two principles were frequently reconciled by ensuring that an elected chief was a close relative of his predecessor, as in the Julien family. Sometimes, however, there was conflict. Noel Antoine Athenase of Richibucto had inherited his chieftainship from an uncle, who had received it in turn from his father. Athenase was set upon by supporters of a rival. They took away his medal and gave it to their man, who went around appointing subchiefs and captains on his own authority.[6] Election versus inheritance was also present in a longstanding rivalry between the Shubenacadie and Cape Breton branches of the tribe for the principal chieftainship. The issue came to a head in 1883 when the election of Noel John of Shubenacadie was challenged as "a gross violation of an old and never before questioned law of the Mic-Mac tribe in this Province that the Chieftainship should be hereditary." It had descended through the Denis family of Cape Breton for 135 years. Noel John remained chief at Shubenacadie, although his authority was limited to peninsular Nova Scotia.[7]

Given these cross-currents, the chiefs were of no use as executors of British policy, but the fact that there were contests for the position indicated that it carried some authority with it. The chief remained important in the internal workings of each band. "His principal duty," one Indian agent explained, "is to correct any public abuses that may have crept into individual conduct and thus reflect disgrace on the Micmac name." He wore no distinctive clothing and received no support from his followers. If lots were cast to determine the distribution of the hunt or the fishery, he had no preference. Chiefs, captains, and the people at large met in councils shortly before each St. Ann's day to review the events of the previous year and discuss the relations of the bands with each other. At this time miscreants were publicly admonished and publicly promised to reform their ways.[8] There were numerous individuals who carried the title "judge," sometimes in connection with a chieftainship, sometimes not. Francis Paul of Shubenacadie, for example, was presented to the consideration of the Nova Scotia assembly for a pension. He was a principal chief and had "long acted and still acts as judge among his people, settling their differences & managing their principal affairs.... in the discharge of these duties he has travelled long journies and spent a great portion of his time."[9] The exact nature of the duties of an Indian judge has not been recorded, and white notions of Indian justice have a rather fanciful quality to them. A story gathered in Shelburne County in 1871 told of an Indian murderer sentenced to death by his own people. He was bound and left lying on the beach while they debated who was to shoot him. Failing to agree, they commuted his sentence and hamstrung him.[10]

Whatever authority Indian chiefs and judges exercised within their bands, it would be of little use in their dealings with whites. There were many obvious points of friction between colonists and Indians. Every local jurisdiction passed ordinances at one time or another to regulate, among other things, the taking of fish in the rivers and the lighting of fires in the woods.[11] In moving around the provinces, the Micmacs would not observe such restrictions. They set their camps regardless of the title deeds of newly arrived settlers. Pioneers did not appreciate arguments that the trees had been there for the use of the Indians long before the whites came. A William Corbett was moved to petition the Nova Scotia assembly over the damages wrought by Indians camped on his fifty acres for a few days, long enough to destroy birch trees for their bark, spruce and ash for staves and baskets, and other varieties for firewood.[12] The only record of a legal remedy being sought against such trespass occurred in Halifax County in 1843 when Peter McNab charged Francis Toney and John Morris with cutting down the trees on his land. Each Indian was fined twenty shillings and neither paid.[13] For their part, whites would move in on forest clearings where Indians had planted a few potatoes and then gone off hunting. One Micmac chief lost two hundred acres of cleared land in that way in various parts of Nova Scotia.[14] Pierre de Powmeville, farming near Shippegan, N.B., in 1841, had ten acres cleared, a small house, a cow, two heifers and some pigs. He did not dare leave home because the neighbouring whites would simply take his farm.[15] Fishing rights were as valuable as land and equally productive of disputes.[16]

The ugly results of these conflicts have been recorded mainly as local oral tradition, impossible to substantiate. For example, it was later claimed that "about 1815" the Indians were accustomed to camp on a certain piece of land at Richibucto and to steal from the nets of the white fishermen. One day the settlers learned that the natives were being drilled under arms by their chief, O'Peter Pearsock. The white militia was called out, and a farmer shot a dog belonging to an Indian. Shortly thereafter he was surrounded by Indians while out ploughing, and they cut the throats of his two oxen. At that, after avoiding an ambush set for them, the militia seized the Indian camp and called on the Indians to surrender. Chief Pearsock bared his breast and defied the whites to shoot him. He was knocked out. There was no further trouble with the Indians in that neighbourhood.[17] It is impossible to say how many different events were rolled into that one reminiscence, but it is obvious that that confrontation was only one of many. In 1786, the first criminal trial held at Fredericton was of two white men who had shot an Indian they thought was stealing their hogs. One of the whites, a Loyalist veteran of the Queen's Rangers, was hanged for murder, and the other was pardoned.[18] This early and admirable example of the impartiality of British justice probably guaranteed that such incidents were thenceforth unreported. Judge Haliburton could write in passing that whenever English soldiers or hunters shot an Indian they "boast of having killed a black duck."[19] Whatever the reason, no crimes of this sort came before the courts.[20]

The colonial courts were routinely concerned with far more mundane matters. The most frequent cases heard before them concerned drunkenness, assault, and verbal abuse. Admittedly, the court records for this period are far from complete. Fairly good for Nova Scotia, they are either lost or inaccessible for the other two provinces. But it would seem reasonable to assume that what held true in one province would be true for the others, and the most singular fact that emerges from the records is that the Indians are highly conspicuous by their absence. No Indian was involved in a verbal exchange that came to court, even though "dirty squaw" was a term of abuse among white women.[21] There are only two cases of assault on Indians on record, and none of an assault by Indians, in the whole period from 1760 to 1867. In the first, Bartholemew Nowat complained of two whites, who were condemned to pay £5 direct to Nowat "as a Recompense for his suffering"; a decision, the magistrate remarked, "with which the Indians were also well satisfied."[22] The year was 1763, hostilities were still fresh in everyone's mind, and the wisdom of placating the Micmacs was obvious to all. The penalty, a payment of damages to the victim, was not the type of punishment meted out for assaults between whites. Indians were treated differently. In the other case, three men were accused of assaulting Molly Tommy in Cumberland County in 1815: two were convicted and fined £10 and costs, just as they would have been for an assault on a white.[23]

Charges of public drunkenness filled the dockets of every minor court. Here again, the Indians are absent. No Micmac in rural Nova Scotia was brought into court on this charge. However, when Halifax became a city and established its own mayor's court, the occasional Indian was brought before it for drunkenness. Between 1841 and 1856, thirty different Indians were charged with drunkenness on thirty-five different occasions, an average of two persons a year. Practically all were admonished and dismissed, presumably to rejoin their bands. Only persistent offenders eventually found themselves imprisoned for up to ninety days. Other occasions on which Micmacs appeared in court, according to this first complete extended run of police records, were vagrancy (three) and begging and larceny (one each).[24]

Another indicator of how few Indians were involved with the law is the "List of Persons Committed to the House of Correction for the City of Halifax" between June, 1854 and April, 1860. Two thousand four hundred and thirty-five committals were recorded in these years, and sixteen of these involved eight different Indians. The charges that brought terms ranging from seven to ninety days were vagrancy (7), drunkenness (6), unstated (3). For every Indian committed, there were 152 non-Indians imprisoned.[25] Police court records for Saint John provide some basis for comparison. A daily listing of courtroom appearances was published in the *Morning Freeman*, and the year 1871 (just outside the period of this study) gives every appearance of being covered comprehensively. Fifty-nine per cent of the charges heard that year were for drunkenness, 807 out of a total 1,361. Twelve different Indians were charged with drunkenness, one of them on three occasions; one was charged with larceny, and another was before the court "in need of protection." Indians, then some 2 per cent of the population, accounted for 1.2 per cent of the cases.[26] The entry book for the Saint John and Dorchester Penitentiary, the only record of its kind extant for New Brunswick, shows that four Indians were imprisoned in the thirty years between 1844 and 1873: one for insanity and the other three, all accorded white occupations—farmer, blacksmith, and seaman—for perjury, larceny, and assault respectively.[27]

If petty offences were rare, serious crimes committed by Indians were, to all intents and purposes, unknown. The reaction of the colonial authorities to two cases of murder among the Micmacs suggests that these were the only major crimes they committed in a hundred years. Peter Paul was charged with the murder of his mother-in-law at Hammond Plains near Halifax late in 1829. He had shot her point blank during a family quarrel. His counsel argued that the gun had discharged accidentally, but the jury found Paul guilty. Judge Brenton Halliburton of the Nova Scotia Supreme Court found himself in a quandary for, as he wrote the lieutenant-governor, "The Prisoner's case must be decided by the same rules of Law which would be applicable to any other of His Majesty's Subjects." To do otherwise would leave a whole class of persons free to roam the countryside without restraint of law. Yet the judge had not passed the mandatory death sentence because the condemned man "appeared so unconscious of the awful consequences" of his deed. The letter was forwarded to the Colonial Office in London, which consulted no less a personage than Sir Robert Peel, who recommended that the sentence be commuted to two years' imprisonment "considering the peculiar circumstances of the case."[28] Peter Paul had been treated differently from other British subjects.

The judge's hesitation about the disposition of this case is ample proof that there were no precedents for dealing with an Indian convicted of a major offence. The judges of Prince Edward Island faced exactly the same problem a few years later. In 1839, Tom Williams was convicted of murdering Joe Louis after a drunken canoe trip. The apparent reason was a quarrel over whether Louis had hurt Williams' son nine years earlier. The jury recommended mercy, for Williams was sixty years old. The judge sentenced him to death, and the lieutenant-governor reprieved him, recommending banishment. Once again, the point was made that Indians should be subject "to those Laws by which the civilized part of the Community is controlled," but Williams had shown no comprehension of his crime and rather exulted in "the savage virtue of revenge." There were no precedents, for no Indian in the colony had ever been convicted of a capital offence. A few had been hanged in the other Maritime provinces, the judges thought, but they were not sure.

In a memorial presented in his name, Williams was made to argue that "being an Indian without education, and almost without religion [he] cannot be considered in the same light as a civilised British Subject." This time the Colonial Office avoided giving any directions.[29] The colonial council mulled over the problem. Some punishment was necessary; otherwise the Indians would assume that their taste for vengeance was officially sanctioned. Should Williams be transported to Australia? He would not survive there for long, however, because of the difference in climate and way of life. Furthermore, no one would know his language. British Guiana was a possibility, since there were Indians down there. Finally, the council decided to banish Williams without specifying where.[30] Once again, a Micmac had been treated unlike other British subjects, and there had been no known precedents to guide those who made the decisions.

It is apparent that the Micmacs and the colonists' criminal laws had little to do with each other. The records of the city magistrates' courts presumably give an accurate picture of the situation with regard to minor offences. These courts maintained a detailed supervision of their jurisdictions as the pettiness of many of the charges indicated. Halifax and Saint John, the two principal cities of the region, were regular places of resort for Indians selling their wares, and a high proportion of the Micmac tribe would pass through one or the other in any given year. Separated from his accustomed life while on these annual visits, an Indian would be much more likely to run afoul of the law than when he was with his band in the countryside. The magistrates recognized this fact in their admonishments and their readiness to see the few Indians who did appear before them return without punishment to their own people.[31] At the same time, the city magistrates would not have ignored assaults or thefts if they had occurred, nor have failed to punish them. The one Indian who, every twenty years or so, was charged with theft was treated the same as a white offender. The record shows that the Micmacs were conspicuously law-abiding citizens.

It is difficult to interpret the significance of the almost total absence of the Indians from legal process in the rural areas. There are two possible explanations: first, that there were no cases of assault, abuse, or drunkenness involving Indians; or, second, that such incidents were ignored by the law because the Indians were seen to stand outside it. The first proposition is absurd, and if the second is correct, it raises the probability of violence that went unreported because the custom was to deal with the Indians informally. Stories are still told about sites in Nova Scotia: "The Indians used to camp here but we burned them out."[32] In one such incident, "two drunken roughs" broke into a camp some eighteen miles from Kentville, beat the occupants and smashed and burned everything they found. The local magistrate arranged a cash payment to the victims but took no criminal action against the whites.[33] But there were advantages to being outside the protection of the laws, for it also meant that no Indian was flogged at a time when thirty-nine lashes remained the standard rural punishment for most offences against property. For better and for worse, the Micmacs were not on the same footing as other British subjects.

The Micmacs could not avoid involvement in the civil law because of their landholdings throughout Nova Scotia and New Brunswick. They frequently entered a complex of legal obligations that was totally alien to them. The most prevalent form of civil action among the colonials was for debt, sometimes for amounts of only a few cents. Again, the records exist for Nova Scotia but not for the other provinces. No Indian appears to have sued or been sued for debt, yet the fact that they could get involved is shown by what happened to the band on the Little Southwest Miramichi River in 1821. Their predicament is known because it was dire enough to engage the attention of the attorney-general of New Brunswick. They had gone into debt for the large sum of £676.6.8 to a number of merchants. They had sold their cattle to make payments, and their hay had been seized. Their crops in the ground were liable to be taken at harvest, and the whole group would face starvation in the winter. Attorney-General Thomas Wetmore was able to scale down the creditors' demands and urged the government to sell a portion of the reserve that was "of very little if any use to [the Indians] but valuable for a Mercantile establishment." He worked out an agreement spreading repayment over three years and leaving the Indians a basic subsistence. However, Wetmore avoided any general consideration of Indian indebtedness.[34] The law allowed them to go into debt, and they would have to learn prudence.

The Micmacs, at least in Nova Scotia, were allowed to own land. Admittedly, most Indian grants were made under licences of occupation, but the deviations from this practice indicate that the distinction between Micmacs and other subjects was somewhat blurred in civil matters. This situation probably arose from ignorance growing out of a casual bureaucracy and a poor filing system that meant that a precedent once established was easily forgotten. One of the first Indian grants in Nova Scotia had included a prohibition against alienation without the governor's consent.[35] But in 1786, Philip Barnard, chief of the Indians at St. Margaret's Bay, jointly with two members of his band, received five hundred acres "for ever in free & Common soccage." The land was deeded to them in the standard form that required the cultivation of three acres in every fifty and a quit rent payment of 2 shillings per hundred acres after the first two years.[36] In 1793, John, Joseph, and Thomas Baul (Paul) received lots 31 and 32 in Chester Township for themselves and their families freehold. The land had been reserved to them previously.[37] Individual Micmacs could own land too. Sarah Thibault, a widow, was granted four hundred acres in Clare County in 1817 and sold off fifty acres for fifty dollars in 1839.[38] Charles Glode of Annapolis County received a licence to occupy two hundred acres in 1824 and added to it by buying a neighbour's hundred acres. He requested a free grant of his original holding and received it, even though his petition was minuted with a caution that some designing white would filch a freehold away from him. Glode held on to his land until his death in 1847, when it was sold for £25.10 to pay his debts.[39] Lewis Lexie of Shelburne County bought freehold land from the government at the standard rate in 1863 and 1865.[40] Even at that late date it was legally possible to be a Micmac and a freeholder in Nova Scotia.

If there were no set rules against Indians owning freehold land, there was nothing to prevent their selling land whether reserved or not. Officials frequently lamented the fact that Indians sold off land, while at the same time they realized that it was often the best thing for them to do before they lost it to aggressive white squatters anyway.[41] There seemed to be no way to stop the process. Since members of the judiciary themselves took advantages of these opportunities on a grand scale, it is not too surprising that the procedure became legal for great and small alike. In 1792, the New Brunswick council confirmed an earlier Nova Scotia grant of a reserve near Fredericton. The Indians leased the land for ten years to Captain Fulton who then sold the lease to Judge Isaac Allen. He renegotiated the lease with the Indians for £25 a year for 999 years and shortly thereafter commuted it for a cash payment of $1,650. The reserve was extinguished with the full approval of the lieutenant-governor and Allen's fellow councillors.[42] Similarly, in Nova Scotia there were no obstacles; Peter Pemninurch and Peter Paul conveyed one square mile of the reserve on the Middle Stewiacke River for £25, and the deed was properly registered at Truro.[43] However, when the Indians along the Miramichi complained in 1815 that their chief was selling off their reserve, the crown lands commissioners ruled that no sale of land was to be permitted and that any white purchaser would have an invalid title.[44]

Sales of lesser amounts of reserve land continued throughout the colonial period. John Larlee bought three hundred acres from the Indians at Tobique for £25 in the mid-1820's,[45] and Donald McKay got a quit claim for two hundred acres from the Eel Ground Indians in 1832.[46] Lewis Lexie sold the reserve near Shelburne for £75 about 1855.[47] Peter and Albert Smith bought a mill site from the Indians on the north side of the Buctouche River and furnished documentary proof that they had the approval of fifteen Indians from the reserve.[48] Sometimes a chief would sell reserve lands to buy supplies to see his people through a hard winter. Chief Thomas Nicholas disposed of a thousand acres of the same Buctouche reserve in small lots. One parcel of a hundred acres went for £9 and a horse. He kept the horse for himself and distributed the money amongst the band.[49] Not all the chiefs were so conscientious, and there were frequent charges that they were alienating communal lands for personal profit.

The most usual method of disposing of land was not through sale but lease, which could amount to the same thing. Lewis Barnaby leased an island in the Southwest Miramichi River to Edward Simonds in 1810 for twenty-one years at twenty shillings a year. At the end of that term, Barnaby bound himself to continue the lease or "pay for all the Buildings and improvements at a fair appraisal." Simonds promptly leased the same land to William Nasmith on the same terms for ten years at £12 a year. Jared Betts took over the lease in 1818 on payment of £700 for the improvements. He was served a writ of trespass two years later, but by then he claimed the improvements had increased in value to £2,000. Simonds had originally gained approval from the council for making a lease, all the steps were legally documented, and Betts had at least an equitable right to the island.[50]

The stipulation that the lessor pay the lessee the value of improvements was basically a reasonable one, but when used in Indian leases it was tainted with fraudulent intent. Joseph Ward rented a lot on the Richibucto reserve for six years at £3 in produce a year. If the Indians did not pay him the value of his improvements at the end of that term, then the lease would continue another six years and so on, indefinitely. Ward paid his rent, but in such a way that it was "expended in unnecessary frolics among detached members of the Tribe."[51] Since the Indians would never have the capital to buy his improvements, Ward had obtained perpetual possession of the land under the guise of a lease. Some Indians, depending no doubt on the quality of the advice they received, were more careful. A lease by the Tabusintac Indians included a proviso that they would maintain their rights of "landing cabining, and staying" on the land as long as they did not disturb the lessee.[52]

Land was not always leased to prospective farmers. One deed, registered in Lunenburg County in 1799, had a Halifax merchant pay five shillings a year for fourteen years for a lot of land he intended to use as a limestone quarry.[53] A barrel of flour and £1 a year gave John Morison the privilege to fish at the Burnt Church reserve.[54] A magistrate, Jacob Powell, leased timber-cutting rights from the Richibucto Indians in 1809. He was rebuked by the provincial secretary for making this arrangement, the very sort of thing that he, as a magistrate, was supposed to stop. It was "a standing Order of this government" that no such bargains be struck "unless the same be made with the full consent of every Man of the tribe" and were later approved by the government.[55] As with sales, so with leases, standing orders were of little effect. And since those who profited from these arrangements might be the very persons who could pronounce them legal, this situation is not surprising.

Some Indians were able to profit from leasing land to whites. Barnaby Julien and his sons left sixty-five leases on record, some informal, some legally registered.[56] Julien was able to make the most of the opportunity by virtue of being elected chief of the Miramichi Indians in 1836. In the following years he was estimated to have made over £2,000 out of the reserve lands. The band finally deposed him.[57] It was the prudent white who did as James Holm did when he wrote the local missionary before concluding a lease with Julien so "that no blame arise hereafter."[58] Many of these and similar arrangements were simply recorded on scraps of paper or by word of mouth, although the fact that some deeds were registered in proper form shows that the Micmacs had a legal right to dispose of land in this way. The requirement that all the men of the band agree to a lease, even if it had been taken seriously, was almost impossible to meet. A tenant who did pay the rent sooner or later ran into the problem of who exactly to pay; there would always be some Indians left out.[59] But it is obvious that the majority of whites who took leases from the Micmacs had no intention of honouring their agreements and simply found it the least troublesome way to squat on the land.

From time to time it was suggested, at least in Nova Scotia, that the Indians would have a much better chance of defending their lands against intruders if they were given the right to vote. There was apparently an attempt to give them the franchise in the Indian Act of 1842, but it met with no success.[60] The Indian commissioner in Cape Breton twice suggested that the Indians receive the vote in order to make their presence felt in the assembly.[61] Yet when a new franchise law was passed in 1854, Indians were excluded from it by name, along with paupers.[62] When the law was rewritten nine years later, there was no mention of Indians, but paupers and anyone who received "aid as a poor person from any public grant of Government money" were forbidden the vote.[63] This clause effectively excluded the Micmacs, for in the following year an assembly committee recommended that if Indians were to be encouraged to abandon their wandering life, anyone who did settle as a farmer should "be treated in every respect as a British subject—to pay taxes, and when having a legal title to his land, he should be allowed to vote at elections."[64] Despite the vagaries that appeared in practice, the Micmacs remained without basic civil rights and duties.

11

The Micmacs and the Churches

If the laws of the white man had little regard for the Micmacs, the same had never been true of his religion. From the earliest days of contact, the missionary had been the harbinger of the arrival of white society. But missionary services had virtually disappeared with the collapse of the French Empire in America, and the few priests in the Maritime provinces saw the Acadians as their first responsibility. The British did not allow religious communities to enter Canada, and the greatest missionary order of all, the self-financing Society of Jesus, had been abolished by the pope. Consequently, the diocese of Quebec, which had jurisdiction over the Micmacs, had none but secular clergy, and no revenues but its own. Yet the faith survived. Faith led the Indians to St. Pierre to meet their priests; faith led them to be the dupes of a pretended missionary, Father Juniper, a lay brother who had run off from a Quebec monastery and was to run off with their savings to Boston.[1] Faith provoked the outburst of exasperation that greeted Bishop Jean-Octave Plessis on his tour in 1815: "We live like dogs, and are in danger of dying without the sacraments. Our children are ignorant of religion. No priest speaks our language. Our old people have not heard a sermon in fifty years. What have we done that we should be abandoned in this way?"[2]

The lack of priests meant that the Micmacs were largely responsible for maintaining their own Catholicism. In doing so, they were guided by Father Maillard long after his death. The hieroglyphs he had perfected were lost to his missionary successors, but they were retained by the Micmacs in birchbark

†Quotations marked with a dagger are translated in the notes.

manuscripts of what they called, simply, "the book." Parents taught their children from this book, and when more copies were needed, they transcribed them. Consequently, many versions existed. One examined in the late 1840's contained historical excerpts from the Bible, a catechism, some psalms, hymns, and prayers.[3] The book had multiple uses, for the power it contained could determine guilt or innocence. One story had it that a father whose son was accused of disobedience read from the book, closed it loudly, and said, "Let him be so!" three times. As his son remained unaffected by this invocation, the father denounced the accusers.[4] Maillard had also prepared his flock to be self-sustaining in some sacramental matters. It had long been the custom for Indian marriages to be consecrated at a later date by the clergy, but he had arranged a special form for Indian baptism, so that parents could save their infants from damnation until such time as a priest were found.[5]

From the first, the Micmacs had incorporated Christian beliefs into their own, and this tendency was confirmed in the absence of missionaries. The second coming of Christ became the second coming of Gluscap to free his people from the troubles and oppressions that bore down upon them.[6] In the circumstances, it is surprising that there is only one story of a Micmac setting himself up as a priest in his own right. At some time in the second half of the eighteenth century, a man named Marten declared he was God and convinced a whole village. People came to kiss his feet; he introduced new doctrines and beliefs and forms of worship; his followers slept by day and worked by night. An uncle put a stop to it all by beating the impostor and calling in a priest. Marten repented, was absolved, and everything returned to normal.[7] Whether Marten was an historical figure or a composite of several individuals, he represented a not unusual reaction to Christian teachings among North American Indians.[8] But in his case the priest triumphed because Catholic Christianity had blended into traditional life to the extent that the Micmacs valued it as they valued themselves. Catholicism continued to define them as a group distinct from the colonists who surrounded them, and their beliefs stiffened their will to fight assimilation.

Many of the new settlers found it hard to accept that the Micmacs had long been Christians and preferred to think of them as pagans. Protestant ministers had predictable comments when it came to the work of Catholic priests. Few went so far as the anonymous correspondent of the *Scottish Missionary Register* who denounced the Jesuits for two hundred years of "fraud and peculation," but all were convinced that the Catholics had done a very inadequate job of conversion. John West, an Anglican priest who visited the region after working at Red River, asked one of his Catholic colleagues what he taught the Indians. He was shown a manuscript copy of a prayer to the Virgin Mary together with a "Confiteor." West commented that this seemed very little to show for two hundred years' work, but matters were put in a proper light by a Micmac who explained to him: "you know in England quakers, when born, all come little quakers, so Indians, all come little Catholics!"[9] Some Protestants generally approved of this state of affairs. Judge Haliburton credited the Catholics' teachings for the "truly astonishing" respect that the Indians showed for the laws and property of the colonists. Peter Fisher, the historian of New Brunswick, shared this opinion, but he added darkly that the Catholics had achieved their control of the Indians by playing on their love of pageantry and by allowing paganism to continue under a veneer of Christianity.[10]

The colonial authorities were moderately sympathetic to a religion that had proved so serviceable under Father Bourg in the American Revolutionary War. This sympathy did not mean that they were ready to support Catholic missions with public money as a matter of course, but only as a matter of crisis. When the wars with France resumed in 1793, the lieutenant-governors of both New Brunswick and Nova Scotia urged the appointment of Catholic missionaries to guard against Indian disaffection. The home government refused to add the cost of priests to the colonial establishments and insisted that it was up to the bishop of Quebec to find the necessary support. But he had no money.[11] As conflict with the United States loomed close in 1808, General Hunter, mindful of this earlier rebuff, wrote Bishop Plessis to offer a stipend of £50 for a priest who would attend the Indians at Meductic Point, New Brunswick, and endeavour "by all proper means to conciliate and confirm the Indians in a peaceable attachment to His Majesty's Government." Plessis sent a young Canadian clergyman to minister to all the Catholics between Madawaska and Fredericton and to spend two or three months a year with the Meductic Indians. Once established, this mission continued to operate from the Chapel of St. Ann near Fredericton.[12] Plessis thoroughly appreciated the British position and the opportunities it offered his church. Ordering Father Morriset of Saint John to undertake a mission to the Indians in 1821, Plessis stated that it was up to the Indians to get the government to make the missionary an allowance. It was, he continued, most certainly in the British interest to do so, for otherwise the Indians might drift down to Passamaquoddy: "il concevra qu'il vaudrat mieux vous donner les £50 que de laisser cette portion du sujets Britanniques gagner les Etats Unis."[13]† When border dispute threatened war in 1838, Sir John Harvey of New Brunswick made a grant of £50 a year for a priest to the Indians of Madawaska with the express purpose of strengthening their attachment to the British government.[14] Catholicism and loyalty was a powerful combination for both church and state. As Bishop McEachern pointed out, "it is of no use to expect to make Protestants out of [the Indians]; for let them once abandon their religion . . . and Government has no further hold of them."[15]

The basic responsibility for financing missions to the Indians was supposed to fall on the Indians themselves. They had traditionally supported their priests with supplies, but the last record of such help was in 1792, and after that date the Micmacs' declining standard of life probably denied them a surplus of any sort.[16] When Father Beaubien was sent in 1812 to the Indians along the coasts of Pictou and Merigomish, he was instructed to collect fifty cents a year from each communicant.[17] The Indians were expected to tithe, but so long as they refused to take up farming, there was little to tithe. This fact, Plessis explained to one group, accounted for their so rarely having the services of a priest.[18] Missionaries had to make do on the sporadic generosity of colonial legislators, which meant that they devoted the bulk of their time to those who would support them, namely the Acadians. When a missionary divided his time thus, a further difficulty arose, for assemblymen refused to give money to any one denomination working amongst whites. In 1828 the New Brunswick assembly, for example, voted £50 for a priest to serve the Indians at St. Ann's, but his bishop insisted that he spend only one Sunday a month there. The legislative grant was not paid.[19]

The clergy were few and the distances great, while the language barrier remained as formidable as ever. Only one Catholic missionary could speak Micmac in 1811, and then with the greatest difficulty. Father Lejamtel, who had spent a week a year amongst the Indians for twenty years, had never bothered to learn the tongue.[20] Priests found it impossible to teach or hear confession except through interpreters, and sometimes they had to use English as the language of communication. And it was not only protestants that thought there was little to teach, for Plessis himself considered the Micmac catechism used by the missionaries to be grossly inadequate.[21] The only source of information about the Micmac tongue was the work of Maillard, for no priest any longer thought to learn it from the Indians. Those of Maillard's papers written in the Roman alphabet were prized and copied extensively; his hieroglyphs were left to the Indians. Jean-Mandé Sigogne, missionary at St. Mary's Bay, was having a six-hundred-page manuscript of the Micmac language transcribed for him in 1804, and he eventually became proficient in the tongue.[22] J.-M. Bellenger worked for years on a copy of Maillard's writings that was in such bad condition that it was falling to pieces. He decided that the original was too long and repetitious; so he abridged the grammar and simplified many Micmac phrases which he thought, para-doxically, were beyond the understanding of "Sauvages simples et idiotes." His aim was to produce a basic Micmac through which new missionaries could learn to converse with their flock: accordingly he devoted many pages to "Phrases détachées pour servir d'instruction et de Reprimande en Confes-sion,"† with French on the right page and Micmac (in the Roman alphabet) on the left. Few profited from these labours. Bellenger completed the first draft of his edition in 1816, and it is probably the anonymous thirty-nine page *Alphabet Mikmaque* published in Quebec in the following year. He worked on two further versions over the next twenty years, but they were not printed until 1864.[23]

Some missionaries bridged the language gap with graphic representations of hell fire. A Trappist, Father Vincent de Paul, showed the Indians of Chezzetcook a transparency depicting souls in torment: "the brilliant and real looking flames were well calculated to produce an impression.... At once penetrated with compassion and charity for the suffering souls in purgatory they began to weep, and to look up the money they had with them so as to have the Holy Sacrifice offered on behalf of these suffering souls." Father Vincent was himself impressed with the religiosity of the Micmacs, for all wore the cross and many carried rosaries, telling their beads several times a day. Their Friday penance, which involved each member of the family having the backs of his hands beaten up to fifty times with a rod, was commendably rigorous.[24]

Of all the methods of putting the Christian message across, none remained more effective than the St. Ann's Day festivities held on 26 July, which was made even more important by the deferral to that date of the rites of Easter.[25] These celebrations became more elaborate as the century progressed, reinforcing the traditional function of bringing the Micmacs together in the presence of the clergy. The eve of St. Ann's Day at Chezzetcook in 1818 was marked with bonfires, dancing, and gunfire, but not until the celebrants had said their evening prayers and sung their hymns and canticles.[26] The priest at Bartabog confessed all the Indians between Pokemouche and Buctouche in a ten-day period around the 1822 observations, and 316 Indians were confessed at Burnt Church in 1824.[27] Twenty years later, Bishop Walsh moved the devotions in from such rural fastnesses and held a special service at the Halifax Cathedral. There he told his congregation of the pope's solicitude for them, and of His Holiness's pleasure at receiving the "pair of mocassins which his simple children had sent him."[28] Bishop Colin F. McKinnon chose to travel to the Micmacs, arriving at Chapel Island in 1852 to be greeted by 8 priests and 3,000 people (including 762 Micmacs) on their knees.[29]

As the religious year reached its climax on St. Ann's Day, Bishop Plessis had originally planned to rationalize missionary work by concentrating on the three centres of this pan-Micmac festivity: Chapel Island on Lake Bras d'Or, Cape Breton, Lennox Island off Prince Edward Island, and Burnt Church in New Brunswick. The most important of these sites was Chapel Island, with its wooden statue of St. Ann and a tradition of continuous use from the beginning of the eighteenth century. Through the initiative of Father Lejamtel, the Cape Breton council had granted this island to the native Indians in 1792 "to hold, Use occupy and possess... during His Majesty's Pleasure."[30] In 1801 Plessis tried to centralize the Indians of Prince Edward Island by instructing the Abbé de Calonne to reunite and settle them on Lennox Island. All Cape Breton Indians were to be directed to Chapel Island, along with those from Nova Scotia; the New Brunswick Indians would meet at Burnt Church, which had become a reserve in 1802.[31] Plessis also made arrangements for the Micmac colony at St. George's Bay, Newfoundland, which the local bishop did not even know existed. These Indians customarily travelled to Chapel Island for the saint's day, but Plessis wanted them to go to Lennox Island or, better still, stay home. The Micmacs were not to be that well regulated. As late as 1839, the Newfoundland Micmacs were still arriving regularly in Cape Breton.[32]

In an ideal world, the several shrines of St. Ann would have become centres for settled agricultural communities of Catholic Indians. Bishop Pierre Denaut made his position crystal clear on a visit to Arichat in 1803. If the Indians wanted missionaries, then they must farm. They were to live in a village, build and maintain a chapel at its centre, get £50 a year from the government for a priest, and pay him a dollar a year for each communicant among them.[33] Bishop Plessis lamented the apathy of the Indians he met on his travels and deplored their utter indifference to the material values that he himself held dear. A barely recognizable village stood at Restigouche on a good site, but the grass was uncut and bush grew all around the derelict cabins dotted at random across the landscape. He found the Indians there querulous about the lack of a missionary and absolutely without the will to help themselves. A plain chapel and a wretched hovel of a priest's house stood forlorn at Burnt Church, while the rest of the village site was overgrown with trees. At least thirty families congregated there each year, but they had done nothing, built nothing, and simply drifted away.[34] There was good agricultural land at Chapel Island going to waste while the local Indians kept themselves in idle penury and spent what little money they did have for tobacco.[35] Good Catholics settled and farmed.

Bishop Plessis hoped he had found the man to set up an Indian farming community when Father Vincent de Paul providentially missed his boat connections and was stranded at Halifax in 1815. As early as 1801, the abbot of La Trappe had written Plessis with a view to establishing his order in the diocese of Quebec, but it had then been politically inopportune. After his first visit to the eastern provinces, Plessis toyed with the idea of bringing over some Irish Trappists to Antigonish to instruct the Indians. When he arrived in Halifax in 1815, he found Father Vincent there, one of a party of monks and nuns returning from the United States to France.[36] Plessis quickly recruited him and sent off letters of recommendation to Lieutenant-Governor Sir John Sherbrooke and to the abbot superior of La Trappe.[37] Father Vincent was ready to meet the challenge and drew up a plan for the salvation of the Micmacs through settlement. He would divide the people into tribes of twenty-five to thirty families each under a chief and each forming a village with a chapel at its core. The government would provide land for the Indians to cultivate. Every month, the tribal chief would render an account to a general-in-chief, who would report to the mission priest. The general-in-chief would be chosen by the priest and tribal elders, the tribal chiefs by the general and the priest. Government supplies, furnished on a regular basis, would be distributed down through the hierarchy; there would be tight controls on who went out among the whites to sell handicrafts and buy goods. Father Vincent hoped to make a start on this project with a Trappist house forming the nucleus of the first settlement.[38]

Impressed with the industry of a group of Indians who cultivated potatoes at Pomquet, Father Vincent decided to locate his mission there. He bought three hundred acres near Tracadie in 1819 and built two houses, one a girls' school and one for his order, with money from Monseigneur Burke of Halifax. Vincent hoped to assemble the Indians around this centre and teach both catechism and agriculture. Since he was unable to get government support, he quickly ran short of funds, and he delayed going to Canada to raise money until it was too late.[39] He was an angular, awkward man, and subject to epileptic fits, and Plessis would rather he had returned to France permanently. In 1823, Vincent visited Clairvaux, the mother house of his order in France, and he returned two years later with another priest and three friars aboard a French naval transport.[40] By then, Vincent wanted to set up his mission in Cape Breton, further removed from the evil influences of white settlement. Such a plan, Plessis remarked, would require government approval, and the manner of Vincent's second coming had probably put an end to that hope.[41]

From then until his death in 1853, Petit Clairvaux, Vincent's monastery at Tracadie, maintained a tenuous existence with the aid of a handful of local Irish lay brothers. He taught no Indians to till the soil, but he did impart some Latin to one student. In 1839 he lost even the moral support of his own order, presumably because his missionary zeal violated the contemplative life to which Trappists were bound. He maintained his contacts with the Indians over the years and had their respect.[42] He changed their lives not one iota.

The only Indian settlement founded with the blessing of the Catholic clergy at this time was the one established at Bear River, Nova Scotia, in the 1820's. This venture was undertaken by Peleg Wiswall of Digby and the Abbé Sigogne. Both these men had official standing with the government, Wiswall as a judge and Sigogne as a justice of the peace, and this fact doubtless smoothed their path. Late in 1825, Wiswall won the support of Lieutenant-Governor Kempt for an experimental settlement where the Indians would learn to "abandon the prejudices and habits of their Fathers." When informed, Sigogne responded to the news with "heartfelt" joy and suggested that from fifteen hundred to two thousand acres were needed, together with a chapel and a burying ground. The government offered to acquire the land, pay the surveying costs, and provide basic supplies to help with the clearing and preparation of the soil. One thousand acres were acquired in 1827, and thirty-acre lots were laid out on each side of a central road. Both Wiswall and Sigogne were realists enough to know that any attempt to change the Indians' way of life would take a long time, and they viewed the proposed settlement more as a rallying point than as an instant agricultural community. Wiswall would be content, he wrote, to see "A Root Cellar near each Winter Wigwam and a patch cleared by each family for the culture of a few Potatoes, Indian Corn & Kidney Beans." The men would still follow their established local seasonal routines, shooting porpoises in the summer and trapping in the winter; the women would continue to make baskets and brooms for sale to the whites. The settlement should remain small, for more than twenty families would put too great a pressure on local resources.[43]

Modest though it was, the settlement got off to a shaky start. Supplies were dumped on the beach and left to spoil in the rain. Quarrels among the Indians in the summer of 1828 nearly drove Sigogne to despair. There was also a continuing problem of how to get support until the community was ready to stand on its own. A visitor recently returned from London, William Bowman of Saint John, wrote to say that Samuel Gurney of the philanthropic Quaker family had enquired whether he could do anything to help. Thirty or forty pounds every so often would be useful if it were spent to promote industry rather than idleness; local cranberries might be marketed in London. Sigogne approved of seeking funds from the Quakers so long as their money did not interfere with religion.[44] He himself felt more optimistic after the legislature voted £100 towards building a chapel. By January 1832 there were seventy-four Indians living at Bear River under the leadership of Chief Andrew Meuse. Two years later, a visitor described the settlement as "chiefly lying covered with logs, brush &c. and growing up with young suckers": the residents had sold their tools and seed for rum and were still improvident as ever. Nevertheless, the settlement endured, and 750 acres were added to it in 1837.[45]

Sigogne's partial success at Bear River contrasted with Vincent's total failure to realize his community, and the difference lay in the measure of official approval each received. Sigogne was the exception, for it was natural that protestant governments would favour protestant causes. While the Catholic Church had few priests and little money, it did not measure its strength by how well it turned Indians into farmers. A Catholic Indian did not have to become a white man; settlement was highly desirable but not essential to the soul's salvation.

The English, however, thought differently, for no protestant could distinguish between assimilation and salvation: the two were as one. This doctrine was embodied in the royal charter of the senior English missionary society known as the Company of New England, or, more formally, the Society for the Propagation of the Gospel in New England. Founded in 1649 and incorporated at the Restoration, its objects were not only the spreading of the gospel amongst the heathen natives but also the

civilizing, teaching and instructing the said heathen natives and their children, not only in principles and knowledge of true religion, and in morality and the knowledge of the English tongue, and in other liberall arts and sciences, but for educating and placing of them or their children in some trade, mistery, or lawfull calling.[46]

Following the American Revolution, this London-based society decided to quit the new republic and concentrate its efforts in the surviving colonies, particularly New Brunswick. The tone was set by Joseph Mauduit in a speech before the company in 1785. He argued that the Americans would probably try to set the Indians on to the new Loyalist settlement. Therefore, common prudence as well as religious duty required that these Indians be educated and assimilated into colonial society.[47] Mauduit was so persuasive that the company appointed nine commissioners in New Brunswick, including the lieutenant-governor, the chief justice, the provincial secretary and the solicitor-general. As a further earnest of their seriousness, the company made an annual grant of £500, rising to £800, in a province that was fortunate to have a total revenue of £2,000 in any given year. No missionary effort could have begun with a more ample endowment of influence and money.[48]

The commissioners made a fine start. They chose sites for Indian schools and, in the first year, appointed five instructors and two missionaries, spent over £50 on supplies for the Indians, and paid for their inoculation against smallpox. They opened correspondence with several Catholic priests, including Father Bourg, seeking their support.[49] Difficulties quickly became apparent, for the Indians did not want to send their children to school. James Frazer reported from the Miramichi that his sudden interest in them caused the Indians to fear "that they were to be compelled to become Sailors & Soldiers." Since he knew no Micmac, he found it difficult to disabuse them of this idea.[50] Gervase Say of Maugerville, who did know the language, had more success. The Indians in his area were sufficiently destitute to give up their children in exchange for supplies. Encouraged, the commissioners offered him £25 a year (in addition to his stipend) for the maintenance of each child enrolled in his school and for the entertainment of the parents. In November 1789, Say claimed to have twenty-five children at school, and thirty a few months later. Walter Dibblee at Meductic reported twenty-five students; he had induced their parents to settle on land near his school.[51] Oliver Arnold had nine Indians at his school at Sussex Vale.[52] Expenditures were going completely out of control. The lavish scale of support offered Say and, subsequently, the others was taxing the generosity of the New England Company, and there was no close accounting of the outlays. The company raised its grant but insisted that no more than three schools be maintained. In 1796 the three surviving schools were concentrated at Sussex Vale.[53]

The central school was placed under the direction of Oliver Arnold, a man of considerable entrepreneurial talents. He had gone to Sussex Vale for the company in 1787 and had been ordained into the Anglican Church in 1790. He became a missionary to the whites for the Society for the Propagation of the Gospel in 1794. His school was supposed to ensure the regular attendance of Indian children, send them to church on Sundays, and serve as a gathering place for their parents, once a quarter, for worship and catechism. He would receive £15 a year for each Indian child enrolled. In 1801 he increased his income by admitting fee-paying white students on a segregated basis. Arnold sent in encouraging reports. When he first went to Indian camps, he wrote the governor of the New England Company, "the Children especially would immediately make their escape to the Wood," but a judicious use of presents had changed fear into friendship. But some of the New Brunswick commissioners did not share his optimism. Chief Justice George Ludlow, Judge Isaac Allen, and Attorney-General Jonathan Bliss resigned from the commission claiming that Arnold had not educated a single Indian in seven years.[55] In March, 1804, Lieutenant-Governor Carleton attended the general court of the company in London and recommended that funding be suspended. The company agreed, closed Arnold's school, and formed a committee to decide what to do next.[56]

The company blamed two major faults for its failure. First, the Indian children who had attended Arnold's school had not been effectively separated from their parents, and the maintenance of these family ties had enabled them to resist instruction. Second, education was simply a preparation for the apprenticeship of Indians to whites to learn useful skills. That scheme had not yet been tried. In July, 1806, the company decided to renew its funding and re-open Arnold's school. Indians were to be apprenticed to white families in the neighbourhood of Sussex Vale, and the masters were to be responsible for sending them to school. Indian parents were to be given a weekly allowance to stay away from their children.[57]

The New Brunswick programme now entered its second and final phase. Each Indian who allowed his child to be apprenticed received an annual allowance of three yards of coarse blue cloth, a blanket, and a shirt; and, as long as his child stayed an apprentice he got a cash allowance, usually two shillings and sixpence a week.[58] Each white who took an Indian apprentice was paid £20 a year to provide board, lodging, clothing, "proper Schooling," and instruction in the principles of the protestant religion. Indian boys were bound out to learn the trade of farming, girls to learn domestic service.[59] Children were taken on at any age from birth to sixteen, and the indentures were out at the age of twenty-one. At that point, each Indian male was supposed to receive fifty acres, two steers, a cow, an ox, and a hoe. By 1814 there were thirty-five children in indentures.[60]

There was enormous scope for abuse in these arrangements. New Brunswick had always been short of farm labourers who, when they could be found, earned £25 a year. To be paid £20 to take on a person who could be made to do the farm chores was, to say the least, a stroke of luck. There was apparently no limit to the number of apprentices in a family: Arnold had six, each bringing him £20 a year. The girls suffered especial abuse, and seduction by the master, or his son, was documented on three occasions and doubtless occurred much more frequently than that. One of Arnold's apprentices, Molly Gell, was seduced by his son, and when the child was born, Arnold simply took him on as another apprentice at the charge of the company.[61] These children, and the offspring of apprentices married to each other, were brought into the programme, which thus became self-perpetuating.[62]

Slowly, the New England Company became aware that its benevolent intentions had once again been perverted into a device for draining money off from the metropolis to the backwoods. In 1816 they decided once again to suspend their operations, but the indentures remained legally valid. The local commissioners tried to save the plan, which also paid them salaries, by expressing just sentiments. The Indians, they agreed, were "a part of the human race and not only entitled to our commiseration, but have strong claims upon the justice of those by whom they have been deprived of their country and former resources for sustenance."[63] The company sent Walter Bromley from Nova Scotia to check on what had in fact been done. He found the results of the programme to be appalling. The Indians were regarded as inferiors, "treated as Menial Servants and compelled to do every kind of drudgery." Although some of the boys had received a smattering of education, none of the girls had. He was especially critical of Arnold for wasting the company's money on his dissipated relatives, and he considered the whites of Sussex Vale totally unfit to have anyone in their power. As soon as their time was up, the former apprentices rejoined the Catholic Church, but since they had grown up without learning their own language, they were not accepted by other Indians; nor were they accepted by whites. Consequently, they became "a peculiar distinct people, shut out from all Society" and doomed to beg from door to door.[64] The company's project had ended in disaster, and it wisely abandoned New Brunswick to try again in Upper Canada.

The attempt to convert the Indians to the protestant faith had been undertaken with full government support and expenditures that totalled some $140,000. After a failure on this scale, it is hardly surprising that little further effort was made to protestantize the Indians. Yet Walter Bromley, who had pronounced the doom of the Sussex Vale experiment, represented another strain of endeavour. He was a religious man, but his faith drove him to undertake good works without seeking immediate sectarian advantage. He was, in other words, the Maritime provinces' first humanitarian.[65]

Captain Walter Bromley, paymaster of the 23rd Regiment, the Welch Fusiliers, had been a soldier since 1790 and had taken his retirement in Halifax. His interest in education led him to the Indians, and in 1813 he proposed the establishment of an "Asylum" where they might be clothed, fed, and instructed. In a speech published as the first of *Two Addresses on the Deplorable State of the Indians*, Bromley claimed that their decline was such that "the British settlers of this colony will be registered with a Cortes and a Pizaro" for sheer destructiveness. The Nova Scotia Micmacs, debauched by liquor and deprived of their hunting grounds, were driven off any lands they tried to cultivate. Basically honest, the Indians were understandably "impenetrably secret" in their dealings with whites. Some right-thinking persons had to win their confidence and teach them to read and write and embrace Christianity. Increase their knowledge, increase their wants, he said, and "honest industry" would be the result.[66]

A response came from Fredericton. There, in January, 1814, a group headed by the president of the council, Sir Thomas Saumarez, formed the "North American Indian Institution." Its objects ranged from providing the Indians with materials to build huts to form small towns to instructing them in literacy and publicizing its activities throughout Britain and the colonies.[67] The group had one success with a purchase of four hundred acres near Fredericton for the Indians, but by June enthusiasm was running low, and their meetings were thinly attended.[68] However, before they expired, they had the good sense to appoint Walter Bromley as their secretary. The New England company commissioners in New Brunswick also consulted Bromley over the problems they were having at Sussex Vale, and he immediately criticized the manner in which Indian children were separated from their parents. If Indians were to be civilized, it could only be done "by the general consent of the whole tribe."[69]

Combining these reponses, Bromley gave his second address, dedicated to Saumarez, in March, 1814. He spoke of the New Brunswick Indians as being far more civilized, more temperate, than those in Nova Scotia, who combined "all the worst features of rude and uncultivated nature, with the vilest habits that can be gathered from the lowest classes." Once again likening the English colonists to the Spaniards of days gone by, Bromley emphasized how much the Indians had cause to complain and called on Christians of all denominations to instruct them in "the advantages of education, of pure and undefiled religion, and the comforts of civilized society."[70]

Events now began to run together. A month after this address, four Micmac brothers, Louis Benjamin, Jean Lucem, Pierre, and Francis Pominout, hearing of an "Indian Society among the good English people," petitioned the lieutenant-governor of Nova Scotia. They spoke, they said, for 120 men who wanted land at Shubenacadie, "not back in the woods," but fit for agriculture. The petition was drawn by the Abbé Sigogne, and consequently it emphasized that the petitioners were all Catholics and did not need any more books, for they had enough of their own to know of Redemption through the Lord Jesus Christ. Any help in transcribing their books, Sigogne added hopefully, would be much appreciated.[71] This clear warning of the dangers ahead did not disturb Bromley. He had already dismissed the idea that the Catholics might oppose his plans as being "as groundless as it is uncharitable."[72]

Bromley's two addresses were published in London and came to the attention of the New England Company. That body, by then wary of its commissioners in New Brunswick but not yet ready to abandon the field, voted Bromley £300 as "Treasurer of the North American Institution of New Brunswick." Then they asked him what he planned to do with the money.[73] He went to Lieutenant-Governor Lord Dalhousie with this largesse, and Dalhousie wrote the company to explain that the grant would be spent in Nova Scotia. Anxious to avoid any repetition of the company's activities in New Brunswick, Dalhousie emphasized that though the Indians were "little better than outcasts of Society... they are Christians" and he would oppose any attempt to convert them from the Catholic faith. He spoke highly of both Sigogne and Bromley and pointedly added that freedom of religion was guaranteed in Nova Scotia. Rather unsurprisingly, considering its charter, the company agreed that conversion was not necessary, and sent a further £300. The London Missionary Society also provided some money.[74]

Bromley had cash; the Shubenacadie Indians had declared themselves; Lord Dalhousie had given his approval; and the New England Company no longer insisted on conversion. By early 1817 Bromley had collected twenty-four Micmac families and was settling them on lands at Shubenacadie. He petitioned the assembly for financial aid to build an access road, hoping "you will even consider the attempt to civilize the Indians a matter not unworthy of your anxious solicitude, patronage and support." He received £25.[75] Ten days after this petition, Lord Dalhousie supported its main thrust in a special message to the legislature concerning the "most wretched and deplorable" state of the Indians and urged the encouragement of those who were willing to farm. The result was a grant of £250 to be applied under his direction.[76] The Shubenacadie settlement got off to a satisfactory start: twenty-two of the families were settled and some fifty acres cleared by August, 1818. When he visited in the autumn, Bromley found twenty-three acres, all fenced, planted with vegetables and grains; one log and two frame houses built; and the six cows he had given the settlers all healthy. A group of Indians from Gold River asked for his support, and they quickly cleared and planted six acres.[77] The work of "civilization" was well under way. Bromley had decided to begin at the beginning and set aside education for the time being. When it came to missionary work, "little is to be expected from preaching abstruse doctrines to men who had never been taught the exercise of their thinking abilities... and I think a liberal plan of education, connected with agricultural pursuits, would produce the happiest effects."[78]

From the point of view of the Catholic Church, the activities sponsored by the New England Company in New Brunswick and Nova Scotia formed a

concerted attack on the Indians' religious faith. Bishop Plessis recruited
Father Vincent to found an Indian settlement while Bromley's plans were
fresh in print. The Abbé Sigogne had initiated the Shubenacadie project, only
to see it completely taken over by Bromley. He was to try again, with greater
success, at Bear River. But the Catholics could not hope to emulate those who
were backed by leading colonials with apparently unlimited funds. Spiritual
weapons were the best counter against this drive to protestantize the Micmacs.
Resistance was a long time coming, and it was only after Bishop Plessis noted
on his travels that the children at Sussex Vale were doomed to become heretics
that one priest began to refuse the sacraments to the parents of those children.[79] On behalf of the New Brunswick commissioners, Jonathan Odell
wrote Plessis to put an end to such obstruction and appealed to him to
understand that the Sussex Vale experiment was carried on "dans l'esperance
de contribuer, peu à peu, à civiliser les pauvres sauvages de ce pays."† Plessis
gave him short shrift: the missionaries civilized by teaching the Indians to fear
God and serve Him; the clergy had every right to resist those who would
destroy the Indians' faith.[80]

Within a year of rebuffing Odell, the bishop was casting a jealous eye on
Walter Bromley's attempt to "decatholicize" the Indians of Nova Scotia. With
the "Methodist" Bromley in complete control of the settlement, Father
Vincent happily reported that the Indians were so angry at their chief for
accepting aid that they thought of killing him. But Chief Benjamin personally
won over Vincent by explaining: "The potatoes, cows, and other provisions of
Bromlet [*sic*] . . . are good. I have taken them and made use of them, but his
religion is worthless, I will have none of it." Benjamin then went before the
assembled Indians, repeated his explanation, professed his faith in the
Catholic Church, and so won them over too.[81]

Protestant efforts to convert the Micmacs had failed, and protestant
missionaries henceforth kept much to their own people. The Rev. Joshua
Marsden noted with some asperity that when he left England in 1822 prayers
were said for the success of his mission among the savages. He wished to make
it quite clear, he told those who read his reminiscences, "once for all, that the
Wesleyan missions in North America are not missions to [the] Indians of the
country but to the colonists." There simply was no time to spare.[82] An "Indian
Civilization Society" was formed at Pictou in 1828 to encourage agriculture,
discourage vice, and promote education among the Micmacs. An offshoot of
the local Auxiliary Bible Society, it apparently got no further than its
organizational meeting.[83] From Charlottetown, a Catholic layman, Thomas
Irwin, fought a lonely campaign in the early 1830's for the establishment of
"Philo-Indian Societies" with the same virtuous ends in view. A student of the
Micmac tongue, he was anxious to promote school books in Micmac of his
own devising, but since he planned to incorporate Catholic texts he ran afoul
of the protestants. He received no help from the Catholic clergy. The Micmacs

belonged to them, and to them alone.[84] In 1837 the *Christian Messenger* of Halifax gave its opinion that the moral state of the Indians had sunk beyond hope of redemption. When protestant missionary societies were formed, it said, they devoted themselves to the spiritual welfare of Hindus and Burmese and Africans.[85]

The only sustained challenge to this state of affairs came from the Micmac Missionary Society, an essentially one-man operation run by a Baptist minister, Silas Rand. A self-educated Nova Scotian who had mastered French, German, Latin, Greek, and Hebrew, he began to study Micmac in 1846. Sent to Charlottetown on a mission to the whites, he visited the local Micmacs to learn at first hand. By March, 1847, he was proposing to translate the Bible direct from Hebrew into Micmac.[86] When the mission to Charlottetown ran out of funds, he tried to convince his church to sponsor work among the Micmacs. They suggested he accept a call to Burma, but his wife put her foot down.[87] In 1849 he launched his Micmac Missionary Society at well-attended public meetings in Halifax and Charlottetown, seeking support on an interdenominational basis. He spoke at length on the history and customs of the Micmacs and the evil deeds of the whites who had taken their lands and given them only liquor and disease in return. He published the address in 1850.[88] For the next twenty years he toured the Maritimes on behalf of this mission. He reported regularly on the progress of his work and the extent of his translation of the Gospels. He brought encouraging news of awakening interest among the Indians: one had bought a Bible, another had made a donation to the cause. He told and retold the misdeeds of those who had dispossessed the Indians and urged the granting of adequate reserves to remedy these wrongs. His meetings often featured conversations in Micmac and a recital of Micmac melodies.[89] He was the first man to publicize the Micmacs amongst the whites, and he published an annual report to ensure the widest possible audience.[90]

For a few years Rand enjoyed interdenominational support until his own church abandoned him over the issue of the correct translation of the word "baptism."[91] This setback did not diminish his energy. Supported entirely by the money he was able to collect at his public appearances, the society began to purchase land at Hantsport for a school and "industrial establishment" where Indians would be encouraged to work by the receipt of good wages. A depot was set up in Halifax for the sale of their artifacts, but the enterprise seems to have been neither durable nor profitable.[92] Yet by 1856 the society had amassed 458 acres and grandiloquently named them "Mount Mic-mac." Rand reported that the Indians there were being instructed in "agricultural art and mechanical improvement." However, the school never was founded; the New England Company turned down his application for support.[93]

Rand frequently maintained that his prime object was to enable the Micmacs to read the Bible in their own language and that the Christian denomination they then chose was of no concern to him. But he was also convinced that any advance in the Micmacs' spiritual welfare could take place only within the context of their material well-being. His work inevitably aroused the opposition of the Catholic clergy. As Reverend James McDonald, missionary at Lennox Island, put it: "Education without religion makes man more powerful for evil." Rand's emphasis on material improvement could only undermine the Micmacs' faith, for they had been taught that their "poverty will not exclude [them] from the kingdom of heaven."[94] This fatalism was beyond Rand's understanding: did it mean that everything must always remain the same? The Indian "eats and sleeps in the midst of confusion— bundles, blankets, kettles, papooses and dogs tumbled pell mell, and huddled together amidst smoke and filth and vermin. . . . We seize upon their country. We rob them of their lands. We drive them from their homes." Have we no obligations to them?[95]

The Indians themselves resented Rand's attentions. He ran into great and predictable difficulties. "I am to explain to them the New Testament doctrine of Salvation through the atonement of the Redeemer. They refer to crossing themselves, to purgatory, and to the fasts of Friday."[96] Sometimes the Indians teased their would-be instructor:

> "Tell us," said one old man, "where is heaven."
> "It is above," said I. "And don't the earth turn over every day?" he rejoined. "Yes, it does." "Well then, if heaven is up at noon, where is it at midnight?" This was a difficulty, truly, but he seemed satisfied with my explanation.[97]

Another listened to Rand denouncing purgatory and masses for the dead and then remarked that it was not the custom of Indians to contradict a speaker. Whites might "learn a little good manners from them."[98] A correspondent from Liverpool reported to the *Halifax Catholic* that a "wild *hairy looking* character" had been annoying the local Indians, trying to get their money by pretending to sell them land at Mount Mic-Mac. The "Rev. Ranny" or "Mrs. Granny," as he was known, had departed and good riddance to him.[99] "'How long you intend to stop?' asked a shrewd fellow at Annapolis Gut. 'I don't know,' I replied; 'are you tired of me?' 'We been that all along. . . .'"[100] Rand faced physical violence as well as derision on these visits. Children at play would sound the alarm: "The devil is coming." Mothers appeared in doorways brandishing axes; men picked up clubs and threatened to turn the dogs on him. He recalled that his very first visits to the Indians near Charlottetown had been so perilous that he frequently went in fear of his life.[101]

Despite opposition, Rand seemed to be making significant progress with the recruitment of Ben Christmas, who became widely known as his "Micmac assistant." He was the only Micmac that any Christian sect ever entrusted with missionary work. Christmas had worked with Rand on the translation of the Gospel of St. Matthew as early as 1852, and he made his public debut in 1856. He gave an effective speech, in heavily accented English, on the material and moral plight of the Indians and their need to read the Scriptures to learn how to come to God.[102] He toured the Maritimes giving public addresses and accompanied Rand on a visit to the protestant Indians of Canada. In 1859 the Society hired him as a missionary at £125 a year. Like Rand, Christmas had to earn his salary out of the collection plate, and in his first year he took in £40 more than his stipend.[103] Then, disaster struck. He began to send the money direct to his wife and family and to use it to pay off debts. By 1861 he had left the society and was lecturing in his own right on Indian manners and customs.[104] From then on it was "poor Ben Christmas." He took to the bottle and became a regular in various police courts. In 1867 he joined a Temperance Society at Yarmouth and added a temperance lecture, "Alcohol and its Power," to his repertoire.[105] His fame was such that in 1870 he was reported to be out at Red River rebelling against the government, a charge he indignantly denied.[106] The degradation of Ben Christmas tarnished the whole mission. Rand suffered: he had placed his faith in conversion "only to be betrayed, and to result in bitter disappointment. Poor 'Ben Christmas' is of universal notoriety."[107]

Measured in terms of conversion, Rand's mission was an abject failure: the only Micmac he ever baptized was Susan, the long-suffering wife of Ben Christmas.[108] The true worth of Rand's work lay in his philological enthusiasms. His translation of St. Matthew's Gospel was printed in Charlottetown in 1852 and reprinted the following year. In 1854 he began an association with Pitman's in England (which was experimenting with phonetic spelling) and published the *Ferst ridin buk in Mikmak*. Pitman's subsequently brought out his translation of Saint Luke (sent Lwk) in 1856, of Genesis (Djenesis) in 1857, and the Psalms (samz) in 1859. Then there was a ten-year interval before the translations resumed in the 1870's. Rand published a dictionary of the Micmac language in 1888 with support from the dominion government. Undoubtedly his most famous work was the collection of Micmac tales that appeared posthumously, the result of over forty years of interviews and conversations with Micmacs in their camps.[109] "Devil books!" expostulated Mary Pictou when asked about Rand's work in 1923: "Was he not a Methodist clergyman? Devil books!"[110]

The Catholic Church had never shared protestant enthusiasm for the dissemination of the Bible, and the Indians Rand talked to had never heard of it as such. However, his success finally prompted a major Catholic effort to publish the Micmacs' book of devotions. Father Christian Kauder came to live at Tracadie in 1856 and set about the task. Rand had used the Roman alphabet, but Kauder made the important decision to retain Maillard's heiroglyphs for his work. It was an enormous undertaking for, quite apart from the translation, no less than 5,703 characters had to be especially cut for the printer. The work was financed by a grant from Ludwig-Verein in Vienna and appeared late in 1866. Most of the edition was lost in a shipwreck while on its way to Nova Scotia, and the text was not reprinted until 1921.[111]

Print did not preserve Catholicism amongst the Micmacs. They preserved that faith because it had become part of themselves. On 23 October 1867, Thomas Noel was crossing the railway tracks at the Richmond Railway Depot, Halifax. A runaway car pinned him against the wall of the freight office, and he was taken to hospital where he died within a few hours. The hospital physician spoke of his last moments in testimony before the Coroner's inquest. "The deceased was Sensible & Expressed a Wish to see a priest. The Priest was sent for, who administered to him the Rites of his Church."[112]

Many years separated the age of Membertou from the age of steam. Biard, LeClerq, and Maillard had done their work well.

Epilogue: The Last Hundred Years

The Micmacs had been in contact with Europeans for some 350 years, far longer than any other Indian people, by the time the colonial period in the Maritime provinces came to an end. The contact process had been spread out over generations. Almost one hundred years elapsed between the time the first Europeans touched the shore and the first French came to establish trading posts and mission stations. In the following century, whites made little impact on the face of the land; the handful of Acadian French were no challenge to the Micmacs. European goods and spiritual beliefs wrought changes in their society, but the Micmacs remained in control of their fate. After France ceded Acadia to Great Britain in 1713, the Micmacs fought the newcomers to a standstill. The British held only the semblance of sovereignty since they did not have the military strength to pave the way for settlement. Micmac resistance was successful only so long as Nova Scotia remained on the periphery of the British Empire, and it was broken once Halifax was created to fit into a global strategy. But even after their defeat in 1760, the consequences were postponed for another twenty years. It was not until 1783 that settlers arrived with such a surge that they swept away whatever stood before them.

The interval between the arrival of the first whites and the disruption of Indian life by extensive settlement has varied greatly across North America. Some Indians had only a few years to adapt to the new conditions; few had more than two or three generations. None had the long experience of the Micmacs in coping with changes introduced from the outside world. The very gradualness of white penetration into their homeland had allowed them to come to terms with change, to accept what they could use, to reject what they could not. They had traded as equals, received and modified Christianity, played white off against white, and fought for their territory. They had learned over centuries a resilience that other Indians had no time to acquire. This knowledge did not mean that they were able to retain control of their land in the face of a determined opponent, but it did allow them to retain their identity in the face of catastrophe.

After 1783 the Micmacs had to accept that they were under the political jurisdiction of three separate governments which responded to the interests of the settlers. The Micmacs' way of life was totally disrupted by settlement on farm and riverbank. They could no longer support themselves by fishing or hunting or trading. Colonists were concerned about this situation only sporadically, and then only in the context of how the Indians affected the "progress" of the colonies. The new authorities accepted that not even Indians should be allowed to starve and belatedly distributed a grudging relief to those whom progress had pauperized. The occasional attempts to assimilate the Micmacs into the sedentary farmer ideal of white society invariably foundered on their preference for the traditional life. They retained their mobility, the most cherished aspect of their past independence, and became peddlers of handicrafts and woodenware. They retained their own blend of Catholic Christianity which clearly marked them off from the protestant majority among the colonists. They maintained their tribal authority, with its structure of chiefs and captains chosen by election. They remained responsible to each other.

After Confederation, the new Dominion of Canada took sole responsibility for the administration of Indian peoples across its broad expanse, but this change had little practical effect on the Micmacs. Canada looked westward for its future, and the new Department of Indian Affairs was quickly preoccupied making treaties with prairie Indians to open new land for settlers. A bureaucracy that had to persuade many thousands of fierce and pagan warriors to give up their territory in peace had little time to spare for a tribe on the eastern fringes of the Dominion. The Micmacs were a harmless and tractable Christian people, few in numbers, who lived in an area long settled by the white man. They were no challenge to Canada, and they no longer held anything to covet.

It was not only the Micmacs who lived on the periphery of the new government's vision. Many white Maritimers felt that their whole area was slighted by the drive to the west, which absorbed a disproportionate amount of Canada's energies. There were some initial benefits for the region as the establishment of a rail link to central Canadian markets, coupled with preferential freight rates, led to rapid industrial development in the 1880's and 1890's. The population of towns quickened into life by the railways—Moncton, Amherst, New Glasgow, Sydney—almost doubled. Coal mines were expanded, steel factories and their attendant secondary industries came into production, and a host of smaller enterprises appeared to produce everything from textiles to pianos. But by 1900 many of these new ventures had fallen under the control of central Canadian business, which showed a tendency to close down its branch plants. Emigration told the story: some 150,000 left the region in the first twenty years of the century, mostly to the United States. In 1920 the preferential railway rates were abolished and the result was catastrophic: a further 150,000 left in the following ten years. Even before the onset of the Great Depression, the Maritime provinces had been effectively deindustrialized and indelibly stamped as the poorest part of Canada.[1]

The sudden rise and even swifter collapse of the Maritime economy were events that impinged on the lives of the Micmacs far more than any actions of the Department of Indian Affairs. Their fortunes reflected those of the community as a whole. They had long since learned to supplement the meagre support the land afforded by selling handicrafts or working, where possible, in the forest industry. The railways that brought prosperity to the region had an immediate impact, for whole bands camped near the various stations and found a new outlet for traditional wares by sales to passengers. Soon, the Micmacs were sharing in the general benefits of the railway. They took employment as labourers building and maintaining the lines, as stevedores offloading coal and iron ore at the ports, as workers in steel foundries, sawmills, and lobster canneries. The increase in coal production created a steady demand for pick handles, and, in another development of their wood-working skills, they began to make hockey sticks that were sold across Canada. The general collapse of the economy deprived the Micmacs of these various sources of income. The government agents who had recorded their entry into the industrial world had nothing to report in the 1920's. When the Depression came, those Indians who still had jobs were the first to be fired.[2] Admittedly, most of their work had been at the lowest end of the industrial scale, unskilled and seasonal. But that was to be the fate of all too many Maritimers, of whatever origin, all too soon.

As with other poor people, war offered the Micmacs a chance to escape from the grinding routine of poverty. Over 150 signed up during World War I, and enlistments in some areas were phenomenally high. Every eligible male Micmac in Sydney went to the front, as did thirty of the sixty-four adult males on Prince Edward Island.[3] For a few, the war presented opportunities of a different kind. Joe Cope invented a device that would allow aerial bombs to glide onto their targets; he sent the plans to the Ministry of Munitions in London, which rejected them but expressed its pleasure that "in such a far away spot as Mossman's Grant, the call is heard to do something for the good of the Empire."[4] Among the war casualties were eight Micmacs in a small settlement at Tuft's Cove, killed instantly in the explosion of a munitions ship that destroyed much of Halifax in 1917.[5] World War II saw no such domestic tragedies; its insatiable demands meant that there was once again employment for all on the farms, in the lumber camps, and even in the revitalized steel mills. In addition, some 250 men joined the armed forces, and officials described 1945 as the most prosperous year the Micmacs ever enjoyed.[6] Came the peace, and jobs disappeared as the veterans returned. Not surprisingly, over 60 Micmacs enlisted in the Canadian forces for service in Korea in the early 1950's.[7]

Following World War II, the Department of Indian Affairs made a determined effort to find work for the Micmacs. Each veteran was entitled to receive a house valued at $2,320, and these homes were built by Indians on their reserves from wood they cut and processed.[8] But such employment was limited and Micmacs began to seek work in the United States, taking advantage of their longstanding right of free access under Jay's Treaty of 1794. Individuals worked in factories and warehouses and on construction sites. Boston became a second home to many who worked there for years before retiring to the reserves, and in 1969 there were between two and three thousand Micmacs in the area.[9] Apart from these more or less permanent employments, seasonal work was available in the state of Maine. Families began to pick potatoes there in the early 1940's and continued to do so for almost twenty years before mechanization cut down the demand for labour. Blueberry picking continued strong into the mid-1970's. A "fair sized family" at the beginning of the decade could earn $500 a week for three weeks, but much of the money was advanced by growers before the season began and little went home with the workers themselves. Indian entrepreneurs recruited pickers from distant Nova Scotia and made "a substantial profit... by providing transportation, board and booze."[10]

With the single exception of veterans' housing, the Department of Indian Affairs did not take any responsibility for assisting the Micmacs to earn a living. The Indian Act of 1876, which established the department, had the "object of aiding the Indian to raise himself from the condition of tutelage and dependence; and of encouraging him to assume the privileges and responsibilities of full citizenship."[11] A bureaucracy's work inevitably falls into an administrative routine, and the Micmacs had little to be administered. Trust funds financed departmental spending. In 1895 the Indians of the Eel Ground had exactly $138.84 to their account, and the total for all the Indians in Nova Scotia was only $226.51.[12] The poverty of the Micmacs and their resulting lack of consequence to a bureaucracy can be seen from another set of figures taken at random. The average per capita value of all real and personal property held by the Indians of Nova Scotia in 1919 was $120.67, a stark contrast to the $2,121.78 average for the Alberta Indians that same year.[13] Officials spent little time on people of such small worth, as perfunctory and repetitious reports demonstrated year after year.

When the Department of Indian Affairs took over the responsibilities of the individual provinces, it tried to systematize the conduct of Indian policy. Nova Scotia was divided into nineteen administrative districts, each with a part-time official; New Brunswick was organized into three large areas with full-time officials, the northeast being exclusively Micmac, and the north and southwest departments predominantly Malecite; Prince Edward Island was accorded one agency located on Lennox Island. The first major change did not come until 1941, with the consolidation of the Nova Scotian agencies into two, at Eskasoni and Shubenacadie. Centralization, it was argued, would permit greater efficiency and the use of full-time officers. Under examination by a parliamentary committee, a rather embarrassed director of Indian Affairs admitted that the Indians had required considerable persuading to agree to this arrangement, but what could he do? He had received many complaints from whites living near small bands of Indians "about the moral relations, the temptations besetting their sons... really very, very disturbing."[14] Centralization was a failure. The various bands showed a tenacious desire to stay where they were throughout Nova Scotia. Nor did they welcome living close to each other: when Micmacs moved in to Eskasoni from Whycocomagh "fights were waged day and night."[15] By 1953 the department had given up its attempt to reduce the Indians to living in tidy administrative units.

The Micmacs had always refused to stay put on the reserves set aside for them by the old colonies, and they resisted the earnest desire of the Canadian government that they be sedentary. Settlement remained the touchstone by which the bureaucrats judged their success in helping the Indian "raise himself" in the community. Down to the 1950's one section of the required annual report was invariably headed "Progress of the Indians," and progress continued to mean settling on a farm on a reserve. But mobility remained the rule; in 1904, for example, five of the New Brunswick reserves were entirely devoid of Indians.[16] The "migratory habits" of these people, wandering at will throughout the Maritime provinces, remained a perennial source of complaint. Nothing happened to reverse the process, and in 1968 official statistics showed 693 Indian families in Nova Scotia living on reserves and 606 off; the figures for Prince Edward Island were 56 and 27 respectively, and amongst the New Brunswick Micmacs, 528 and 281. The failure of settlement as a policy was further emphasized by the fact that only 8 per cent of the reserve land had been cleared, and much less had been put into cultivation.[17]

The department devoutly hoped that Indians settled permanently on reserves would benefit from education as part of their preparation for a better life. Reservation schools came and went with monotonous regularity: a good start followed by more or less rapid oblivion. In 1908 there were seventeen such schools operating in the Maritime provinces, but their effect was minimal.[18] The dispersion of the Micmacs meant that at any given time at least half of their children attending school were in the regular provincial system. Few ever reached the eighth grade, and it was a rare year when one crossed that line. As late as 1949, with 1,035 Indians at school in the region, there were 22 children in Grade 8 and 6 in the higher grades.[19] Elsewhere in Canada, the department placed great faith in church-run boarding schools which would educate the children in white ways while keeping them separated from the corrupting influence of their parents. There was no such school in the Maritimes for years, although one, just across the border at Restigouche, Quebec, did enroll Micmacs.

In theory, sedentary life and education led to "enfranchisement"—assimilation into the white community. The Indian Act provided that once an Indian was capable of supporting himself and his dependents he could be "enfranchised," that is, given the full duties and responsibilities of Canadian citizenship. An Indian woman who married a white was enfranchised whether she wished it or not. The Department of Indian Affairs kept a register of all those with Indian status. When a person was enfranchised he or she left the reserve forever, taking a share of the band funds as an endowment, and was struck off the roll. Few Micmac men were enfranchised, but marriage removed some women from the bands every year. These women did not find it easy to assimilate into white society, and they and their children became a new group, non-status Indians. A considerable number of people who were culturally Micmac no longer counted as such because of a legal technicality in the Indian Act. Despite this continuing loss of women of child-bearing age, the registered Micmac population grew steadily. There were 4,706 in Nova Scotia and 440 in Prince Edward Island in 1970. New Brunswick, where Micmacs and Malecites were grouped together, accounted for a further 4,468. With a birthrate of 33.1 per thousand and a death rate of 7.6, their numbers were increasing by 2.4 per cent a year.[20] Law and policy had both failed to assimilate the Micmacs.

The Catholic Church continued to play an important part in the life of the Micmacs. St. Ann's Day has remained the high point of the year, with the festivities being held across the Maritimes. Towards the end of the nineteenth century the celebrations became something of a tourist spectacle and, consequently, a trying time for Indian department officials. The agent at Bear River noted in 1887, with a sigh of relief, that the day had passed "without any infringement of the law, which was something remarkable as there were over 1000 Indians and French assembled, besides the English sight-seers." A visitor to the Richibucto celebrations observed: "It would scarcely be an exaggeration to say that at this season all the men are making love to other men's wives or to single girls."[21] The religious character of the day was obviously in danger of being lost, but it was saved as the result of the efforts of the Reverend Father Pacifique. Early in the twentieth century, he established a mission at Restigouche and set about making it the focal point of Micmac life. The tercentenary of the baptism of Chief Membertou was celebrated there with great pomp in 1911. Father Pacifique published prayer books, hymnals, and catechisms in hieroglyphs and edited a Micmac language monthly, *Le Messager Micmac*.[22] He also wrote on the history of the people, but with a rather undue emphasis on the centrality of Restigouche to their life. At his passing, Restigouche dwindled in importance, and Chapel Island reasserted its primacy as a religious centre. Tragically, the church there, which contained the historic statue of St. Ann, was destroyed by fire during a lightning storm in December, 1976.

Micmac notions of Christianity continued to be a blend of traditional and acquired beliefs: St. Ann took on the role of a culture-hero. Interviewed in the year following the tercentenary celebrations, one woman explained that St. Ann had taught the Indians to weave moose hair. The saint was the wife of an Indian of very good family and mother of the Virgin Mary. "At her very first meeting with Micmac she told them that she wanted to show them how to do things and said she would like to meet them again on July 26."[23] More recently, there has been a renewed interest in the spiritual values of the Indians as they existed before the coming of the missionaries. Noel Knockwood of the Micmac Association for Cultural Studies eulogized the Great Spirit in a series of articles: "He made us Indians and treats us as such. He gradually shows himself to the Medicine Men in their vision quests. He tells them that he desires to free the Indians of their bondage." Such sentiments drew a rebuke from the missionary at Chapel Island, who feared that the Micmacs might be led astray: "We do not have a vague, wispy spirit but A Divine Person Who dwells in His Children, those who have accepted personally Jesus Christ as their own Lord and Savior."[24] The debate continues.

Knockwood's articles reflect the continent-wide resurgence amongst the Indians that began in the middle of this century. The Micmacs' self-esteem remained at a low ebb until late in the 1960's, and up to that time they appeared to accept their position as poor people on the extremities of Canada. Their passivity was shown, for example, by their failure to resort to court action to define their rights. Only twice did Micmacs challenge the many restrictions that obstructed their life. In the first case, in 1928, the defendant pleaded not guilty to a charge of hunting out of season by virtue of the 1752 treaty between Governor Hopson and Major Jean-Baptiste Cope that guaranteed his tribe "free liberty to hunt and fish as usual." The magistrate held that the treaty was local in character and in any case beyond Hopson's power to make.[25] The decision was not appealed, and it formed the precedent thirty years later for deciding against a New Brunswick Micmac who unsuccessfully pleaded his treaty rights when charged with violating fishery regulations.[26] There the matter rested. Micmac disinterest was clearly shown when the federal Indian Act was being revised in the late 1940's. A parliamentary committee heard or read thousands of pages of testimony from Indians in British Columbia, the Prairies, Ontario, and Quebec; two Micmac bands contributed a total of four pages of sparse comment on the narrowest of local interests.[27] When the enquiries were repeated for a further revision between 1959 and 1961, four volumes were filled with position papers and argument from Indian unions, associations, brotherhoods, and individuals: not one voice was raised from the Maritimes.[28]

As a result of that second round of parliamentary hearings, an Indian claims commission was created "to settle grievances and claims of Indian bands arising out of past transactions with the Crown."[29] The federal government was not impressed with what it learned and in 1969 proposed to move to complete assimilation by repealing the Indian Act, abolishing the Department of Indian Affairs, and giving the Indians full control over their reserves. Land claims presented in the previous five years were dismissed as too "general and undefined" and the treaties on which they were based were "limited and minimal promises" that could not be expanded.[30] The result was furor among the Indians across Canada. The National Indian Brotherhood was formed to refute the charges and demand the natives' right to a distinctive life within Canada. The government withdrew its proposals.

The Micmacs finally cast aside their lassitude. They were ready to accept the challenge hurled at all Indians: prove yourselves. The Micmacs discovered that they did have it within themselves to protest and that they did have leaders who could organize and direct their energies. Decision-making had been spread widely in the previous twenty years following changes in the Indian Act that saw elective band councils take a variety of responsibilities previously reserved for chief and government agent. Councils made by-laws concerning health, traffic, disorderly conduct, public works, and game and fish management. They also controlled the expenditure of reserve income, still meagre at $15,498 for the whole of the Maritimes in 1969 as compared to the Alberta Indians' $2.6 million.[31] This training in self-government was reinforced by an annual folk school sponsored by the department and St. Francis Xavier University to encourage "the development of the individual as a community leader."[32] Further, although the failure rate in school remained appallingly high, a few individuals, fifteen in 1968, were beginning to attend university.[33] The result was the appearance of a new young leadership typified by Chief Denis Nicholas: "Before ... you were that quiet Indian Chief who sat in the corner and didn't say a damned thing. That's finished."[34]

These new men had their chance because the federal government responded to the outrage it had generated by pouring money into Indian causes. A department whose budget had hovered around $5 million for years was handling $435 million in 1975 and providing services to the value of $2,000 for each Indian man, woman, and child in Canada. When other sources of government support were added in—family allowances, economic development and cultural grants, guaranteed mortgages and health care—that average rose to $2,500. Beginning in 1970, a five-year core programme to create Indian organizations and finance research cost a further $31 million.[35] The Micmacs received their fair share of this largesse, and people who previously handled tens of dollars were suddenly accounting for hundreds of thousands. The Union of Nova Scotia Indians was founded in 1969 and immediately argued that since aboriginal right to Nova Scotia had never been extinguished, the Micmacs were owed compensation for white use of the entire province. The Union of New Brunswick Indians followed in 1970 to "safeguard the aboriginal treaty and residual rights of the Indians of New Brunswick."[36] Both began to take over programmes of concern to their people: community development, education, alcohol and drug abuse treatment, treaty and rights research. Both received federal funding, $150,000 and $165,000 respectively in 1971.[37] The Union of Nova Scotia Indians' budget grew to $1,067,235 for the fiscal year ending 31 March 1975.[38]

The federal government also assumed responsibility for creating employment among the Indians. The unions and their ancillary services provided work for the new leadership, but this did not reach very far down into the community. A newly created Indian Economic Development Fund had, however, invested $3.5 million in Nova Scotia by the end of 1975 to start some sixty new enterprises including an oyster farm, a motel, auto-body shops, supermarkets, and a karate school. A good example of these new undertakings was the Glooscap Sawmill, owned and operated by the Shubenacadie band council, which paid each of its eighteen employees the same wages.[39] Similar investments were made in New Brunswick, yet the unemployment rate amongst Micmacs in 1977 was reported to be 94.3 per cent.[40]

According to the Indian unions, the only answer to the problem of unemployment lay in the satisfaction of their land claims. These fell into three broad categories: for land which belonged to the Indians by aboriginal right and had been taken from them before the Royal Proclamation of 1763; for land taken from them by the colonies after the Proclamation had established the usufructuary right of the Indians under English law; and for land taken by Canada following Confederation. There were also specific claims against power companies and highway departments that had obtained rights-of-way on Indian land and also claims for the right to hunt and fish without government regulation. The assembling and documentation of these claims was a monumental task, and a proportion of it was done by whites hired for the purpose, new advocates of Indian rights who filled the role once played by missionaries. The value of this extensive research was demonstrated when it proved that 3,000 acres of the Big Cove reserve had been taken over illegally by the federal government in 1879. Only eleven members of the band had put their mark to the deed, and experts testified that the marks were forged. Half the acreage was promptly returned, but the future of the remainder, owned by white farmers, was left undecided.[41] The 4,500 acres of the Wagamatcook reserve had been whittled down to 650 when a rapid tourist development that included a motel and a Lick-a-Chick restaurant alerted the local Indians to their loss. The band council put in a claim, proved it, and were offered $1 million in compensation by the federal government. They refused, insisting on the return of the precise land in contention.[42]

A heightened awareness of grievance raised the possibility of direct action by various groups. When offered $900 for nine acres of the Gold River reserve needed for road widening, the local band demanded $200,000 and threatened to block the existing highway if its price was not met.[43] In April, 1975, some armed Micmacs took over Muless Island in Merigomish harbour and promised to stay until their claims were recognized. The department agreed that the island probably was reserve land, and the owner, whose title went back to a crown grant of 1761, offered to sell out. The Indians retired after a week, claiming victory.[44] In a somewhat similar exploit, Chief Peter Barlow, in full regalia, staged a media event when he occupied Indian Island in the Richibucto River with a force consisting of Micmacs, journalists, and a television camera crew.[45] Compared to the demonstrations and activism elsewhere in Canada, the Micmacs asserted themselves peacefully.

By October, 1973, the Union of Nova Scotia Indians had filed fifty-six claims for redress for the illegal use of Indian lands.[46] In January, 1974, the union launched its campaign for "a formal claim to aboriginal title for all of Nova Scotia," listed seventy-five properties being used illegally by whites, and demanded compensation for damages arising out of "a phase of cultural genocide . . . in the centralization of the 1940s." Delegates met the provincial cabinet in October and five months later had a formal hearing with the Indian Claims Commission in Ottawa.[47] The Union of New Brunswick Indians was further behind and launched only thirteen land claims between 1971 and 1975.[48] Prince Edward Island did not create its own Indian union, although non-status people there were organized.

The cause of native rights received powerful support in 1975 when the Appeals Division of the Nova Scotia Supreme Court reversed the conviction of an Indian for having a rifle in his possession on a reserve, contrary to the Lands and Forests Act. Chief Justice MacKeigan held that the provincial law did not apply because the Indian had "a usufructuary right in the reserve land" by virtue of the Royal Proclamation of 1763. MacKeigan went further and found that British title to Nova Scotia was defective because, in acquiring the land from France, no attention had been paid to the "burden of Indian rights" that overlay that title. In other words, neither France nor Britain had ever extinguished Indian rights in the Maritime provinces.[49] This was the first time that any court had construed the Proclamation as applying to the Maritime region. The proposition that the Indian unions had been advancing now had full judicial backing.

Pointedly enough, the Union of New Brunswick Indians took the opportunity of Queen Elizabeth II's visit to Fredericton to present her with a copy of her predecessor's Proclamation.[50] The Union of Nova Scotia Indians pressed on with compiling its claims, which now included a demand for immediate "managerial control" of provincial crown lands.[51] The completed claim, entitled "Nova Scotia Micmac Aboriginal Rights Position Paper," was presented to the minister of Indian affairs, Warren Allmand, at Eskasoni on 25 April 1977.[52]

The position paper was an exhaustive review, some 130,000 words in length, of the Micmacs and their rights. Chapters dealt with the prehistory, anthropology, history, and legal position of the tribe and MacKeigan's recent judgment was reprinted in full. The bulk of the material was excerpted from studies by contemporary scholars. Both the force and quantity of the argument was impressive:

The Micmac concept that the free use and occupancy of the land, air, water and its resources to maintain a [*sic*] Social—Economic—Cultural—Educational and Political areas of Micmac life has anthropologically, historically and legally been accepted. [The Canadian government] must compensate for Micmac aboriginal title by guaranteeing through statute, aboriginal rights in the cultural, social, economic and political fields. These aboriginal rights must compensate for the loss of a way of life *and* must contribute positively to a lasting solution of cultural, social, economic and political concerns *as felt and as advanced by the Micmacs* of Nova Scotia.

The minister received the claim courteously. It would, he said, "be processed through regular federal channels."

Appendix

Micmac Indian Reserves
in the Maritime Provinces, 1972

NEW BRUNSWICK

Reserve	No.	Band	Location	Acreage (approx.)
Big Hole Tract (North part)	8	Red Bank	13 miles west of Newcastle, on east bank of Northwest Miramichi River	3,450
Big Hole Tract (South part)	8	Eel Ground	13 miles west of Newcastle, on east bank of Northwest Miramichi River	4,300
Buctouche	16	Buctouche	2 miles southwest of Buctouche, on north shore of Buctouche River	137
Burnt Church	14	Burnt Church	20 miles northeast of Chatham, on north shore of Burnt Church River	2,052
Eel Ground	2	Eel Ground	3 miles west of Newcastle, on north bank of Northwest Miramichi	2,651
Eel River	3	Eel River	2 miles south of Dalhousie, on north bank of Eel River	240
Indian Island	28	Indian Island	5 miles northeast of Rexton, on south bank of Richibucto River	100
Indian Point	1	Red Bank	12 miles west of Newcastle; 1 mile northeast of Little Southwest and Northwest Miramichi rivers	600
Pabineau	11	Pabineau	5 miles south of Bathurst and along both banks of Nepisiquit River	1,053
Palmers Pond	1	Fort Folly	One mile southeast of Dorchester	100
Pokemouche	13	Burnt Church	7 miles west of Inkerman, on south shore of Pokemouche River	680

Reserve	No.	Band	Location	Acreage (approx.)
Red Bank	4	Red Bank	14 miles west of Newcastle and south of junction of Little Southwest and North-west Miramichi rivers	3,600
Red Bank	7	Red Bank	15 miles west of Newcastle and 3 miles northwest of junction of Little Southwest and North-west Miramichi rivers	2,500
Renous	12	Eel Ground	17 miles southwest of New-castle; 1 mile east of junction of the Renous and main South-west Miramichi rivers	25
Richibucto	15	Big Cove	5 miles southwest of Rexton on north shore of Richibucto River	2,940
Tabusintac	9	Burnt Church	25 miles northeast of Chatham; 5 miles west of Tabusintac and along both banks of the Tabusintac River	8,077

NOVA SCOTIA

Reserve	No.	Band	Location	Acreage (approx.)
Bear River	6	Bear River	On the Bear River; on the Digby-Annapolis Co. Line; 11 miles southeast of Digby	1,594
Bear River	6A	Bear River	Near Annapolis Royal; adjoins Grand Lake on the south	196.2
Beaver Lake	17	Truro	49 miles northeast of Halifax on road from Sheet Harbour to Upper Musquodoboit	100
Boat Harbour West	37	Pictou Landing	5 miles north of New Glasgow near C.N. Railway	200
Cambridge	32	Annapolis Valley	Near Cambridge Station; 55 miles northwest of Halifax	37
Caribou Marsh	29	Sydney	5 miles southwest of Sydney	536
Chapel Island	5	Chapel Island	Island near south shore Bras d'Or Lake, 43 miles southwest of Sydney	1,233
Cole Harbour	30	Truro	6 miles east of Halifax at Minister Lake	44

Reserve No.	No.	Band	Location	Acreage (approx.)
Eskasoni	3	Eskasoni	On north shore of east Bay of Bras d'Or Lake; 25 miles southwest of Sydney	8,660
Eskakoni	3A	Eskasoni	On peninsula on north shore of east Bay of Bras d'Or Lake; 25 miles southwest of Sydney	68
Fishers Grant	24	Pictou Landing	On south shore of entrance to Pictou Harbour; 6 miles north of New Glasgow	241
Fishers Grant	24G	Pictou Landing	On southeast shore of Boat Harbour, 2 miles southeast of Pictou Landing, Pictou County	142
Franklin Manor	22	Afton 48% Pictou Landing 52%	West of Hebert River, 20 miles southwest of Amherst	1,000
Gold River	21	Acadia	On west bank of Gold River, near northwest shore of Mahone Bay; 38 miles west of Halifax	900
Horton	35	Annapolis Valley	West of Avon River, 43 miles northwest of Halifax	423
Malagawatch	4	Sydney, Eskasoni, Chapel Island, Middle River, Whycocomagh	At entrance of Denys Bay on Bras d'Or Lake; 39 miles southwest of Sydney	1,634
Margaree	25	Middle River	Near junction of southwest and northwest Margaree rivers; 43 miles northwest of Sydney	2
Medway River	11	Acadia	On west bank of Medway River at outlet of Ponhook Lake; 68 miles southwest of Halifax	10
Merigomish Harbour	31	Pictou Landing	Two islands in Merigomish Harbour; 8 miles east of New Glasgow	35
Middle River	1	Middle River	At mouth of Middle River; 32 miles west of Sydney	833
Millbrook	27	Truro	5 miles south of Truro on east side of C.N. Railway	760
New Ross	20	Shubenacadie	At Walaback Lake, 40 miles northwest of Halifax	1,000
Pennal	19	Shubenacadie	At west end of Walaback Lake, 47 miles northwest of Halifax	100

Reserve	No.	Band	Location	Acreage (approx.)
Pomquet & Afton	23	Afton	7 miles west of Inkerman, on south shore of Pokemouche River	500
Ponhook Lake	10	Acadia	On east bank of Medway River at outlet of Ponhook Lake; 68 miles southwest of Halifax	200
Port Hood	26	Whycocomagh	Near Port Hood, south of Margaree #25	Undetermined
St. Croix	34	Annapolis Valley	At north end of Lake St. Croix; 29 miles northwest of Halifax	263
Sheet Harbour	36	Truro	On both shores of Sheet Harbour; 57 miles northeast of Halifax	77
Shubenacadie (Grand Lake)	13	Shubenacadie	On west shore of Shubenacadie Lake, just south of Hants-Halifax line, 20 miles north of Halifax	1,018
Shubenacadie (Indian Brook)	14	Shubenacadie	3 miles west of Shubenacadie River; 18 miles southwest of Truro	2,957
Sydney	28A	Sydney	2 miles east of Sydney Harbour; 1 mile northeast of city of Sydney	15
Sydney	28B	Sydney	1 mile east of Sydney Harbour; 1 mile south of city of Sydney	66
Truro	27A	Truro	Adjoins south limit of Corporation of Truro	40
Truro	27B	Truro	Adjoins Truro Indian Reserve No. 27A on the south	40
Truro	27C	Truro	Adjoins Truro Indian Reserve No. 27B on the south	40
Whycocomagh	2	Whycocomagh	At southwest end of St. Patrick Channel; 44 miles west of Sydney	2,043
Wildcat	12	Acadia	On Wildcat River, west of Malaga Lake and north of Ponhook Lake; 69 miles southwest of Halifax	1,150
Yarmouth	33	Acadia	2 miles east of Yarmouth	21

PRINCE EDWARD ISLAND

Reserve	No.	Band	Location	Acreage (approx.)
Lennox Island	1	Lennox Island Abegweit	15 miles north of Summerside at northwest end of Malpeque Bay	1,320
Morell	2	Lennox Island	24 miles northeast of Charlottetown on Morell River	198
Rocky Point	3	Lennox Island	On south shore of Charlottetown Harbour	3
Scotch Fort	4	Lennox Island	15 miles northeast of Charlottetown on the Hillsborough River	140

Source: Department of Indian Affairs and Northern Development, *Schedule of Indian Reserves and Settlements* (Ottawa, 1972), Part 1, pp. 276–90.

Letter of Chief Pemmeenauweet to Queen Victoria

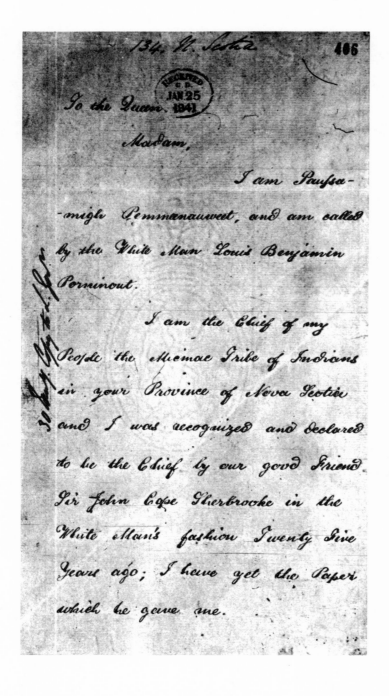

134. N. Scotia   406

To the Queen.

    Madam,

        I am Pausa-
migh Pemmenauweet, and am called
by the White Man Louis Benjamin
Porminout.

        I am the Chief of my
People the Micmac Tribe of Indians
in your Province of Nova Scotia
and I was recognized and declared
to be the Chief by our good Friend
Sir John Cope Sherbrooke in the
White Man's fashion Twenty Five
Years ago; I have yet the Paper
which he gave me.

Sorry to hear that the King is dead. Am glad to hear that we have a good Queen whose Father I saw in this Country. He loved the Indians.

I cannot cross the great Lake to talk to you for my Canoe is too small, and I am old and weak. I cannot look upon you for my eyes not see so far. You cannot hear my voice across the Great Waters. I therefore send this Wampum and Paper talk to tell the Queen I am in trouble. My people are in trouble. I have seen upwards of a

407

Thousand Moons. When I was young I had plenty: now I am old, poor and sickly too. My people are poor. No Hunting Grounds — No Beaver — no Otter — no nothing. Indians poor — poor for ever. No Store — no Chest — no Clothes. All these Woods once ours. Our Fathers possessed them all. Now we cannot cut a Tree to warm our Wigwam in Winter unless the White Man please. The Micmacs now receive no presents, but one small Blanket for a whole family. The Governor is a good man but he cannot help us now. We look to you the

Queen. The White Waumpum tell that we hope in you. Pity your poor Indians in Nova Scotia.

White Man has taken all that was ours. He has plenty of everything here. But we are told that the White Man has sent to you for more. No wonder that I should speak for myself and my people.

The man that takes this talk over the great Water will tell you what we want to be done for us. Let us not perish. Your Indian Children love you, and will fight for you against all

your

.408

your enemies.

My Head and my Heart
shall go to One above for you.

Pausauhmigh Pemmcenau-
-weet, Chief of the Micmac
Tribe of Indians in Nova Scotia
His mark

✝

This was signed in my presence,
as witness

Goram, Second Chief of the
Micmacs His mark

#

And in mine

Francois, first Captain of
the Micmac Warriors, His
mark ✝

Abbreviations

AAQ	Archives de l'archdiocese de Québec, Quebec
AC	Archives des Colonies, Bibliothèque National, Paris
APS Papers	Papers of the British and Foreign Anti-Slavery and Aborigines' Protection Societies, Oxford
ASQ	Archives du Seminaire de Québec, Québec
CASNPF	Canadian Association in Support of Native Peoples Files
CMNF	*Collection de Manuscrits ... historiques relatifs à la Nouvelle-France, recueillis aux Archives de la Province de Québec ou copiés à l'étranger*
CO.	Colonial Office Series, PRO, London
DIAAR	Department of Indian Affairs Annual Report, Ottawa
HAR	Halifax Archdiocesan Records, Halifax
HILA	Harriet Irving Library Archives, University of New Brunswick
JLANB	Journals of the Legislative Assembly of New Brunswick
JLANS	Journals of the Legislative Assembly of Nova Scotia
JLAPEI	Journals of the Legislative Assembly of Prince Edward Island
JLCNS	Journals of the Legislative Council of Nova Scotia
NBHS	New Brunswick Historical Society, Saint John
NBM	New Brunswick Museum, Saint John
NEC	New England Company Papers, Guildhall Library, London
NSM	Nova Scotia Museum, Halifax
PAC	Public Archives of Canada, Ottawa
PANB	Provincial Archives of New Brunswick, Fredericton
PANL	Provincial Archives of Newfoundland and Labrador, St. John's
PANS	Public Archives of Nova Scotia, Halifax
PAPEI	Public Archives of Prince Edward Island, Charlottetown
PR	Moses Perley, *Reports on Indian Settlement*
PRO	Public Records Office, London
SPG	Society for the Propagation of the Gospel
SRO	Scottish Records Office, Edinburgh
RAPQ	Rapport de l'Archiviste de la Province de Québec

Notes

NOTES TO CHAPTER ONE

1. Marc Lescarbot, *Nova Francia: A Description of Acadia*, ed. H. P. Biggar and trans. P. Erondelle (1609; London: Routledge, 1928), p. 84. The standard work on the Micmacs is W. D. Wallis and R. S. Wallis, *The Micmac Indians of Eastern Canada* (Minneapolis: University of Minnesota Press, 1955). Alfred G. Bailey, *The Conflict of European and Eastern Algonkian Cultures 1504-1700*, 2d ed. (Toronto: University of Toronto Press, 1969), is an excellent study of the early period. For a brief but comprehensive review of the factors involved in white contact, see Calvin Martin, "The European Impact on the Culture of a Northeastern Algonquian Tribe: An Ecological Interpretation," *William and Mary Quarterly*, n.s. 31 (1974): 3–26, and his *Keepers of the Game* (Berkeley and Los Angeles: University of California Press, 1978). Bernard G. Hoffman's doctoral dissertation, "The Historical Ethnography of the Micmac of the Sixteenth and Seventeenth Centuries" (University of California, Berkeley, 1955) is an admirable work of such massive proportions as to beggar description. Harold F. McGee, "Ethnic Boundaries and Strategies of Ethnic Interaction: A History of Micmac–White Relations in Nova Scotia" (Ph.D. diss., Southern Illinois University, 1963), provides an interpretative overview of the subject.

2. John M. Hooper, "The Culture of Northeastern Indian Hunters: A Reconstructive Interpretation," in *Man in Northeastern North America*, ed. Frederick Johnson (Andover, Mass.: Phillips Academy, 1946), pp. 272–305; R. G. Thwaites, ed. *The Jesuit Relations and Allied Documents*, 73 vols. (Cleveland: Burrows, 1886–91), 2: 73; 3: 105. Hoffman, "Ethnography," p. 230, suggests

6,000, and Henry F. Dobyns, "Estimating Aboriginal American Population," *Current Anthropology* 7 (1966): 395–416, advances a "hemispheric average population density" that would put the Micmac population at the high figure of 100,000. A more modest estimate of 35,000 is made by Virginia Miller, "Aboriginal Micmac Population: A Review of the Evidence," *Ethnohistory* 23 (1976): 117–27.

3. The hunting life is described in *Jesuit Relations*, 3: 79–83; and in Nicolas Denys, *The Description and Natural History of the Coasts of North America (Acadia)*, ed. William F. Ganong (Toronto: Champlain Society, 1908), pp. 428–35. See also Hoffman, "Ethnography," pp. 129–32.

4. Lescarbot, *Acadia*, p. 131.

5. Denys, *Acadia*, p. 405; *Jesuit Relations*, 2: 167; 3: 109.

6. Virgil J. Vogel, *American Indian Medicine* (Norman: University of Oklahoma Press, 1970), pp. 152, 159.

7. Lescarbot, *Acadia*, pp. 192, 197, 198; *Jesuit Relations*, 3: 74.

8. *Jesuit Relations*, 8: 159; Denys, *Acadia*, p. 411; Lescarbot, *Acadia*, pp. 187–88, 189, 192–93, 195, 204, 211.

9. Lescarbot, *Acadia*, p. 148; Denys, *Acadia*, pp. 400–403; Sieur de Dièreville, *Relation of the Voyage to Port Royal in Acadia or New France*, ed. J.C. Webster (Toronto: Champlain Society, 1933), pp. 146, 155; Father Chrestien Le Clerq, *New Relation of Gaspesia*, ed. W. F. Ganong (Toronto: Champlain Society, 1910), pp. 118–21.

10. Lescarbot, *Acadia*, p. 218; Hoffman, "Ethnography," p. 590; Frank G. Speck, "The Family Hunting Band as the Basis of Algonkian Social Organization," in *Cultural Ecology*, ed. Bruce Cox (Toronto: McClelland and Stewart, 1973),

pp. 58–75. For a study of a neighbouring people, see Eleanor Leacock, "The Montagnais-Naskapi Band," ibid., pp. 81–100.

11. Dièreville, *Relation*, p. 142; Lescarbot, *Acadia*, pp. 216, 219; Denys, *Acadia*, pp. 407–10; Bailey, *Conflict*, p. 104.

12. Lescarbot, *Acadia*, pp. 220, 222, 252, 253; Denys, *Acadia*, p. 409; LeClerq, *Gaspesia*, pp. 100, 227–28; Dièreville, *Relation*, p. 162.

13. Lescarbot, *Acadia*, pp. 151, 252; Denys, *Acadia*, pp. 403–4; Le Clerq, *Gaspesia*, pp. 89, 228–29; Dièreville, *Relation*, p. 146.

14. Denys, *Acadia*, p. 404; Lescarbot, *Acadia*, pp. 152, 253; Dièreville, *Relation*, pp. 145, 147–48.

15. *Jesuit Relations*, 3: 93; A. I. Hallowell, "Some Psychological Characteristics of the Northeastern Indian," in *Man in Northeastern North America*, pp. 195–225; LeClerq, *Gaspesia*, pp. 242–43.

16. LeClerq, *Gaspesia*, pp. 101–2; *Jesuit Relations*, 1: 75; 3: 87–89, 101; Hoffman, "Ethnography," pp. 574–75; Francis Jennings, *The Invasion of America: Indians, Colonialism and the Cant of Conquest* (Chapel Hill: University of North Carolina Press, 1975), pp. 102–3.

17. Hoffman, "Ethnography," pp. 522–72.

18. LeClerq, *Gaspesia*, pp. 192–93; Lescarbot, *Acadia*, p. 84.

19. Lescarbot, *Acadia*, pp. 98–101, 308; LeClerq, *Gaspesia*, p. 269.

20. Dièreville, *Relation*, pp. 163–64.

21. Lescarbot, *Acadia*, pp. 308, 309, 311, 312, 314; Hoffman, "Ethnography," pp. 649, 658–59.

22. Hoffman, "Ethnography," p. 420; Martin, European Impact," passim; Bailey, *Conflict*, pp. 136, 143: Denys, *Acadia*, p. 419; Samuel de Champlain, *The Works of Samuel Champlain*, ed. H. P. Biggar, 6 vols. (Toronto: Champlain Society, 1912–36), 1: 317.

23. Bailey, *Conflict*, p. 136; *Jesuit Relations*, 2: 75.

24. Vogel, *Indian Medicine*, pp. 24–25; Bailey, *Conflict*, p. 75; Dièreville, *Relation*, pp. 176–77; LeClerq, *Gaspesia*, pp. 90, 275, 297, 299; Denys, *Acadia*, p. 416; *Jesuit Relations*, 3: 115; 2: 279.

25. *Jesuit Relations*, 1: 259, 2: 147; Denys, *Acadia*, pp. 417–18; Lescarbot, *Acadia*, pp. 173, 238–39; Bailey, *Conflict*, p. 80; Hallowell, "Some Psychological Characteristics," passim.

26. LeClerq, *Gaspesia*, pp. 220–23.

27. Lescarbot, *Acadia*, p. 173; Dièreville, *Relation*, pp. 157–58.

28. LeClerq, *Gaspesia*, p. 136; Bailey, *Conflict*, pp. 97, 138; Hoffman, "Ethnography," pp. 370–72.

29. LeClerq, *Gaspesia*, p. 144; Hoffman, "Ethnography," pp. 388–89.

30. *Jesuit Relations*, 2: 77; 3: 127–31; LeClerq, *Gaspesia*, p. 300; Champlain, *Works*, 1: 444–46; Denys, *Acadia*, pp. 437–38.

31. Denys, *Acadia*, p. 438; LeClerq, *Gaspesia*, pp. 299–302; *Jesuit Relations*, 1: 203.

32. Champlain, *Works*, 1: 444–46; Lescarbot, *Acadia*, pp. 318–28.

NOTES TO CHAPTER TWO

1. Robert F. Berkhoffer, *Salvation and the Savage* (Lexington: University of Kentucky Press, 1965), p. ix.

2. *Jesuit Relations*, 3: 111.

3. LeClerq, *Gaspesia*, p. 116; *Jesuit Relations*, 2: 79.

4. Lescarbot, *Acadia*, pp. 161–63.

5. *Jesuit Relations*, 6: 231; 3: 12.

6. Champlain, *Works*, 1: 272.

7. Ibid., p. 292.

8. Lescarbot, *Acadia*, p. 24.

9. Ibid., p. 139.

10. Ibid., p. 260; LeClerq, *Gaspesia*, pp. 104–5.

11. *Jesuit Relations*, 3: 123.

12. Denys, *Acadia*, pp. 445–49.

13. Ibid.

14. Bailey, *Conflict*, pp. 13, 14, 46–52; Denys, *Acadia*, pp. 399–422; Martin, "European Impact," passim; Leacock, "Montagnais-Naskapi Band," passim.

15. Eleanor Leacock, *The Montagnais "Hunting Territory" and the Fur Trade*, American Anthropological Association Memoir 78, [1954]; Rolf Knight, "A Reexamination of Hunting, Trapping, and Territoriality among the Northeastern Algonkian Indians," in *Man, Culture*

and Animals: The Role of Animals in Human Ecological Adjustments, ed. A. Leeds and A. P. Vayda, American Association for the Advancement of Science Publication 78 (Washington, D.C.: the Association, 1965), pp. 27–42.

16. LeClerq, *Gaspesia*, p. 246; *Dièreville*, Relation, pp. 150–52.

17. For an overview of the missionary impact, see Robert Conkling, "Legitimacy and Conversion in Social Change: The Case of French Missionaries and the Northeastern Algonkian," *Ethnohistory* 21 (1974): 1–24.

18. Angus A. Johnston, *A History of the Catholic Church in Eastern Nova Scotia*, 2 vols. (Antigonish, N.S.: St. Francis Xavier University Press, 1960, 1972), 1: 8–25.

19. LeClerq, *Gaspesia*, pp. 288–89.

20. *Jesuit Relations*, 2: 89, 155.

21. Ibid., 1: 167.

22. LeClerq, *Gaspesia*, pp. 172–75.

23. *Jesuit Relations*, 2: 19.

24. Ibid., 3: 269.

25. Ibid., 2: 53.

26. Ibid., 3: 145.

27. Ibid., 8: 160.

28. LeClerq, *Gaspesia*, p. 220; Bailey, *Conflict*, p. 145.

29. LeClerq, *Gaspesia*, p. 220.

30. Ibid., pp. 229–33.

31. [Pierre Maillard], *An Account of the Customs and Manners of the Mickmackis and Maricheets, Savage Nations*

(London: Hooper and Morley, 1758), p. 37.

32. Bailey, *Conflict*, p. 137; Cornelius Jaenen, *Friend and Foe* ([Toronto]: McClelland and Stewart, 1976), pp. 50–57, 65.

33. Lescarbot, *Acadia*, p. 183.

34. *Jesuit Relations*, 2: 9.

35. Ibid., 3: 247.

36. Ibid., 8: 169.

37. Ibid., 2: 11, 73.

38. See pp. 169–70.

39. Bailey, *Conflict*, pp. 100, 135, 140.

40. *Jesuit Relations*, 3: 73.

41. LeClerq, *Gaspesia*, pp. 126–35; Martin, "European Impact," passim.

42. The best brief account of early Acadia is in Andrew H. Clark, *Acadia: The Geography of Early Nova Scotia to 1760* (Madison: University of Wisconsin Press, 1968).

43. Ibid., pp. 113–21.

44. Ibid., pp. 91, 115; Jaenen, *Friend or Foe*, p. 160.

45. The purchase was never completed (W. F. Ganong, "Richard Denys, Sieur de Fronsac, and his Settlements in Northern New Brunswick," New Brunswick Historical Society, *Collections* 7 [1907]: 7–54).

46. Rameau de Saint Père, *Une Colonie féodale en Amérique, L'Acadie 1604–1881*, 2 vols. (Paris: E. Plon, Nourrit et Cie, 1889), 1: 205–10.

NOTES TO CHAPTER THREE

1. Jérome Phélypeaux, Comte de Pontchartrain, minister of marine, to Governor Phillippe Rigaud de Vaudreuil, 29 March 1713; Pontchartrain to Father Antoine Gaulin, 29 March 1713, MG1, series 2, B series, transcripts, 35: 3, pp. 158–69, 179–83, PAC. For an account of Micmac resistance and its connection with the French, see Olive M. Dickason, *Louisbourg and the Indians: A Study in Imperial Race Relations 1713–1760* (Ottawa: National Historic Parks and Sites Branch, 1976).

2. Minister of marine to Baron de St. Castin, 8 April 1713, MG1, series 2, B series, transcripts, 35: 3, pp. 188–89, PAC. I have used the translation in the

Public Archives of Canada, *Report 1889* (Ottawa, 1890), supplement, p. 648, which is somewhat more eloquent than the original.

3. Minister of marine to Governor Philippe de Costebelle, 4 June 1715, ibid., 37: 3, pp. 828–52. "With much discretion and secrecy in order to give the English no occasion to complain."

4. For example, Lieutenant-Governor John Doucett to Vaudreuil, 15 April 1718; Governor Brouillon de St. Ovide to Doucett, 21 July 1718, CO. 217/31, ff. 71–75.

5. "Council sur les Sauvages," 4 December 1716, AC, C11B, vol. 2, ff. 54–60, microfilm, PAC: Le Normant de Mézy to

council, 27 December 1722, ibid., vol. 6, ff. 72–76.

6. St. Ovide to minister, 1 November 1729 and 18 October 1733, ibid., vol. 10, ff. 114–20, vol. 14, ff. 83–90; president of Navy Board to M. Le Normant, 27 April 1734, ibid., B, vol. 61, ff. 587–89; "Memoire sur les Mikmaques," c. 1739, unsigned, ibid., C11B, vol. 1, pt. 2, ff. 384–97; "Description de l'Acadie" and "Documents sur l'Acadie," *Le Canada-Français* 1 (1888): 44–47.

7. "Lettre du M. L'Abbe Maillard," in *Les Soirées Canadiennes*, ed. H. Casgrain (1863): 294. "It is necessary that I encourage them continually to practise religious acts, that I make them as much as can be, tractable, sociable, faithful to the King our prince, of whom they have constantly a high and sublime notion, people of integrity, and especially that I apply myself to making them live on good terms with the French."

8. Micheline Dumont Johnson. *Apôtres ou Agitateurs* (Trois Rivières: Boreal Express, 1970), p. 77. This book is a study of the role of the missionaries in eighteenth-century Acadia. "An almost-savage, one of their own in some way."

9. Gaulin to [St. Ovide], 17 November 1719, AC, C11B, vol. 4, ff. 132–37.

10. "Memoire sur les Mikmaques," ff. 384–97.

11. Maillard, "Lettre," pp. 355–58, 364. "They would doubtless abuse this knowledge . . . to know evil things rather than good ones."

12. Governor Pierre-Auguste de Soubras to minister of marine, 4 December 1716, AC, C11B, vol. 1, pt. 2, ff. 588–91; "As much by drunkenness as by the continual frequenting of the French houses by the women." "Council sur les Sauvages," ibid., vol. 2, ff. 54–60.

13. Gaulin to Doucett, 13 March 1722, CO. 217/4, ff. 132–34; Le Normant de Mézy to council, 12 December 1722, AC, C11B, vol. 6, ff. 69–71.

14. St. Ovide to minister, 24 December 1724 and 10 December 1725, ibid., vol. 7, ff. 33–41, 149–52; Jean Frédéric Phélypeaux de Maurepas, minister of marine, to St. Ovide, 28 May 1726, ibid., B, vol. 49, ff. 705–7. "To send them to disturb the English."

15. D. C. Harvey, *The French Régime in Prince Edward Island* (New Haven: Yale University Press, 1926), p. 226.

16. "Memoire sur les Mikmaques," ff. 384–97.

17. Le Loutre to unknown, 1 October 1738, "Documents sur l'Acadie," pp. 19–25. "The combination of savage inconstancy, fickleness and sloth, aggravated by their trade with the French."

18. Johnson, *Apôtres*, p. 86.

19. St. Ovide to council, 5 September 1720, 15 September 1721, AC, C11B, vol. 5. ff. 56–60, 147–52.

20. Maillard, "Lettre," pp. 338–40, 346. "to preserve your country for you, to leave you masters of your own free will, at peace. . . . Do you not see that once this nation is destroyed, we will then remain peaceful owners of the whole country? . . . It is absolutely necessary that we rid the land where we are now living of these wicked animals. Thus did one of our kings, in former times, have every last wolf destroyed in the land we come from."

21. Gaulin to [St. Ovide], 17 November 1719.

22. Ibid. "These savages are of little account as our allies but could become quite important as enemies."

23. Maillard, "Lettre," p. 365. "But when we consider still that we have to live with a nation, which although it has always been up to the present very attached and very submissive to the French government, could perhaps in the future fail us, betray us, in short break away from our interests, who knows if they might not make use to this end of this art of writing that we will have imparted to them."

24. "Memoire sur les Mikmaques," ff. 384–97; "much less as warriors than the savages of Canada, they would be little capable of conducting a considerable undertaking." La Galissonière to unknown, 6 November 1747, *CMNF*, 3: 399–400; "If we are attacked, we will be abandoned and perhaps betrayed by our most trustworthy savages."

25. Vaudreuil to minister, 6 September 1716, ibid., pp. 19–21; memoire du roy to Sieurs Vaudreuil and Michel Begon, 15 July 1718, ibid., p. 28.

26. "Answer of Indians of Penobscot to the Commisioners." April 1714, CO. 217/1, ff. 364–66. "I have my own kings and governors, my chief and my elders. . . . I do not wish nevertheless that any

stranger erect any fort or establishment on my land. They would embarrass me. I am [strong] enough to occupy the land on my own."

27. Vaudreuil to minister, 6 September 1716.

28. Governor Richard Philipps to Mr. Secretary James Craggs, 26 May 1720, CO. 217/3, ff. 31–39.

29. Lieutenant-Governor Lawrence Armstrong to Duke of Newcastle, 9 October 1733, CO. 217/39, ff. 65–66; Lords of Trade to Armstrong, 11 September 1734, CO. 218/2, ff. 150–52.

30. Doucett to Lords of Trade, 10 February and 15 November 1718, CO. 217/2, ff. 194–96, 230–31; Doucett to Philipps, 13 December 1718, CO. 217/31, ff. 67–68; Lords of Trade to Mr. Secretary Craggs, 30 April 1719, CO. 218/1, f. 197; Colonel Gardener to Lord Stanhope, 27 August 1719, CO. 217/38, ff. 43–44.

31. Armstrong to Newcastle, 9 October 1733; Lords of Trade to Armstrong, 11 September 1734; Lords of Trade to Philipps, 13 September 1734, CO. 218/2, ff. 150–53; Philipps to Lords of Trade, 30 November 1734, CO. 217/7, ff. 136–41.

32. St. Ovide to council, 15 September 1721, AC, C11B, vol. 5, ff. 147–52.

33. Major de Bourville to minister, 30 November 1730, ibid., vol. 11, ff. 56–63; "this nation, governed by self-interest, adjusts itself to both French and English, whom they welcome from all over and, without the slightest regard, are very capable of [doing] all sorts of harm." St. Ovide to minister, 14 November 1732, ibid., vol. 12, ff. 170–86; president of the Navy Board to St. Ovide and Le Normant, 19 May 1733, ibid., B, vol. 59, ff. 517–18.

34. Memoire sur les Limites de l'Acadie by Père Charlevoix, 29 October 1720, CMNF, 3: 49–54. "With a sneer—Know ...that when we all want, as many nations as we are on this vast continent, we will unite to drive out from it all the strangers, whoever they may be."

35. Col. Philipps' Conference with the Indians, July 1720. CO. 217/3, ff. 147–51.

36. Doucett to Lords of Trade, 6 November 1717, CO. 217/2, ff. 174–77; Philipps to Mr. Secretary Craggs, 26 May 1720.

37. Gaulin to [St. Ovide], 17 November 1719; "for the maintenance of the savages who would be English today without me." See also Vaudreuil to minister, 14 October 1716, CMNF, 3: 23–24.

38. David Jefferies to Captain Robert Mears, 6 July 1715, extract, CO. 217/2, f.5.

39. Governor Costebelle to minister, 9 September 1715, AC, C11B, vol. 1, pt. 1, ff. 189–202.

40. St. Ovide to council, 5 September 1720; "these nations followed no advice or council except that of their own wilfulness and their chiefs." Subsequent French documents about the Canso affray are in ibid., ff. 95–127. Philipps to Lords of Trade, 27 September 1720, CO. 217/3, ff. 117–27; other English documents are in CO. 217/4, ff. 69–116. For a detailed account of the controversy over Canso that preceded the Indian attack, see W. A. B. Douglas, "The Royal Navy and the Canso Station," unpublished typescript.

41. Antoine and Pierre Couaret to Governor Philipps, 2 October 1720, CO. 217/3, ff. 155–56. "This land here that God has given to us of which we can be accounted a part as much as the trees are born here cannot be disputed by any-one....We are masters independent of everyone and wish to have our country free."

42. François de Salle to Philipps, 10 November 1720, CO. 217/3, ff. 204–5; Philipps to Lords of Trade, with enclosure, 24 November 1720, ibid., ff. 198–203.

43. St. Ovide to council, 15 September 1721.

44. Report of Vaudreuil and Begon to minister, 8 October 1721, CMNF, 3: 57–61; unknown to Cardinal Dubois, 28 December 1721, AC, B, vol. 44, ff. 120–24; memoire du roy to Vaudreuil and Begon, 8 June 1721, CMNF, 3: 54.

45. The exchange of letters between Governors Samuel Shute and Vaudreuil is in ibid., pp. 55–56, 63–67, 70–84.

46. Vaudreuil to council, 10 November 1721, ibid., pp. 61–62.

47. Report of Vaudreuil and Begon, 17 October 1722, ibid., pp. 85–88; Vaudreuil to Shute, 2 October 1723, ibid., pp. 89–91; "Decision des Ministres sur le Rapport de Canada du 14 Octobre 1723," 18 January 1724, ibid., pp. 101–2; memoire du roy aux Sieurs Marquis de Vaudreuil et Chazel, 15 May 1725,

ibid., pp. 123–24. "The French must not appear to enter into this war, but they must secretly inspire other nations to help the Abenakis."

48. Vaudreuil to minister, 7 August 1725, abstract, in *Documents Relative to the Colonial History of the State of New York*, ed. E. B. O'Callaghan, 15 vols. (Albany: Weed, Parsons, 1853–87), 9: 947–49.

49. Philipps to Lords of Trade, 27 September 1720. 16 August 1721 (CO. 217/4, ff. 42–44), and 30 November 1734.

50. Gaulin to Doucett, 13 March 1722 ("where we will be able more easily to deter their evil enterprises") and Doucett to Gaulin, 14 March 1722, CO. 217/4, ff. 132–35; Doucett to Lords of Trade, with enclosure, 2 July 1722, ibid., ff. 125–31.

51. Philipps to Lords of Trade, 19 September 1722, CO. 217/3, ff. 155–59; Le Normant de Mézy to minister, 7 August 1722, AC, C11B, vol. 6, ff. 61–63.

52. Vaudreuil to minister, 25 October 1724, *CMNF*, 3: 108–10; St. Ovide to minister, 24 August 1724 and 17 August 1725, AC, C11B, vol. 7, ff. 33–34, 133–34; Armstrong to Newcastle, 24 October 1725, CO. 217/38, ff. 88–89; Douglas, "Royal Navy and Canso."

53. Report of Longueuil and Begon to minister, 31 October 1725, *CMNF*, 3: 125–26. "This war did not concern the French at all."

54. Articles of Submission, Port Royal, 4 June 1726, CO. 217/4, ff. 99–103, 320–21.

55. Memoire du roy to Beauharnois and Dupuy, 24 May 1728, *CMNF*, 3: 140–41; "an unexpected inconvenience." Navy Board to St. Ovide, 10 June 1727 and 20 June 1728, AC, B, vol. 50, ff. 581–83, vol. 52, ff. 586–88; "is only too true."

56. St. Ovide to minister, 11 September 1726, 20 September 1727, and 3 November 1728, ibid., C11B, vol. 8, ff. 25–30, vol. 9, ff. 22–29, vol. 10, ff. 79–89.

57. St. Ovide to minister, 18 November 1726 and 13 September 1727, ibid., vol. 8, ff. 38–43, vol. 9, ff. 15–16; St. Ovide to minister, 20 September 1727; Navy Board to St. Ovide, 10 June 1727; "I have no doubt that this affair will rekindle more strongly than ever the hatred and distrust which exists between the two nations." St. Ovide to Armstrong, 3 October 1727, Armstrong to

St. Ovide, 13 November 1727, CO. 217/38, ff. 203–6.

58. St. Ovide to minister, 1 November 1729; president of Navy Board to St. Ovide, 27 June 1730, ibid., B, vol. 54, ff. 517–18.

59. St. Ovide to minister, 14 November 1732; president of the Navy Board to St. Ovide and Le Normant, 19 May 1733.

60. Council meeting, 25 July 1732, in *Selections from the Public Documents of the Province of Nova Scotia*, ed. Thomas B. Akins (Halifax: Annand, 1869), pp. 97–98; Armstrong to Newcastle, 15 November 1732 (ibid., p. 101), and 9 October 1733.

61. St. Ovide to minister, 1 November 1734, AC, C11B, vol. 15, ff. 228–41; Bourville to minister, 3 October 1738, ibid., vol. 20, ff. 58–67.

62. "A State of the French Fishery at Cape Breton, June, 1739," in *The Royal Navy and North America*, ed. Julian Gwyn ([London]: Navy Records Society, 1973), pp. 10–12.

63. Proclamation, 20 October 1743; Major Paul Mascarene to Alexandre Bourg, 21 October 1743, CO. 217/31, ff. 193–95, 189–90.

64. Conference, 5 May 1744, Brown Manuscripts, BL, Add. MS 19071, ff. 74–76, microfilm, PANS.

65. Mascarene to Lords of Trade, 27 July 1744, CO. 217/31, ff. 212–14; minutes of council, 6 and 8 December 1744, CO. 217/39, ff. 288–89; Mascarene to Lords of Trade, 25 September 1744, Akins, *Public Documents*, pp. 133–34; Mascarene to unknown, December 1744, ibid., pp. 146–50.

66. [Pierre Maillard], "Motifs des sauvages mickmaques et marichites de continuer la guerre contre les Anglois depuis la dernière paix," in *Les Derniers Jours de l'Acadie*, by Gaston de Bosq de Beaumont (Paris: Lechevalier, 1899), pp. 248–58. Mascarene reported that a "distemper" had carried off hundreds of Le Loutre's Indians and nearly as many of Maillard's late in 1746, Gwyn, *Royal Navy*, pp. 364–65.

67. Mascarene to Newcastle, 9 December 1745, CO. 217/39, ff. 314–15.

68. Maillard, "Motifs," passim; Le Loutre to unknown, 12 July 1747, "Documents sur l'Acadie," pp. 31–33.

69. Beamish Murdoch, *A History of Nova-Scotia*, 3 vols. (Halifax: J. Barnes, 1865), 2: 106–10.

NOTES TO CHAPTER FOUR

1. Murdoch, *Nova-Scotia*, 2: 279, and *passim*.
2. J. B. Brebner, *New England's Outpost* (New York: Columbia University Press, 1927), p. 178.
3. *The Memorials of the English and French Commissioners concerning the Limits of Nova Scotia, or, Acadie*, 2 vols. (London, 1755).
4. Johnson, *Apôtres*, p. 118.
5. President of Navy Board to Desherbiers, 14 June 1750, AC, B, vol. 91, ff. 352-53; "without compromising yourself to cut off the establishments of the English."
6. Comte de Raymond to J. B. de Marchault d'Arnonville, minister of marine, 19 November 1751, ibid., C11B, vol. 31, ff. 81-84.
7. Marquis de La Jonquière to Philipps [*sic*: Spencer Phips, president of the Massachusetts Council], 7 March 1751, *CMNF*, 3: 502-4; "very far from stirring the savages up against the English, I am doing my utmost to keep them at peace with you."
8. Abbé de l'Isle Dieu to Minister Rouillé, 1 April 1750, *RAPQ*, 1935-36, pp. 293-94; "must not undertake anything except in concert with the ministry and the people on the spot who are invested with the authority of the king."
9. Governor Edward Cornwallis to bishop of Quebec, 1 December 1749, AC, C11B, vol. 29, pt. 1, ff. 94-95.
10. Maillard to Abbé du Fau, 18 October 1749, Carton P, item 66, ASQ.
11. Maillard to unknown, 13 October 1751 and 21 June 1752, P, items 68, 69, ASQ. After training with Maillard at Louisbourg. Jean Manach went to join Jean-Louis Le Loutre at Beauséjour.
12. Maillard to unknown, 7 October 1750, P, item 67, ASQ; Charles Desherbier de la Ralière and Jacques Prevost to minister, 27 November 1749, AC, C11B, vol. 28, ff. 68-71. Maillard eventually received his pension (president of Navy Board to de Raymond, 21 July 1752, ibid., B, vol. 95, f. 294).
13. Maillard to M. de Surlaville, 21 February 1753, Beaumont, *Derniers Jours*, p. 85. "I do not give more than fifty years to them and to the Marichites before one

sees them so mixed with the French colonists that it will no longer be possible to tell them apart."
14. Maillard to unknown, 21 June 1752; "he alone gives courage to all."
15. Resumé of a letter from Le Loutre, 29 July 1749, AC, C11C, vol. 9, ff. 60-64; "to incite the savages to continue the war against the English and to make them say that they would not tolerate any new establishment in Acadia."
16. Cornwallis to Lords of Trade, 11 September 1749, CO. 217/9, ff. 89-93.
17. Prevost to minister, 16 August 1753, AC, C11B, vol. 33, ff. 229-36.
18. Johnson, *Apôtres*, pp. 124-26; Maillard, "Lettre," pp. 388-407.
19. President of Navy Board to de Raymond, 21 July 1752.
20. Abbé de l'Isle Dieu to Bishop Pontbriand, 3 March 1753, *RAPQ*, 1935-36, pp. 368-71; Abbé de l'Isle Dieu to president of the council of marine, 5 September 1753, ibid., 1936-37, pp. 340-42.
21. Governor Augustin de Boschenry du Drucour to minister, 8 November 1755, AC, C11B, vol. 35, ff. 146-47. "It is a nation that one can lead only with presents and provisions in hand."
22. This attitude is explained in Governor William Shirley to d'Arnonville La Galissonière, 9 May 1749, CO. 217/32, ff. 47-50.
23. Cornwallis to Duke of Bedford, 23 July 1749, Akins, *Public Documents*, pp. 561-64.
24. Cornwallis to Bedford, 20 August 1749, CO. 217/40, ff. 118-21; Akins, *Public Documents*, pp. 573-74, 577-79.
25. Cornwallis to Lords of Trade, 11 September 1749.
26. Maillard to Abbé du Fau, 18 October 1749; ASQ; declaration printed in *Le Canada Français* 1 (1888): 17-19.
   The place where you are, where you are building dwellings, where you are now building a fort, where you want, as it were, to enthrone yourself, this land of which you wish to make yourself now absolute master, this land belongs to me, I have come from it as certainly as the grass, it is the very

place of my birth and of my dwelling, this land belongs to me, the Indian, yes I swear, it is God who has given it to me to be my country for ever... show me where I the Indian will lodge? you drive me out; where do you want me to take refuge? you have taken almost all this land in all its extent. Nothing remains to me except Kchibouktouk. You envy me even this morsel.... Your residence at Port Royal does not cause me great anger because you see that I have left you there at peace for a long time, but now you force me to speak out by the great theft you have perpetrated against me. The use of "tu" throughout the passage indicates the contempt of the speaker for the English.

27. Cornwallis to Bedford, with enclosures, 17 October 1749, CO. 217/40, ff. 142–44.
28. Corwallis to Lords of Trade, 7 December 1749, CO. 217/9, ff. 127–30.
29. Cornwallis to Bedford, 17 October 1749.
30. Orders to Captain Silvanus Cobb, 13 January 1750, CO. 217/9, f. 207.
31. Cornwallis to Lords of Trade, 19 March 1750, CO. 217/9, ff. 188–94.
32. Lords of Trade to Cornwallis, 16 February 1750, CO. 218/3, ff. 95–98.
33. Cornwallis to Lords of Trade, 19 March 1750.
34. Lords of Trade to Cornwallis, 2 April 1750, CO. 218/3, ff. 109–16.
35. Paper dated Piziquid, 12 December 1749, CO. 217/9, f. 202.
36. Cornwallis to Lords of Trade, 27 November 1750, CO. 217/11, ff. 3–7.
37. Murdoch, *Nova-Scotia*, 2: 230–31.
38. Prevost to minister, 24 June 1751, AC, C11B, vol. 30, ff. 154–58; Governor Charles Lawrence to Lords of Trade, 29 December 1753, CO. 217/15, ff. 3–8.
39. Council minutes, 14 and 16 September 1752, Akins, *Public Documents*, pp. 671–74; "The Answer of the Govr. & Council," 16 September 1752, CO. 217/13, ff. 305–6.
40. Governor Peregrine Hopson to Secretary of State Holdernesse, 18 October 1752, CO. 217/40, f. 225.
41. Council minutes, 22 November 1752, Akins, *Public Documents*, pp. 682–85; printed proclamation, 24 November 1752, RG1, vol. 430, doc. 2, PANS.
42. Hopson to Lords of Trade, 6 December 1752, CO. 217/13, ff. 384–89; Lords of Trade to Hopson, 28 March 1753, CO. 218/4, ff. 213–25.
43. Abbé de l'Isle Dieu to president of council of marine, 19 July 1753, *RAPQ*, 1936–37, pp. 336–38; Prevost to minister, 12 May 1753, AC, C11B, vol. 33, ff. 186–91.
44. Prevost to minister, 12 May 1753; extract of letter from Surveyor-General Charles Morris to Cornwallis, 16 April 1753, Brown MSS, Ad. MS 19071, ff. 12–20.
45. Statement of Anthony Casteel, 30 July 1753, CO. 217/14, ff. 199–202.
46. Murdoch, *Nova-Scotia*, 2: 225–26.
47. Governor Marquis Duquesne de Menneville to minister, 10 October 1754. *CMNF*, 3: 515–18; "to strike without it appearing that it comes from me."
48. [Thomas Pichon to Captain T. Hussey], 27 December 1754, in John C. Webster, *Thomas Pichon "The Spy of Beauséjour"* (Halifax: Public Archives of Nova Scotia, 1937), pp. 76–77.
49. Murdoch, *Nova-Scotia*, 2: 235–37; Lawrence to Hussey, 8 November 1754, Akins, *Public Documents*, pp. 237–38.
50. Chief Algimou to Hussey, 19 January 1755, Webster, *Pichon*, p. 8.
51. Murdoch, *Nova-Scotia*, 2: 257–58.
52. Lawrence to Lords of Trade, 25 May and 3 November 1756, CO. 217/16, ff. 61–78. Le Loutre went to Quebec and thence departed for France only to be captured a second time on the high seas; until 1763 he was a prisoner on Jersey.
53. Prevost to minister, 27 September 1756, AC, C11B, vol. 36, ff. 163–65; M. des Bourbes to Surlaville, 18 April 1756, Beaumont, *Derniers Jours*, pp. 185–88.
54. du Drucour to minister, 12 July 1757, AC, C11B, vol. 37, ff. 81–82; "the extreme need that we have for each other." President of Navy Board to du Drucour, 18 February 1758, ibid., B, vol. 107, f. 365. B, vol. 107, f. 365.
55. Prevost to minister, 10 December 1757, ibid., C11B, vol. 37, ff. 189–93; du Drucour to minister, 15 January 1758, ibid., vol. 38, ff. 17–19; Dickason, *Louisbourg and the Indians*, p. 101, n. 54.
56. Dickason, *Louisbourg and the Indians*, pp. 102–3; Maillard to unknown, [August 1758], P, item 70, ASQ.
57. Lawrence to Lords of Trade, 25 Decem-

ber 1758, CO. 217/16, ff. 305–8.

58. Maillard to unknown, [August 1758]; [George Townshend], "Journal," 2 May 1759, in *The Siege of Quebec*, eds. A. Doughty and G.W. Parmalee, 6 vols. (Quebec: Dussault and Proulx, 1901), 5: 231.

59. "Treaty of Peace and Friendship," 23 February 1760, CO. 217/18, ff. 18–31.

60. Council meetings, 14 and 16 February 1760, CO. 217/20, ff. 115, 126–27; instructions to Commissary Benjamin Garrish, 10 February 1760, ibid., f. 120.

61. Council meeting, 15 May 1761, ff. 132–34; Lieutenant-Governor Jonathan Belcher to Lords of Trade, 10 April 1761, CO. 217/18, ff. 131–34 puts the figure at £2,000.

62. Passes in RG1, vol. 165, pp. 54, 55, 74, PANS.

63. Maillard to unknown, [1760], P, item 71, ASQ. "For my part, having been made victim for all, and having fled in circumstances where it was not possible to act otherwise I keep inviolably the

word that I have given. Such is my way of thinking."

64. Letter of Colonel Frye, 7 March 1760, *Pennsylvania Gazette*, 1 May 1760.

65. Maillard to [Lawrence], April 1760, P, item 72, ASQ; Belcher to Lords of Trade, 9 April 1761, CO. 217/18, f. 170.

66. "Ceremonials at concluding a Peace . . .," 25 June 1761, ibid., ff. 277–84.

67. This account was given fifty years after the event and based on the recollections of an eye-witness (Abbé Jean-Mande Sigogne to Lieutenant-Governor Sir John C. Sherbrooke, 5 May 1812, with enclosure, RG1, vol. 430, docs. 20, 21, PANS).

68. Additional instructions to Governor Henry Ellis, 9 December 1761, ibid., vol. 30, doc. 58.

69. Belcher to Lords of Trade, 2 July 1762, CO. 217/19, ff. 22–26. The assembly's London agent saw the hand of Maillard in the proclamation (Joshua Mauger to Lords of Trade, 28 September 1763, CO. 217/20, ff. 202–4).

NOTES TO CHAPTER FIVE

1. Belcher to Col. Denson, 17 July 1762; S. Zouberbuhler, J. Creighton, L.C. Rudolf to Belcher, 15 and 21 July, 1762, CO. 217/19, ff. 116–23; Council of War, 16 July 1762, ibid., ff. 94–95.

2. Address of House of Assembly to Belcher, 7 September 1762, ibid., f. 126.

3. Belcher to Lords of Trade, 7 September 1762, ibid., ff. 70–78.

4. Joshua Mauger to Lords of Trade, 28 September 1763, CO. 217/20, ff. 202–4.

5. Governor Montagu Wilmot to Lords of Trade, 28 January 1764, CO. 217/21, ff. 7–8.

6. Lieutenant-Governor Michael Francklin to Earl of Hillsborough, 20 July 1768, CO. 217/45, ff. 161–64.

7. Hillsborough to Governor Lord William Campbell, 1 March 1769, CO. 217/46, ff. 38–40. I have found no mention of Nova Scotia in Sir William Johnson's correspondence.

8. Manuscript copy of the act in CO. 217/45, f. 167.

9. Exhaustive enquiries into the truckhouse deficits are recorded in CO.

217/20, ff. 56–176; as late as 1766 Gerrish was insisting that the government owed him over £750 (petition of 19 February 1766, CO. 217/21, ff. 148–50).

10. Belcher to Lords of Trade, 20 February 1763, CO. 217/20, ff. 60–62.

11. Wilmot to Lords of Trade, 5 November 1764, CO. 217/21, ff. 96–98.

12. Captain Samuel Thompson to Philip Stevens, secretary to the Lords of the Admiralty, 16 April 1764; Stevens to John Pownall, secretary to the Lords of Trade, 21 April 1764, CO. 217/20, ff. 318–21; Pownall to Stephens, 1 May 1764; Lords of Trade to Wilmot, 8 May 1764, CO. 218/6, ff. 204–6.

13. Wilmot to Halifax, 10 December 1763 and 29 August 1764, CO. 217/43, ff. 183–86, CO. 217/21, ff. 91–92.

14. Wilmot to Lords of Trade, 24 June 1764, CO. 217/21, ff. 118–204.

15. Lords of Trade to Wilmot, 13 July 1764 and 24 June 1765, CO. 218/6, ff. 224–27, 238–39.

16. Francklin to Lords of Trade, with enclosures, 17 January 1768, CO. 217/22,

ff. 15–72.

17. Benjamin Green, president of the council, to Lords of Trade, 24 August 1766, CO. 217/21, ff. 260–71.

18. Francklin to Lords of Trade, 3 September 1766, CO. 217/21, ff. 342–49.

19. Governor Hugh Palliser to Lt.-Col. Pringle, 22 October 1765, letter books of the colonial secretary, GN2/1/3, p. 345, PANL.

20. Francklin to Palliser, 11 September 1766, ibid., GN2/1/4, p. 40.

21. Palliser to Francklin, 16 October 1766, CO. 217/44, ff. 81–83; Palliser to Lords of Trade, 21 October 1766, CO. 194/27, ff. 287–92; Palliser to Shelburne, 5 December 1767, ibid., ff. 320–21.

22. Dr. Bearcroft, secretary of the SPG, to Lords of Trade, 26 February 1750, CO. 217/9, ff. 146–47.

23. [Pierre Maillard], *Customs and Manners of the Mickmakis and Maricheets.*

24. Rev. Thomas Wood to SPG, 27 October 1762, Lambeth MSS, 1124–2, f. 120, PAC, in H.-R. Casgrain, *Les Sulpiciens et les Prêtres des Missions-Etrangères en Acadie* (Quebec: Pruneau and Kirouac, 1897), p. 443.

25. Wilmot to Lords of Trade, 10 December 1763, CO. 217/20, ff. 354–59.

26. Pownall to the Rev. Dr. Daniel Burton, 20 June 1764, CO. 218/6, ff. 216–17; Lords of Trade to Wilmot, 13 July 1764; Burton to Lords of Trade, CO. 217/21, ff. 23–24.

27. Rev. J.-B. Moreau to Pownall, 20 June 1764, CO. 217/21, ff. 226–28; general meetings of SPG, 15 March and 20 December 1765, Lambeth MSS., transcripts, MG11, n.s., A74, pp. 89–92, A75, pp. 156–59, PAC.

28. Claim of J.-B. Moreau for £20.15.6, 1766, CO. 217/22, f. 50.

29. General meeting of SPG, 19 December 1766, Lambeth MSS, MG11, A78, pp. 108–11, PAC. A similar story is told by Gamaliel Smethurst. A letter from Jesus Christ to the pope said that the French were coming to drive the English out of Nova Scotia, and in the meantime the Indians should abstain from rum and cider and drink only French claret and brandy. Indians carried copies of this precious letter, sold for 30 pounds of beaver skins, around the neck in bark purses (*A Narrative of Extraordinary Escape* [London, 1774], reprinted in New Brunswick Historical Society, *Collections* [1905]: 358–90).

30. Maillard's will makes no mention of these papers. He bequeathed his vases and altar ornaments to L.-B. Petitpas who had given him shelter after the fall of Louisbourg. In 1778 Petitpas sold them to the Seminary of Quebec for 724 livres. Maillard left a silver sun, a silver chalice, two copper candelabra, a missal, and a chasuble to his missionary successor (will, 12 April 1759, with codicils, Seminaire IV, no. 91, ASQ). The sale by Petitpas is recorded ibid., no. 89.

31. General meeting of SPG, 21 December 1764, Lambeth MSS, MG11, A75, pp. 47–52, PAC.

32. General meeting of SPG, 21 February 1766, ibid., A76, pp. 174–77, PAC. Roma had received a deathbed bequest of £15 from Maillard (codicil of 5 August 1762); Roma was paid £5 a month to instruct Wood in the Micmac language (CO. 217/22, f. 25). Presumably Wood knew nothing of Roma's involvement in spurious letter writing.

33. General meetings of SPG, 17 October and 21 November 1766, Lambeth MSS, MG11, A77, pp. 180–82, A78, pp. 95–96, PAC. The manuscript essay is in the Thomas Wood MSS, packets 8, 10, J.C. Webster Collection, NBM.

34. Wood to SPG, 15 October 1765, Lambeth MSS, MG11, A76, pp. 174–77, PAC.

35. Wilmot to Lords of Trade, 9 October 1765, CO. 217/21, ff. 179–81.

36. Francklin to Lords of Trade, 3 September 1766.

37. Rev. Charles François Bailly to Bishop Jean Oliver Briand, 20 June 1768 and 22 July 1769, Ev. Q. 2, 62, 62, AAQ; general meeting of SPG, 19 December 1766, pp. 97–99; Johnston, *Catholic Church*, 1: 92–95.

38. W. O. Raymond, *The River St. John* (Saint John: J. A. Bowes, 1910), p. 416.

39. Campbell to Hillsborough, 22 December 1770, CO. 217/48, ff. 11–12. Hillsborough agreed to the settlement as long as no public expense was involved (Hillsborough to Campbell, 4 May 1771, ibid., f. 13).

40. Bailly was presented to the Grand Jury at Halifax on 15 July 1771 as "a Popish Priest" who frequently exercised his office "against the Peace of our said

Lord the King" (Supreme Court Records, RG39, PANS).

41. "A Description of the Island of Cape Britain," 1 November 1768, CO. 5/70, ff. 14–45.

42. Francklin to Shelburne, 19 November 1766, CO. 217/22, ff. 4–5.

43. Francklin to Hillsborough, 20 July 1768. Micmacs may have asked for land, but no grants were made to them.

44. Campbell to Hillsborough, 13 January 1769, CO. 217/46, ff. 24–26.

45. Moses Perley, "The Indians of New Brunswick," 1848, CO. 188/106, ff. 206–23.

46. Council minutes, 18 July 1768, CO. 217/45, ff. 169–70; Francklin to Hillsborough, 20 July 1768; Land Grants, Old Book, 6, pp. 763–64; Old Book 9, pp. 54–55, PANS. The grant was reissued on 2 August 1779, with the names of seven trustees but otherwise identical (Old Book 12, pp. 106–7, PANS).

47. Raymond, *St. John*, pp. 309, 319.

48. Memorial of Charles Jadis, 27 August 1771, in Campbell to Hillsborough, 9 October 1771, CO. 217/48, ff. 90–93.

49. Memorial of John Cunningham to Governor John Parr, 11 November 1782, CO. 217/56, ff. 69–72.

50. Governor Francis Legge to Dartmouth, 31 July 1775, CO. 217/51, ff. 274–77.

51. Frederic Kidder, ed., *Military Operations in Eastern Maine and Nova Scotia during the American Revolution* (1867; reprint ed., New York: Kraus Reprint Co., 1971), pp. 51–55.

52. Legge to Dartmouth, 11 November and 26 December 1775, CO. 217/52, ff. 7–9, 54–56; Captain John Stanton to Legge, 4 December 1775, CO. 217/52, ff. 60–61.

53. George Washington to the president of Congress, 30 January 1776; Washington to Philip Schuyler, 1 February 1776, in George Washington, *The Writings of George Washington*, ed. John C. Fitzpatrick, 39 vols. (Washington, D.C., 1931–44), 4: 286–93, 301–2; Kidder, *Military Operations*, p. 170.

54. Ibid., pp. 170–71.

55. Ibid., p. 65.

56. Washington to president of Congress, 4 July 1776; Washington to Massachusetts Legislature, 11 July 1776, *Writings*, 5: 218–24, 261–62.

57. *Resolves of the General Assembly of the Colony of Massachusetts-Bay* [29 May–

13 July 1776] (Boston, 1776), p. 57; Kidder, *Military Operations*, pp. 60–61, 95n; Sir Richard Hughes to Germain, 16 January 1779, CO. 217/54, ff. 151–52.

58. Kidder, *Military Operations*, pp. 166–79, 57–58.

59. Francklin to John Pownall, 4 May 1776, CO. 217/52, ff. 142–45.

60. Admiral Marriott Arbuthnot to Lord George Germain, 8 July 1776, ibid., ff. 190–92.

61. Admiral Sir George Collier to Germain, 21 November 1776, ibid., ff. 250–51; accounts of the expedition are in Kidder, *Military Operations*, pp. 67–72; and "Extract of a Journal. The Proceedings at Fort Cumberland," CO. 217/53, ff. 33–44.

62. Kidder, *Military Operations*, p. 59. Raymond, *St. John*, has an extended account of the Malecites in the Revolutionary War, pp. 428–81. On p. 430 he wrongly implies that Thomas visited Washington's camp on the Delaware at the time the letter was written.

63. Arbuthnot to Germain, 12 June 1777, CO. 217/53, f. 104.

64. "Arthur Goold, Councillor to 'Mes Amis,'" 11 May 1777, ibid., ff. 110–13.

65. Kidder, *Military Operations*, pp. 180–84; appendix "Containing sundry RESOLUTIONS for carrying on an Expedition to *St. John's* in *Nova Scotia*," *Resolves of the General Assembly of the State of Massachusetts-Bay* (Boston, 1777).

66. Kidder, *Military Operations*, pp. 85–124.

67. Ibid., p. 251; Raymond, *St. John*, pp. 454–55.

68. Kidder, *Military Operations*, p. 193.

69. Raymond, *St. John*, p. 456.

70. Ibid., pp. 456–62; Sir Guy Carleton to Arbuthnot, 23 February 1778, CO. 217/54, ff. 46–47; Hughes to Germain, 12 October 1778 ibid., ff. 131–32, and 16 January 1779.

71. Manuscripts Relating to the American Revolution, RG1, vol. 364, doc. 78, PANS. Joseph Claude's copy was acquired by the Capuchin Museum, Restigouche, in 1945, and printed in *Revue d'Histoire de la Gaspésie* 2, no. 4 (1964): 219–21.

72. Kidder, *Military Operations*, pp. 261–62, 265–68.

73. Expenses, 20 October 1779, CO. 217/54,

ff. 225–26; Land Grants, Old Book 12, pp. 106–7, PANS.

74. Germain to Francklin, 3 May 1779, CO. 217/54, ff. 178–79; Francklin to Germain, 3 August 1779, ibid., ff. 202–4.

75. Francklin to Germain, 8 and 26 September 1779, ibid., ff. 206–7, 219–22.

76. Council minutes, 11 September and 11 October 1779, CO. 217/55, ff. 17–19.

77. Kidder, *Military Operations*, pp. 274–76, 293–95; Germain to Francklin, 4 December 1779 and 7 July 1780, CO. 217/54, ff. 237–38, CO. 217/55, ff. 169–70; Germain to Brigadier Francis Maclean, 5 July 1780, ibid., ff. 44–46; Francklin to Germain, 18 May and 21 November 1780, ibid., ff. 109–10, 111–13.

NOTES TO CHAPTER SIX

1. Anthony Blackwood, "Observations upon Lord Falkland's despatch of the 15th of July, 1841," CO. 217/178, ff. 78–88. Chapters 6–8 are revised versions of articles that first appeared in *Acadiensis*.

2. Monk received the post as compensation for having raised the Loyal Nova Scotia Regiment at his own expense (draft petition, George H. Monk to Sir George Prevost, July, 1816, Monk Papers, MG23, G11–19, pp. 1384–86, PAC).

3. Monk Letter Book, ibid., pp. 1030–31, 1035–36.

4. Monk to Edward Barron, 19 July 1784; Barron to Monk, 12 August 1784, ibid., pp. 1029–31.

5. For exceptions, see below, pp. 149–52.

6. 24 June 1782, Licence to Philip Bernard et al., RG20, series "C," vol. 95, pp. 72–73; RG1, vol. 430, doc. 26 1/2, PANS.

7. Licences of occupation dated 18 December 1783, ibid., doc. 23 1/2.

8. Richard Cumberland to Lord Sydney, 4 March 1784, CO. 217/35, ff. 220–21.

9. S. Hollingsworth, *The Present State of Nova Scotia*, 2d ed. (Edinburgh: Creech, 1787), p. 71.

10. Monk to Lieutenant-Governor Sir John Wentworth, 23 July 1793, Monk Papers, p. 1037, PAC.

11. Wentworth to Monk, 18 October 1793, ibid., pp. 295–98.

12. Major George Deschamps to Monk, 4 November 1793; Monk to Wentworth, 17 November 1793; ibid., pp. 1040, 819–21; the contract for issuing supplies at Windsor went to Deschamps, a former business partner of Monk (ibid., p. 1073).

13. Notes on conversations with Indians, ibid., pp. 1047–60.

14. Monk to Wentworth, 23 January 1794; Monk's petition on behalf of the Indians, 24 January 1794, ibid., pp. 1051–55.

15. Wentworth to Monk, 14 January 1794; Monk to Ross, 2 February 1794, ibid., pp. 307–12, 1058.

16. Wentworth to Henry Dundas, 3 May and 9 November 1793, letter books of Governor Wentworth, RG1, vol. 50, n.p., PANS; Dundas to Wentworth, CO. 218/27, ff. 108–11.

17. Wentworth to Dundas, 19 May 1794; Dundas to Wentworth, July 1794, letter books of Governor Wentworth, RG1, vol. 51, pp. 107–9; vol. 33, doc. 67, PANS.

18. Wentworth to Duke of Portland, 8 October 1796, ibid., vol. 51, pp. 345–47; Portland to Wentworth, 14 December 1796, 9 March 1797, and 18 June 1800, CO. 218/27, ff. 112–14, 117–19, 175–76.

19. "Report of a Committee to take into consideration Health Officer's Accounts—demands on Government & Transient Poor Account 8 Apr 1800," RG5, series A, vol. 7; "Report of the Committee on the Condition of the Indians," 15 April 1800, RG1, vol. 430, doc. 33 1/2; PANS; *JLANS*, 1800, pp. 75–76.

20. 1 May 1800, ibid., pp. 102–3. The point of distribution was in Sydney county, as "it is much to be desired that Indians should be kept as far from the Capital as possible" (Committee to administer relief to Messrs. Edward Irish and Timothy Hurley, 10 December 1800, RG1, vol. 430, doc. 34, PANS).

21. Report of Joint Committee, n.d., RG1, vol. 430, doc. 72 1/2, PANS; an example of the better reply is Jonathan Crary to Messrs. Benton, Morris and Wallace, 6 June 1801, ibid., doc. 72.
22. 14 July 1801, *JLANS*, 1801, p. 68; 4 July 1803, *JLANS*, 1803, p. 58.
23. Commissioners to James Archibald, 11 January 1803, RG1, vol. 430, doc. 139, PANS.
24. Edward Cooke to Major-General Martin Hunter, 3 October 1807, CO. 218/28, f. 127.
25. Wentworth to Monk, 15 October 1807, Monk Papers, pp. 517–20, PAC; Monk to commissioners (circular), 20 October 1807, RG1, vol. 430, doc. 143, PANS.
26. Digest of answers, n.d., RG1, vol. 430, doc. 145, PANS; Prevost to Cooke, CO. 217/82, ff. 196–205.
27. "The Interests of Humanity might require that we should resign the benefit of their alliance and active Cooperation with us in the Field" (Lord Bathurst to Sherbrooke, 26 August 1812, CO. 217/89, ff. 431–33; Sherbrooke to Bathurst, 7 October 1812, CO. 217/90, ff. 45–47; Bathurst to Sherbrooke, 16 November 1812, CO. 218/29, ff. 138–41).
28. "Petition of Eleven Families of Indians to Lieutenant-Governor Wentworth [1807]," Vertical Manuscript File: Indians: Land, PANS.
29. Charles Morris to Deputy Surveyor-General Crandle or Vaughan, 16 June 1810, RG10, vol. 459, folder 3, PAC.
30. The locations listed were at Shubenacadie, Pugwash, Antigonish, St. Margaret's Bay, Chester, Pomquet, Manchester, Sissaboo; on the La Have River, Petit Rivière, St. Mary's River and "several harbours" (Morris to Henry Cogswell, 7 March 1815, RG1, vol. 430, doc. 151, PANS).
31. Minutes of council, 22 December 1819 and 8 May 1820, RG3, vol. 214 1/2A, pp. 91, 136–39, PANS.
32. For example, the long career of Francis Glode as a land petitioner, RG10, vol. 461, folder 14, PAC.
33. Message of Lieutenant-Governor Kempt to the assembly, 9 March 1827, *JLANS*, 1827, pp. 74–75.
34. 5 April 1827, ibid., p. 142.
35. Letter of "Micmac," *Nova Scotian*, 6 March 1828.

36. For example, Thomas Trotter to William Hill, 29 November 1825, RG1, vol. 430, doc. 23 1/2, PANS.
37. Petition to Sir Peregrine Maitland, 15 December 1830, ibid., vol. 330, doc. 139.
38. Wentworth to Michael Wallace, 23 September 1802, ibid., vol. 430, doc. 117.
39. For example, petition of Pictou Indians, 2 March 1829, ibid., doc. 168.
40. Thirteen white families were cultivating 135 acres of intervale and "good upland" on the three-thousand-acre reserve by 1837 (List of Trespassers, 1 May and 8 July 1837, ibid., vol. 432, p. 250; printed *Notice to Trespassers*, 1 May 1837, ibid., vol. 431, doc. 36; Report of Assembly Committee, 19 April 1838, ibid., vol. 430, doc. 187).
41. 16 January 1821, *JLANS*, 1821, p. 36; Francis Meuse's petition in RG5, misc. A, series P, vol. 2, PANS; *Halifax Journal*, 27 December 1824; *Halifax Morning Post*, 1 February 1842.
42. Judge Peleg Wiswall to William Hill, 14 December 1829, RG1, vol. 430, doc. 169 1/2, PANS.
43. 12 February and 3 March 1828, *JLANS*, 1828, pp. 208, 254; *Acadian Recorder*, 16 February 1828.
44. "An Act to prevent the Sale of Spirituous Liquors to Indians, and to provide for their Instruction," 10 Geo. 4, c. 29, (*Statutes of Nova Scotia 1827–1835* [Halifax, 1836], p. 53); 20 February, 7 and 14 March 1829, *JLANS*, 1829, pp. 386, 424, 450. Successive drafts of the bill show that the title changed from "restrain" to "regulate" to "prevent" the sale of liquor while the provisions remained the same; clause IV, concerning instruction, was pencilled in (RG5, series B, vol. 10, PANS).
45. Description and plans of reserves dated between 5 December 1832 and 5 August 1833, RG1, vol. 432, pp. 235–45, PANS.
46. Minutes of council, 3 October 1829, RG3, vol. 214 1/2B, pp. 262–63, PANS.
47. Abstract of letters in reply to circular dated 29 October 1835, [*sic* 1838], RG1, vol. 432, pp. 19–27, PANS; the same, with background information, are in Lord Falkland to Lord Russell, 15 July 1841, CO. 217/177, ff. 74–76, 89–95.

48. Petition, undated, but stamped "Received 25 January 1841," CO. 217/179, ff. 406-8.
49. Russell to Falkland, 30 January 1841, CO. 217/177, ff. 128-29.
50. Some late replies to this circular are R. N. N. Henry to John Whidden, 10 January 1842; Charles R. Ward to Whidden, 11 January 1842; E. F. Harding to Whidden, 26 January 1842, MG15, vol. 1, docs. 22-24, PANS.
51. Falkland to Russell, 15 July 1841. The memorandum was published with commendation in the *Yarmouth Herald*, 5 August 1842.
52. Howe to Falkland, November 1841, RG1, vol. 432, pp. 1-6, PANS.
53. Speech of 20 January 1842, *JLANS*, 1842, p. 201; the act is 5 Vict. c. 16 (*Statutes of Nova Scotia 1836-1846* [Halifax 1846], pp. 23-24); the draft shows that a clause obliging the assembly to provide £300 in each of the five following years was struck out (RG5, series B, vol. 20, Bills 1842, PANS).
54. Falkland to Lord Stanley, 9 March 1842, CO. 217/180, ff. 215-16; observations in Falkland to Stanley, 1 July 1842, CO. 217/181, ff. 153-55.
55. Stanley to Falkland, 12 July 1842, CO. 217/180, ff. 294-301.
56. Commission to Joseph Howe, 2 April 1842, RG1, vol. 432, pp. 13-14, PANS.
57. 11 May 1842, ibid., pp. 68-73.
58. Ibid., pp. 77-119.
59. For example, Howe's correspondence with James Dawson between 26 January and 8 December 1842, ibid., pp. 138-58.
60. Report on Indian Affairs, 25 January 1843, *JLCNS*, 1843, appendix 7, pp. 17-25.
61. Report on Indian Affairs for 1843. *JLANS*, 1844-45, appendix 50, pp. 119-26; samples of later complaints are those of Abraham Gesner in his report 4 March 1852, *JLANS*, 1852, appendix 32, pt. 2, pp. 274-75, and William Chearnley, Report, 20 February 1861, *JLANS*, 1861, appendix 34, pp. 1-4.
62. Howe to Thomas Irwin, 27 May 1843, RG1, vol. 432, pp. 231-32, PANS.
63. This was a perennial complaint, e.g., Samuel P. Fairbanks to Hector Langevin, 3 April 1868, RG10, vol. 451, folder 5, PAC.
64. Bishop William Fraser to Patrick Power, 15 February 1845, MG15, vol. 3, doc. 85, PANS.
65. Report on Indian Affairs for 1843, passim.
66. For example, William Walsh to Howe, 9 February 1843, RG1, vol. 432, pp. 205-6, PANS.
67. James Dawson to Howe, 25 June 1842, reporting on a visit to Merigomish Island, ibid., pp. 146-51.
68. Dr. Robert Leslie to Alfred Whitman, 30 October 1846, MG15, vol. 3, doc. 102, PANS.
69. Edward Jennings to Sir Rupert George, 15 February 1847, ibid., vol. 4, doc. 16.
70. W. H. Crawley to George, 17 October 1846, ibid., vol. 3, doc. 111.
71. Report of James McLeod, Sydney, 12 January 1853, *JLANS*, 1853, appendix 30, pp. 319-20.
72. *Halifax Morning Post*, 14 January 1846.
73. For example, petition of the overseers of the poor, Horton, 11 January 1847, RG5, series P, vol. 83, PANS.
74. For example, petition of Thomas Belcher Desbrisay, Dartmouth, February 1847, ibid.
75. Report on Indian affairs, 21 December 1847, *JLANS*, 1847, appendix 24, pp. 114-26; Minutes of council, 11 June 1847, vol. 214 1/2, PANS.
76. Report on Indian affairs, 8 February 1849, *JLANS*, 1849, appendix 36, pp. 336-39.
77. Ibid.; petition of Pelancea Paul and nine others, Chebucto, 8 February 1849, *Times & Courier*, 27 February 1849; received 10 February, *JLANS*, 1849, p. 262.
78. *Acadian Recorder*, 24 February 1849; *Church Times*, 2 March 1849; *Times & Courier*, 27 February 1849.
79. *Times & Courier*, 7 June 1849; *Nova Scotian*, 11 June 1849.
80. Gesner to Howe, 13 April 1853, RG1, vol. 431, doc. 69, PANS; *Daily Sun*, 3 June 1853.
81. Report of Indian commissioner, 4 March 1854, *JLANS*, 1854, appendix 26, pt. 2, pp. 211-12.
82. Report of the committee on Indian affairs, 13 April 1857, *JLANS*, 1857, appendix 63, pp. 379-80; *Evening Express*, 28 May 1858.

83. Howe to Dawson, 1 October 1842, RG1, vol. 432, p. 152, PANS.
84. Report of the committee on Indian affairs, n.d., *JLANS*, 1849, appendix 88, pp. 498–500; assembly resolution, 22 March 1850, *JLANS*, 1850, p. 581.
85. H. Shaw to unknown, 7 February and 3 March 1854, MG15, vol. 5, doc. 24, PANS.
86. Petition of Peter Paul Toney Babey, physician, chemist and alchemist, 27 February 1852, ibid., vol. 4a, doc. 126; *JLANS*, 1852, p. 93. The house debated the petition with "some merriment" (*Nova Scotian*, 1 March 1852). See also petition of Peter Bobbeie, 16 January 1855, MG15, vol. 5, doc. 42, PANS.
87. Petition of John McKinnon Sr., 21 January 1856, MG15, vol. 5, doc. 71, PANS.
88. Report of the committee on Indian affairs, 13 April 1857, *JLANS*, 1857, appendix 63; resolution of assembly, 29 April 1857, ibid., p. 373.
89. Report of W. H. Crawley, 1 February 1849, *JLANS*, 1849, appendix 45, pp. 354–58; report of W. A. Hendry, 8 February 1862, ibid., 1862, appendix 30, pp. 5–10.
90. For some typical squatter responses when their title was challenged, see Widow Mackenzie to S. P. Fairbanks, 10 December 1858, RG10, vol. 461, folder "Petitions"; Quarrie McQuarrie to Fairbanks, 27 December 1858, ibid., vol. 460, folder 10; Donald McLean to Fairbanks, 30 September 1864, ibid., folder 8, PAC.
91. Inhabitants of Indian River to Crawley, 27 August 1850; Peter Gougou et al. to Crawley, 17 November 1850, MG15, vol. 4, doc. 87, PANS; the same petitioners, 24 January, RG10, vol. 460, folder 19, PAC. Indian complaints against whites at Whycocomagh went back at least to 1821 (F. Cranwell to George, 5 November 1821, RG1, vol. 430, doc. 158, PANS).
92. In W. A. Hendry to attorney-general, 9 October 1852, RG1, vol. 431, doc. 65, PANS.
93. As the sequel to the complaints from Ingraham's River once again proved: Chearnley to Messrs. Webber &c., 25 July 1853, ordering him to lower his dam, ibid., doc. 72; proceedings were instituted in August but still had not begun by May, 1854, ibid., docs. 73, 82.
94. Report by W. S. Morris of Gold River survey, 13 November 1852, RG10, vol. 459, folder 3; William Faulkner to J. B. Uniacke, 20 January 1857, ibid., vol. 460, folder 12, PAC.
95. Minutes of council, 13 April 1852, RG3, vol. 214 1/2G, p. 35; a manuscript order vesting title in the crown lands commissioner, 15 March 1852, RG1, vol. 431, doc. 98; memorandum on Indian reserves, 7 April 1852, ibid., doc. 67; Uniacke's report, 9 June 1854, copy in ibid., doc. 98 1/2, PANS; original in RG10, vol. 460, folder 19, PAC. See also Uniacke to Seth Williams, 24 May 1854, RG1, vol. 431, doc. 83, PANS.
96. *Daily Sun*, 3 June 1853.
97. Fairbanks to provincial secretary, 12 August 1858, RG1, vol. 431, doc. 99, PANS.
98. 22 Vict. c. 14 (*Statutes of Nova Scotia 1859* [Halifax, 1859], pp. 19–21); draft bill in RG5, series U, vol. 35, PANS.
99. Charles Tupper to Fairbanks, 22 August 1859, *JLANS*, 1859, appendix "Indian Reserves," p. 392; report of Indian commissioner, 10 February 1859, *JLCNS*, 1859, appendix 27, pp. 424–27; *JLANS*, 1860, appendix, "Indians," p. 322; report on crown lands, 25 January 1861, *JLCNS*, 1861, appendix 7, pp. 2–8.
100. Chearnley to provincial secretary, 26 May 1862, RG1, vol. 431, doc. 136, PANS; report of Indian commissioner, 9 February 1863, *JLCNS*, 1863, appendix 16, pp. 1–2.
101. "Of Indians," c. 57 (*Revised Statutes of Nova Scotia 1864* [Halifax, 1864], pp. 205–8; report of crown lands commissioner, 25 January 1861, *JLCNS*, 1861, appendix 7, pp. 2–6; report of committee on Indian affairs, n.d., *JLANS*, 1864, appendix 37, pp. 5–7.
102. Report of Indian commissioner, 1 February 1864, ibid., pp. 1–2.
103. Hendry to Fairbanks, 8 February 1862, *JLANS*, 1862, appendix 30, pp. 5–10; Hendry to Fairbanks, quoting the missionary J. Courteau, 25 February 1863, *JLCNS*, 1863, appendix 16, pp. 3–4.
104. Report of Indian commissioner, 31 December 1866, *JLCNS*, 1867, appendix 6, pp. 1–2.

105. Ibid.; *JCLNS*, 1863, appendix 16, p. 5; printed circulars are in RG10, vol. 460, folder 11; unissued deeds, ibid., folder 9, PAC; Vertical Manuscript Files: Provincial Treasury: Indian Affairs, PANS.

106. Report of Indian commissioner, 31 December 1866; Report of Indian affairs committee, 29 April 1867, *JLANS*, 1867, appendix 39.

NOTES TO CHAPTER SEVEN

1. Lord Dorchester to Lt.-Gov. Thomas Carleton, 3 January 1787, in *Winslow Papers*, ed. W.O. Raymond (Saint John: New Brunswick Historical Society, 1901), pp. 338–39. Carleton to Dundas, 20 November 1792, CO. 188/5, ff. 3–4; he put much of the blame for the disturbances on "Canada traders" selling liquor to the Indians (Carleton to Dorchester, 1 October 1790, CO. 188/4, ff. 325–26).

2. Licence to John Julien, 20 August 1783, RG20, series C, vol. 95, PANS.

3. Benjamin Marston to Thomas Knox, 29 August 1785, RG2, RS8, Indians, PANB; 8 July 1785, Records of Crown Lands, Journal of Proceedings, 1785, no. 4, f. 13, PANB.

4. Moses H. Perley, "The Indians of New Brunswick," [1848], CO. 188/106, ff. 206–23.

5. Ibid., Licence of occupation to John Julien, 5 March 1804, New Brunswick— Indian Affairs, MGH54, HILA; 5 March 1805, Records of Crown Lands, Journal of Proceedings, vol. 11, 1803–6, ff. 26–27, PANB.

6. 28 February 1807, ibid., vol. 12, 1806–8, f. 19.

7. William F. Odell to G. Sproule, 16 September 1808, MGH54, HILA; Perley, "History," passim.

8. Proclamation, 28 June 1788, MGH54, HILA.

9. Certificate of George Sproule, 29 January 1802, ibid.

10. Petition of Tabusintac Indians, 26 September 1801, with endorsements, ibid.; Perley, "Indians," passim.

11. Certificate of Jonathan Odell, 29 January 1802, MGH54, HILA.

12. "Schedule of Indian Reserves," 31 January 1838, *JLANB*, 1837–38, appendix 12.

13. Memorandum of examination of Indians at St. Andrews, October 1796, Maine Historical Society, The Barclay Collection, papers of the St. Croix Commission....1796–1827, folder 1, box 1, microfilm.

14. Minutes of commissioners, 7 October 1796, ibid.

15. Hunter to Castlereagh, 25 May 1808, RG1, RS2, PANB.

16. Lord Castlereagh to Hunter, 8 April 1809, CO. 189/111, ff. 199–200.

17. Minutes of the executive council, 22 June and 10 July 1812, RG2, RS6, vol. 2, pp. 53, 59, PANB; *Royal Gazette*, Fredericton, 13 July 1812.

18. Agreement with marks of Lewis Thomas Ganis et al., 20 August 1812; proclamation by Major-General G. S. Smyth, 20 August 1812, MGH54, HILA.

19. Minutes of the executive council, 19 July 1813, RG2, RS6, vol. 2, p. 76, PANB.

20. Minutes of 6 May 1814, ibid., pp. 88–89. The assembly later protested that this was a misuse of public money (*JLANB*, 1816, 29 February 1816); memorandum by Jonathan Odell, n.d., Odell Papers, box 13c, item 10, NBM.

21. Lieutenant-Governor Sir Howard Douglas to Bathurst, 25 January, Bathurst to Douglas, 30 June 1825. These were the only contributions from New Brunswick to the "Reports from Governors...on the present state of the Aboriginal Tribes," House of Commons, *Sessional Papers* (1834), 44: 485–86.

22. Report of the Indian commissioners to Douglas, 28 February 1827, S35–M12.1, RG4, RS24, PANB.

23. Sir George Murray to Douglas, 15 March 1830, CO. 189/12, ff. 419–21.

24. Proclamations by Lt.-Gov. Sir William Colebrooke, 29 July and 16 August 1841, RG2, RS7, vol. 40, pp. 226, 229, PANB.

25. "Return of the number of Persons who have settled upon, and occupy portions

of the Indian Reserves, in the Province of New Brunswick, 1841," RG2, RS8, Indians, PANB; *PR*, appendix, p. cxxviii.

26. Report of attorney-general and solicitor-general, 22 February 1842, CO. 188/76, ff. 122–23.

27. 21 and 29 March 1843, *JLANB*, 1843, pp. 206–8, 235–36.

28. Richard McLaughlin to Thomas Baillie, 6 August 1832; agreement, 23 August 1832, with marks of Mitchell, Diny, and Barnaby Julien, MGH54, HILA. The reserve remained unsold.

29. 24 January 1838, *JLANB*, 1837–38, pp. 87–88.

30. 23 February 1838, ibid., 187–89. Perley asserted that the land sales were not made as a result of vigorous protests from the Richibucto Indians, "Indians," passim.

31. 3 March 1838, *JLANB*, 1837–38, p. 219.

32. Glenelg to Harvey, 22 August 1838, CO. 189/15, ff. 252–54.

33. Harvey to Lord Normanby, 14 May 1839, enclosing commissioners' reports, CO. 188/64, ff. 146–63.

34. In a report three years later, the Gloucester county commissioners noted the reluctance of the Indians to provide any information concerning their numbers, means of support, or exact location on their lands (A. Barberrie and T.M. Deblois to Odell, 4 June 1841, RG2, RS8, Indians, PANB).

35. Harvey to Normanby, 14 May 1839.

36. Normanby to Harvey, 27 July 1839, CO. 189/15, ff. 342–46.

37. In 1823, at the age of eighteen, Perley accidentally killed an Indian while at target practice, see pp. 145–20. There may have been an element of atonement in his later championing of the Indians' cause.

38. Alfred Reade to Perley, 16 and 23 June 1841, *PR*, pp. cxxi–xxii.

39. Ibid., p. xcviii.

40. Ibid., p. c. Perley was reprimanded for using his title in correspondence with the colonial secretary (Odell to Perley, 18 May 1844, provincial secretary's letter book, 1842–45, pp. 216–17, RG3, RS13, PANB).

41. *PR*, pp. civ, cvii–ix.

42. L.F.S. Upton, "The Origins of Canadian Indian Policy," *Journal of Canadian Studies* 8, no. 4 (1973): 51–61.

43. For example, Lord Glenelg to Earl of Durham, 22 August 1838, where the colonial secretary contrasted the noble efforts of Jesuit missionaries to the disinterest of the British ("Copies or Extracts of Correspondence," House of Commons, *Sessional Papers* [1839], 34: 223–27; *PR*, p. cvi).

44. *PR*, p. cvi.

45. Ibid., p. xcvi, for one example.

46. Colebrooke to Lord Falkland, 3 May 1842, Colebrooke letter book, pp. 18–19, RG1, RS2, PANB.

47. Lord Stanley to Colebrooke, 26 August 1842, CO. 189/16, ff. 328–29.

48. Reade to Perley, 17 February 1843; Perley to Sir Hesketh Fleetwood, 25 February 1843, "Transcripts of Moses Perley Letters 1813–1854," Ganong Papers, box 38, NBM.

49. Report of attorney-general and solicitor-general, 22 February 1842.

50. Minutes of council, 4 and 5 May 1842, RG2, RS6, vol. 4, pp. 325, 328–29; Odell to Perley, 6 May 1842, provincial secretary's letter book, 1838–42, p. 255, RG3, RS13, PANB; *Royal Gazette*, Fredericton, 18 and 25 May 1842.

51. 15 March 1843, *JLANB*, 1843, p. 174; however, £50 was voted for a missionary to the Malecites "at Fredericton" and £25 for a missionary at Madawaska, 21 March 1843, ibid., pp. 205–6.

52. Committee report, 21 and 29 March 1843, ibid., pp. 206–8, 235–36.

53. Minutes of council, 10 June 1843, vol. 5, pp. 89–90, RG2, RS6, PANB.

54. In *Statutes of New Brunswick, 1844* (Fredericton, 1845), pp. 147–49.

55. Report of council on Indian Act, 29 July 1844, RG2, RS7, vol. 40, pp. 269–73, PANB.

56. Stanley to Colebrooke, 1 and 24 August 1844, CO. 189/17, ff. 239–41, 249–50.

57. John S. Saunders to John Dibblee, 25 July 1845, provincial secretary's letter book, 1845–47, pp. 35–39, RG3, RS13, PANB.

58. Saunders to Perley, 13 September 1845, ibid., pp. 66–67.

59. In particular, Perley was afraid the commissioners would be too tender to squatters; see, for example, his strictures on William Salter, and the latter's defence (Perley to Saunders, 22 July 1847, Salter to Baillie, 30 November 1847, RG2, RS8, Indians, PANB).

60. Perley to Saunders, 14 February 1846, ibid.; Perley's draft of "A Bill for the Management and disposal of the Indian Reserves in this Province," n.d., ibid., RS7, vol. 40, pp. 214–22.
61. Perley to Baillie, 30 December 1847, ibid., RS8, Indians.·
62. Advertisement in *Royal Gazette*, Fredericton, 11 August 1847.
63. 12 April 1847, *JLANB*, 1847, pp. 357–58; report of 3 March 1848, *Indian Affairs in New-Brunswick* (Fredericton, 1848), pp. 5–6. The earlier report did note that Indians should be allowed to retain "suitable" woodlands and campgrounds in addition to the fifty-acre farms available to families.
64. Report of 3 March 1848.
65. Minutes of council, 4 April 1848, RG2, RS6, vol. 6, pp. 210–11, PANB.
66. Colebrooke to Lord Grey, with notations, 8 April 1847, CO. 188/104, ff. 375–77.
67. Sir Edmund Head to Grey, 17 August 1848, CO. 108/106, ff. 180–201.
68. Ibid.
69. Perley, "Indians," passim.
70. Grey to Head, 11 November 1848, CO. 189/18, ff. 328–31.
71. General Regulations, 7 July 1849, RG2, RS8, Indians, PANB.
72. Dibblee to John McMillan, 20 May 1862, ibid.
73. Report on Tobique Indians, 11 May 1865, ibid.
74. R. Sutton to Langevin, 2 December 1867, with enclosures, ibid.
75. 19 March 1858, *JLANB*, 1858, pp. ccclxxxiii–xxxv.
76. Report of Stafford Benson, ibid., 1854 (1), pp. cclxviii–ix; Samuel Tilley to Dibblee, 31 July and 8 August 1855, provincial secretary's letterbook, 1854–57, pp. 168, 172, RG3, RS13, PANB.
77. Tilley to Dibblee, 8 August 1855, p. 173; Benjamin Close to J. B. Toldervey, 21 June 1851, RG2, RS7, vol. 40, pp. 196–97, PANB.
78. 1 September 1855, provincial secretary's letterbook, 1854–57, p. 189, RG3, RS13, PANB.
79. John Partelow to Perley, 2 April 1851; Partelow to Dibblee, 30 July 1851, ibid., 1850–54, p. 156.
80. Louis Robichaud to Tilley, 12 October 1858, RG2, RS7, vol. 40, p. 44, PANB.
81. 14 February 1854, *JLANB*, 1854(1), p. 19.
82. Report on Tobique Indians, 11 May 1865.

NOTES TO CHAPTER EIGHT

1. For the French period, see D. C. Harvey, *The French Régime in Prince Edward Island*, pp. 212–32; John H. Maloney, "And in the Beginning...," *Canada's Smallest Province*, ed. Francis W. P. Bolger (Charlottetown: P.E.I. Centennial Commission, 1973), pp. 1–10.
2. Andrew H. Clark, *Three Centuries and the Island* (Toronto: University of Toronto Press, 1959), pp. 261, 269.
3. Certificate of Edmund Fanning, 14 July 1806, CO. 226/21, f. 196; abstract of title to Lennox Island, 1 October 1772, CO. 226/94, f. 30; Clark, *Island*, p. 233, n. 19; James Douglas to Sir James Montgomery, 24 November 1800 and 26 August and 23 November 1802; Fanning to Montgomery, 14 November 1804, GD. 293/2/20, 17, 18, SRO.
4. Abbé de Calonne to Fanning [?], 16 July [1806]; memorial to Secretary of State William Windham, [1806], CO. 226/21, ff. 192–95; A. B. Warburton, *A History of Prince Edward Island* (Saint John: Barnes, 1923), pp. 231–32.
5. Report of Survey, 1841, *JLAPEI*, 1841, appendix K, p. 35.
6. Chief Francis had protested Yeo's conduct in 1827 (J. L. Hurdis to Captain Francis, 10 December 1827, MG1, vol. 449, file 230, PANS); *Royal Gazette* Charlottetown, 21 February 1832 and 28 March 1843; 12 April 1841, *JLAPEI*, 1841, p. 119; Robert Stewart to John Prendergast, 2 December 1835, letter books of Robert Stewart, vol. 2, pp. 348–52, PAPEI.
7. Petition of Oliver Thomas Le Bone, May 1838; Lieutenant-Governor Sir Charles A. Fitzroy to Lord Glenelg, 8

October 1838, *JLA PEI*, 1840, appendix N, pp. 111–13.

8. [S. Hill], *A Short Account of Prince Edward Island* (London: Madden and Co., 1829), pp. 54–55.

9. 8 and 9 April 1831, *JLA PEI*, 1831, pp. 20–22.

10. 7 January 1832, ibid., 1832, pp. 11–12.

11. *Royal Gazette*, 21 February 1832; David Stewart to Lord Normanby, 2 August 1839, *JLA PEI*, 1840, appendix N, p. 114.

12. The negotiations for the sale were carried out by David's brother, Robert Stewart (Stewart to John Lawson, 30 December 1833 and 6 August 1834, letter books, vol. 1, pp. 337–43, 413–15; Stewart to Prendergast, 4 February and 1 July 1835 and 12 November 1834, ibid., vol. 2, pp. 109–13, 217–21, 35–42).

13. The petition and ensuing correspondence are in *JLA PEI*, 1840, appendix N.

14. Fitzroy to Russell, 5 May and 25 November 1840 and 11 May 1841, CO. 226/60, ff. 240–41, 383–84, also 475–76, CO. 226/61, f. 211: 10, 14, 15, and 20 April 1840, *JLA PEI*, 1840, pp. 110, 124, 135, 136; 12 April 1841, ibid., 1841, p. 119, appendix K.

15. 20 January and 6 April 1843, *JLA PEI*, 1843, pp. 69, 121.

16. 20 January 1843, ibid., 1843, p. 68; 2 April 1846, ibid., 1846, p. 87; 25 April 1848, ibid., 1848, p. 151.

17. 19 Vic., c. 10, "An Act relating to the Indians of Prince Edward Island," passed 4 April 1856 (*Revised Statutes of Prince Edward Island* [Charlottetown, 1862], pp. 164–65); Lieutenant-Governor Dominic Daly sent the law on to the Colonial Office without comment (14 June 1856, CO. 226/87, ff. 123–25); [Theophilus Stewart], "The Micmacs of Prince Edward Island," *Aborigines' Friend and Colonial Intelligencer* (London), (1865): 508–10.

18. *JLA PEI*, passim.

19. Henry Palmer to Cornelius Howat, 7 April 1862, *JLA PEI*, 1862, appendix Y, n.p.

20. For an example of Stewart's accounts, see ibid., 1860, appendix L; Stewart, "Micmacs," pp. 508–10.

21. Report of Theophilus Stewart, 4 March 1861, *JLA PEI*, 1861, appendix S; 10 February 1862, ibid., 1862, appendix Y.

22. Reports of Stewart, 22 February, and Palmer, 11 March 1858, ibid., 1858, appendix R; petition of James Louis and others, 7 May 1866, ibid., 1866, p. 86.

23. Stewart, report, 22 February 1858, ibid., 1858, appendix R; petition of Stewart and Palmer, 4 March 1858, ibid., pp. 30–31, 90–91; Stewart, report, 19 March 1860, ibid., appendix L; Stewart, "Micmacs," pp. 508–10; Stewart to superintendent of Indian affairs, 5 January 1875, *DIAAR*, 1874, 51–52.

24. Stewart, report, 19 March 1860, *JLA PEI*, 1860, appendix 1; petition of Peter Francis, 8 April 1861, ibid., 1861, pp. 109, 143; William and Francis Herring to Charles Desbrisay, 6 July 1861, ibid., 1862, appendix L, p. 115; address to His Excellency, 8 May 1866, ibid., 1866, pp. 89–90, 93, 111.

25. "The Indians," *The Examiner*, 21 August 1860; "Princely Munificence Impeded in Its Course," ibid., 10 December 1860.

26. Lieutenant-Governor George Dundas to Duke of Newcastle, 15 October 1860, CO. 226/92, ff. 331–32.

27. *The Examiner*, 21 August, 10 September 1860, 26 August 1861; report of the land commissioners, *JLA PEI*, 1862, appendix O; petition of John Trenamen, 28 March 1862, ibid., p. 78.

28. Newcastle to Dundas, 2 September 1861, enclosing R. B. Stewart to Newcastle, 27 August 1861, CO. 226/94, ff. 26–29; abstract of title, ibid., f. 30.

29. *JLA PEI*, 1862, p. 129; ibid., 1864, p. 114.

30. Petition of Stewart and Palmer, 19 March 1860, ibid., 1860, pp. 56, 79; petition of John Mitchell, 19 April 1861, ibid., 1861, p. 146; petition of James Louis and other Micmacs, 20 April 1859, ibid., 1859, p. 66; order of 20 April 1861, ibid., 1861, p. 148.

31. Stewart, report, 10 February 1862, ibid., 1862, appendix Y.

32. 25 March 1868, ibid., 1868, p. 30; ibid., passim; Stewart, report, 25 March 1869, ibid., 1869, appendix T; *DIAAR*, 1874, p. 52.

33. Stewart, "Micmacs," pp. 508–10.

34. Aborigines' Protection Society, Seventh and Eighth *Annual Reports* (London, 1844, 1845), appendix, pp. 34–57; *Aborigines' Friend* (1861): 230–32.

35. *Aborigines' Friend* (1865): 112.

36. When Stewart returned the conveyance and other documents, they were all lost in the wreck of the SS *City of Boston* (Stewart to Richard Smith, 3 March 1870, enclosing duplicates of his letters of 19 and 22 January together with the minutes of the Micmac Society meeting of January 20); Stewart to Smith, 5 March 1870, APS Papers, MSS Br. Emp., S22, G83, Rhodes House, Oxford. Stewart to F.W. Chesson, 26 December 1870, ibid., S18, C148, f. 99; Chesson to Lord Kimberley, 19 August 1871, CO. 226/108, ff. 330–31; Stewart, report, 13 April 1870, *JLAPEI*, 1870, appendix AA; *The Islander*, 10 June 1870; *Quebec Mercury*, 7 June 1870.

One benefaction begat another. In 1872, Lady Wood of Bath left her estate to be divided amongst the deaf and dumb of Prince Edward Island and the Micmacs. The bequest was widely reported. Ten years later, after the lawyers had finished, there was a little over £2,000 left. A provincial committee decided in 1886 to invest the money in the Dominion Government Savings Bank; half of the interest would go annually to the Nova Scotia Deaf and Dumb Institute, half to the dominion superintendent of Indian affairs for Prince Edward Island (folder "Re Estate of Lady Wood," APS Papers, S22, G83; *Harbour Grace Star*, 11 June 1872; *Saint John Daily News*, 1 June 1872.

37. "Mr. T. Stewart's account of Indian disbursements &c," *JLAPEI*, 1872, appendix P; *DIAAR*, 1874, pp. 51–52.

38. As can be seen from the flurry of correspondence; the basic letters are: Chesson to Kimberley, 19 August 1871, (draft in APS Papers, S18, C149, f. 351); Kimberley to William Robinson, 23 August 1871, CO. 227/12, f. 77; Robinson to Kimberley, 19 September 1871 and 20 September 1872, CO. 226/109, f. 113, CO. 226/110, ff. 24–25. The APS had earlier been concerned about fishing rights at Lennox Island, Stewart to Richard Smith, 22 January 1870, APS Papers, S22, G83.

39. Superintendent-General of Indian affairs to J.C. Aikins, 21 August 1873; E.P. Meredith to Stewart, 22 August 1873, 15 January and 9 May 1874, RG10, vol. 4,386, pp. 115–16, 134, vol. 4,387, pp. 886–88, vol. 4,390, pp. 157–58, PAC.

40. *DIAAR*, 1874, pp. 51–52.

NOTES TO CHAPTER NINE

1. Alexander Monro, *New Brunswick with a Brief Outline of Nova Scotia, and Prince Edward Island* (Halifax: R. Nugent, 1855), p. 278; Abraham Gesner, Report on Indian Affairs, 21 December 1847, *JLANS*, 1847, appendix 24, pp. 114–26; Fitzroy to Lord Glenelg, 8 October 1838, *JLAPEI*, 1840, appendix N, pp. 111–13. This chapter is a revised version of my article "Colonists and Micmacs," *Journal of Canadian Studies* 10, no. 3 (1975): 44–56.

2. *PR*, appendix, p. xcvii.

3. Wiswall to George, draft, 22 March 1823, Wiswall Papers, PANS.

4. For examples, see pp. 92–93.

5. *Morning Journal*, 20 April 1856.

6. William Pearson to unknown, 4 January [*sic*: February] 1861, MG15, vol. 6, doc. 63, PANS.

7. Winthrop Bell, "A Hessian Conscript's Account of Life in Garrison at Halifax at the time of the American Revolution," Nova Scotia Historical Society, *Collections*, 27 (1947): 125–46. [Written by Johann Seume.]

8. Titus Smith Jr., "Report of the Eastern and Northern Parts of the Province [Nova Scotia] in the Years 1801 & 1802," RG1, vol. 380, pp. 113, 116, PANS.

9. Council minutes, 9 March 1790, RG20/319, p. 315, PANS.

10. Titus Smith, "Report," p. 117.

11. Petition of eleven families to Wentworth, [1807], Vertical Manuscript File: Indians; Land, PANS.

12. Charlotte Phelan to Walter Bromley, 7 February 1818, in Walter Bromley, *An Appeal ... in behalf of the Indians of North America* (Halifax: Ward, 1820),

pp. 26–28.

13. *Quebec Gazette*, 4 March 1836.

14. Wallis and Wallis, *Micmacs*, p. 92.

15. Sir John Harvey to Grey, with minutes, CO. 217/202, ff. 291–92.

16. Joseph Barrett, *The Indians of New England* (Middletown, Conn., 1851), p. 4. Tenesles was married to a Micmac at the time.

17. "A New Brunswicker" to the editor of the *London Sporting Review* in *The Times* (Halifax), 20 August 1839. Perley is using the term "boys" in the derogatory sense that whites often applied to grown men of a different race. The letter was based on his experiences on a hunting expedition described in the Saint John *Courier*, 18 November 1837.

18. "Arthur, H.R.H. Prince," Vertical Manuscript File, PANS.

19. Macworth Shove, *Two Months on the Tobique* (London, 1866), p. 101.

20. Arthur Gordon, "Wilderness Journeys in New Brunswick," in *Vacation Tourists and Notes of Travel in 1862-3*, ed. Francis Galton (London: Macmillan 1864), pp. 515–22.

21. Titus Smith, "Report," pp. 131–32.

22. *PR*, pp. cii, civ.

23. Ibid., p. xcviii.

24. *The Gleaner*, 6 January 1851.

25. Letter of "Philanthropus," *Nova Scotian*, 16 August 1827; Bromley, *Appeal*, p. 16.

26. *Acadian Recorder*, 19 October 1833; for a similar lament, ibid., 19 April 1834.

27. Coroner's inquest, RG41-22, PANS.

28. Comments of Moses Delesdernier in Brown MSS, Add. MSS 19071, ff. 259–63, microfilm, PANS.

29. Letter to Rev. Silas Rand from Shediac, N.B., 17 October 1850, *Christian Messenger*, 25 October 1850.

30. Charles Ward to John Widden, MG15, vol. 3, doc. 72, PANS.

31. *Halifax Morning Post*, 14 January 1846.

32. Wallis and Wallis, *Micmacs*, pp. 461–63.

33. Ibid., pp. 307–8.

34. Ibid., pp. 471–72, 476–77.

35. Statement of Joseph Malli (Murray) for Lord Stanley, 9 February 1842, New Brunswick Papers, 1840–49, RG10, vol. 469, PAC.

36. Monk Papers, MG23, G11-19, pp. 1046–50, 1053–55, 1067–77, PAC.

37. Captain W. Moorsom, *Letters from Nova Scotia* (London: H. Colburn and R. Bentley, 1829), p. 111.

38. Petition of Chief Pemmeenauweet, [January 1831], RG1, vol. 430, doc. 176, PANS.

39. Petition of Chief Pemmeenauweet, [received at the Colonial Office 25 January 1841], CO. 217/179, ff. 406–8. See also p. 89.

40. Petition of chiefs and captains of the Indians, 5 January 1848, MG15, vol. 4, doc. 57, PANS. Several whites commented on the Indians' tendency towards the indiscriminate slaughter of game, for example Abraham Gesner, *The Industrial Resources of Nova Scotia* (Halifax: A. and W. MacKinlay, 1849), pp. 222–23.

41. Petition of John Battis, Joseph Battis, and Francis Cope to Lord Falkland, 6 April 1845, MG15, vol. 3, doc. 81, PANS.

42. Petition of Gorham Paul to Lord Falkland, 15 July 1842, CO. 217/178, ff. 101–3.

43. *Acadian Recorder*, 8 and 24 February 1849.

44. Petition of Francis Paul, Gorham Paul, Louis Paul, et al., 25 July 1853, CO. 217/213, ff. 8–25. The Colonial Office considered the whole document "written & conceived in English" and was not impressed (ibid., ff. 3–4); *Christian Messenger*, 16 March 1854.

45. Indian Address, [23 July] 1860, RG2/114, no. 114, PANS.

46. Petition of Peter Charles, March 1866, MG15, vol. 6, doc. 73, PANS.

47. *Nova Scotian*, 7 May 1840.

48. J.W. Dawson, *A Handbook of the Geography and Natural History of the Province of Nova Scotia for the Use of Schools and Families*, 2d ed. (Pictou: Macpherson and Co., 1851). Twenty years later, J. B. Calkin, *The Geography and History of Nova Scotia*, new ed. (Halifax: A. and W. MacKinlay, 1873), gave the Indians 81 words in 110 pages.

49. Moorsom, *Letters*, p. 109.

50. Bell, "A Hessian Conscript's Account of Life," p. 136.

51. Lieutenant Campbell Hardy, *Sporting Adventures in the New World; or Days and Nights of Moose-Hunting in the Pine Forests of Acadia*, 2 vols. (London: Hurst and Blackett, 1855), 1: 30–31.

52. Monro, *New Brunswick*, p. lv: James F. W. Johnston, *Notes on North America:*

Agricultural, Economical, and Social, 2 vols. (Edinburgh and London: Blackwood, 1851), 2: 190.

53. Abraham Gesner, *New Brunswick; with Notes for Emigrants* (London: Simmonds and Ward, 1847), ch. 5, pp. 106–18.

54. W. R. M. Burtis, *New Brunswick as a Home for Emigrants* (Saint John, 1860).

55. G. W. Atkinson, *A Historical and Statistical Account of New Brunswick, B.N.A., with Advice to Emigrants,* 3d ed. (Edinburgh: Anderson and Bryce, 1844), pp. 209–14.

56. Rev. John Sprott in *Nova Scotian,* 6 April 1846.

57. Ibid., 6 March 1828.

58. T. C. Haliburton, *A General Description of Nova Scotia* (Halifax: C. H. Belcher, 1823), p. 56.

59. Raymond, *St. John,* p. 472; Moses H. Perley, "On the Early History of New Brunswick," *Educational Review* [Fredericton?], (1891): 174.

60. Hardy, *Sporting Adventures,* 1: p. 41.

61. Petition of inhabitants of Whycocomagh, January 1856, MG15, vol. 5, doc. 70, PANS.

62. *Guardian,* 30 January 1839.

63. "Letter on Mickmack Indians," *Nova Scotian,* 29 August 1832.

64. *Free Press,* 11 March 1817.

65. Haliburton, *Nova Scotia,* p. 55.

66. *Nova Scotian,* 6 April 1846.

67. William Bowman to Wiswall, 30 October 1828, Wiswall Papers, PANS.

68. Gesner, Report on Indian Affairs, *JLANS,* 1847.

69. John Monk to George Monk, 7 September 1783, pp. 231–32, Monk Papers, PAC.

70. Jonathan Odell to Gervas Say, 11 May 1789, RG2, RS8, Indians, PANB.

71. See pp. 160–65.

72. "Publicola," *Free Press,* 11 March 1817.

73. Anthony Lockwood, *A Brief Description of Nova Scotia* (London: G. Hayden, Cadell and Davies, 1818), pp. 7–10.

74. Bromley, *An Appeal,* passim.

75. *Great Exhibition of the Work of Industry of all Nations, 1851; Official Descriptive and Illustrated Catalogue,* 3 vols. (London, 1851), 2: 969–70.

76. Monro, *New Brunswick,* pp. iii–iv.

77. "Biography of Peter Paul—Written February 16th 1865 From his own statement" (unidentified press clipping, scrapbook of Dr. George Patterson, scrapbook no. 5, PANS).

NOTES TO CHAPTER TEN

1. Haliburton, *Nova Scotia,* p. 55.

2. 28 April 1814, framed original document, item 31.24, NSM.

3. Proclamation, September 1836; undated paper; election statement, 5 August 1836, signed Michael Egan, Indian Affairs—New Brunswick, MGH54, HILA; Perley to Odell, 2 October 1843, RG2, RS7, vol. 40, pp. 7–9, PANB.

4. Deposition of Robert Christie, 24 February 1838, GII–90; Charles Buller to Bishop [Signay], 16 August 1838, GII–96, AAQ.

5. 7 August 1815, memorial to Major-General George Smyth, RG2, RS8, Indians, PANB.

6. 29 September 1847, petition, NBHS Papers, packet 6, NBM.

7. Petition of Jacob Brooks et al. to Lieutenant-Governor Adam George Archibald, 5 February 1883; petition of Christopher Paul et al. to Archibald, 29 March 1883, RG2-9, documents 1815, 1820, PANS; "Micmac Indians," notes ca. 1911, Harry Piers Papers, NSM.

8. R. Macdonald to superintendent-general of Indian Affairs, 28 July 1881, *DIAAR,* 1881, pp. 29–30.

9. Petition signed by 42 whites, 9 February 1856, MG15, vol. 5, doc. 56, PANS.

10. Thomas Robertson, "History of Shelburne County," Akins Prize Essay 1871, King's College Library, Halifax.

11. For example, Horton Township, 1787, RG34–316, P5; Digby County 1830, RG34–310, P2, p. 25, PANS.

12. Petition of W. D. Corbett, 5 February 1855, MG15, vol. 6, doc. 73, PANS.

13. "Return of Criminal & Penal Suits before Edw H Lowe Esq., Year 1843. Halifax," RG34–312, J3, PANS.

14. Walter Bromley, *An Appeal,* p. 35n.

15. *PR*, appendix p. ci.
16. For example, John Henderson threatened to shoot the first Indian he caught fishing the Pisabeque River (Petition of Chief Matthew Andrew, [ca. 1800], RG2, RS8, Indians, PANB.
17. Unidentifiable press clipping, ca. November 1883, NBHS, SB, C27, p. 127, NBM.
18. *Royal Gazette & New-Brunswick Advertiser*, 27 June 1786. The pardon for William Harbord, 27 June 1786, "for divers and good Causes" is in RG2, RS8, "Crime," PANB.
19. Haliburton, *Nova Scotia*, p. 48.
20. Moses Perley accidentally killed an Indian while at target practice near Saint John in 1823. He was tried for manslaughter and fined £10. The local Indians accepted Perley's explanation ([Walter Bromley], "Report of the Indians in New Brunswick....," J.C. Webster Collection, packet 31, NBM).
21. *Morning Freeman*, 10 June 1871.
22. Court of General Sessions, Kings County, Proceedings, 1760–64, RG34–316, P1, PANS.
23. Court of General Sessions, Cumberland County, RG34–309, P2, PANS.
24. Halifax Police Court Records, RG135/102, PANS.
25. Ibid.
26. *Morning Freeman*, 1871, passim.
27. Entry Book, Westmoreland County Historical Society, on loan to PANB. Gabriel Meuse, farmer, had been committed for perjury despite a plea for clemency: he had acted "under the pressure of extreme poverty." The one-year sentence was considered a light punishment for the crime (Petition of Gabriel Meuse, [April 1859], RG1, vol. 431, doc. 103, PANS). In 1969, with less than 1 per cent of the population of New Brunswick, Indians accounted for 3.3 per cent of those convicted for indictable offences; in Nova Scotia, 0.6 per cent and 1.8 per cent respectively; in Prince Edward Island, 0.4 per cent and none. Most offences concerned alcohol and motor vehicle violations (Law Reform Commission of Canada, *The Native Offender and the Law*, [Ottawa, 1974], p. 15).
28. Judge Halliburton to Maitland, 12 May 1830, CO. 217/150, ff. 161–64; Sir George Murray to Maitland, 28 August 1830, RG1, vol. 430, doc. 170½, PANS.
29. The correspondence resulting from this case runs from 18 March to 27 May 1839, CO. 226/58, ff. 41–58.
30. Normanby to Fitzroy, 27 May 1839, CO. 229/10, ff. 32–34.
31. In his study of urban Indians at the present day, Mark Nagler, *Indians in the City* (Ottawa: Canadian Research Centre for Anthropology, St. Paul University, 1970), p. 79 quotes a Toronto police sergeant: "On practically any day of the week we could load up the paddy wagon" with drunken Indians, but "we have more important matters to be concerned with." Even if this attitude were in existence in colonial Halifax and Saint John, the absence of Indian involvement in "more important matters" is striking.
32. J.S. Erskine, "Their Crowded Hour: The Micmac Cycle," *Dalhousie Review* 38 (1959): 443–52.
33. J.E. Beckwith to superintendent-general of Indian affairs, 17 July 1884, *DIAAR*, 1884, p. 41. I know of only one camp burning that came to court, and that involved murder near Georgetown, P.E.I. (T. Stewart to Chesson, 2 January 1871, APS Papers, S18, C148, f. 99). The disposition of the case is not recorded.
34. Attorney-General Thomas Wetmore to Lieutenant-Governor Smyth, with enclosures, 24 September 1822, RG2, RS7, vol. 40, pp. 245–53, PANB.
35. 20 August 1768, Land Grants, Old Book 6, pp. 763–64, PANS.
36. 10 March 1786, ibid., Old Book 18, no. 24, PANS.
37. 3 September 1793, ibid., Old Book 20, no. 7, PANS.
38. 11 April 1817, Land Grants, Letter Book G, no. 84; 12 February 1839, Digby County Deeds, RG47, vol. 14, pp. 275–76, PANS.
39. Petition of Charles Glode, 10 February 1840, RG1, vol. 430, doc. 188; Index to Crown Land Grants: Glode, Charles 1840; Annapolis County Deeds, RG47, vol. 33, p. 400, vol. 38, p. 278, vol. 44, p. 166, vol. 45, pp. 95–96, PANS.
40. 31 July 1863, Land Grants, New Book, vol. 31, no. 251; 16 May 1865, ibid., vol. 33, no. 71, PANS.
41. For example, Charles Morris to Deputy Surveyor-General Crandle, 16 June

1810, RG10, vol. 459, folder 3, PAC.

42. Grant to Francis Xavier et al., 25 October 1792, Department of Lands and Mines, Fredericton, Land Grants IV, no. 269; 24 January 1795, ibid., Grants Book B, grant 300, pp. 443–48; W. O. Raymond, ed., *Winslow Papers* (Saint John: New Brunswick Historical Society, 1901), p. 333n.

43. William Faulkner to James B. Uniacke, 20 January 1857, RG10, vol. 460, folder 12, PAC.

44. Records of crown land commissioners, Journal of Proceedings, 1815, no. 17, f. 4, PANB.

45. Petition of John Larlee to Lieutenant-Governor Sir Archibald Campbell, 16 July 1832, MGH54, HILA.

46. Donald McKay to Richard McLoughlin, 28 July 1832, ibid.

47. Alexander Hamilton to Fairbanks, 2 December 1862, RG10, vol. 460, folder 13, PAC.

48. Petition of Peter and Albert Smith to Campbell, 10 April 1832, MGH54, HILA.

49. Paper endorsed "Indian Office at Buctouche," [ca. 1858], RG2, RS8, Indians, PANB.

50. Papers under date of original lease by Lewis Barnaby, 3 August 1810, ibid.

51. Petition of Richibucto Indians to Sir John Harvey, 12 October 1837, ibid. The lease is in ibid.

52. 26 March 1811, lease from Tabusintac Indians to Benjamin Stymest Jr., ibid.

53. 25 March 1799, Lunenburg County Deeds, RG47, vol. 5, pp. 24–25, PANS.

54. Certificate, 18 September 1841, RG2, RS8, Indians, PANB.

55. Jonathan Odell to Jacob Powell, 6 June 1809, MGH54, HILA.

56. RG2, RS8, Indians, PANB, passim.

57. Perley to Jonathan Odell, 2 October 1843, RG2, RS7, vol. 40, pp. 7–9, PANB.

58. James Holm to Reverend Michael Egan, 13 January 1840, RG2, RS8, Indians, PANB. Egan's advice is not on record.

59. Donald McLean to S. P. Fairbanks, 20 September 1864, RG10, vol. 460, folder 8, PAC.

60. *Halifax Morning Post*, 1 February 1842.

61. W. H. Crawley to Joseph Howe, 1 February 1849 and 13 February 1852, *JLANS*, 1849, appendix 45, pp. 354–58, ibid., 1852, appendix 32, p. 272.

62. 17 Vict. c. 6, *Statutes of Nova Scotia 1854* (Halifax, n.d.), pp. 12–15. The original draft read "No Indian shall be entitled to vote (under the qualification of residence)," but this wording was presumably too loose for the final version read "nor any Indian shall be entitled to vote" (series B, vol. 30, PANS).

63. 26 Vict. c. 28, *Statutes of Nova Scotia 1863* (Halifax, 1863), pp. 49–68.

64. Report on Indian Affairs, n.d., *JLANS*, 1864, appendix 37, pp. 5–6. John Garner, *The Franchise and Politics in British North America* (Toronto: University of Toronto Press, 1969), pp. 32, 160, gives the mistaken impression that the Indians were enfranchised by the 1863 law.

NOTES TO CHAPTER ELEVEN

1. P. F. Thorne to John Sullivan, 26 February 1803, CO. 194/43, ff. 274–76; [J.-O. Plessis], *Journal des Visites Pastorales de 1815 et 1816 Par Monseigneur Joseph-Octave Plessis Evêque de Québec* (Quebec: Têtu, 1903), p. 136.

2. The Indians at Chapel Island, quoted in Johnston, *Catholic Church*, 1: 306.

3. Silas T. Rand, *A Short Statement of Facts Relating to the History, Manners, Customs, Language, and Literature of the Micmac Tribe of Indians* (Halifax: James Bowes and Son, 1850), p. 24.

4. Silas T. Rand, *Legends of the Micmacs*, ed. Helen L. Webster (New York: Longmans, Green, [1893]), p. 231n.

5. Bishop Plessis to Rev. J.-M. Bellenger, 12 February 1818, Registre des Lettres, vol. 9, pp. 324–25, AAQ.

6. Rand, *Legends*, pp. 228–29.

7. Ibid., pp. 242–43. Marten was also one of the animals that played a large part in Micmac folklore.

8. Alexander F. Chamberlain, "'New Religions' among the North American Indians," *Journal of Religious Psychology* 6 (1913): 1–49.

9. Letter from Halifax, 25 April 1823, *Scottish Missionary Register*, 1823, pp. 274–75; John West, *A Journal of a Mission to the Indians of the British Provinces of New Brunswick and Nova Scotia* (London: Seeley, 1827), pp. 224, 247.

10. Haliburton, *Nova Scotia*, p. 53; Peter Fisher, *History of New Brunswick* (1825), ed. W. S. Fisher (Saint John: New Brunswick Historical Society, 1921), p. 94.

11. Lieutenant-Governor Thomas Carleton to Dundas, 14 June 1794; Dundas to Carleton, 8 August 1794, CO. 188/5, ff. 184–85, 188–89; Carleton to Duke of Portland, 19 December 1794, CO. 188/6, ff. 5–6.

12. Hunter to Plessis, 8 July 1808, Cartables: Gouvernement, I, no. 87; Plessis to Hunter, 7 September 1808, Registre des Lettres, vol. 6, pp. 236–37, AAQ; Plessis, *Journal... de 1815 et 1816*, pp. 126–27.

13. Plessis to Rev. Morriset, 25 October 1821, Registre des Lettres, vol. 10, pp. 285–88, AAQ. "He will think that he would rather give you the £50 than to let this group of British subjects take off for the United States."

14. Lieutenant-Governor Sir John Harvey to Lord Normanby, 14 May 1839, CO. 188/64, ff. 146–48. The grant continued for ten years before it was challenged as a misuse of public money (assembly debates of 9 March 1848, *Morning News*, 15 March 1848).

15. Quoted in John C. Macmillan, *The History of the Catholic Church in Prince Edward Island* (Quebec: L'Evénement, 1913), p. 251.

16. Johnston, *Catholic Church*, 1: 150.

17. Plessis to Beaubien, 10 August 1812, Registre des Lettres, vol. 7, p. 421, AAQ.

18. Johnston, *Catholic Church*, 1: 306.

19. Rev. Panet to Sir Howard Douglas, 26 May 1828, Registre des Lettres, vol. 13, pp. 395–96; Panet to Hon. William Black, 12 October 1830, ibid., vol. 14, pp. 285–86, AAQ.

20. Joseph-Octave Plessis, "Deux Voyages apostoliques dans le Golfe Saint-Laurent et les provinces d'en bas, en 1811 et 1812," *Le Foyer Canadien* 3 (mai–novembre 1865): 187–88; Plessis, *Journal... de 1815 et 1816*, p. 53.

21. Plessis to Rev. Orfroy, 23 October 1808, Registre des Lettres, vol. 6, pp. 276–78, AAQ; Plessis, *Journal... de 1815 et 1816*, p. 55.

22. Sigogne to Plessis, 28 June 1804, Nouvelle-Ecosse, V–51, AAQ.

23. [J.-M. Bellenger], *Alphabet Mikmaque* (Quebec: C. Le François, 1817); "separate phrases to serve in instruction and in reprimanding in confession." Pierre Maillard, *Grammar of the Mikmaque Language of Nova Scotia*, ed. Rev. J.-M. Bellenger (New York: Cramoisy Press, 1864), reprinted 1970. A manuscript of 296 pages, dated Restigouche, 9 October 1816, is in Fonds J.-M. Bellenger: Manuscrits Micmacs, AAQ; Bellenger to Bishop Signay, 16 September 1837, 26CP, 7:7A; Plessis mentions the printed Micmac alphabet in a letter of encouragement to Bellenger, 12 February 1818, Registre des Lettres, vol. 9, pp. 324–25, AAQ.

24. Vincent de Paul, *Memoir of Father Vincent de Paul*, trans. A. M. Pope (Charlottetown: Coombs, 1886), pp. 16–17.

25. Johnston, *Catholic Church*, 2: 8.

26. *Memoir of Father Vincent*, p. 46.

27. Johnston, *Catholic Church*, 1: 485; T. Cook to Bishop Plessis, 5 August 1822, Nouveau-Brunswick, VI–76, AAQ.

28. *The Cross*, 2 August 1845.

29. *The Casket*, 19 August 1852.

30. Council minutes, Cape Breton Island, 28 November 1792, RG1, vol. 319, p. 381, PANS.

31. Plessis to de Calonne, 24 June 1801, Registre des Lettres, vol. 3, pp. 193–94; Plessis to Beaubien, 10 August 1812; "Schedule of Indian Reserves," *JLANB*, 1838, appendix 12, n.p.

32. Plessis to Bishop of Chytre [Newfoundland], 12 August 1812, Registre des Lettres, vol. 7, pp. 421–22; Chytre to Plessis, 14 September 1812, Terre-Neuve, I–41, AAQ: Johnston, *Catholic Church*, 2: 239.

33. Ibid., 1: 202–3.

34. Plessis, "Deux Voyages... en 1811 et

1812," pp. 262, 171.

35. Plessis, *Journal... de 1815 et 1816*, p. 54.

36. *Memoir of Father Vincent*, p. 12; Plessis to de Calonne, 24 June 1801, Registre des Lettres, vol. 3, pp. 193–94; Plessis to Mgr. Edmund Burke, 31 August 1813, ibid., vol. 8, pp. 96–97, AAQ. Burke to Plessis, 9 February and 6 July 1813, Bishop Burke Papers, nos. 175, 176, HAR. See also Rev. Luke Schrepfer, *Pioneer Monks in Nova Scotia* (New York: St. Augustine's Monastery, N.S., 1947).

37. Plessis to Sherbrooke, 27 July and 4 August 1815, Registre des Lettres, vol. 8, pp. 346–48, 351; Plessis to Vincent, 6 August 1815, ibid., pp. 351–52; Plessis to Abbott Superior, 1 August 1815, ibid., pp. 348–51, AAQ.

38. Anon., "Life of Father Vincent de Paul," typescript, Oka, Quebec, [c. 1904], ch. 8, p. 3, ch. 13, p. 2.

39. Plessis to Father Vincent, 20 May 1823, Registre des Lettres, vol. 11, pp. 209–11, AAQ; Johnston, *Catholic Church*, 1: 371–72; "Life of Father Vincent," ch. 8, pp. 4–5, ch. 9, p. 4.

40. Ibid., ch. 12, p. 6; Plessis to Father Vincent, 20 May 1823, Registre des Lettres, vol. 11, pp. 209–11, AAQ.

41. "Life of Father Vincent," ch. 13, p. 1; Plessis to Vincent, 3 September 1825, Registre des Lettres, vol. 12, pp. 326–27, AAQ. Bishop Plessis had originally preferred a Cape Breton site and had written Lieutenant-Governor George R. Ainslie on 18 October 1817 (ibid., vol. 9, pp. 240–41).

42. "Life of Father Vincent," ch. 13, pp. 3–4, ch. 14, p. 1. For an example of his standing with the Indians, Denis, chief at Bras d'Or, to Vincent, 4 October 1851, asking him to draw a petition— which he did not do (Bishop Walsh Papers, 207i, HAR). Father Vincent's papers were destroyed in a fire at Petite Clairvaux in 1892 (J. M. O'Connor to A. M. Kinnear, 2 February 1929, MS File "Tracadie," PANS).

43. Kempt to Wiswall, 1 December 1825; Sigogne to Wiswall, 30 January 1826; J. S. Harris to Wiswall, 9 November 1827; R. D. George to Wiswall, 7 December 1827, 12 May 1828; Wiswall to George, draft, 22 March 1828, MG1, vol. 979, Papers of Peleg Wiswall,

folder 8, PANS.

44. Sigogne to Wiswall, 27 December 1828; William Bowman to Wiswall, 10 October 1828, 20 January 1829, ibid.

45. William Roach to Wiswall, 25 March 1830; loose sheet dated 1832, ibid. T. C. Haliburton to Sigogne, 10 March 1827, Bishop Burke Papers, no. 39, HAR; *Acadian Recorder*, 29 March 1834; paper dated 2 November 1837, RG10, vol. 460, folder 17, PAC.

46. Quoted in [W. O. Raymond], "The New England Company," New Brunswick Historical Society, *Collections* (1899): 110–22.

47. The text of this speech is in MSS 7959, NEC. The *Royal Gazette*, New Brunswick, reprinted excerpts and noted that "a considerable sum of money will be annually expended here" as a result (16 and 23 January 1787).

48. See J. Fingard, "The New England Company and the New Brunswick Indians," *Acadiensis* 1, no. 2 (1972): 29–42.

49. Minutes of the commissioners, Saint John, 19 February, 2 and 3 May, 3 October, and 21 December 1787, 7 February 1788, MSS 7954; George Leonard to Rev. Joseph-Maturin Bourg, 24 August 1787, MSS 7956, NEC.

50. Minutes, 8 February 1789 and 18 February 1790, MSS 7954, NEC.

51. Minutes, 19 February 1787 and 4 February 1790; George Leonard to Alexander Champion, 18 February 1790, ibid.

52. Minutes, 8 February 1791, ibid.

53. Minutes, 9 February 1791 and 23 February 1795, ibid.

54. Minutes, 11 February 1801, ibid.; Oliver Arnold to Benjamin Way, 12 October 1803, MSS 7956, NEC.

55. George Ludlow and Isaac Allen to Way, 7 April 1803, MSS 7954, NEC.

56. "Statement of the Commencement progress and present State of the Plan...," n.d., ibid.

57. Ibid.

58. Minutes, 17 October 1808, ibid.

59. A printed indenture form is in Sussex School Papers: Indian Academy, doc. 11, NBM.

60. "Situation as of December, 1814," MSS 7954, NEC.

61. "Return of Indians in the Province of

New Brunswick placed out by Lieut. General Coffin, in English Families, by Indentures of Apprenticeship, to be educated agreeably to the direction of the Incorporated Society for propagation of the Gospel in New England and parts adjacent in America 24th Sept. 1813," Sussex School Papers: Indian Academy, doc. 42, NBM.

62. Minutes, 28 January 1813, MSS 7954, NEC.

63. Minutes, 26 February 1816, ibid.

64. [Walter Bromley], "Report of the State of the Indians in New Brunswick under the Patronage of the New England Company, 14th Aug.–22 Sept. 1822," lithograph. J.C. Webster Collection, packet 31, NBM. Bromley's findings were confirmed three years later by the Rev. John West.

65. See J. Fingard, "Walter Bromley in Nova Scotia, 1813–1825," *Canadian Historical Review* 54 (1973): 123–51.

66. Walter Bromley, *Two Addresses on the Deplorable State of the Indians* (London: T. Hamilton, 1815), pp. 3, 7, 9, 15.

67. [Walter Bromley], *Mr. Bromley's Second Address on the Deplorable State of the Indians* (Halifax: Recorder Office, 1814), pp. 50–55.

68. *Royal Gazette* supplement to the *City Gazette*, 20 June 1814.

69. Bromley, *Second Address*, pp. 46–48.

70. Ibid., pp. 5, 42. He attributed these sentiments to the Duke of Kent.

71. Petition to Sir John Sherbrooke, 5 April 1814, press clipping in MSS 7956, NEC.

72. Bromley, *Second Address*, p. 43.

73. Secretary, NEC to Bromley, 21 November 1816 and 4 March 1817, MSS 7956, NEC.

74. Dalhousie to Joseph Stonard, 10 March 1817; H.J. Sayer to Bromley, 8 August 1817, ibid. Walter Bromley, *An Appeal*, p. 46.

75. Petition of 27 February 1817, MG15, vol. 3, doc. 24, PANS; 11 March 1817, *JLANS*, 1817, p. 273.

76. 21, 25, and 29 March 1817, *JLANS*, 1817, pp. 306, 315, 316, 333.

77. List of families at Shubenacadie, Vertical Manuscript File: Indians: Shubenacadie, PANS; Bromley, *An Appeal*, pp. 46–48 states that there were twelve families in the autumn of 1818.

78. Ibid., p. 40.

79. Plessis, *Journal...de 1815 et 1816*, p. 123; "in the hope of contributing, little by little, to civilizing the poor savages of this country." Arnold to Ward Chipman Jr., 26 February 1816, MSS 7956, NEC. Bishop Denaut had visited the Sussex Vale school in 1803 and, according to Oliver, had expressed himself well satisfied (Arnold to Benjamin Way, 12 October 1803).

80. Odell to Plessis, 15 April 1816, Cartables: Gouvernement, I, no. 134; Plessis to Odell, 31 August 1816, Registre des Lettres, vol. 8, pp. 538–39, AAQ.

81. Plessis to Mignault, 26 March 1817, ibid., vol. 9, pp. 133–34; *Memoir of Father Vincent*, pp. 18–19. Bromley described himself as a "Dissenter within the Church," i.e., the Church of England, and made a point of stating that he had not become a Methodist (Bromley, *Second Address*, p. 41n).

82. Joshua Marsden, *The Narrative of a Mission to Nova Scotia, New Brunswick and the Somers Islands*, 2d ed. (London: J. Kershaw, 1827), p. 56.

83. *Colonial Patriot*, 14 March 1828.

84. For Irwin's career, see L.F.S. Upton, "Indians and Islanders: The Micmacs in Colonial Prince Edward Island," *Acadiensis* 6, no. 1 (1976): 21–42.

85. *Christian Messenger*, 22 December 1837, 10 July 1846.

86. Ibid., 26 March 1847; for Rand see J. Fingard, "Silas Rand," forthcoming in *Dictionary of Canadian Biography*, vol. 11.

87. Rand, Journal, 1 April 1849, in J.S. Clark, *Rand and the Micmacs* (Charlottetown: Examiner Office, 1899), p. 12.

88. Rand, *Short Statement of Facts*; for his lectures in Halifax see, e.g., *The Guardian*, 23 November 1849 and 20 December 1850; in Charlottetown, Haszard's *Royal Gazette*, 18 December 1849.

89. For examples, Haszard's *Royal Gazette*, 18 January 1853; *Christian Messenger*, 1 November 1850 and 24 January 1866.

90. The Micmac Missionary Society *Reports* ran from 1850 to 1867.

91. *Wesleyan*, 18 October 1851.

92. *Nova Scotian*, 14 August 1854.

93. Ibid., 10 November 1856, Micmac Missionary Society *Report*, 1859, p. 34.

94. Letters in Haszard's *Royal Gazette*, 9 November and 3 December 1853.

95. Silas Rand, "The Claims & Prospects of the Micmacs," *Christian Messenger*, 15 March 1855.

96. *Guardian*, 16 August 1850.

97. *Wesleyan*, 25 October 1851.

98. *Christian Messenger*, 22 August 1851.

99. Quoted in ibid., 28 December 1854.

100. Micmac Missionary *Report*, 1857.

101. *Christian Messenger*, 8 February 1865 and 25 April 1882.

102. *Nova Scotian*, 10 November 1856; according to the *Christian Messenger*, 5 November 1856, the *Halifax Catholic* tried to turn the event into a burlesque.

103. For Christmas on tour see, for example, *Nova Scotian*, 20 September 1858, Micmac Missionary Society *Report*, 1859, passim.

104. Ibid., 1861; letter of Rand in the *Christian Messenger*, 19 September 1860.

105. *Unionist & Halifax Journal*, 22 November 1867; *Morning Chronicle*, 28 March 1872.

106. Ibid., 15 and 22 January 1870.

107. Silas T. Rand, *A Brief Statement Concerning the Micmac Mission*, (n.p., n.d.), [dated January 1880], p. 7.

108. Ibid., p. 9.

109. Rand Bibliography in *A Catalogue of the Maritime Baptist Historical Collection in the Library of Acadia University*, (Kentville, N.S., 1955), pp. 32–35.

110. Elsie Clew Parsons, "Micmac Folklore," *Journal of American Folklore* 38 (1925): 55–133.

111. Christian Kauder, *Buch des gut enthaltend den Katechismus Betrachtung, Gesang* (Vienna, 1866); new edition, together with a *Manuel de Prières, instructions et chants sacrés en Hiéroglyphes Micmacs* (Restigouche, Quebec, 1921); Johnston, *Catholic Church*, 2: 344, 448; John G. Shay, "Micmac or Recollet Hieroglyphs," *Historical Magazine* 5, no. 10 (1861): 289–92.

112. Inquest of 24 October 1867, Coroners' Inquests, RG41, box 41, PANS.

NOTES TO EPILOGUE

1. Ernest R. Forbes, "Misguided Symmetry: The Destruction of Regional Transportation Policy for the Maritimes"; and T. W. Acheson, "The Maritimes and 'Empire Canada,'" in *Canada and the Burden of Unity*, ed. David J. Bercuson (Toronto: Macmillan, 1977), pp. 60–86, 87–114.

2. *DIAAR*, 1875–1936, passim.

3. Ibid., 1919, p. 18.

4. Harry Piers Papers, Cope MSS, NSM.

5. *DIAAR*, 1918, p. 33.

6. Ibid., 1946, p. 195.

7. Ibid., 1952, p. 50.

8. Ibid., 1953, p. 50.

9. Jeanne Guillemin, *Urban Renegades: The Cultural Strategy of American Indians* (New York: Columbia University Press, 1975), p. 65. The title is somewhat misleading, since the book is exclusively concerned with Micmacs in Boston. See also *Micmac News*, January 1977, "Boston's Micmac Indians' Struggle in Isolation—Ignored, Misunderstood."

10. Indian-Eskimo Association to Union of New Brunswick Indians, 2 September 1970, CASNPF, 1971.

11. *DIAAR*, 1876, p. 8.

12. Ibid., 1895, pp. 70, 90, 92.

13. Ibid., 1919, p. 17.

14. *Minutes of Proceedings*, Special Joint Committee on Indian Act, 29 June 1947, no. 39 (Ottawa, 1947), p. 1961.

15. Wallis and Wallis, *Micmacs*, p. 276.

16. *DIAAR*, 1904, p. 62.

17. Department of Indian Affairs and Northern Development, Statistics Division, Tables 17.1, 18.1/Maritimes/1968–69.

18. *DIAAR*, 1908, p. 63.

19. Ibid., 1949, pp. 215–16.

20. Department of Indian Affairs and Northern Resources, Estimates of Vital

Rates for Canadian Indians, 1960–70.

21. Freeman McDonald to superintendent-general, 28 August 1887, *DIAAR*, 1887, p. 41; W. H. Mechling, "The Malecite Indians, with Notes on the Micmacs," *Anthropologica* 7 and 8 (whole issues), 7: 160.

22. John M. Clarke, "The Micmac Tercentenary" (Albany, 1912).

23. Wallis and Wallis, *Micmacs*, p. 184.

24. *Micmac News*, February 1977.

25. Rex. v. Syliboy, 1928, 50 C.C.C. 389 [Nova Scotia County Court].

26. Regina v. Simon, 1958, 124 C.C.C. 110 [New Brunswick Supreme Court].

27. Namely, the Millbrook and Shubenacadie bands; *Minutes of Proceedings*, Special Joint Committee on Indian Act, 13 August 1946, no. 21 (Ottawa, 1946), pp. 854–55, 868–69.

28. Joint Committee of the Senate and the House of Commons on Indian Affairs, *Minutes of Proceedings and Evidence 1959–1961*, 4 vols. (Ottawa, 1959–1961).

29. Department of Citizenship and Immigration: Indian Affairs Branch, *The Administration of Indian Affairs* ([Ottawa, 1964]), p. 24.

30. *Statement of the Government of Canada on Indian Policy 1969* (Ottawa, 1969), p. 11.

31. *DIAAR*, 1968–69, p. 45.

32. Ibid., 1958–59, p. 85.

33. Department of Indian Affairs and Northern Development, Statistics Division, Table 12.1/Maritimes/1968–69.

34. *Telegraph Journal*, 14 June 1975. Nicholas is a Malecite from Tobique, but he spoke for the whole region.

35. *London Evening Free Press*, 6 December 1975.

36. UNSI *Newsletter*, [Easter, 1970]; UNBI Constitution, [1970], CASNPF.

37. Department of Indian Affairs, *Facts and Figures* (Ottawa, 1971).

38. *Micmac News*, July 1975.

39. *Chronicle-Herald*, 29 and 30 December 1975.

40. *Micmac News*, May 1977.

41. *Ottawa Citizen*, 5 December 1973; *Agenutemagen*, December 1973.

42. Aborigine Land Claims, Maritimes, 1973, CASNPF.

43. *4th Estate*, 28 October 1971.

44. *Chronicle Herald*, 28 and 30 April and 5 and 6 May 1975.

45. *Ottawa Journal*, 17 September 1975.

46. *Chronicle-Herald*, 29 October 1973.

47. *Mail Star*, 12 January 1974, *Chronicle-Herald* 11 October 1974 and 19 March 1975. Text of the meeting with the provincial cabinet is in *Micmac News*, October 1974.

48. *Telegraph Journal*, 14 June 1975.

49. *Isaac v. the Queen*, 1975, S.H. No. 05763. The full text of the judgment is in *Micmac News*, March 1976.

50. *Chronicle-Herald*, 16 July 1976.

51. *Micmac News*, April 1976.

52. Ibid., May 1977; the position paper had already been printed as a supplement to the December 1976 issue.

Bibliography

1. Manuscript Sources

Charlottetown, Prince Edward Island. Public Archives of Prince Edward Island. Letter Books of the Lieutenant-Governor, LG2.
———.———.Letter Books of Robert Stewart
Edinburgh. Scottish Records Office. GD. 293/2/17 Montgomery Papers.
Fredericton, New Brunswick. Department of Lands and Mines. Land Grants IV. Grants Book B.
———.Harriet Irving Library Archives, University of New Brunswick. MGH54, Indian Affairs—New Brunswick.
———.Provincial Archives of New Brunswick. RG1, RS2. Letterbooks of the Lieutenant-Governors.
———.———.RG2, RS6. Minutes of the Executive Council.
———.———.RG2, RS7. Executive Council Papers, Indians.
———.———.RG2, RS8, Indians. Records of the Executive Council, Indians.
———.———.RG3, RS13. Letterbooks of the Provincial Secretaries.
———.———.RG4, RS24. Assembly Papers.
———.———.RG10, RS107. Records of the Crown Land Commissioners.
Halifax, Nova Scotia. Archdiocese of Halifax Offices. Halifax Archdiocesan Records. Bishop Burke Papers and Bishop Walsh Papers.
———.Nova Scotia Museum. Harry Piers Papers.
———.Killam Library, Dalhousie University. Papers of the St. Croix Commission 1796–1827, microfilm.
———.Public Archives of Nova Scotia. Brown Manuscripts, BL, Add. MSS 19071, microfilm.
———.———.MG1, vols. 979–80. Papers of Peleg Wiswall.
———.———.MG1, vol. 1189a. Journal of Rev. John Payzant.
———.———.MG4, vol. 141. Shelburne County Records.
———.———.MG15, vols. 3–6. Indian Manuscripts.
———.———.RG1, vols. 50–51. Letter Books of Governor Wentworth.
———.———.RG1, vol. 214 1/2A, 214 1/2B. Council Minutes.
———.———.RG1, vols. 221–22. Miscellaneous Documents.
———.———.RG1, vols. 318–23. Council Minutes, Cape Breton.
———.———.RG1, vol. 330. Manuscript Documents, Cape Breton.
———.———.RG1, vol. 364. Transcripts of Manuscripts Relating to the American Revolution.
———.———.RG1, vol. 380. Titus Smith Jr., "Report of the Eastern and Northern Parts of the Province in the Years 1801 & 1802."
———.———.RG1, vols. 430–32. Indian Manuscripts.
———.———.RG3. Minutes of the Executive Council.
———.———.RG5. Series A, Assembly Papers; Series B, Bills; Series P, Petitions.
———.———.RG17. Indian Treaties.
———.———.RG20. Series B, Cape Breton Land Papers.
———.———.RG34. Court of General Session of the Peace.
———.———.RG39. Supreme Court Records.
———.———.RG41. Coroners' Inquests and Medical Reports.
———.———.RG47. Registry of Deeds.
———.———.RG135–102. City of Halifax Records.
———.———.Vertical Manuscript File, Arthur, H.R.H. Prince; Indians: Land; Indians: Shubenacadie; Micmac Language; Provincial Treasury: Indian Affairs; Tracadie.

————.————.Index to Crown Land Grants.
————.————.Land Grants, Letter Book G.
————.————.Land Grants, Old Book 6, 9, 12, 18, 20.
————.————.Land Grants, New Book 31, 33.
Ottawa, Ontario. Public Archives of Canada. MG1, Series 2, B Series. Archives des Colonies, transcripts.
————.————.MG11. Nova Scotia Transcripts.
————.————.MG23, G11–19. Monk Papers.
————.————.RG10, vols. 459–61. Indian Affairs. Nova Scotia Papers.
————.————.RG10, vols. 304–82. Indian Affairs Register.
————.————.RG10, vols. 527, 528, 722, 723. William Spragge Letter Books.
————.————.Archives des Colonies C11B. Correspondance générale. Ile Royale 1712–1763, microfilm.
————.————.Archives des Colonies B. Lettres envoyées 1663–1789, microfilm.
————.————.Archives des Colonies C11C. Amérique du Nord, microfilm.
————.————.Archives des Colonies C11D. Correspondance générale. Acadie, microfilm.
————.————.Colonial Office Papers, Series 188, 189. New Brunswick, microfilm.
————.————.Colonial Office Papers, Series 217, 218. Nova Scotia, microfilm.
————.————.Colonial Office Papers, Series 226. Prince Edward Island, microfilm.
————.————.New England Company Records, microfilm.
Oxford. Rhodes House. MSS Brit. Emp. S18, C148. Papers of the Aborigines' Protection Society.
Quebec, Quebec. Archives de l'Archdiocese de Québec. Cartables: Gouvernement: Nouveau-Brunswick; Nouvelle-Ecosse; Terre-Neuve.
————.————.Manuscrits Micmacs.
————.————.Registre des Lettres.
————.Archives du Séminaire de Québec. Lettres. Carton P. Séminaire IV.
Saint John, New Brunswick. New Brunswick Museum. Ganong Manuscripts.
————.————.Jarvis Papers.
————.————.Mahood Field Book No. 19.
————.————.Milner Miscellaneous notes.
————.————.Milner Scrapbook.
————.————.New Brunswick Scrapbook No. 1.
————.————.Odell Papers.
————.————.Sussex School Papers: Indian Academy.
————.————.J.C. Webster Collection.
St. John's, Newfoundland. Provincial Archives of Newfoundland and Labrador. GN2. Letter Books of the Colonial Secretary.

2. Government Publications

Canada. The Administration of Indian Affairs. [Ottawa, 1964.]
————.Department of Citizenship and Immigration. Indian Affairs Branch. *Annual Report*, 1950–65.
————.Department of Indian Affairs. *Annual Report*, 1880–1936.
————.Department of Indian Affairs and Northern Development. *Annual Report*, 1966–1976.
————.Department of the Interior. Indian Affairs. *Annual Report*, 1874–79.
————.Department of Mines and Resources. Indian Affairs Branch. *Annual Report*, 1937–49.
————.Department of Secretary of State. *Annual Report*, 1868–73.
————.*Facts and Figures.* Ottawa, 1971.
————.*Indian Treaties and Surrenders.* 3 vols. Ottawa, 1891.
————.Joint Committee of the Senate and the House of Commons on Indian Affairs. *Minutes of Proceedings and Evidence 1959–1961.* 4 vols. Ottawa, 1959–61.
————.*Minutes of Proceedings, Special Joint Committee on Indian Act.* 6 vols. Ottawa, 1947–49.
————.*Statement of the Government of Canada on Indian Policy 1969.* Ottawa, 1969.

Massachusetts. *Resolves of the General Assembly of the Colony of Massachusetts-Bay*. Boston, 1776.
————.*Resolves of the General Assembly of the State of Massachusetts-Bay*. Boston, 1777.
New Brunswick. Human Rights Commission. *Some Personality Factors of Matched Groups of New Brunswick Indians and Whites*. Fredericton, 1972.
————.*Journals of the Legislative Assembly of New Brunswick*.
————.*Statutes of New Brunswick 1844*. Fredericton, 1845.
Nova Scotia. *Journals of the Legislative Assembly of Nova Scotia*.
————.*Journals of the Legislative Council of Nova Scotia*.
————.*Statutes*. 1836–46, 1854, 1859.
Prince Edward Island. *Journals of the Legislative Assembly of Prince Edward Island*.
————.*Revised Statutes of Prince Edward Island*. Charlottetown, 1862.
Quebec. *Rapport de l'Archiviste de la Province de Québec*, 1929–1938.
United Kingdom. *Great Exhibition of the Work of Industry of all Nations 1851; Official Descriptive and Illustrated Catalogue*. 3 vols. London, 1851.
————.House of Commons, *Sessional Papers*, 1834, 1839.

3. Published Primary Sources

Akins, Thomas B., ed. *Selections from the Public Documents of the Province of Nova Scotia*. Halifax: Annand, 1869.
Barrett, Joseph. *Indians of New England*. Middletown, Conn., 1851.
Bell, Winthrop, ed. "A Hessian Conscript's Account of Life in Garrison at Halifax at the time of the American Revolution." Nova Scotia Historical Society, *Collections* 27 (1947): 125–46.
Bellenger, J.-M. *Alphabet Mikmaque*, Quebec: Le Français, 1817.
Bromley, Walter. *An Appeal . . . in behalf of the Indians of North America*. Halifax: Ward, 1820.
————.*Mr. Bromley's Second Address on the Deplorable State of the Indians*. Halifax: Recorder Office, 1814.
————.*Two Addresses on the Deplorable State of the Indians*. London: T. Hamilton, 1815.
Canadian Association in Support of Native Peoples. *Files*.
Champlain, Samuel de. *Works*. Edited by H. P. Biggar. 6 vols. Toronto: Champlain Society, 1922–36.
Collection de documents inédits sur le Canada et l'Amérique publiés par le Canada-Français. 3 vols. Quebec: Coté, 1888–90.
Collection de manuscrits . . . historiques relatifs à la Nouvelle-France, recueillis aux Archives de la Province de Québec ou copiés à l'étranger. 4 vols. Quebec: Coté, 1884.
David, Albert. "Une Autobiographie de l'Abbé Le Loutre." *Nova Francia* (1931): 1–34.
Denys, Nicolas. *The Description and Natural History of the Coasts of North America (Acadia)*. Edited by W. F. Ganong. Toronto: Champlain Society, 1908.
Dièreville, Sieur de. *Relation of the Voyage to Port Royal in Acadia or New France*. Edited by J. C. Webster. Toronto: Champlain Society, 1933.
"Documents sur l'Acadie," *Le Canada-Français* 1 (1888).
Doughty, A. G., with G. W. Parmelee, eds. *The Siege of Quebec*. 6 vols. Quebec: Dussault and Proulx, 1901.
Gallatin, Albert. Micmac vocabulary in "A Synopsis of the Indian Tribes of North America." American Antiquarian Society, *Transactions* (1836): 228–32.
Ganong, W. F. "Richard Denys, Sieur de Fronsac, and His Settlements in Northern New Brunswick," New Brunswick Historical Society, *Collections* 7 (1907): 7–54.
Ganong, W. F., ed. "The Cadillac Memoir on Acadia of 1692." New Brunswick Historical Society, *Collections* 13 (1930): 76–97.
Gwyn, Julian, ed. *The Royal Navy and North America: The Warren Papers 1736–1752*. [London]: Navy Records Society, 1973.
Hamilton, W. D., and W. A. Spray, eds. *Source Materials Relating to the New Brunswick Indians*, Fredericton: Hamray Books, 1977.
Kidder, Frederic, ed. *Military Operations in Eastern Maine and Nova Scotia during the Amer-*

ican Revolution. 1867. Reprint. New York: Kraus Reprint Co., 1971.

Lafitau, Father Joseph François. *Customs of the American Indians compared with the Customs of Primitive Times*. Edited by W. N. Fenton and E. L. Morse. 2 vols. Toronto: Champlain Society, 1974, 1977.

LeClerq, Father Chrestien. *New Relation of Gaspesia*. Edited by W. F. Ganong. Toronto: Champlain Society, 1910.

Lescarbot, Marc. *Nova Francia: A Description of Acadia*. Edited by H. P. Biggar. London: Routledge, 1928.

McGee, Harold F., ed. *The Native Peoples of Atlantic Canada*. Toronto: McClelland and Stewart, 1974.

[Maillard, Pierre]. *An Account of the Customs and Manners of the Mickmacks and Maricheets, Savage Nations*. London: S. Hooper and A. Morley, 1758.

―――. *Grammar of the Mikmaque Language of Nova Scotia*. Edited by Rev. J. M. Bellenger. New York: Cramoisy Press, 1864.

―――. "Lettre du M. L'Abbé Maillard." Edited by H. Casgrain. *Les Soirées Canadiennes* (1863): 291–426.

Maine Historical Society. *Documentary History of the State of Maine*. 24 vols. Portland, 1869–1916.

Mechling, W. H. *Malecite Tales*. Department of Mines, Geological Survey Memorandum 49. Ottawa, 1914.

Memorials of the English and French Commissioners concerning the Limits of Nova Scotia, or, Acadie. 2 vols. London, 1755.

O'Callaghan, Edmund B., ed. *Documents Relative to the Colonial History of the State of New York*. 15 vols. Albany: Weed, Parsons, 1853–87.

"Papiers Amherst (1760–1763) concernant les Acadiens." La Société Historique Acadienne, 27ième cahier (1970): 256–320.

Perley, Moses H. *Indian Affairs in New-Brunswick*. Fredericton, 1848.

―――. *Reports on Indian Settlements*. *JLANB*, 1841. Fredericton, 1841.

Prince, J. D. "A Micmac Manuscript." Congrès Internationale des Americanistes, *XVe Session*, Quebec (1906), pp. 87–124.

Plessis, Mgr. Joseph-Octave. "Deux Voyages dans le Golfe Saint-Laurent et les provinces d'en bas, en 1811 et 1812." *Le Foyer Canadien* (1865).

―――.*Journal des Visites Pastorales de 1815 et 1816 Par Monseigneur Joseph-Octave Plessis Evêque de Québec*, Quebec: Têtu, 1903.

Rand, Silas T. *Legends of the Micmacs*. Edited by Helen L. Webster. New York: Longmans, Green, [1893].

Raymond, W. O. "The New England Company." New Brunswick Historical Society, *Collections* 2 (1899): 110–22.

Raymond, W. O., ed. *Winslow Papers*. Saint John: New Brunswick Historical Society, Sun Printing Co., 1904.

Sayres, William C., ed. *Sammy Louis: The Life History of a Young Micmac*. New Haven: Compass Publishing Co., 1956.

Smethurst, Gamaliel. *A Narrative of an Extraordinary Escape*. (London, 1774.) New Brunswick Historical Society, *Collections* 2 (1905).

Thwaites, Reuben G., ed. *The Jesuit Relations and Allied Documents*. 73 vols. Cleveland: Burrows, 1886–91.

Vincent de Paul. *Memoir of Father Vincent de Paul*. Translated by A. M. Pope. Charlottetown: Coombs, 1886.

Washington, George. *The Writings of George Washington*. Edited by John C. Fitzpatrick. 39 vols. Washington, D.C., 1931–44.

West, Rev. John. *A Journal of a Mission to the Indians of the British Provinces of New Brunswick and Nova Scotia*. London: Seeley, 1827.

4. Newspapers

Acadian Recorder. Halifax.

Agenutemagen. Fredericton.
Casket. Antigonish.
Christian Messenger. Halifax.
Chronicle-Herald. Halifax.
Church Times. Halifax.
Colonial Herald. Charlottetown.
Colonial Patriot. Pictou.
Cross. Halifax.
Daily Sun. Halifax.
Evening Express. Halifax.
4th Estate. Halifax.
Free Press. Halifax.
Gleaner. Miramichi.
Guardian. Halifax.
Halifax Journal.
Halifax Morning Post.
Haszard's Royal Gazette. Charlottetown.
Islander. Charlottetown.
London Evening Free Press.
Mail-Star. Halifax.
Micmac News. Sydney.
Morning Chronicle. Halifax.
Morning Freeman. Saint John.
Morning Herald. Halifax.
Morning Journal. Halifax.
New Brunswick Courier. Saint John.
Nova Scotian. Halifax.
Ottawa Citizen.
Ottawa Journal.
Presbyterian Witness. Halifax.
Prince Edward Island Register. Charlottetown.
Protestant, and Evangelical Witness. Charlottetown.
Quebec Gazette.
Royal Gazette, Charlottetown.
Royal Gazette, Fredericton.
Royal Gazette and New-Brunswick Advertiser. Saint John.
Scottish Missionary Register. Edinburgh.
Telegraph-Journal. Saint John.
Times and Courier. Halifax.
Unionist and Halifax Journal.
Wesleyan. Halifax.
Yarmouth Herald.

5. Published Secondary Sources

Atkinson, Christopher W. *A Historical and Statistical Account of New Brunswick, B.N.A., with Advice to Emigrants.* 3d ed. Edinburgh: Anderson and Bryce, 1844.

Bailey, Alfred G. *The Conflict of European and Eastern Algonkian Cultures, 1504-1700.* 2d ed. Toronto: University of Toronto Press, 1969.

Baird, William T. *Seventy Years of New Brunswick Life.* Saint John: Day, 1890.

Bannon, Rev. Richard V. "Antoine Gaulin 1674-1730: An Apostle of Early Acadie." Canadian Catholic Historical Association, *Report* (1952): 49–59.

Beaumont, Gaston de Bosq de. *Les Derniers Jours de l'Acadie.* Paris: Lechevalier, 1899.

Belliveau, Pierre. "Indians and Some Indian Raids on Massachusetts about 1690-1704." La Société Historique Acadienne, *2ème cahier* (1962): 15–33.

Bercuson, David J., ed. *Canada and the Burden of Unity.* Toronto: Macmillan, 1977.

Berkhoffer, Robert F. *Salvation and the Savage.* Lexington: University of Kentucky Press, 1965.

Bock, Philip K. *The Micmac Indians of Restigouche.* National Museum of Canada, Bulletin no. 213. Ottawa, 1966.

———."Micmac." *Handbook of North American Indians.* Vol. 15. *Northeast.* Washington, D.C.: Government Printing Office, 1978.

Bolger, Francis W. P., ed. *Canada's Smallest Province.* Charlottetown: PEI Centennial Commission, 1973.

Brebner, John B. *New England's Outpost.* New York: Columbia University Press, 1973.

———."Micmac." *Handbook of North American Indians.* Vol. 15. *Northeast,* pp. 109–22. Washington, D.C.: Government Printing Office, 1978.

Burtis, W. R. M. *New Brunswick as a Home for Emigrants.* Saint John, 1860.

Calkin, J. B. *The Geography and History of Nova Scotia.* New ed. Halifax: A. and W. Mackinlay, 1873.

Campeau, Lucien, ed. *La Première Mission d'Acadie.* Quebec: Les Presses de l'Université Laval, 1967.

Casgrain, H.-R. *Les Sulpiciens et les Prêtres des Missions-Etrangères en Acadie.* Quebec: Pruneau and Kironac, 1897.

Chamberlain, Alexander F. " 'New Religions' among the North American Indians." *Journal of Religious Psychology* (1913): 1–49.

Chouinard, Rev. E. P. *Histoire de la Paroisse de Saint-Joseph de Carleton (Baie des Chaleurs) 1755-1906.* Rimouski: Impr. générale de Rimouski, 1906.

Clark, Andrew H. *Acadia: The Geography of Early Nova Scotia to 1760.* Madison: University of Wisconsin Press, 1968.

———. *Three Centuries and the Island.* Toronto: University of Toronto Press, 1959.

Clark, Jeremiah S. *Rand and the Micmacs.* Charlottetown: Examiner Office, 1899.

Clarke, John M. "The Micmac Tercentenary." *Eighth Report of the Director of the Science Division 1911,* pp. 1–9. Albany, 1912.

Conkling, Robert. "Legitimacy and Conversion in Social Change: The Case of French Missionaries and the Northeastern Algonkian." *Ethnohistory* 21 (1974): 1–24.

Cooke, Sherburne F. "The Significance of Disease in the Extinction of the New England Indians." *Human Biology* 45 (1973): 485–508.

Cooper, John M. "Is the Algonquin Family Hunting Ground System pre-Columbian?" *American Anthropologist* (1939): 66–90.

Cox, Bruce, ed. *Cultural Ecology.* Toronto: McClelland and Stewart, 1973.

Crosby, Alfred W. *The Columbian Exchange,* Westport, Conn.: Greenwood Publishing, 1972.

———."Virgin Soil Epidemics as a Factor in the Aboriginal Depopulation in America." *William and Mary Quarterly* (1976): 289–99.

Cumming, Peter A., and Neil H. Mickenburg. *Native Rights in Canada.* 2d ed. Toronto: Indian-Eskimo Association of Canada, 1972.

David, Albert. "L'Apôtre des Micmacs." *La Revue de l'Université d'Ottawa* (1935): pp. 49–82.

———. "Messire Pierre Maillard, Apôtre des Micmacs." *Bulletin des recherches historiques* (1929): 365–75.

Dawson, J. W. *A Handbook of the Geography and Natural History of the Province of Nova Scotia for the Use of Schools and Families.* 2d ed. Pictou: McPherson and Co., 1851.

Day, Gordon M. "The Indian as an Ecological Factor in the Northeastern Forest." *Ecology* 34 (1953): 329–46.

Dickason, Olive P. *Louisbourg and the Indians: A Study in Imperial Race Relations, 1713-1760.* National Historic Parks and Sites Branch, History and Archaeology 6. Ottawa, 1976.

Dobyns, Henry F. "Estimating Aboriginal Population." *Current Anthropology* 7 (1966): 395–416.

Elder, William. "The Aborigines of Nova Scotia." *North American Review* 112 (1871): 1–30.

Erskine, J. S. "Early Culture of Nova Scotia: III. The Transitional Period 1000 BC to AD 600." *Journal of Education* [Halifax], (March 1970): 17–24.

————. "Early Culture of Nova Scotia: IV. The Bow and Arrow People." *Journal of Education* [Halifax], (May 1970): 50–56.

————."Their Crowded Hour: The Micmac Cycle." *Dalhousie Review* 39 (1959): 443–52.

Fingard, Judith. "The New England Company and the New Brunswick Indians." *Acadiensis* 1, no. 2 (1972): 29–42.

————."Walter Bromley in Nova Scotia 1813–1825." *Canadian Historical Review* 54 (1973): 123–51.

Fisher, Peter. *History of New Brunswick* (1825). Edited by W. S. Fisher. Saint John: New Brunswick Historical Society, 1921.

Garner, John. *The Franchise and Politics in British North America.* Toronto: University of Toronto Press, 1969.

Gesner, Abraham. *New Brunswick; with Notes for Emigrants.* London: Simmonds and Ward, 1847.

————. *The Industrial Resources of Nova Scotia.* Halifax: A. and W. MacKinlay, 1849.

————."The Native Indians of New Brunswick." *Simmond's Colonial Magazine* (1846): 398–407.

Gilpin, J. B. "Indians of Nova Scotia." Nova Scotia Institute of Science. *Proceedings and Transactions* 4 (1877): 260–81.

Gordon, Arthur. "Wilderness Journeys in New Brunswick." In *Vacation Tourists and Notes of Travel in 1862–3.* Edited by Francis Galton. London: Macmillan, 1864.

Gross, Fred. "Indian Island: A Micmac Reserve." In *Native Peoples.* Edited by J. L. Elliott. Scarborough: Prentice-Hall, 1971, pp. 89–98.

Guillemin, Jeanne. *Urban Renegades: The Cultural Strategy of American Indians.* New York: Columbia University Press, 1975.

Haliburton, T. C. *A General Description of Nova Scotia.* Halifax: C. H. Belcher, 1823.

Hallowell, A. I. "Some Psychological Characteristics of the Northeastern Indian." In *Man in Northeastern North America.* Edited by Frederick Johnson. Andover, Mass.: Phillips Academy, 1946, pp. 195–225.

———— "The Size of Algonkian Hunting Territories: A Function of Ecological Adjustment." *American Anthropologist* 51 (1949): 35–45.

Hardy, Campbell. *Sporting Adventures in the New World; or Days and Nights of Moose-hunting in the Pine Forests of Acadie.* 2 vols. London: Hurst and Blackett, 1855.

Harper, Allan G. "Canada's Indian Administration." *América Indígena* 5 (1945): 119–32; 5 (1946): 297–314; 7 (1947): 129–48.

Harvey, D. C. *The French Régime in Prince Edward Island.* New Haven: Yale University Press, 1926.

Hill, S. *A Short Account of Prince Edward Island.* London: Madden, 1829.

Hoffman, Bernard G. *Cabot to Cartier.* Toronto: University of Toronto Press, 1961.

Hollingsworth, S. *The Present State of Nova Scotia.* 2d ed. Edinburgh: Creech, 1787.

Hooper, John M. "The Culture of the Northeastern Indian Hunters: A Reconstructive Interpretation." In *Man in Northeastern North America.* Edited by Frederick Johnson. Andover, Mass.: Phillips Academy, 1946, pp. 272–305.

Hutton, Elizabeth. "Indian Affairs in Nova Scotia, 1760–1834." Nova Scotia Historical Society, *Collections* (1963): 33–54.

Jack, I. Allen. "Acadienses: The Indians of Acadia." *The Canadian Indian* 1 (1891): 331–37.

Jacobs, Wilbur R. "The Tip of an Iceberg: Pre-Columbian Indian Demography." *William and Mary Quarterly* (1974): 123–32.

Jaenen, Cornelius. *Friend and Foe* [Toronto]: McClelland and Stewart, 1976.

————. "Amerindian Views of French Culture in the Seventeenth Century." *Canadian Historical Review* 55 (1974): 261–91.

Jennings, Francis. *The Invasion of America: Indians, Colonialism and the Cant of Conquest.* Chapel Hill: University of North Carolina Press, 1975.

Johnson, Frederick, ed. *Man in Northeastern North America.* Andover, Mass.: Phillips Academy, 1946.

————. "Notes on Micmac Shamanism." *Primitive Man* 16 (1943): 53–80.

Johnson, Micheline Dumont. *Apôtres ou Agitateurs.* Trois Rivières: Boreal Express, 1970.

————. "Pierre Maillard." *Dictionary of Canadian Biography* 3. Toronto: University of Toronto Press, 1974, pp. 415-19.

Johnston, Rev. A. A. *A History of the Catholic Church in Eastern Nova Scotia*. 2 vols. Antigonish: St. Francis Xavier University Press, 1960, 1971.

Johnston, James F. W. *Notes on North America: Agricultural, Economical, and Social*. 2 vols. Edinburgh and London: Blackwood, 1851.

Knight, Rolf. "A Re-examination of Hunting, Trapping, and Territoriality among the Northeastern Algonkian Indians." In *Man, Culture and Animals*. Edited by A. Leeds and A. P. Vayda, pp. 27-42. Washington: American Association for the Advancement of Science, 1965.

Koren, Rev. Henry J. *Knaves or Knights? A History of the Spiritan Missionaries in Acadia and North America 1732-1839*. Pittsburgh: Duquesne University Press, 1962.

Law Reform Commission of Canada. *The Native Offender and the Law*. Ottawa, 1974.

Leacock, Eleanor. *The Montagnais "Hunting Territory" and the Fur Trade*. American Anthropological Association Memoir 78 [1954].

Lockwood, Anthony. *A Brief Description of Nova Scotia*. London: G. Hayden, Cadell and Davis, 1818.

MacFarlane, R. O. "British Indian Policy in Nova Scotia to 1760." *Canadian Historical Review* 19 (1938): 154-67.

McGee, Harold F. "White Encroachment on Micmac Reserve Lands 1830-1867." *Man in the Northeast* 8 (1974): 57-63.

Macmillan, John C. *The History of the Catholic Church in Prince Edward Island*. Quebec: L'Evénement, 1913.

MacNutt, W. S. *New Brunswick: A History*. Toronto: Macmillan, 1963.

Marsden, Rev. Joshua. *The Narrative of a Mission to Nova Scotia, New Brunswick and the Somers Islands*. 2d ed. London: J. Kershaw, 1827.

Marshall, M. V. "Silas Tertius Rand and His Micmac Dictionary." *Nova Scotia Historical Quarterly* (1975): 391-410.

Martin, Calvin. "The European Impact on the Culture of a Northeastern Algonquian Tribe: An Ecological Interpretation." *William and Mary Quarterly* (1974): 3-26.

————. "The Four Lives of a Micmac Copper Pot." *Ethnohistory* 22 (1975): 111-33.

————. *Keepers of the Game*. Berkeley and Los Angeles: University of California Press, 1978.

Mechling, W. H. "The Malecite Indians, with Notes on the Micmacs." *Anthropologica* 7 and 8 (1958-59).

Miller, Virginia P. "Aboriginal Micmac Population: A Review of the Evidence." *Ethnohistory* 23 (1976): 117-27.

Monro, Alexander. *New Brunswick with a Brief Outline of Nova Scotia, and Prince Edward Island*. Halifax: R. Nugent, 1855.

Moorsom, Captain William S. *Letters from Nova Scotia*. London: H. Colburn and R. Bentley, 1829.

Morse, William I. *Acadiensa Nova*. 2 vols. London: B. Quaritch Ltd., 1935.

Murdoch, Beamish. *A History of Nova-Scotia*. 3 vols. Halifax: J. Barnes, 1865.

Nagler, Mark. *Indians in the City*. Ottawa: Canadian Research Centre for Anthropology, St. Paul University, 1970.

Narvey, Kenneth M. "The Royal Proclamation of 7 October 1763." *Saskatchewan Law Review* 38 (1974): 123-249.

Pacifique, Father. "Quelques Traits caractéristiques de la Tribu des Micmacs." Congrès Internationale des Americanistes. *Xve Session*. Quebec, 1906, pp. 315-28.

————. "Restigouche: Metropole des Micmacs." *Bulletin de la Société de Géographie de Québec* 19 (1925): 129-62.

Parsons, Elsie C. "Micmac Folklore." *Journal of American Folklore* 38 (1925): 55-133.

————. "Micmac Notes." *Journal of American Folklore* 39 (1926): 460-85.

Patterson, George. *Memoir of the Rev. James McGregor DD*. Philadelphia: Joseph M. Wilson, 1859.

Perley, Moses H. "On the Early History of New Brunswick." *Educational Review* [Fredericton?] (1891): 172-75.

Piers, Harry. "Brief Account of the Micmac Indians of Nova Scotia and Their Remains." Nova

Scotian Institute of Science, *Proceedings and Transactions* 13 (1910-14): 99-125.

Rand, Silas T. *A Short Statement of Facts Relating to the History, Manners, Customs, Language, and Literature of the Micmac Tribe of Indians.* Halifax: James Bowes and Son, 1850.

Ray, Roger B. "Maine Indians' Concept of Land Tenure." *Maine Historical Society Quarterly* 13 (1974): 28-51.

Raymond, W. O. *The River St. John.* Saint John: J. A. Bowes, 1910.

Rogers, Norman M. "Apostle to the Micmacs." *Dalhousie Review* 6 (1926): 166-76.

———. "The Abbé Le Loutre." *Canadian Historical Review* 11 (1930): 105-28.

Ronda, James P. "'We are well as we are': An Indian Critique of Seventeenth Century Christian Missions." *William and Mary Quarterly*, n.s. 34 (1977): 66-82.

Saint Père, Rameau de. *Une Colonie féodale en Amérique, L'Acadie 1604-1881.* 2 vols. Paris: E. Plon, Nourrit et cie, 1889.

Saunders, Marshall. *The House of Armour.* Philadelphia: A. J. Rowland, 1897.

Shay, John G. "Micmac or Recollet Hieroglyphs." *Historical Magazine* 5, no. 10 (1861): 289-92.

Shove, Macworth. *Adventures in Canada, being Two Months on the Tobique, New Brunswick.* London: Smith, Elder, 1866.

Speck, Frank G. *Beothuck and Micmac.* New York: Museum of the American Indian, Heye Foundation, 1922.

———, and Ralph W. Dexter, "Utilization of Animals and Plants by the Micmac Indians of New Brunswick." Washington Academy of Sciences, *Journal* 41 (1951): 250-59.

———, and Loren C. Eiseley, "Significance of Hunting Territory Systems of the Algonkian in Social Theory." *American Anthropologist* 41 (1939): 269-80.

Stewart, Theophilus. "The Micmacs of Prince Edward Island." *Aborigines' Friend and Colonial Intelligencer* (London), (1865): 508-10.

Trigger, Bruce G. *The Children of Aataentsic.* 2 vols. Montreal: McGill-Queen's University Press, 1976.

Upton, L. F. S. "Colonists and Micmacs." *Journal of Canadian Studies* 10, no. 3 (1975): 44-56.

———. "Indian Affairs in Colonial New Brunswick." *Acadiensis* 4 (1974): 6-26.

———. "Indians and Islanders: The Micmacs in Colonial Prince Edward Island." *Acadiensis* 6 (1976): 21-42.

———. "Indian Policy in Colonial Nova Scotia 1783-1871." *Acadiensis* 8 (1975): 3-31.

———. "The Extermination of the Beothucks of Newfoundland." *Canadian Historical Review* 58 (1977): 133-53.

———. "The Origins of Canadian Indian Policy." *Journal of Canadian Studies* 8, no. 4 (1973): 51-61.

Vachon, André. *Eloquence Indienne.* Ottawa: Fides, 1968.

Van Wart, A. F. "The Indians of the Maritime Provinces; Their Diseases and Natural Cures." Canadian Medical Association, *Journal* (1948): 573-77.

Vogel, Virgil J., *American Indian Medicine.* Norman: University of Oklahoma Press, 1970.

Wallis, W. D. "Historical Background of the Micmac Indians of Canada." National Museum of Canada, Bulletin no. 173, *Contributions to Anthropology 1959.* Ottawa, 1961, pp. 42-63.

Wallis, W. D., and R. S. Wallis. *The Micmac Indians of Eastern Canada.* Minneapolis: University of Minnesota Press, 1955.

Warburton, A. B. *A History of Prince Edward Island.* Saint John: Barnes, 1923.

Washburn, Wilcomb E. *The Indian in America.* New York: Harper and Row, 1975.

Webster, John C. *Thomas Pichon, "The Spy of Beauséjour."* Halifax: Public Archives of Nova Scotia, 1937.

Wood, William. *The Great Fortress.* Toronto: Brook, 1915.

Woods, Nicholas A. *The Prince of Wales in Canada and the United States.* London: Bradbury and Evans, 1861.

6. Dissertations and Unpublished Material

Anon, "Legal Status of Indians in the Maritimes: Report of Discussions." Typescript. Halifax,

16 October 1970.

Anon. "Life of Father Vincent de Paul." Typescript. Oka, Quebec, c. 1904.

Anon. "Micmac Aboriginal Title." Eskasoni, 4 March 1974. Typescript.

Chute, Janet E. "A Comparative Study of the Bark, Bone, Wood and Hide Items Made by the Historic Micmac, Montagnais/Naskapi and Beothuk Indians." Master's thesis Memorial University, 1976.

Douglas, W. A. B. "The Royal Navy and the Canso Station." Typescript.

Hoffman, Bernard G. "The Historical Ethnography of the Micmac of the Sixteenth and Seventeenth Centuries." Ph.D. dissertation, University of California, Berkeley, 1955.

McGee, Harold F. "Ethnic Boundaries and Strategies of Ethnic Interaction: A History of Micmac-White Relations in Nova Scotia." Ph.D. dissertation, Southern Illinois University, 1973.

Pastore, Ralph T. "Micmac Colonization of Newfoundland." Presented at the meetings of the Canadian Historical Association, 1977. Typescript.

Robertson, Thomas. "History of Shelburne County." Akins Prize Essay 1871. Manuscript. King's College Library. Halifax.

————."History of Digby County." Akins Prize Essay 1873. Manuscript. King's College Library. Halifax.

Index